SPYING FROM THE SKY

At the Controls of U.S. Cold War Aerial Intelligence

ROBERT L. RICHARDSON

CASEMATE

Philadelphia & Oxford

Published in the United States of America and Great Britain in 2020 by
CASEMATE PUBLISHERS
1950 Lawrence Road, Havertown, PA 19083, USA
and
The Old Music Hall, 106–108 Cowley Road, Oxford OX4 1JE, UK

Hardcover Edition: ISBN 978-1-61200-836-3
Digital Edition: ISBN 978-1-61200-837-0

A CIP record for this book is available from the British Library

Printed and bound in the United States of America

Typeset in India for Casemate Publishing Services. www.casematepublishingservices.com

For a complete list of Casemate titles, please contact:

CASEMATE PUBLISHERS (US)
Telephone (610) 853-9131
Fax (610) 853-9146
Email: casemate@casematepublishers.com
www.casematepublishers.com

CASEMATE PUBLISHERS (UK)
Telephone (01865) 241249
Email: casemate-uk@casematepublishers.co.uk
www.casematepublishers.co.uk

Cover image: Image taken from the U-2 Dragonlady based at Beale Air Force Base in California. (Ross Franquemont)

Contents

Author's Note

This biography has been made possible by the more than 100 interviews, commentaries, and phone conversations with William Gregory during the period 2014–2019. Each tape recording has been archived, and carefully transcribed, mostly verbatim. In the interest of brevity, in the text all direct quotations from William Gregory are italicized, but do not include specific source references. Citations from other sources are indicated by quotation marks.

Acknowledgments

This book is the result of countless interviews, email exchanges and phone conversations with William Gregory, and I am deeply grateful for the opportunity to have written this account of Greg's life, and for a chance to become his friend. And to Greg's family, who also contributed commentary, recollections, and many family photographs, I am also very indebted.

Research has necessitated deep excursions into Air Force archives, and the staff at the Air Force Historical Research Agency (AFHRA), in particular Archivist Cathy Cox and Microfilm Processor Tammy Horton, have been of great help. Notable Air Force historian George Cully, deeply knowledgeable about the AFHRA archives, provided much useful material for the book.

John Oliver of the Trousdale County Historical Society is deserving of special thanks for the many contributions he has made to this book, and to my understanding of life in northcentral Tennessee in the early decades of the twentieth century. His guidance was always given readily and has been most welcome. Also at the Trousdale County Historical Society, special thanks are due to Annie Farris Welch, the woman who went to some effort to first put me in touch with William Gregory.

Several academic institutions provided material for this book. Dr. Wendy Beckman, Chair of the Aerospace Department at Middle Tennessee State University (MTSU), and Christy Groves at the Walker Library there, were of great help in uncovering Greg's years at State Teachers College in the late 1930s. Donna Baker, University Archivist at the Albert Gore Research Center at MTSU, generously digitized issues of the student newspaper, *Side Lines*, which lent a solid basis for the section on Greg's college years. Lynn Whitfield, Archivist at Texas Tech University (TCU), contributed material related to aviation in West Texas in the early war years, and Brooke Nichols of TCU's Southwest Collection Special Collection Library facilitated much useful information about Uvalde and Garner Field. Dr. Julie Martenson, Director of the University of Texas Osher Lifelong Learning Institute, was very helpful in providing background information and current details on the LAMP program that has been so much a part of Greg's retirement years.

The Air Force and Department of Defense were also very helpful in many instances in the preparation of this book. Abigail Gardner at the National Defense University Library and Learning Center provided a copy of the thesis Greg wrote while attending the National War College, together with Greg's profile from the NWC student annual. Dr. Jeremy Prichard, Historian of the 19th Airlift Wing, provided archival information on the 19th Bomb Group. Brett Stolle, Manuscript Curator of the National Museum of the US Air Force, was helpful in locating information related to the 4080th SRW.

Museums have been rich sources of information. Leroy Walther at the Aviation Museum at Garner Field was very helpful in providing a better understanding of Garner Field at the time Greg was a cadet there. Annie Hogeboom of the Travis AFB Heritage Center provided details on the PT-19 aircraft Greg flew at Garner AAB in 1942. Virginia Davis with the Archives of Southwest Texas was more than helpful in providing material related to the City of Uvalde and Garner Army Air Base from the time of Greg's training. And Jim Long, Chairman Emeritus of the Laughlin Heritage Foundation, has been of inestimable help in understanding the organization and operations of the 4080th Strategic Reconnaissance Wing, and the 4025th Strategic Reconnaissance Squadron.

Special thanks to the estimable Thornton D. Barnes of Roadrunners Internationale, whose guidance and many contributions strengthened the book immeasurably. John Sheehan of the International Plastics Modeling Society Special Interest Group provided very helpful information related to RB-57D ELINT systems. Nicholas Roche, NATO Archives, was helpful in securing information related to Greg's service with the NATO Tactical Air Reconnaissance sub-committee. Former Air Force pilot Tony Martinez flew RB-57D-2s with Greg at Laughlin AFB, and on deployments in Turkey and the UK. For his insights and perspective, my sincere thanks. To Anthony Asterita, Commander of the 49th Fighter Squadron Association, the author extends his sincere thanks and appreciation for his careful manuscript review.

And thanks to the staff of the Spokane Public Library who arranged for over 30 interlibrary loans over the period of research for this book. This biography would be paler without the valuable source material they made available.

I sincerely appreciate the Casemate Group, and the contributions of Ruth Sheppard (Publisher), Isobel Fulton (Editor) and Alison Griffiths (Copy Editor). Many thanks for your support, guidance, and expertise.

William Gregory and the author also wish to express their thanks to Francis Gary Powers, Jr., founder and Chairman Emeritus of The Cold War Museum, for his friendship and for his contribution to both this book and to the broader historical record of the Cold War. We are most grateful.

Preface

It's an interesting thing to be part of the process of capturing one's own life story. I had never even considered this prospect when I first met author Robert (Bob) Richardson on August 5, 2014. He was conducting research for a book about a member of the 49th Fighter Squadron from North Africa during World War II. His call came on my birthday, and I knew he was going to be a special friend. Bob's research had uncovered the fact that there were two remaining members of the 49th, and I was one of the two. Over the course of the research period I came to know Bob quite well. By the time his book was complete, I had become the only living member of the 49th, and Bob suggested that my life story might be next.

But thinking back on my youth spent in Tennessee, I remember well my early teen years. I suffered the impact of my family's low-income status, and during this time the idea of a book ever being written about my life was impossible. Though those years were challenging, I have never forgotten my high school principal, Mr. Stone. One day at the end of my freshman year, near the Hartsville Courthouse, Mr. Stone saw me and said, "James I am expecting great things of you." I was so surprised that he specifically sought me out to tell me this. I had great respect for him, and sadly he lived for just one more year. But that one comment unlocked something in me.

On one hand I knew my daughters Cookie and Gretchen would be happy with the idea of the project. On the other was the realization that my military career had included top-secret clearances and covert operations. While the operations discussed in this book were declassified in the mid-1970s, the discipline of protecting information was hard to reprogram, even when the information in question had become the subject of books and other reports.

I was 56 years old when the CIA made the decision to declassify events that had taken place in 1962 in which I was involved. I would be 92 years old before I shared my first public comments at the request of a friend asking me to give a talk to a small group. From this initial invitation followed a series of presentations in rapid succession. My daughter Cookie created a 100-slide PowerPoint to accompany the speech which made it much better than it could have been. Over the months, we figured out how to sync the comments to the images, travelling to various venues to make presentations in response to requests.

I was extremely surprised by the interest in this topic as I began to speak to larger and larger groups. A section of my talk included my acquaintance with former U-2 pilot Francis Gary Powers. Through an interesting twist of fate our paths crossed on a number of occasions, including a couple of times after Powers was returned to the United States in exchange for Russian spy Rudolph Abel, which was on February 10, 1962. Though Powers died in a helicopter accident on August 1, 1977, his son, Francis Gary Powers, Jr. (FGP Jr.) had dedicated his life to clearing his father's name, and insuring that posthumous awards were made for his father's service.

In the course of this work, F. G. P. Jr. eventually found me, and as a result of this association, I was invited to address a national conference in Dallas. Gary and I met to discuss questions about his father. Our friendship and a relationship continued.

Sometimes I think of my life in three parts: the years before Helen; the 46 magical years I shared with her; and the time beyond her life. Our time together brought us our daughters Gretchen and Cookie and later their husbands, Dr. Gene Davis and Lieutenant Colonel Phil Ruiz. Cookie and Phil were blessed with their own two daughters, J.R. and Boo, and Gretchen and Gene with two sons, Greg and Grant. And now J. R. and Boo have added Jaxson Warrick and Kyle Wong to our family, and in the past two years J. R. and Jaxson have also added my great-grandchildren, Parker Helen and Wade Warrick. Helen and I started our lives as two, and today there are a dozen members of this family.

Ultimately I have enjoyed the opportunity to reflect on the many chapters of my life that started in 1920. Aviation was coming of age at that time, and the radio and automobile were invented; nearly 100 wonderful years later my business transactions are digital, and I have an iPhone in my pocket.

William James Gregory
November 2018

Introduction

William Gregory knows how to keep a secret. And he has had some serious secrets to keep. Even as undisclosed CIA and NSA reports began to be declassified, and as his security strictures began to ease, Colonel Gregory remained silent about a central part of his life and career: his clandestine service during the hottest years of the Cold War. And while details of America's critical overhead spying programs gradually came to light, the mechanics of Cold War surveillance operations, and the stories of those in command—the Cold Warriors—were still largely unrecorded.

Today, as he prepares to enter his eleventh decade, and sixty years after commanding those fateful Cold War reconnaissance missions, Gregory is ready to have his story told. A story of Air Force and CIA service that began in the early days of World War II, and spanned nearly the entirety of America's Cold War with the Soviet Union.

It is the tremendous arc of his life and service that makes his story so compelling. How is it possible that so much could occur in one lifetime, even a long one like Gregory's? Many of the most salient events in the Cold War occurred during his time in the service. The Doomsday Clock reached its nadir of two minutes to midnight as he entered service with the Strategic Air Command, and the minute hand would not budge for seven tense years. For most of Gregory's career, the United States and the Soviet Union were never far from war. The work undertaken by Greg and his colleagues in developing and carrying out overhead surveillance would make a historic contribution not just to the security of the United States, but to the survival of the world.

Gregory's life can only be fully appreciated by clearly understanding his roots, including his early years growing up a sharecropper's son in 1920s Tennessee. That roughly corrugated landscape—a region of great natural beauty, steeply sided hills, and crystal springs—speaks through its native sons of hard work and sometimes deprivation, of self-reliance, abiding faith, and deep kinship. Great achievement is sometimes rooted in difficult places and harsh circumstances, and that is certainly true of William Gregory.

Greg himself might feel that his life has been something of a conundrum: in retrospect he feels deeply blessed by the life he has led. And the same time, if pressed, he would be unsurprised that his hard work, strong faith, and constancy would inevitably lead to success, achievement and happiness. Throughout his life, he has been well equipped with a disarming self-confidence.

This book tells the story of William Gregory's military career in all its unique turns and achievements, but always within the context of the Air Force within which he served, and in light of the challenges and policies of the American civilian and military leadership. It is only by an understanding of that context that the reader will understand Greg's true place in history, and the contributions he made to world peace.

Greg's service to the nation has been recognized by leaders in both the military and civilian spheres, including by President John F. Kennedy. His career has been marked by a continually ascending arc always characterized by a commitment to the mission and to his country, and an inerrant professionalism. His many commendations often cite his "meritorious service conspicuously beyond normal duties."

At the same time, Greg has faced the unavoidable consequences of war. Many of his closest friends were killed in training accidents and during combat missions. How, Greg has been asked, can a person continue in the face of such loss? And his answer: "You just have to keep on going... " To this day, Greg still feels many of those losses deeply, with regret but also with a pride in having called them his friends.

The narration that follows will also serve as a testament to his abiding faith, and to his commitment to family. And, perhaps strangely for a man who has been at the sharp end of America's nuclear deterrent force, it will also serve to underscore Greg's lifelong desire for peace, and his commitment to fairness and equity among men.

Greg's story continues with his life after separation from the Air Force at the still-very-young age of 55. While he did not know it at the time, he had just reached the halfway point in his long life, with much more work to be done, and with innumerable new experiences lying ahead. For many of the young men with whom he served, the second half of Greg's life might be surprising, if not completely unrecognizable.

And, from the age of 24—a combat veteran returned from the war—for Greg there was always Helen. His wife and the mother of his children, Helen was the stalwart of the family: tolerating his many absences, keeping the family tight, and always supporting Greg in his service. The epitome of an "Air Force Wife," Helen shares Greg's history in the pages that follow.

Spying from the Sky was written with Greg's family in mind. But it is hoped that military historians and aviation enthusiasts—and anyone looking for a hero—will also appreciate his experiences, his perspective, and his service.

CHAPTER I

Early Years

William James Gregory's Tennessee ancestors understood what has come to be known in this more erudite age as *terroir*: the concept that fruits, vegetables, and other crops and farm products are shaped by their genetics, horticulture, and environment. Just as hops, tomatoes, and good Tennessee tobacco bear their own *terroir*, so too does the character of a Tennessean. Regardless of what unimagined future may await him, a man born of Tennessee soil is forever the product of that place and his people. And that is undoubtedly true for William James Gregory, whose own *terroir* would inform every stage of his most astonishing life.

The Gregory lineage is reportedly traced to the shores of Loch Lomond, in Northern Scotland, in the ninth century. Family histories link the Gregory ancestors to Alpine, king of the Picts and later of Scotland, and by descent to the current queen of England, Elizabeth II, though those same histories report "it is our honest opinion that all the royal blood in the veins of the Gregory family has long since 'run out'."[1]

The family's migration took it from Scotland to Northern Ireland, thence to England, and in 1620, to Jamestown. By 1800 the family had set permanent roots near the village of Pleasant Shade in north-central Tennessee, an area referred to as the "Upper Cumberland." Latticed with creeks, rivers, and hollows in a matrix of steep-sided hills and fertile bottom land, the area was generally unsuited to large-scale farming, such as the cotton farms in western regions of Tennessee. Instead, the Upper Cumberland was home to hundreds of small subsistence farms.[2]

The region was populated with little ethnic diversity, leading one wag to comment that it was home to the "purest Anglo-Saxon stock in the nations." Ownership of slaves was common, but because of the prevalence of small-scale subsistence farming in Trousdale County and the Upper Cumberland,

Pleasant Shade, TN. (Tom Dickerson)

the practice was hardly universal, and there is no record of William James' own direct forebears having owned slaves.[3]

Generation by generation, farms were passed down to sons and daughters and frequently subdivided, resulting in family farms of decreasing size. At the time of the Civil War, the average size of a Tennessee farm was 251 acres. By 1900 this was reduced to just 91 acres.[4] In keeping with this tradition, Greg's great-grandfather ceded a portion of the Gregory farm to Greg's grandfather, and later, in 1913, provided a portion of the farm to his mother Creola on the occasion of her marriage to Sam Gregory.

The portion of the farm on which Sam and Ola would live and work was in the hill country in the Peyton Creek river valley region, along Big Creek Road a couple of miles north of Pleasant Shade, Tennessee. That part of Tennessee is remarkable for its topography—innumerable steep hills interspersed with hollows and webbed with creeks and rivers of all sizes. *Kind of a rough place,* as Gregory would later describe it, the farm included a bit of flat land near the river bottom, with the less fertile fields extending up the hillside. They lived in a two-room cabin set back on a hill. A nearby spring supplied their drinking and wash water, and milk, butter, and cheese were stored in the small spring houses, sharing space with resident newts and frogs. No running water, no indoor plumbing, and no electricity. Midway to nothing, and on the way to nowhere, but it was a start.

In that two-room cabin would be born William James Gregory on August 5, 1920. A first-born son named after both of his grandfathers, he went by "James" or "Jimmy" in his early years and came to be called "Greg" only later in life. The second child, Greg was bracketed by sisters.

Farming was hard for Sam and Ola, but it was a life they both knew. As with most of the state's farmers in the 1920s and 30s, being a farmer meant a subsistence living, and that meant living in poverty, in one form or another, and to one degree or another. The Gregorys lived like everyone else along the creek. Farming land owned by Ola's father meant that they were poor, but not dirt poor. The living was harsh, but it was not without hope or joy. The old adage "Tough times don't last, but tough people do" was hardly a cliché for the Gregorys—it was how they lived each day.

At that time, cotton was still king in western Tennessee and was the most important cash crop. But the largest crop in the state was corn, and that was true also in the northern hill country. Corn was used as stock feed, ground into meal for use in cornbread or cornmeal mush, and occasionally converted into whiskey in a local still. Folks also grew whatever else they needed to live—hay, a bit of wheat, hogs, cattle, sheep, and fowl. Men cultivated the fields and tended livestock while women helped with chores, reared children, saw to the family garden plot and any non-working livestock, and put up food for winter. Like all the neighboring farmers, Sam would wait for a cold spell in the fall to kill the hogs, which were first cured with salt and then hung in a smokehouse. "Farm families sold little, bought less, and ate what they produced at home."[5]

Illness and injury took their toll, and the Gregory family did not escape their share of traumas. Greg himself was stricken at the age of three by an unknown malady, and was saved only when his uncle rode horseback 30 miles to Carthage, TN in a winter storm to secure medicine for his recovery.

Greg's younger sister, Robbie Neil, was born in December 1927 and was premature. *My grandmother, Mammy Nixon, knew quite a bit about childbirth, having given birth to 11 children of her own. She came to assist my mother and reckoned that it was going to be a bad birth.*

Soon after she arrived, she took my sister, Agnes, and I into a private room, and said "I don't want you to get too close to your little sister, as she is not going to live. I don't want you to get too attached to her."

Under Ola's continuing good care, Robbie struggled but did survive. The family credits a medicine available at the time, Castoria, with helping her survival, and she eventually thrived.[6]

Sam was eager to succeed in farming and knew that a larger acreage would be needed to raise the crops and livestock he had in mind. But getting started in farming was expensive: land prices had increased fourfold in the previous 20 years, and by 1920 the average value of an acre of land was $64. Finding the 150 acre-or-so farmstead that Sam required would take a large mortgage. But farming was what he knew, and so in 1925, Sam bought a farm on Little Creek, a tributary of Peyton Creek, about two miles north of Pleasant Shade in northern Smith County. And with the farm came a large house—a most welcome change from the two rooms the family had been living in for years.

It was a nice farm and a nice house, and my dad made good progress for about two or three years. He had lots of hogs, cattle, sheep and it appeared that he was going to be successful. But he had a loan with a high interest rate and despite his and the family's hard work, his cash income was not sufficient to keep up with the mortgage payments. In the end, we had to give up the farm.

At this point, Sam's only option was to become a working tenant on someone else's farm—a sharecropper. Across the south, over 1.8 million southerners had become sharecroppers: in Tennessee in the 30s, farming for shares had become increasingly common, due in part to crop failures leading to mortgage defaults. At the time Sam lost the farm, more than one-third of Tennessee farms were operated by sharecroppers.[7]

So in 1928, in one day we lost the farm, and all the livestock, and the nice home that we had on the farm to (become) a sharecropper. So many young kids in rural Tennessee dropped out of school early when they were stuck with farming. There was no way to get ahead financially in this new role. And with the loss of the farm came a social stigma that was to have a profound effect on Sam and his family. As landowners, Greg and his friends and cousins were equal in each other's eyes—all were poor, but their lives were similar. As tenant farmers, Greg's family had slipped a rung. It was a harsh change for the seven-year-old Greg.

This was a terrible event that happened in our early life. We went from a very nice home to become sharecroppers. We lived on someone's farm, tilled their land for a fraction of the proceeds—usually ⅓ to ½.

Sam and Ola moved the family and everything they owned from Smith County to the adjacent county—Trousdale County, about 30 miles from Pleasant Shade. At the time, the population of the state of Tennessee had grown to over two million, but Trousdale, the smallest of Tennessee's 95 counties at just 110 square miles, never had a population much above six thousand.[8]

They settled on a small farm owned by Mrs. Allie Mae Payne, six miles west of Hartsville, population at the time just 1,015: a town which was then, and remains today, the only officially constituted municipality in Trousdale County. The widow Payne lived in Gallatin, twelve miles to the west, and rarely visited the farm, which was something less than 100 acres in size.[9]

We had a good garden there, and we grew about two acres of tobacco and got a fraction of it on shares. Much of the acreage was in trees and in wild grove. It was an old house with four or five rooms. One room we did not use because it was about to fall in. But it was all we could afford.

Greg attended a two-teacher school at another community—Walnut Grove—about a mile down the road.

We used to pick blackberries there. Blackberries were ripe about July, and we received fifteen or twenty cents for a gallon of these berries—that is a lot of berries, but 15 cents was a lot of money, which we were always short of at that time.

Early settlers had reached middle Tennessee from Virginia and North Carolina in the 1780s, bringing with them a crop that would come to shape much of the agriculture and economy in the region—tobacco. Burley tobacco began to be grown in Trousdale County around 1915. By the time Greg was old enough to help around the farm, tobacco had become an important cash crop, and Sam planted it every year.

Seeds were started in covered beds, and then transplanted in rows—a very labor-intensive process that involved the whole family in planting season. In late summer, the now-tall plants would be cut and hung on poles in the tobacco barn to air dry, and in the fall the farmers stood at stripping tables from early to late, six days a week, pulling leaves from the stalks. By Thanksgiving the roads were busy with flatbed trucks, pickups and hay wagons piled high with golden tobacco leaves, making deliveries to one of the five tobacco markets in nearby Hartsville.

These markets, like the other principal markets in Carthage, Gallatin, and Springfield, served farmers in a 30–40 mile radius, catering to principal tobacco buyers like R.J. Reynolds, American Tobacco, and Lorillard, who regularly visited for the tobacco auctions.

Like other sharecroppers, the Gregorys lived off credit from a local store, and the sale of their tobacco crop in the fall was a big event. Depending on the farmer's agreement with the landowner, his share of the crop would be 30–50 percent. A typical tobacco crop would yield about 700 pounds per acre, and sold for $0.22 per pound, generating around $750 in total revenue for a five-acre plot—about what the Gregorys planted each year. With hard work, reasonable soil, and a bit of rain, Sam could earn about $400 for his crop, about enough to pay off his grocery bill for that year.[10]

Each September, many sharecropping farmers looked for new opportunities for the coming crop year, visited new farms, met the owners and discussed the sharecropping terms. Typically, the sharecroppers made a move to a new farm and home in January, well ahead of the year's planting, and all on the basis of a handshake with the owners. And if their move took them to a new community, they made new arrangements with the owners of the local grocery store.

Sam was no exception, and moved his family frequently: five times in the 13 years Greg remained with the family, always hoping to secure better terms from a different landowner, or a better parcel with higher yields.

Greg learned to plow as soon as he was big enough to reach the handles. *While plowing on the farm in June, July, and August I could see people driving up and down the highway, looking like they were having a much better life than we were having. It gave me the thought that there must be a better way to make a living than we had to put up with. This was the first time I thought I must find something that I can do better than being a farmer.* His dad was always in support of Greg's ambition and did nothing to tie Greg to a life of farming. Sam's attitude was "Let me help you go…"

Wrestling with a mule-drawn plow, or sweating over the 'baccer crop, Greg began gradually, probably imperceptibly, to develop an approach to living that would characterize much of his life. Foremost was the recognition that creating change in his life would inevitably require risk and consequence—whether for good or for ill. He was able, even at a young age, to recognize unfairness when he saw it, and to value kindness. He was becoming increasingly aware that he could trust his judgment, a judgment informed by the firmly rooted ethics that grew from family and faith. And finally, he acquired the habit of making his decisions based mostly on his own counsel—in important matters of his early life, he did not especially seek the counsel of others. This was a trait that would serve him well, but would, in at least one noteworthy situation, cause some consternation.

From the earliest settlements in the Upper Cumberland, religion had always been an essential part of Tennessee life, and that was indeed true for the Nixon and Gregory clans. Sam and his family were members of the Baptist church and participated in camp meetings and revivals in the summers. Local revivals were normally week-long and held in the evening, with the current preacher delivering the message. Greg, even as a young boy, was able to sit through the sometimes interminable sermons and meetings.

I had attended church a lot over the years and sometimes went to church meetings with my grandparents at a Baptist church called Mount Tabor. It was a different kind of church than we normally attended. The church at Mount Tabor started at about 9:30 and the preacher would deliver three-hour fire-and-brimstone sermons full of predictions of hellfire and eternal damnation. The pastor would get the congregation so fired up that we actually had people shouting during the service. That was quite common. He would also talk about the end of times, and gave me, and everyone else, the impression that the end of times would come soon. He convinced me that if we got through Monday, we certainly would not get through the rest of the week before the world would end. That was a tactic that was used back then. I didn't appreciate those meetings. They were more radical, and it was a different type of Baptist. I was always so hungry that I wanted the service to end before it did. But at my church, it was quite different than that. We had a good pastor.

I grew up having a strong belief in Jesus, although I had resisted joining the church up to that point because I did not feel the push to do it. But one Sunday night when I was 12 years old, I had a religious experience that was really unbelievable. I was praying, and all of a sudden, the spirit seemed to descend on me. I had never had a feeling like it. It was such an outstanding feeling. It was as if all my troubles were removed. I was no longer sinful, as I had been told I was, and as we all were, I guess. This was just a great, great experience, and I felt so relieved and felt the spirit descend upon me.

It was such a marvelous feeling, and I felt that way for several days. Since that time I have believed in the 22nd Psalm, verses 9, 10, and 11. "Lord how you have helped me before. You took me safely from my mother's womb, and brought me through the years of infancy. I have depended on you since birth. You have always been my God." It was a strange feeling—I felt like all of a sudden the Holy Spirit had descended upon me, and for the first time I felt free, and that I had become a child of God. For days I felt that wonderful feeling.

That was a terrific experience, and since that time I have had a strong belief in God. I've remembered it frequently throughout my life. He has really blessed me over the years and has taken care of me through my lifetime.

Greg was no longer troubled by the fire-and-brimstone, doom-and-gloom preaching he often heard. *I realized that I didn't need to believe that anymore.* This spiritual awakening gave Greg's self-confidence a tremendous boost. *I thought, God is on my side, and I can do a lot of things. It was a confidence builder.*

This spiritual epiphany, shared with almost no one over the years since, remained with Greg though all his challenges, his triumphs, and his heartfelt losses.

Greg attended the Hartsville High School. *I really liked our principal, Mr. Pullias. He was the principal, but he also taught a really forward-looking class. He told us one time in class—no one believed him—that farmers would one day be making $5 a day. At that time, my dad was making $1 a day. None of us believed this farfetched idea of $5 a day, but of course, it was true, and then some.*

One day near the end of his freshman year, Greg was standing at the fence near the Hartsville courthouse. *Professor Stone, the principal at the high school prior to Mr. Pullias, came over to me. I had not had any classes from him and was surprised when he spoke to me: "James, I am expecting great things from you." That was something I remember to this day. He only lived another year, dying of pneumonia. Wow, to have someone say something like that, at that time of my life, was really awesome. I didn't know that he even knew me. I have remembered that ever since.*

Greg remembers his life from age seven to 18 as being a somewhat degrading experience. *We never had any money. We survived, but we never had any surplus money. At one time we shared a farm with a black farmer and his wife. They were actually older and did not have any kids. They were pretty nice people, and we had an identical deal (with the landowner) as the black family. Most at that time in that area, the white people had the upper hand, but we did not feel like we did so much.*

Greg joined the 4-H program in high school and raised hogs. *I had a prized hog during that time, a female that I had raised from a piglet, and who later gave me a litter or two. For that time, 4-H was a good thing, and all of my friends were in 4-H as well. With the 4-H we would go (to an auction) and buy a piglet, take it home and with the full support of my father, rear it up.*

Summer days were spent either working on his farm or hiring out to other farmers. Working every daylight hour, turning the soil behind a mule or planting and tending tobacco, Greg would earn 75 cents for a hard day's work.

Diversions were few. There was no radio on the farm, and no newspapers delivered. In Greg's household, there were no musical instruments, no camera, and no particular interest in sports. They never attended a movie.

Temperance advocates had been active in Tennessee since the late 19th century, and while the cities of Nashville, Memphis, Chattanooga, and La Follette continued to allow alcohol, by 1907 many rural counties had banned alcohol entirely. But a county's "dry" status meant little for those with a taste for "white lightning"—moonshining had a long tradition in Tennessee because homemade liquor, when legal, was not taxed. One writer noted: "Middle-Westerners turn corn into hog to make it portable; with the same object a very limited class of mountaineers turn corn into whiskey. There was a lot of bootlegging in those days, and in those hills, they would produce alcohol and often got caught because of the wood smoke that resulted from cooking the corn they were brewing."[11]

As for the Gregorys, Sam was a drinking man—not a heavy drinker, but he would on occasion have a taste. But Greg's mother did not approve, and it was illegal. So Sam always drank in private.

Greg was 13 years old before he ever went through a full year without hunger, but recalls these challenging years with no rancor. *It wasn't all bad. I can remember good times. During those years there were a lot of good times. We had a pretty good outlook, even though times were pretty grim.*

Poverty has many faces, and although Greg was at that time living in degraded conditions, he and his family were not themselves degraded. Poor did not mean, for the Gregorys, poor in spirit, poor in family relations, poor in experiences or education, nor as will be seen, opportunities. The Gregorys endured poverty without despair or desperation. Even with the severe circumstances they sometimes experienced, Sam and Ola might have felt, at times, pride in knowing that they could sustain their family in the face of the unrelieved adversity.

But if Greg could accept his lot without bitterness, he was not blind to the harshness of his life. *We were sharecroppers in those years, and so I worked hard in the fields as a teenager, and I just felt like there was a better life than that. I was just looking for opportunities to do something different.*

Greg was 18 before they had electricity—none of their former farmhouses had it. They got by mostly with kerosene lamps. He would occasionally hear radio programs at other family's homes, but his own family did not own a radio.

By this time, Sam had acquired a car, and the family went to town regularly. But not having money to spend, they would just stay for a couple of hours and then go back to whichever farm they were living in at the time. At Christmas time, with the prior year's grocery credit recently paid up, Sam and Ola would treat the family to bananas—about 10 cents a dozen. Greg recalls his family trading at Owen's Grocery Store. *We never had a bar of candy. Sometimes we would have broken stick candy—you could get quite a bit for three cents.*

Throughout all his travails, Sam held firm to his desire that his children get a good education. His own education had ended at the third-grade level and Ola's after eighth grade. He never allowed Greg to miss a day of school, no matter how busy things were on the farm. *His had not been a good life, and he wanted things better for us kids. He was willing to make any sacrifice to keep his children in school. There were many days when he really needed my help. I was the only son in the family, and my two sisters couldn't do much of the field work. But my dad would not let me stay home, and I always thanked him so much for that later, that he had the foresight to see the value of education, and he wanted to ensure that I at least got through high school. And his commitment to education was the same for his two daughters.*

William James Gregory, graduation photo, Trousdale County High School. (Gregory)

With his father's encouragement, Greg was a good student and graduated Trousdale County High School in the spring of 1938, fourth in a class of 30. He was elected "most handsome"—the caption on his senior picture read: "All handsome men are dying and I don't feel so well myself."[12]

The book salesman

It was during the summer of 1938 when Greg, having graduated high school, made a decision that reflected his hunger for new experiences and his yearning for a way out of tenant farming. A decision that had the potential to be a big step along the pathway to improving his life, but one which would lead first to one of the most difficult short periods he experienced. He was about to learn that the adage "no pain no gain" acquired longevity because of the truth it contained.

The year prior a friend had begun successfully selling books for a Nashville company, and recruited Greg to give it a try. *I went to Nashville for a week's training on how to sell books. They gave us sample books to show our prospective customers what they would be buying. They had several copies of bibles—from really deluxe bibles down to ordinary. They had a New Testament, a cookbook, and one or two other books. Mostly it was bibles.*

At the time Greg left for Nashville, neither he nor his parents knew where he would be posted—it could have been anywhere in the South. *At the end of the week (Saturday), the training was over, and we were all to hitchhike to the place where we had been assigned. My group of five was assigned to Shreveport for the summer. I had never traveled further than Nashville before. It took me a little over two days to get to Shreveport. I didn't use the phone in those days, so I wrote my parents from Nashville and told them I was going to Louisiana.*

Greg and his team occupied a house in Shreveport, but only on weekends. *The rest of the days we traveled along out in the field. Our travel kit made a neat package—it had a steel case with all our sample books and was great protection against dogs.*

I started out on Monday to sell books and continued every day. The bad part was that none of us had any money. About sundown, I would start looking for a place to stay. It might take quite a while to find a place, and I had to do that every night throughout the summer.

I'd just ask the farmers if they could put me up for the night. These were depression years, and the economy of Louisiana was no healthier than the rest of the country. But there was some sympathy for a young kid who was trying to make his way. I never failed to find a place during the summer. It was a learning experience, for sure.

The families would have Greg join them for supper, and he'd sometimes do a chore or two. *I would ask if there was anything I could do to help them. That was what I did all summer—it was quite a long summer. I liked selling and did OK at it. My territory was near Benton and Plain Dealing—all given to cotton fields. At the end of the summer, I had to deliver the books that I had sold. I netted about $125, which was pretty good. I look back on that summer and the difficult nights I had in all the strange houses. It was an interesting summer, and it was helpful in other times.*

The tale of two bridges

Greg had a strong desire to go to college, but knew that his parents would not be able to contribute any help. He had heard of Berea College in Kentucky that offered a work-study program for students. He thought this was a great opportunity and resolved to make the 175-mile trip to Berea.

It was audacious for Greg to imagine that he could go to college—this was not generally a part of the consciousness of the community of sharecroppers to which the Gregorys belonged. But it was surely in keeping with Greg's nature—he yearned for new experiences, he was not afraid of the risks involved, and he was confident in himself.

But time was running out for Greg—it was already the third week of September 1938, and most college students would already have registered for classes.

Greg caught a ride to Berea, arriving late on September 21. The next morning he walked across the city bridge over Brushy Fork Creek to the admissions office at the college. *When I arrived, the dean of admissions welcomed me, asked what county I was from, and when I told him Trousdale County in Tennessee, he seemed very disappointed. He told me that he was so sorry, but that county was outside the area that his college covered. He seemed to be really concerned that I didn't qualify.*

More than a little dejected, Greg turned his back on Berea and began to hitchhike back home, miserable at his trip's outcome. The trip home took two days, and he arrived back in Hartsville late in the afternoon of Friday, September 23.

Many years later, Greg's daughter Cookie would recall: "The only time I have heard him, in his life, use the word depressed was in reference to that night." At this time in young Gregory's life, his options were few, with a strong likelihood that his future would involve farming, and perhaps a long period of continued sharecropping. A bright young man, he seemed likely to be overwhelmed by his miserable circumstances, with a desperate future shaped by endless poverty.

But viewed in retrospect, and from a brighter perspective, it might be said that Greg had a lot going for him. He had the full support of the father and mother he loved; he had just returned from a trying summer selling books far distant from home—a summer when he learned that survival was often the result of unflinching persistence; he had a solid education, with an excellent academic record; he had, since his spiritual awakening just a couple of years earlier, the sense that his God was watching over him, caring for him. And he recognized that any improvement in his life would necessarily involve taking a chance. For him, the greater risk lay in doing nothing.

He reached the bridge over Little Goose Creek on the outskirts of Hartsville late in the afternoon of the second day of travel, and there yet remained a four-mile hike to his house out in the country. It was the second bridge Greg met on this trip. Earlier, he had eagerly crossed the bridge to the campus of Berea College, full of hope that a good result waited for him on the other side. And now this bridge, the one he knew so well. Crossing this bridge would bring a far different prospect, dreary by comparison. For Greg, it smacked of giving up, of surrendering to that grim future.

As I was walking across the bridge over Little Goose Creek, I had a sudden inspiration. I decided to visit my high school principal, Mr. Pullias. I would never have considered bothering him with my problem, but he was the last person that I knew that might be able to help.

So I walked the mile to his house, arriving at about 5 in the afternoon, and knocked on his door, disheveled and road-weary. Fortunately, his principal was home, answered the door, and greeted Greg warmly. Greg entered to the smell of home cooking.

I told him about my failure at Berea, and he said he might be able to help. His offer to make a long-distance call to Dean Beasley at Middle Tennessee State Teacher's College (STC) surprised me—it was more than I had expected. Luckily he was able to reach Dean Beasley immediately, explained that he had a graduating senior who wanted to go to college, and asked if he had a program that would help provide for a beginning freshman. The dean said that he had a program that would offer 100 hours of work monthly that would pay $30 and was sufficient for room, board, and tuition.[13]

The program described by Dean Beasley was offered through the National Youth Administration, a New Deal agency sponsored by President Roosevelt

to provide work and education for young people. Because of the work requirement, the program restricted students to 12 credit hours per term, making it
necessary for Greg to attend classes year-round.

Just the day before, Dean Beasley had presided over the new student orientation for incoming freshmen, and classes had begun earlier that very day.
*The 1938 academic year had already started, but he said if I could be there on
Monday he could get me started. It was already Friday. I thanked Mr. Pullias so
much, and the four-mile walk home was a pleasure.*

*On Sunday I hitchhiked the 75 miles south to Murfreesboro, Tennessee and I
was in Beasley's office on Monday morning when he arrived. Even though school
had started, I was able to get courses scheduled and was enrolled in a college for
the first time.*

Greg's 13 years of living with a sharecropping family had come to an end
as he joined 700 other students, including 200 fellow freshmen, for the fall
term at STC. Greg's late arrival meant that he missed the brief address to
students by the College's new President, Q. M. Smith, who said in part: "The
College exists for you; college life prepares you for constant change. It's a
training school to prepare you for a changing social order. The aim of STC is
to prepare people to deal with people…"[14] It was a message that seems now
to have been tailored just for Greg.

CHAPTER 2

The Origins of an Aviator

What is now known as Middle Tennessee State University originated in 1909 when the Tennessee legislature authorized three new "normals," or teacher-training institutions. Middle Tennessee Normal School evolved into a four-year teachers college in 1925, to a State College in 1943, and to a State University in 1965.

Arriving at Middle Tennessee State Teachers College, Greg stepped into a different world. The town of Murfreesboro itself was four times larger than Hartsville, with broad, well-paved, and tree-lined streets, and homes that were "modern and artistic." The student newspaper, *Side Lines*, reminded students "…these pillars of stone, vine bearded dormitories and white lanes of concrete will whisper with the wind the stories of your heritage as a student here, of the prestige that has been set up and what you are expected to do here."[1]

Arriving completely unprepared, Greg set about finding lodging. With the sole male dormitory already full, he explored the campus and town and soon found a boarding house advertising rooms available for students. He made arrangements with the owner, Mrs. Falkenberry, to live there for the academic year. He soon met another of Mrs. Falkenberry's tenants, Buford "Breezy" Foster, a sophomore from Franklin, Tennessee who would figure prominently in Greg's college life and beyond. He also met and became friends with William Neely, who would likewise be a central figure in Greg's future.

Greg registered for classes, and as promised by Dean Beasley, was enrolled in the National Youth Administration (NYA). *We didn't get much money for it—twenty-seven cents an hour—but it was enough to pay tuition, room rent, and board, and have a bit left over for incidental expenses, and that was all that mattered. My first job was in the College cafeteria. I worked there from the beginning but was always looking for new things to do.*

Breezy, Neely, and Greg at Middle Tennessee. (Donna Baker, Albert Gore Research Center, MTSU)

Very early in his time at Murfreesboro, he began to glimpse a much larger world than he had imagined before. *I really benefited going to college, learning things that I could actually do.* He was even able to play a bit of tennis in college.

For someone with a hunger for new experience, a college campus like STC was a perfect home. Fifteen student clubs, including boys' and girls' glee clubs, drama club, debating club, and the science club were eagerly recruiting new members. STC also had an active intramural sports program, and throughout the academic year offered touch football, badminton, ping pong, track and field, tennis, and basketball. Autumn was hayride season, and many were sponsored by various student clubs. A new, open-air roller skating rink opened downtown, and Murfreesboro offered a good number of eateries and soda fountains. *There were so many opportunities that I was not aware of before, and I wanted to check all these opportunities out.*

And if *Side Lines* is to be believed, the two central themes for the fall term were Romance and Football. Love was in the air at STC, with couples rapidly pairing off, and lively social events were frequently available.

Because NYA students were limited to 12 course credits per term, they worked and attended classes year-round. As the fall term of 1939 approached with every indication of another enrollment increase, the NYA boys were occupied making desks and chairs for the classrooms, doing landscaping, and adding an extension to the cafeteria. "(Returning students) can readily see what the NYA did during the summer. The grounds have been turned into a beautiful campus. Hedges trimmed, grass planted, and the boys' dorm painted. The NYA stayed after the summer term was completed, getting everything ready for fall quarter. Not everyone had a two weeks' vacation, as some did not leave at all."[2]

And by his sophomore year, Greg was hitting his stride with the STC coeds. He was mentioned in the November 8 edition of *Side Lines*: "Jimmy Gregory must think that the way to a girl's heart is through her stomach, for he serves the girls first in the lunchroom (Printed by request of the boys)."[3]

Greg became increasingly involved in campus activities in his second year. He was elected to the STC Student Congress for the 1940–41 academic year, along with another Hartsville student, Lewis Lockhart.

War news and student views

Underlying the active social, sporting and academic scene at STC was a growing recognition of the ominous developments in Europe. While most Americans strongly opposed becoming involved in European politics, much less armed conflict, the young men and women at STC knew that the situation in Europe could have a profound effect on their lives. An article in a November *Side Lines* asked: "What will be the outcome of Europe's powder keg? Today the world stands at the crossroads of destiny. Germany, led by Hitler, is the predominating influence of this world and its destiny!"[4] On campus, the students listened to radio reports and avidly consumed print news, keenly interested in the latest developments in Europe.

In a later November edition, the paper included details of a report by the Associated Collegiate Press: "…a summary that tells you just how the wind is blowing so far as the nation's undergraduates are concerned." Ninety-six percent were against US involvement in a European war, while 78 percent said they would not volunteer for service if the US went to war on the side of the Allies. "The pacifist views of the nation's collegians have changed little since the opening of hostilities in Europe."[5,6]

With each succeeding issue of the student newspaper, the focus on European affairs sharpened. By the middle of Greg's freshman year, the students were reading of America's war mobilization programs, and of defensive actions taken in both North and South America. Noting that the "great deluge of radio bulletins and news stories made it virtually impossible for the average college student to get a comprehensive view of any situation," with the December 7, 1938 edition, the student newspaper began an exceptionally well-written interpretive column that provided students with a global summary of world and national events, and their mutual impacts and relations. As the students entered the second semester of the year, their student newspaper included this: "There is growing belief among international observers that the major war, which has been averted in the past two or three years, will break out in the spring."[7]

By the end of Greg's freshman year, the tone of the newspaper had turned decidedly more ominous: "In these trying days when history is being recorded by hours rather than by decades…collegians are forming the following platform as their stand on world events: First, last, and always, they do not want the US to participate in any war of aggression or in any war outside the nation's boundaries; neutrality should be observed, subject to economic cooperation…a European war is almost inevitable, and (we students) have little faith in the appeasement policy."[8]

Neither were the students blind to the international situation in the Pacific. Citing commentary from the *Daily Northwester*, a publication from Northwestern University: "There can be no doubt that a situation is fast developing in the east which could very possibly end in war with Japan. It certainly means that we have abandoned any pretense of neutrality in the Sino-Japanese struggle. It also means that we are perhaps closer to war today than we have been since 1918."[9]

Throughout his freshman year, Greg came to grasp the gathering storm across the Atlantic and believed that the events in Europe made it increasingly likely that war would erupt. *There was a strong element in our country to stay out of it… Let the Europeans fight their own war. In 1938 and 1939 the public opinion was for us not to get into it. My father agreed with that, at that time. But at the beginning of my second year at STC war had started in Europe, and the American public began to change its views. Our government had done nothing to improve the military since the severe cutbacks from World War I. In 1940, with the unexpected success of the German forces, attitudes began to gradually change, and during the year some very modest changes began.*[10]

Seeking a break from his work at NYA, his studies at STC, and from the inexorable war news, and flexing new confidence following a successful freshman year, Greg and his friend Harbor McClarron hitchhiked to the World's Fair in New York. *We also went to Boston and back—we were really broke by the time we got back. But it was really a great trip, and one of the things that I did which was not the smartest thing to do.*

A Navy man

At the end of spring quarter in 1940, Greg saw a notice that students who had a couple of years' college were invited to apply for a summer cruise on a Navy ship—part of the US Navy's attempt to increase its officer corps in anticipation of hostilities breaking out in Europe. *I thought this would be interesting, applied for the program and was accepted. I was the only person to apply from STC, but six students from Vanderbilt in Nashville were also accepted. The seven of us traveled from Nashville to New York City and were welcomed aboard the battleship USS New York, a ship that would be our home for most of the summer.*[11]

Greg's life was increasingly characterized by a willingness to take a chance if it might lead to a new and valuable experience. His readiness to "take a shot" was evidence of his own growing self-confidence and his belief that he could manage the consequences if they were negative, and benefit from them if they were positive. As the possible upside consequences grew in significance, so too did the downside.

The first thing they did was to give us a number of immunization shots which made most of us very sick. A huge storm was hitting the area just then, and as we pulled out of the Hudson River, the ship was really rolling. It pitched for a couple of days until we cleared the storm, and it was not only us novices that were sick—some of the experienced seamen were sick as well.

Our first port of call was Guantanamo, Cuba, where we spent a month and a half. We then went to Panama, where we rode a train across the canal, seeing the Panama Canal from both ends. Toward the end of the summer, the ship went into dry-dock back in Virginia. They had us scrubbing down the sides of this big battleship, scraping barnacles off the bottom of the boat—not a very pleasant job.

After we finally finished that, they released us to return home and I hitchhiked back to Murfreesboro. It was a risk I had taken to do these things, but I was always able to get back into school and the NYA program.

The war in Europe was by then going strong, and Greg was a vastly different person than the young man who had graduated high school just two years earlier. Prior to his stint selling books in Shreveport during the summer of 1938, he had never been further afield than Nashville—just 40 miles away from his hometown. His growing experiences began to bring a real change to his outlook on life. The world he had begun to experience surprised him with its depth and breadth. *Once I was in college, it just seemed to open up so many opportunities. Prior to that, I was so limited during the days when we were so poor. This was a great eye-opener for me—there were so many possibilities for all of us at that time, even though the Depression was still on, and this was a good place to start.*

An Air Corps man

Middle Tennessee State was primarily a teacher's college, and teaching would have been a logical career choice for Greg. *I was really trying to find a career, and of course there was the possibility that I could become a teacher. But I had not settled on that. I was looking for other options, and that led me to try several things during my time at STC.*

Returning from his naval cruise, Greg learned that Middle Tennessee State, along with many other academic institutions in the country, had begun offering an aviation program under the Civil Aviation Authority's (CAA) Civilian Pilot Training Program (CPT). At this point, Greg could have been accepted into the Navy's officer candidate program, but he was intent on exploring his other service options, including the new CPT program. At the beginning of his sophomore year, with the Battle of Britain raging, Greg joined the CPT Program and discovered immediately his love of flying. *It was what might be considered Aviation 101. Aviation was really a new thing in those years. Actually it was the impending war in Europe that caused me to go into the CPT Program because even though the war wasn't going on at that time, it was obvious that we were going to get in it sooner or later.*

The CPT Program was initially intended to give a boost to the flagging civilian aviation industry—particularly small flying schools and light plane manufacturers—and to serve as a vocational training program for American youth. But with the disturbing news coming from Europe, the military value of an expanded flight program for young American men was obvious. Following President Roosevelt's unveiling of the program in December 1938, the CAA launched the experimental CPT Program with a goal of providing pilot training to 20,000 college students annually. Following very positive results in an initial trial program that encompassed 330 student pilots at 13 universities, it was expanded quickly: within a year the number of universities offering the course had increased to 116, and by the end of 1940 to 450 schools. Flight training was open to anyone between the ages of 18 and 25. Students were charged a $40 fee, which covered life insurance and the cost of a physical examination.

In 1940, anticipating the huge demand for aircraft that would result from any US involvement in the European war, President Roosevelt called for the production of 50,000 aircraft, creating an equally urgent need for pilots to fly them. Already well-positioned, the CPT Program was able to respond dramatically. Between June 1939 and June 1942, over 42,000 trained pilots graduated from CPT, many of whom entered the Army or Navy. At the time the program ended, it encompassed 1,132 academic institutions, 1,460 flight schools, and had trained over 435,000 pilots.[12,13]

The CPT bought no airplanes, rented no classrooms, and hired no instructors. Its genius was in fostering consortia from academic institutions, local airfields, and private flight training programs already in operation. Within the consortium, the institution provided academic ground instruction, the flight operator provided additional ground instructors, aircraft and flight instructors, and the airport administrator provided the necessary ground facilities and supplies. The program paid the academic institution $20 per student for the ground school instruction, and the flight operators a minimum of $270 per student for flight instruction. The flight instruction was provided by a private business, and instructors were compensated for trainees who "completed the flight instruction." This placed great importance on delivering solid flight instruction to each student subject to the hourly limitations of both the Primary and Secondary course schedules.

I didn't know if I could (fly) or not, or I might get sick as a lot of people do, but it was a test. At Middle Tennessee we had two government-furnished Piper Cubs and two instructors in a program that could accommodate about 20 students. This was the Preliminary training program—small 50 horsepower airplanes, two-seaters, with tandem seats. I didn't volunteer for this program at first; there were about four CPT classes before I joined in the fall of 1940. Flying this little 50-horsepower airplane was really a step, and I found out that I liked it and I was pretty good at it. So aviation became something I wanted to pursue—I guess I could never quite see myself (as a teacher). I never quite could see myself in that role.

Among the early students were Greg's friends Bill Neely and Frank Sheppard. Regarding airsickness, Neely proved to be a sufferer. Aside from feeling miserable, and having to listen to the good-natured kidding from his fellow cadets, Bill also had to clean the aircraft's interior. On landing, it was not uncommon to see Neely hunting up a bucket of soapy water: "Yeah, there's ole Neely, he's got to clean up the airplane again…"[14]

The Preliminary flight program at Middle Tennessee followed a standardized curriculum for both ground schools and flight, and was organized in four phases: Ground Instruction, Dual Flight Instruction, Primary Solo Flight Instruction, and Advanced Solo Flight Instruction.[15]

The Ground Instruction phase was given three evenings a week. Forty-eight hours were delivered by the institution, in meteorology and navigation. Twenty-four hours of instruction were delivered by the flight instruction contractor, familiarizing the student with the function of an airplane, controls and instruments, including engine starting and warm-up, shutdown, and importantly, warnings—the danger of propellers, the difference between ground speed and airspeed, parking a plane during a strong wind, and running an engine with no one in the cockpit.

Piper Cub, Model J-3. Eighty percent of the close to half-million pilot trainees had their first flights in Cubs, soloed in Cubs, and were certificated in Cubs. (Wikimedia Commons)

Instruction in both Dual and Solo phases focused on taxiing, takeoffs and landings, spins and stalls, forced landings, and "air work"—level flight, gentle climbs and turns, 70-degree turns, and landing approaches.

The final phase—Advanced Solo—focused on precision landings, 70-degree power turns and 30 and 70-degree figure eights around pylons, stalls, spins and slips, and power landings. A two-hour solo cross-country flight of 50 miles minimum distance, including two full-stop landings at different airports, was also required as the student neared completion of the program. The flight course required a minimum of 35 cockpit hours, and a maximum of 50, as determined by the instructor's assessment of each student's need. Students flew least 14 solo hours.

In CPT, students could advance more or less at their own pace and could repeat course sections if necessary. In contrast, students who later joined the Air Corps found the instruction faster-paced, and students who did not learn quickly enough were eliminated from the program.

Greg completed all classes of the Preliminary CPT course at Middle Tennessee on May 16, 1941. Attesting to his early piloting proficiency, he had soloed in six hours and logged 37 hours and 35 minutes of flight time in the Piper Cub J-3—close to the minimum hours established for the instruction. He had become "really hooked" on flying.

Specifications: Piper J-3 Cub[16]

Powerplant: 50 hp Continental A-50
Airspeed:
   Max (Dive): 122 mph
   Cruise: 90 mph
Service ceiling: 11,500 ft.
Range: 220 m.
Empty weight: 1100 lbs.
Wing span: 35 ft. 3 in.
Length: 22 ft. 5 in.
Height: 6 ft. 8 in.
First produced: 1937
Production: Nearly 20,000

Greg continued to fly whenever the opportunity arose. The CPT planes were kept in Nashville over the weekend, and sometimes I would go down to Nashville to fly one of them back on Sunday afternoon to have them available on Monday morning. Other times he would deliver the aircraft to Nashville from Murfreesboro. During July and August 1941, he made the run between those two cities nine times, taking the bus to and from Nashville as needed.

Greg recalls two special events that occurred while in CPT. *Not many people were flying in those days, and even if a small plane landed in a city like*

CPT Class, 1941 (Greg third from right). (Donna Baker, Albert Gore Research Center, MTSU)

Hartsville, everyone in town came out to see who the pilot was and to learn what brought the airplane down. My instructor and I flew in the vicinity of Hartsville on the return leg of a cross-country training flight. We found this small strip near town and landed. It was a great feeling. There were just a lot of people who came down, including several friends who came by to see the airplane.

Later Greg completed a solo three-leg cross-country flight that began and ended in Murfreesboro with intermediate stops in Gallatin and Smyrna, landing on the strip near Jones Hall at Middle Tennessee State. *It was special because it was solo and it was a wonderful feeling. After that, the program ended for me, but I always did everything I could to get more flying time.*

An instructor from Alabama was flying an airplane—a Taylorcraft—to Minneapolis and he stopped at Murfreesboro overnight. I went out to greet him, and we had dinner together. He was not very much interested in flying himself and offered me a trip from Murfreesboro as far as we could go. I had to decide if it was the smart thing to do, and it really wasn't. I had a test Monday morning, and this was already Friday night, and we would take off Saturday morning, and I would have to go a long way to get back for that test.

We took off on August 21 and flew all day. We stopped two or three times for fuel and landed at Waterloo, Iowa right at dark after logging 5:30 hours of flight time. I had to get back for my Monday class, and Waterloo was the farthest I reckoned I could go so I got on the highway to try to get a ride. It was 300 miles back to Chicago, another 500 miles back to Murfreesboro, it was dark already, and I only had about $3. About 10 at night I caught one ride for a little way. I had flown all day, and I was bone tired from all this flying.

Fortunately, a big truck, a semi, pulled up and gave me a ride to Chicago and then I started out going south on the way back to Nashville. It was about 2:30 on Sunday afternoon when I started hitchhiking. I hadn't gotten a ride for about two hours and was getting discouraged again. But then a car pulled up and asked me if I could drive, and I said: "Oh yeah, I am a good driver." I got behind the wheel, and the car owner said he was going to Nashville and beyond, and then went to sleep. It was a big win to get to Nashville. I arrived around 10:30 pm and was able to catch the last bus to Murfreesboro.

I got into the dormitory about midnight, took a shower, went to bed, got up the next morning and took the test.

It was not the smart thing to do, but young pilots would go to great extremes in order to get flights in those years. As it happened, his flight to Waterloo would be his last at Murfreesboro, and his last as a civilian.

The Army Aviation Cadet Program had in March sent a team of examiners to Middle Tennessee State to administer aptitude and physical examinations to students with two years of college who wished to apply for admission to the student pilot training program.[17] Beyond proficiency in flying an aircraft, the Army Air Corps (AAC) knew exactly what sort of individual it needed: "Success as a military aviator required specialized abilities, including a strong desire to fly and fight, and a combination of courage, determination, and endurance. Successful airmen needed a keen sense of balance, a talent for marksmanship, quick reflexes, alertness, and emotional stability or 'nerve'."[18]

About 35 of us applied and completed the exams, and we were told we would hear within six weeks. But months passed, and by mid-August, we had still had not heard anything.

At the time, Middle Tennessee State offered only the Preliminary aviation course, and by the end of his sophomore year there, Greg had taken all the CPT courses. In order to receive advanced aviation training, he would need to transfer to a different university.

The Advanced flight course was of great interest to these young pilots because it offered the opportunity of a much more intensive ground school, and a flight course of up to 50 hours. And they would fly much more performant aircraft, such as the sleek, low-winged Fairchild PT-19, which was equipped with a 200 hp engine—four times the power of the Piper Cubs they had been flying.

The University of Tennessee (UT) in Knoxville was offering the advanced course of CPT, and in early September, just a week after returning from his lark to Waterloo, Greg and his friend and fellow CPT cadet "Breezy" Foster decided to hitchhike the 180 miles to Knoxville to apply for admission. They were quickly accepted and were told they could begin the Advanced flight course later in the month.

With the fall term at UT not beginning for three weeks, Greg returned home and on his arrival found a letter from the Army Air Corps confirming his admission into the Aviation Cadet Program. Greg was faced with two enviable choices, each with a downside: completing the Advanced course at UT would have allowed him to complete his college degree, but the CPT Program would not have shielded him from the draft. Accepting the AAC offer would significantly improve his chances of flying in the coming war, but it would require that he defer his education.

I was leaning going to UT. But this was September of '41, and it was not a matter of if but when we were going to get into it at that point. I figured we would get into it within a year. No one dreamed of Pearl Harbor at the time, but the government had started the draft, and it seemed like the war was getting closer. I really couldn't discuss this with my family. They wouldn't have wanted me to do either, especially my mother who did not like me flying—it was a dangerous undertaking, and there were a lot of accidents.

While Greg could not look to his father for any particular insights into his future plans, neither did his father urge Greg to a cautious path. Greg's father had seen tremendous personal growth in Greg during his college years. *He wanted me to go as far as I could. He never tried to get me to put on the brakes.* Choices. At this time, Greg had the opportunity to pursue joining the Navy or the Army via the National Guard. Or he could have gone to UT to complete the CPT aviation program. Or he could accept the Army Air Corps offer of a place in the pilot training program—so many choices, and with so much on the line, it is little wonder that Greg had to think long and hard about which direction to go.

I had reached the age of 21 in August and finally decided to accept the cadet appointment.

Since it had been so long since his initial physical exam, Greg was sent to Maxwell Field in Montgomery, Alabama to take a second physical, and from there he and 30 other cadets were sent to Fort Oglethorpe, Georgia, just across the state line from Chattanooga, for enlistment. Included were Greg's good friend and future squadron mate, William Neely, and his college roommate Breezy Foster. Greg, Neely, and Foster had attended college together, had flown with the CPT together, and now would enter the Army Air Corps together.

They were slow swearing us in—we had to wait for about a week. A few of the group threatened to go home if they didn't swear us in the next day, which they did. On September 27, 1941 Greg and his close friends Bill Neely and Breezy Foster, along with 25 other cadet candidates, joined the Army Air Force.[19]

CHAPTER 3

Army Air Force Flight
Training and Combat

Greg and his cohort of 50 cadets had been assigned to Class 42-D at Garner
Field in Uvalde, TX for Primary Flight Training. Garner was one of many new
Air Force training grounds, and Greg was in its first class. Their instruction
would be in PT-19A aircraft which had only arrived at Garner a few days earlier.

*The day after our swearing-in at Fort Oglethorpe we boarded the Chattanooga
Choo-Choo for the 1,100-mile train ride to the west Texas town of Uvalde. The
train station that serves Uvalde is a few miles from the town, and when got there,
it was just like one of these Wild West stories. It was out in the middle of nowhere.
A bus arrived at the train station to take us to Uvalde, at the time a city of about
7,000 located 80 miles west of San Antonio, and since the barracks had not been
finished at that time, we lived in the Kincaid Hotel for about a week. We drove
out to the base every day and did military drills and ground school. We didn't
start flying until we had moved out onto the base.[1]*

Like Greg, many arriving cadets had completed all or part of the Civilian
Pilot Training Program. Others had never flown, much less sat at the controls.

The principal commonality at all training airfields was that the program started
fast and never slackened. Ground schools in Primary included ninety-six hours
of instruction in a five-course curriculum, with half of that instruction devoted
to the principles and workings of the various operating systems of an aircraft.
Navigation, particularly planning for cross-country flights, was emphasized.
Pilots continued to train in aircraft and naval recognition, as well as in radio
code. In all courses, theory was held to a minimum, the emphasis being on the
practical—teaching the student how to perform necessary operations.[2]

Before mounting their PT-19s, the cadets reviewed the four forces at work
on an aircraft in flight—thrust, drag, lift, and gravity—and were lectured on
the aircraft's control surfaces—ailerons, to control movement of the aircraft
around the longitudinal axis, the elevators to control the movement around
the lateral axis, and the rudder, which controls movement around the vertical

First PT-19s arrive at Garner Field, Uvalde, TX. September 1941. (Virginia Davis, Archives of Southwest Texas)

axis. Cadets were reminded incessantly that the proper use of these control surfaces is essential to achieving "coordinated" flight of the airplane. A smooth turn required that the rudder and ailerons be used in concert.

The entire day was tightly structured: awake at 5:45 a.m., breakfast at 6:00, inspection, classroom instruction until noon, followed by afternoon flight instruction. Cadets flew every day, and also practiced in the LINK Trainer—a simulator in which the cadet could practice navigation, altitude flying, and spin recovery, and learn how to maintain airspeed and attitude using the "needle and ball". After supper, cadets could choose to study, attend chapel or play sports. All returned to barracks for an evening inspection before the 9:30 taps.

Under this rigorous program, cadets soon began to exhibit all the signs of exhaustion. One cadet, Arthur R. Driedger Jr., commented: "Flying in an open cockpit kept one awake until he landed. After landing, almost everyone fell asleep at the table in the waiting room. I never knew whether it was the open air blowing on us, or the release of tension of flying that caused us to fall asleep, but it was a universal phenomenon."[3]

In Primary training, the airfields were operated by private contractors: Basic and Advanced training were entirely Army Air Force operations. As with every cadet, at all Primary schools, Greg was assigned to a single flight instructor for the entire duration at Garner Field. *Our instructor, Jim Counsel, was a small person, about five foot two inches. I towered over him at my small size. His size did not detract from his dedication. He took life pretty seriously, and he took flying pretty seriously. He did not tolerate smiles or laughter.*

The flight instruction used in Primary worked well: when airborne the instructor first explained, then demonstrated each new maneuver. Students would then attempt to replicate the new maneuver, receive the instructor's critique, then practice. Supervisors made important progress checks after 20, 40, and 60 hours of flight time. Every cadet received 60–65 hours of flight training, half of which would be solo hours, and the cadets would make at least 175 landings while in Primary school. After 30 flight hours cadets qualified for a civilian private pilot's license.

Good fliers, even these green cadets, were expected to develop a "feel for flight." As William Mitchell notes in *From the Pilot Factory, 1942*: "As any pilot knows, the relationship between stick and rudder is critical. This is especially true in a turn. Apply too much rudder and the airplane skids. Too much stick and the airplane slips. Apply the right amount of each, and the turn is very smooth. It's a landmark moment when the student discovers how silky smooth the airplane will respond when the controls are well coordinated."[4]

Greg had been taught that, rather than moving the controls through long ranges to create any desired reaction in the attitude of the airplane, a good pilot applies a steadily increasing pressure in the desired direction, easing off that pressure as the airplane reaches the desired heading. Pressure on each control is "coordinated." A rhythm, not independent movements of each flight control. *Pressure, not movement, is what counts.*

Counsel insisted that I do coordination turns even when we were flying to a practice area. He thought flying straight and level was a waste of time. This emphasis was very beneficial to me later during a check ride with the senior officer on the base. He said that he had not seen anyone with my limited experience who could do coordinated turns as well.

Like tens of thousands of future AAF pilots, Greg had flown a J-3 Piper Cub in the CPT Program. For his first flight at Garner Field, Greg climbed into an open-cockpit Fairchild PT-19A—a 200 hp two-seat trainer that had four times the power of the Piper Cub. Praised for its easy handling, the PT-19 was widely used at Primary training fields, and was aptly nicknamed "Cradle of Heroes."

Specifications: Fairchild PT-19A[5]

Powerplant: Ranger 6 cylinder, 200 hp
Airspeed:
    Max (Dive): 132 mph.
    Cruise: 113 mph

PT-19 on landing in Garner Field, 1941. (Wikimedia Commons)

Service ceiling: 15,300 ft.
Range: 400 miles
Empty weight: 1,845 lbs.
Wing span: 36 ft.
Length: 28 ft.
Height: 10 ft. 6 in.
First produced: 1941
Production: Over 3,000

With the huge demand for qualified pilots, instructors were quick to assess a cadet's suitability as a pilot. Airsickness, or poor coordination, led to immediate washouts. Cadets who could not catch on fast enough were also expelled. During the course of the war, over 40 percent of cadets were washed out—more than 120,000 cadet pilots—many of whom would serve as bombardiers or navigators.

Samuel Hynes, in his book *Flights of Passage*, notes: "I think not so much that the people they washed out couldn't learn to fly, but they couldn't learn to fly fast enough. You were expected to solo within 8 or 10 hours, there were tests, but not like any test that I had taken at school or university. You couldn't cram for it, and you couldn't fake it. You weren't even being tested on something that you had studied, really, but on what you were. If you were a flier, you passed; if you weren't, you washed out—fell out of the air, and became a lower order of being. It became clear that some people were natural fliers, and some weren't. The athletes usually were; they used their bodies easily and naturally, and they seemed to make the plane a part of themselves"[6] For cadets who failed to make the grade, washing out could be devastating.

For Greg, a CPT-trained pilot, the first phase of instruction was a refresher of his college instruction: taxiing, takeoffs and landings, turns, gliding, stalls and spins, and flying in traffic. Cadets were taught that pilot awareness was critical—recognizing an impending stall, knowing when a stall has occurred, and being able to recover effectively were learned skills. "See it, hear it, and feel it."

Cadets later learned to fly standard courses or patterns, like figure 8s, lazy 8s, pylon 8s and chandelles, and practiced steep turns, maximum performance power glides, stalls and spins. In the "accuracy" phase, the cadets practiced various landing approaches and landings, and the last bloc of instruction was the "acrobatic" phase, where the cadets learned loops, Immelmann turns, slow rolls, half rolls, and snap rolls—maneuvers they would need in combat.[7]

I enjoyed acrobatic flying, but I don't think my instructor, Jim Counsel, liked it very much. He would often show me one or two things, and then send me up solo where I could do acrobatics by myself. I asked my buddy Breezy Foster if he enjoyed flying solo acrobatic. He said, "Heck no, I don't want to set the world on fire, especially right under me."

At various points in the course, detailed instruction was also given in the methods of bailing out of an aircraft, controlling descent, and avoiding obstacles. Limited instruction in navigation and instrument flying was also included.

Cadets also got a taste of Army regime—marching, ceremonies, inspections, military customs and courtesies, and vigorous PT. Cadets would first encounter the "real" Army at their next schools in Basic flight instruction.[8]

Greg steadily progressed through Primary, in effect honing flight skills he had acquired in the 37 hours of flying time he had accumulated during his CPT Program at Middle Tennessee. *I had no trouble in the Primary phase, and the experience I received at Middle Tennessee helped.*

Primary Flight School was easy for me, and I woke up on December 7 as a very happy person, having finished the course the day before. Four of my buddies and I decided to walk into downtown Uvalde for one last visit, as we were scheduled to be bussed to Randolph Field at 2 p.m. that day. We stayed for an hour or two in town, and when we returned to the base, we learned that the Japanese had bombed Pearl Harbor. The sudden realization that our country was at war was truly, truly shocking.

The somber 102-mile bus ride from Garner Field to Randolph Field, just outside of San Antonio, was not what Greg had expected when he awoke that morning. During Primary, everyone assumed that their country would soon be at war, but would have been surprised that war would come to the United States in the Pacific. Their minds had become prepared for a much more likely European war, but within days of arriving at Randolph, with Germany, Italy, and Japan all declaring war on the United States, the cadets now knew that they would soon be part of the war that had finally engulfed the world.

It was really a sad day because we were really excited about going to Randolph and we thought we were just going to the next phase routinely, but things had changed a lot in that one day. When we got into Randolph, it was a different ballgame. Our tempo really picked up, and we were going seven days a week from early morning, about 5:30, to 9:30 at night, drilling, military formations, and ground school, and flying. We made up quite a bit of time because we were doing so much training, ground school, and flying.

Basic incorporated a transition phase, wherein the cadets became familiar with their new, more performant aircraft, and a diversified phase, which included accuracy maneuvers and acrobatics, formation, instruments, navigation, and night flying. Link simulator training was also included.

Instrument training was the most important part of the basic curriculum—cadets would eventually fly combat missions at night, and under all weather conditions. Greg's training focused on three key instruments: the needle, or rate-of-turn indicator, the ball, or bank indicator, and the airspeed indicator. As will be seen, developing a strong proficiency in these three instruments would be a key to Greg's survival later in his flight career. Only after Greg had completed Basic would the instrument training curriculum upgrade to what was termed a "full panel" system, which included a directional gyroscope and artificial horizon.[9]

Cadet William Gregory. (Gregory)

My group operated out of hanger "O" on the east side of the field, and the planes were parked outside. We walked the 200 yards from our barracks to the flight line every time we flew. There was a fairly constant drone of aircraft engines around the base all the time.

Contrary to what the cadets had experienced at Garner Field during Primary, all instruction was completely controlled and operated by the military, and immediately upon arrival, cadets experienced a higher order of discipline in a more rigorous military setting—the Army's intention of making "military pilots" our of the Primary graduates.[10] The cadet corps was organized much like an operating AAF group, with cadet commandants, squadron commanders, and flight leaders. To his surprise, Greg was named cadet lieutenant, a rank that would remain with him through Advanced training. This new rank included a responsibility to contribute to the discipline of his fellow cadets. He wore cadet lieutenant's stripes and carried a saber at dress formations.

The pace of the curriculum was relentless: reveille, breakfast, inspection, ground school, drill, noon mess, PT and athletics, flying, link training, then supper and a return to barracks to study and prepare for inspections, with an occasional lecture from 8:00–10:00 p.m. In the Army now, they marched in formation wherever they went, and never had enough sleep. Aviation was ever so much a young man's game.

Aerial view of Randolph Army Air Field. Postcard, North American BT-9. "Hello Folks. All is well here. James." (Gregory)

In Basic flight instruction, cadets flew aircraft of greater weight, power, and complexity. At Randolph, Greg flew the North American BT-9, a low wing single-engine aircraft with tandem seating and a glass canopy. The BT-9 had double the horsepower, double the weight, and a significant increase in service ceiling and maximum speed compared to the PT-19A. It was equipped with a two-way radio, and unlike the Piper Cubs and PT-19 that Greg had flown previously, the planes he would fly at Randolph were equipped with a two-pitch propeller. The BT-9 was one significant step closer to the type of aircraft that these pilots would fly in combat.[11] It was altogether a much more complex aircraft than those the cadets had flown in Primary.

Greg began transitioning to the BT-9 with his first flight on December 20: a 35-minute check ride. He flew almost daily, would solo on his ninth flight, and on occasion had two flights in a single day.[12]

We didn't have a runway at Randolph—it was a grass field, and we always landed at an angle, across the field. Sometime later they put paved landing strips at Randolph—one on the east side and one on the west side of the field.

The Basic program included 70 hours of flight instruction, half of which would be solo hours. Following a brief transition to the new aircraft, the cadets underwent a review of flight fundamentals in the BT-9—landings, stalls, spins, forced landings, and maneuvers. Next came further work in acrobatics, accuracy approaches, aerial navigation, strange field landings, instrument flying "under the hood," night landings, formation flying and cross-country flying for long distances. And as always, LINK training. Their flight instruction would include at least 125 landings.

The packed curriculum did not permit extensive aerobatic training, but Greg reveled in the limited aerobatic instruction he received. *They were teaching maneuvers that I had never done, in a larger airplane. Acrobatics always excited me. I thought it was fun, so I never feared acrobatics.* The pattern of instruction was familiar: instructors would first exhibit a particular flight maneuver to perform and then the students would do it on their own as a solo.

As cadets moved from Primary to Basic, the enterprise became more deadly. Primary had a high elimination rate, but a relatively low casualty rate. In Basic, the "washout" rate was half that of Primary, but the mortality rate started to increase.[13] As Samuel Hynes records: "Few airmen in Basic escaped seeing or knowing about somebody who died in a training accident. The grisly statistics…demonstrated that flying, even in the relatively benign early stages, was a highly dangerous occupation. Possibly during Primary, and certainly during Basic, the cold-blooded numbers took on visceral meaning."[14]

North American BT-9 Basic Trainer. (Wikimedia Commons)

Eighteen separate training accidents involving Greg's cohort occurred during his time at Randolph, and two of his classmates were killed in crashes that resulted from stalls or spin maneuvers.[15]

The airfield at Randolph was illuminated for night landings. They had the outline of the field quite clearly. I had my first night flight while at Randolph, taking off in the dark and completing three or four landings. It was really exciting. All of a sudden it was pitch black—Randolph was quite a ways from San Antonio, and there were no (roadway) lights. I wondered if was going to be able to handle this night flying, but my eyes adjusted and I thought "Oh, I can do this," and it wasn't that bad after all. After that, I really never had any trouble at all with the night flying.

Specifications: North American BT-9[16]

Powerplant: Wright 400 hp radial engine
Max speed: 170 mph
Service ceiling: 19,750 ft.
Range: 882 mi.
Empty weight: 3,314 lbs.
Wing span: 42 ft.
Length: 27 ft. 7 in.
Height: 13 ft. 7 in.
First produced: 1937
Production: 750

Gregory at the controls of a BT-9. (Gregory)

Greg was not particularly challenged by any of the instruction, and easily passed all his check rides. He had logged 45 flights in the BT-9, with over 77 flight hours—32 hours of instructor time, and 45 hours of solo flying time.[17]

My mother and father came down to Randolph Field for just a weekend when I was in Basic. It was a great trip for them. It was a long trip from Tennessee to San Antonio, and they had never been that far. I got to spend a little time with them, and they got to see the base. They saw me in uniform for the first time, saw that I was a cadet lieutenant, and they were proud of that. It was a nice reunion.

Instruction and practice in formation flying continued to be of high importance. In combat, a pilot's ability to maintain formation could determine whether he lived or died. But formation flying came easier to some pilots than to others. In training, three aircraft would assemble at 6,000 ft., one taking lead position, and the other two in "trail." Then the formation would shift to echelon, then again to V-formation, and back to trail—always maintaining position through very fine adjustments to the throttle. As Aviation Cadet Bob Norris would later note, "A number of the pilots were challenged; they would over control, fighting to hold the proper formation position with wild

Cadet Lieutenant William Gregory. (Gregory)

bursts of power, or by yanking the throttles back to idle to avoid chopping the lead's wing or trying to hold lateral position by using the rudders. They would end up all over the sky."[18]

Ten weeks after arriving at Randolph Field, Greg and his friends Foster and Neely completed the Basic Training program and were assigned to Moore Field at Mission, TX for Advanced Flight Training. Their posting to Moore, a single-engine flight school, most likely meant they would fly fighters.

As with his experience at Garner Field, Greg's cohort of 85 cadets would again be the first class at the new airfield at Moore Army Air Field (AAF). *It was a brand-new field again, in the lower Rio Grande Valley, 15 miles north of Mission, Texas. I arrived there in the spring, and it was beautiful there. All the citrus were in full bloom, and it was just a beautiful area at that time.*

Moore was equipped with the North American AT-6 "Texan," and a few canopy-equipped PT-19s for use in simulated aerial combat exercises. The Texan was 1,000 lbs. heavier than the BT-9, came with a 600 hp engine that was 50 percent larger than anything Greg had flown at Randolph, had a service ceiling a mile higher, and boasted a maximum speed of over 200 mph.

Specifications: North American AT-6[19]

Powerplant: Pratt & Whitney 600 hp radial engine
Max speed: 208 mph
Service ceiling: 24,200 ft.
Range: 730 miles
Empty weight: 4,158 lb.
Wing span: 42 ft.
Length: 29 ft.
Height: 11 ft. 8 in.

Greg liked flying the AT-6—it represented one more significant step closer to the type of aircraft he would mount in combat missions in just a few months. The curriculum was now familiar—transition, instruments, navigation, formation flying and acrobatics—the specific skills that would be critical to fighter pilots. Ground school included thirty-two different courses crammed into eight weeks. Eighteen- to twenty-hour days were common.

Acrobatics were singularly important for pilots who had been assigned to single-engine Advanced Flight Schools. Cadets trained in all conventional combat maneuvers within the performance limits of the advanced trainer. The instruction stressed the handling of maneuverable, speedy training planes and the development of instantaneous control reactions in students.

Training accidents continued, with increasing severity. About his own flight training, Norris recalls: "We flew extensive cross-country flights at night on instruments and honed our formation flying. We lost two of our pilots when they collided in midair during a solo formation flying session: it was a sober memorial service. Our instructor said, 'Get used to it; you will see death time and time again.'"[20]

Fifteen accidents occurred during Greg's tenure at Moore, with a variety of causes, and a range of lethality: the majority were taxiing, takeoff, or landing accidents, but two cadets were killed in mid-air collisions, and one in a ground collision.[21]

Perhaps oddly, gunnery instruction was not given to Greg's cohort at Moore. He would receive minimal ground gunnery training before going abroad, and no aerial gunnery training.

As Greg had progressed through each stage of flight school, he and his fellow cadets were fully cognizant of what lay ahead for them. *We knew that the Germans had been very successful, and had already been in combat for several years at this time. We knew that if we were transferred to the European campaign, we would be facing serious opposition because these pilots were very, very good.*

North American AT-6 Advanced Trainer. (Wikimedia Commons)

Thirty weeks after joining the AAC at Fort Oglethorpe, Greg graduated from Advanced Flight School at Moore Airfield, Class 42-D, on April 29, 1942, and was commissioned the next day. *We flew a big review that day on graduation. Since our class was the first to graduate from Moore, it was sort of a new thing there in the valley, so a lot of people turned out for that.*[22]

In receiving their commission as second lieutenants, and their rating as Pilot, Greg and his fellow pilots represented the leading edge of what would soon become a tsunami of trained combat pilots. By the end of the war, a total of 193,440 pilots graduated from AAF advanced flying schools, including over 35,000 fighter pilots.

Transition

Despite the fact that Greg's class had done all their training in single-engine aircraft, and normally would have expected to transition into single-engine fighters, every graduate of Class 42-D was assigned to the P-38 twin-engine fighter—the world's most performant production aircraft.

The school at Moore Field was a fighter preparation school, and when seventy-eight of us graduated in April, all of us—the entire class—were selected for P-38s and assigned to one of six squadrons at Hamilton field, eighteen miles north of the Golden Gate Bridge.

The day following their graduation as newly minted second lieutenants, Greg and his friends Harold Ed Brown and Bill Neely left Texas, driving for the California coast and San Francisco. Other pilots had taken the train to California and arrived before Greg and his friends.

At the time of Greg's graduation, the AAF had two fighter groups based at Hamilton Field waiting for new pilots: the 14th and the 78th, each with three squadrons. Arriving a few days later than other new graduates, Greg learned that the 14th had already been fully staffed with new pilots and that he and Bill Neely had been assigned to the 83rd Fighter Squadron (FS) of the 78th Fighter Group (FG). The new pilots were all equally qualified, and the commander of the 14th, Colonel Olds, did not hand-select his pilots: *He just got what he got until his squadron was filled, then the rest of us went to the 78th Fighter Group.*[23]

A short period of "transition" was included in all phases of flight training, as well as later in a pilot's career, when new assignments included unfamiliar aircraft. Cadets accustomed to the low horsepower aircraft in Primary training were challenged by the complexity of the BT-13s, and more so by the much more complicated and complex AT-6s in Advanced training.

In the early days of aviation, this transition to combat aircraft could be done in a few days. But with the increasing complexity of combat aircraft, and as the aircraft became more specialized, the period of the final transition had to be extended. For pilots completing Advanced school in the spring of 1942, the transition to single-engine fighters like the P-47 would take a full two months. Transition to the more complex P-38 would take longer. The pilots viewed this training as critical: in their minds, it represented their last combat training before deployment overseas, and would be essential to their later success, and survival, in combat.

Pilots' views on transitioning to the P-38 were expressed in William Gray's article in the August 16, 1943 issue of *Life Magazine,* addressing what could be a daunting transition for pilots: "Double controls (for twin engines) worried student pilots and bred the talk of "too much plane." The cockpit is about the size of a very deep bathtub fitted with a bus seat. In front on a black instrument panel are 21 clock-like dials, and the maze of other gadgets in the cockpit includes three dozen switches, 22 levers, five cranks, two plungers, half a dozen thumb buttons and radio controls. One pilot peered into the cockpit and gasped, 'It looks like a plumber and an electrician got together and had a nightmare.'"

Greg liked fighters and flying formation, enjoying the tactics. Flying in formation was essential for fighters, but not all pilots were suited to become fighter pilots. Greg remembers flying in formation in Advanced

Lockheed P-38 Lightning fighter. (Wikimedia Commons)

school with his good friend, Harold Ed Brown. *It was dangerous to be in the same sky with him when he was trying to fly formation. He just never had a knack for it at all. I think he would have made it in other type flying, but not in the P-38.*[24]

After a few days at the overcrowded Hamilton Field, the 78th Fighter Group was assigned to Mills Field, 15 miles south of San Francisco, and now the site of San Francisco International Airport. Joining Greg at Mills was his longtime friend, Bill Neely. By now Greg and Bill had attended Middle Tennessee together, had joined the Army Air Corps together, and had completed all three phases of flight training together. Now assigned to the same squadron, it was likely that they would remain together for the duration of their upcoming combat tour.

In early May Greg was introduced to the P-38. At this time in the war, transition training varied among the fighter squadrons. Some new P-38 squadrons benefited from a "piggy-back ride" in a P-38 in which the radio had been removed from behind the pilot, making room for a student observer.

Flight controls and instruments became increasingly complex as aviation cadets advanced through their flight instructions, culminating in the twin-engine, high-performance P-38 fighter. (Richardson)

But not for the new 83rd squadron. Greg, and all his squadron mates, went from the single-seat AT-6 to the twin-engine P-38, and would solo the P-38 in their first flight.

Greg received one-on-one instruction for operating the P-38 on just one occasion. With Greg seated in the cockpit and the instructor perched next to him on the wing, he was familiarized with the flight controls and instruments.

2nd Lt. William Gregory, P-38 pilot. (Gregory)

There really wasn't (much ground instruction) with the P-38. It was very limited. It was terrible. They showed us the cockpit and what all the instruments stood for, and they showed us how to start the airplane. I think they felt that if we could start the airplane and taxi it, we should be able to fly it. So we cranked it up and took off. It was awesome. That was kind of the way our training went.

We never were in a twin-engine aircraft up to that time. We went from a slow airplane (AT-6) to the fastest production airplane in the world at that time. It was a really big step—we all felt it. From flying an AT-6 with one 600 hp engine to the P-38 with two huge Allison engines, each producing 1,425 hp. It was exciting, I guess you might say. On my very first flight, I felt like the airplane was at least a half a mile ahead of me for the first 30 minutes. I really had to stay focused in the early transition phase for the P-38.

Specifications: Lockheed P-38 Lightning[25]

Powerplant: Twin Allison engines 12 cylinders, 1,600 hp ea.
Max speed: 400 mph
Service ceiling: 39,000 ft.
Range: 1,750 miles
Empty weight: 12,200 lbs.
Wing span: 52 ft.
Length: 37 ft. 10 in.
Height: 9 ft. 10 in.
Production: Over 10,000

The dangers of flight training continued, and the 78th Fighter Group's transition to the P-38 carried a steep and costly learning curve. With new pilots flying dangerous combat maneuvers in still-unfamiliar high-performance aircraft, the level of risk remained high. And the consequences were equally severe.

Greg's squadron was scheduled for their first flight in the P-38 during the first week of May at Mills Field, and their unfamiliarity with their new aircraft became tragically apparent almost immediately.

Greg and Bill Neely, along with their friend Charley Stuart, who had been cadet colonel at Advanced school at Moore Field, were scheduled for a 1:00 p.m. flight with an instructor. The instructor took off, and then Lt. Stuart. *It was my second flight in a P-38; probably Stuart's second flight as well. I lined up for takeoff, and I could see as he was going down the runway that his right engine was cutting out and blowing smoke. I was hoping he would stop, but he went on and got off. He got over the power lines at the end of the runway, made it to about 300 feet, then lost control, crashed nose down and was lost. He went straight in—a big smoke.*

And then, with no pause, it was Greg's turn to take off. He had to fly through the smoke of the downed airplane. *We lost quite a few pilots in part because we just hadn't had much training or much transition. It was just lack of experience. Any one of us, if we'd had that airplane, might have had the same fate. But Stuart was a gung-ho guy and he would have wanted to complete the mission. He just didn't have enough time in the airplane.*

Greg would later reflect on what he might have done in that circumstance. *In this case, it was on takeoff, so if the right engine cut out, I would throttle back the left engine to bring the plane back to level flight, and attempt a controlled crash landing. The first thing to do is get a level flight and see if you could get enough power out of the good engine. Of course, you could dive down a little bit to maintain airspeed. But his airplane stalled. We had received no instruction about what to do in that situation. I later learned that you could not overpower an engine out at low airspeed.*

The 78th suffered ten separate flying accidents during September alone, all in their newly acquired P-38s, and five of which were fatal. There was no pattern to the losses, which resulted from mid-air collisions, uncontrolled spins or stalls, and engine failures. But the pilots learned quickly. In October there were just four flight accidents, none fatal. In November, there were none.[26]

The P-38 that Greg would fly in combat would be used in many combat roles, including bomber escort, dive bombing, and ground attack. Yet despite the fact that the bomber escort would necessarily involve extensive aerial combat against experienced German and Italian fighter pilots, Greg received no aerial gunnery instruction. *We did get some training in ground gunnery experience, and that was good. But I don't think we got any aerial gunnery experience at all. We did our practice firing into targets right near the beach there.* But he was comfortable doing that kind of ground attack. *Yeah, that was "cool," as they say today. I liked that a lot. We really should have had experience with aerial gunnery, but we didn't.*

Transition training in the P-38 emphasized combat preparedness. The pilots flew their aircraft in detailed acrobatic, aerial bombing, and gunnery exercises, and in simulated individual combat. Navigation missions, instrument flying, and night flying were also included in the transition training. And since one of the P-38's principal uses would be as a fighter escort for America's heavy bomber fleet, emphasis was placed on high-altitude, long-range operations, and on developing the awareness and aggressiveness that would become important on later escort missions.

Within the limited hours available, the greatest attention was paid to developing six skills that would be critical for operating within a combat squadron: rapid take-off from dispersed positions and quick assembly into combat disposition; precision landings in rapid succession; formation flying; rapid take-off

Operation Training Unit pilots assigned to the 83rd Fighter Squadron, 78th Fighter Group. Front: Richard Decker, Edgar Yarberry, William Gregory, William Neely, Ralph Hines. Back: Harry Vogelsong, Bruce Cambell, Henry L. Perry, Harold Harper. (Harold Harper Family Archives)

P-38s in "four-finger" combat formation. (Wikimedia Commons)

with ascent through overcast and assembly at altitude; descent through overcast, landing, and dispersing on the ground rapidly; and efficient execution of all known offensive and defensive tactics against hostile air and surface forces.[27]

The 14th was slated to be posted abroad first, and debarked Hamilton Field at the end of September for England. Greg's 78th Fighter Group relocated to Hamilton to continue their training through October and early November. The squadron's last training flights at Hamilton were completed on November 2 and the squadron was alerted to go to the European Theater of Operations; the pilots would not fly again until early January 1943.

The group's embarkation for the European Theater began on November 1 when it entrained for the four-day trip to Camp Kilmer in New Jersey. On arrival, the squadron spent a week in locating, sorting, and re-packing the supplies and equipment it would take overseas, and the men took this time to make final preparation for their departure—making wills, creating pay allotments, and letter writing. On the evening of November 23 the group boarded a ferry for the short trip across the Hudson River to the Port of New York, and by the early hours of the next day had boarded HMS *Queen Elizabeth*, recently refitted for troop movement. Among the 13,000 personnel on board were American, French and British pilots, soldiers, sailors, and 300 nurses. All

Lt. William Gregory, Hamilton Field, 1942. (Gregory)

were given a booklet entitled "Guide to Great Britain," found their bunks, and were awakened five hours later for lifeboat drill.

When I departed the US for England with the 78th FG, I had arranged for my pay to be sent to my bank at Hartsville. The government provided a life insurance policy of $10,000, so I didn't buy any additional life insurance. I did not complete a will because I felt like I was coming back. You don't know that, but I felt like I would return.

We rode the beautiful Queen Elizabeth, *assigned twelve to a stateroom, and made the entire voyage to Scotland unescorted, with frequent course adjustments to confuse any lurking U-boats.*

The *Queen Elizabeth* entered the Firth of Clyde and anchored near the town of Greenock, Scotland in the late afternoon of November 29. The next day, the squadron lightered ashore and boarded trains for the final leg of the nearly four-week journey. Passing through Glasgow and Edinburgh, the squadron arrived in the early morning hours at its destination—the town of Goxhill in Lincolnshire, along the south bank of the River Humber across from the city of Hull on the east coast of England.[28] Greg left the United States a second lieutenant but was promoted to first lieutenant soon after his arrival in England.

With no P-38s at their disposal, they flew P-47s when the situation permitted. New P-38s arrived over the next two months, and the pilots of the 78th began making low-level flights to get oriented to the area. *The weather was terrible. It usually is in England through the winter. I have been there several times in the winter, and the weather was usually bad.*

Pilot Robert Vickers recalls the English weather: "The weather in England is terribly unpredictable. In the winter you got used to flying low ceilings in rain and snow and crud. It is amazing to me as I look back on it now that we could put that many airplanes in the air without mishap in weather that was down to 200–300 foot ceilings and rain and any kind of crud that you can imagine."[29]

For the squadrons of the 78th, flying accidents were seemingly inevitable. After being re-equipped with new P-38s in January, the 78th resumed flight operations and just as quickly the casualties began to mount. On January 13, Lieutenant Richard Wells was killed in a flying accident, and later in the month Lieutenant Lovera crashed on takeoff and Lieutenants Brown and Chavis crashed on landing.[30]

The war was all around them. The city of Hull, just eight miles distant, was a magnet for German bombers who raided weekly. The men of the 78th saw the red tracer fire from Allied antiaircraft batteries, the illuminating flares dropped by the bombers, the crack and flash of bursting flak, and the red flash and roar of exploding bombs that rattled the windows of the men's quarters at Goxhill.

In March, twelve out of the 40 or so pilots of the 78th were assigned to fly to Chelveston, a B-17 base, and to practice for two missions before undertaking regular escort missions over Germany. At Chelveston, Greg happened to meet an old friend, Hoyt Davis, from Trousdale County. Greg's family had been sharecroppers on Hoyt's father's farm in the late 1930s, and the two young men had become good friends. Hoyt was on a bomber crew, a fact that Greg found sobering. At the time, fighter pilots were required to complete a 50-mission tour before redeployment home. For bomber crews, the tour was 25, and German defenses were so strong at that period in the war that few crews reached the end of their tours unscathed.[31]

Just six months earlier, in the spring of 1942, the Allies had begun to implement plans for the invasion of northern Europe, to occur as early as May 1943, under the codename *Roundup*. In support of *Roundup*, a massive movement of men and arms began the transit to England, under the codename *Bolero*. The buildup was planned to include a million American troops, with the Air Force contributing up to 69 combat groups—over 3,600 aircraft, including nearly 1,000 fighters, including Greg and his 78th FG. However, with the buildup of men and materiel reaching a crescendo, Allied plans changed drastically.

We flew one practice mission at Chelveston, but before we could fly the second one, our group commander received orders to send all P-38s to North Africa where Rommel was operating at that time.

Operation *Roundup* had been abandoned. Its D-Day, originally set for mid-1943, was too soon for the Allies to reach a satisfactory state of preparedness. Instead, and mainly at the urging of President Roosevelt, Operation *Torch* was put into place—the invasion of North Africa by Allied forces. Many of the resources that had formed Operation *Bolero* were redirected to support the invasion forces in Morocco and Algeria.

Prior to making the move, the group's P-38s all had to be equipped with dust filters to prepare them for service in the arid North African deserts, a retrofit that would be made at Base Air Depot 3 at Langford Lodge, in Northern Ireland near Belfast, where Lockheed operated a factory.

Late in the afternoon of January 26, Greg's 12-aircraft unit—still at Chelveston—received orders to make the flight to Langford Lodge. They left immediately, making an intermediate stop at their base at Goxhill. *It seemed like a bad decision. It was late in the afternoon when we landed back at Goxhill, and still later when we took off. It was heavy overcast—we had about a 1,000-foot ceiling. We knew we would be landing at a place we had never been before, on a black night, and we were going to be in weather all the way there.*

As we neared the highlands in western England, the elevation rose, and we had to fly through the clouds on instruments. At that point, we hadn't had much instrument flying in the P-38s. Struggling to maintain formation, two aircraft in the flight went down over the high ground of the Trough of Bowland, crashing into the bleak Lancashire moorland. Henry Perry of the 83rd squadron and Stephan White in the 82nd were killed. Some historical documents indicate that the aircraft collided and crashed almost immediately—their crash sites were within a mile and a half of each other. *Greg disagrees. I don't think there is any doubt that Perry and White lost control of their airplanes. I don't think they crashed into each other. There is no way of knowing, but it is my belief that they were just not good enough instrument pilots, and they weren't close enough in formation to go through this overcast. We did break out on top, at about 10,000 feet, and we were in the clear at that point. But Perry and White never got through the clouds. I think they lost control of their airplanes and went in.* The same day, Lieutenant Donald Beals, also of the 83rd, was lost while ferrying a P-38 to North Africa.

Greg's life, already hazardous by virtue of his military service to date, was becoming increasingly dangerous, and often for reasons completely outside his control. Having survived the harrowing flight from England to Ireland to deliver P-38s for refitting, Greg settled into quarters at Belfast, about 30 miles away from the Lockheed airfield, with plans to remain for about a week.

Bill Neely and I were rooming together. One day he was trying to get an extra shell in his .45. He got it in but all of a sudden the gun fired, the round passing right over my head. I thought, boy the police are going to be after us. But no one ever came.

With the filters fitted, the squadron left Belfast, returned to Goxhill, and then went on to Predannack Airfield near Land's End, the southern tip of England. They remained at Land's End for three or four days, waiting for the weather to clear, before making the six-hour flight to Cazes Airfield at Casablanca, Morocco to deliver the aircraft to the Army Air Force units badly in need of fresh equipment following heavy losses during Operation *Torch*.

Greg flew back to England on a transport plane and helped deliver another batch of P-38s to Ireland for retrofitting with dust filters. He was assigned to make a second delivery to North Africa in March, and on his arrival at Casablanca, Greg and his fellow pilots from the 78th Fighter Group were surprised to receive fresh orders permanently assigning some pilots to the 48th Fighter Squadron, Greg to the 49th.[32]

Berrechid, Morocco

The North African Training Center (NATC) was located at Berrechid, just outside of Casablanca in Morocco, and provided brief but highly effective pre-combat flight training in combat aircraft by experts versed in the tactical methods and practices then in actual use at the front. Pilots receiving training at NATC were just days away from their first combat mission. Every fighter pilot in the Mediterranean Theater of Operations (MTO) spent a couple of weeks at Berrechid studying aircraft and naval craft recognition, and escape and evasion techniques.

Pilot George Loving recorded his comments about Berrechid: "My new home was a four-man pyramidal tent, one of dozens beneath a line of lofty palm trees at the edge of the airfield. The terrain was barren except for scattered palms, and in the distance loomed the Atlas Mountains, more than 13,500 feet high, and beyond them the Sahara. Despite the blowing dust and sand, we kept the tent sides rolled up during the day to provide some relief from the July heat. While the daylight temperatures reached high levels, it was an arid heat, easier to tolerate than the humid kind, and since temperatures fell sharply at night, sleep was not a problem."

Pilots at Berrechid would occasionally visit nearby Casablanca, about which Loving recorded: "As we disembarked there was a great deal of excitement, this being the first foreign city most of us had ever visited. To us, Casablanca seemed to radiate an atmosphere of mystery and intrigue kindled by the strange attire of the Moroccans, (and) the exotic Muslim architecture. As we walked the streets and broad boulevards what struck me most forcefully was the extraordinary range of uniforms worn by officers and men of the Army, Navy, or Air Forces of Australia, Britain, Canada, France, India, South Africa, and the United States. These showed the Allied effort against the Germans and Italians."[33]

Pilot Wayne Johnson recorded his recollections a bit less lyrically, but no less vividly: "What a godawful place. Beggars, whores, and every kind of terrible-looking humans—solid milling crowds—I've never seen anything like it. I couldn't believe people could live like this. It was much worse than the movies… What a hell hole—everything stinks and sand over everything. The people are supposed to be our allies but look sinister as hell."[34]

Johnson concurs with Loving in one aspect: "There are lots of interesting militaries though. English, French, Arabs, Indians, black and all shades of brown jabbering away in many different languages."

Aerial training at NATC consisted of 25 flight hours. But before that could begin, pilots were again tasked with classroom instruction, with particular emphasis on aircraft recognition. Pilots were taught in an instant to recognize every aircraft type, friendly or enemy, that they were likely to encounter: fighters, bombers, reconnaissance aircraft, trainers, and transports; Italian, German, French, British and American.

According to Loving, "The approach to this formidable task was as simple as it was ingenious. A plain black silhouette of an airplane—either a front or rear view, side view, or overhead view—was flashed on a screen briefly for the group to observe, and whoever recognized it first called out the name. Initially, the silhouette was flashed on for a few seconds, but as our skill increased the time was reduced to a fiftieth of a second. By the end of the course, we could identify almost all of the aircraft without error or hesitation."

The flight line could be ferociously hot. Pilots flying after mid-morning wore gloves to avoid painful burns from touching the wing surfaces or fuselage, which by then had been baked to scorching in the hot African sun.

On March 28 the squadron moved to the airfield at Mediouna, Morocco, just to the north of Berrechid, for an additional month of training. At Mediouna, the 37th Fighter Squadron was attached to the 14th Fighter Group, bringing it to its full complement of men and aircraft. Operating under a new organization, with new aircraft and pilots, and with a fresh set of "marching orders," Greg and the other "re-start" pilots of the 14th began the task for which they had long trained: wresting air superiority in North Africa from the Luftwaffe and keeping it. At Mediouna, Greg felt the pace quickening, and by early May, the group was ready to rejoin the fight and received orders assigning it to a new forward base at Telergma, not far from Constantine in northeastern Algeria.

On May 5 the squadron made the move to Telergma, and the first combat mission was set for the next day. An escort mission—no bombs. Just loaded for strafing.

CHAPTER 4

Combat Tour

Greg arrived in Morocco as part of a rebuilding program for the battered US air forces in North Africa. The original 14th Fighter Group had first arrived in the theater in mid-November 1942, and flew its first mission on November 20. What followed were 69 days of horrific combat and relentless loss. In its first month of combat, the 14th lost nine pilots. By late January, 19 pilots had been killed due to enemy action, and five others taken as POWs. Of the original 54 pilots who arrived from England at the start of combat operations in North Africa, just 38 remained.[1,2]

The group had arrived in North Africa to an uncertain future, and faced two serious disadvantages. At the time the 14th's pilots entered combat, the German Air Force (GAF) had been flying combat operations for four years, in Spain, continental Europe, in Russia, and in the deserts of northeastern Africa. Their flight tactics had long been perfected, many of their pilots had flown hundreds of missions, and they were operating from well-established bases in North Africa. Greg strongly believes that this imbalance in experience was the most critical factor in the 14th's terrible three months of combat that lay ahead.

I think it was one thing. The Luftwaffe was highly experienced and had as much as 300–400 hours of combat experience, and our pilots had zero. Some of the 14th FG pilots had just 50–70 hours in the P-38, none in combat. That was the difference. They were not a good match for the Luftwaffe. The German pilots were just better qualified than the first group was.

Historians also generally agree that the set of doctrines under which the American Air Forces were operating in North Africa at that time were entirely inappropriate for the situation. The P-38 pilots were operating in a defensive mode, and were not attacking the German forces at their home bases. Until this policy was substantially changed in the spring of 1943, the Luftwaffe continued to hold a substantial tactical advantage.[3]

By mid-January, the 14th could muster just 12 combat-ready aircraft. Its sister squadrons, the 1st and the 83rd Fighter Groups, had suffered similarly high losses. The fighter force in North Africa was in tatters.

For the 14th, the worst came on January 23 when the 48th Fighter Squadron lost six aircraft and five pilots on a strafing mission in Tunisia. It was a terrible loss for the squadron. The 14th's parent command, the 12th Air Force, recognized that the group had ceased to be an effective combat unit, and by February it had been relieved of duty.[4]

A similar fate awaited the 33rd Fighter Group, which was itself down to just 13 aircraft. Two weeks after the 14th stood down, the 33rd was also withdrawn from the theater for reconstitution.

Rebuilding the 14th

Army Air Force headquarters quickly began the process of re-equipping and rebuilding the fighter groups in North Africa, and by early spring of 1943, the rebuilding of the 14th was well underway. Concurrently, the Allied Air Forces had been reorganized into the North African Air Force (NAAF), with all strategic assets, including long-range fighters, organized within the North African Strategic Air Force (NASAF). Allied strategies also changed. NASAF was directed to attain air superiority, and that meant attacking the Luftwaffe in the air and on the ground, and specifically targeting their largely undamaged airfields.

The outcome of the land battles in North Africa was no longer in doubt. German forces had been steadily forced into the northeastern corner of Tunisia, and with their surrender imminent, Germany was taking all measures to evacuate essential equipment and personnel, including pilots and aircraft. By the time the 14th reentered combat operations the German air forces had all evacuated to bases on Sicily, Sardinia, and Italy, and it was there that the American and British air forces carried the fight.

On May 6, the day after they arrived at Telergma, the three squadrons of the 14th were assigned to the first of what would be a series of anti-shipping missions against the German and Italian navies. These missions were aimed at interdicting vessels evacuating German troops and material from their last bastions in Tunisia. The mission was a success, with one ship sunk and another damaged. The American formation received only light flak during the attack, and no enemy aircraft were seen during the bomb run. On return to base, with the 49th's aircraft not having fired a shot, the flight leader of the 49th's twelve

Greg and his fellow pilots of the 49th Fighter Squadron, North Africa, 1943. Rear, from left: Frederick Bitter, Carroll S. Knott, Anthony Evans, Harold T. Harper, Wayne M. Manlove. Front, from left: Marlow J. Leikness, Richard E. Decker, William J. Gregory, Lloyd K. DeMoss. (Gregory)

aircraft elected to take the formation on a strafing run against a German air-field in eastern Tunisia. Despite Germany's evacuation, the remaining airfields were still fiercely defended with large and medium caliber anti-aircraft guns, including the 4-barreled Flakvierling 38—a weapon that had been proven to be devastatingly effective against low-flying aircraft.[5]

The pilots' preflight briefing had included only the bomber escort mission, with no mention of a possible ground attack after the bombers had safely exited German airspace. The pilots were unprepared for the strafing run. Lieutenant Harold Harper later reported: "We weren't ready for strafing... I didn't even have my gun sight on, and I never got a shot off. I looked over my left wing and here is a ball of fire, and I got my tire shot out."[6]

Killed in the attack was Lieutenant Gail Moore, and in a separate mission a pilot with the 37th FS was also killed by ground fire.[7] For the 14th, the loss of two pilots in the Group's first mission was a shocking introduction to combat. The historical record shows a more costly and more tragic end to the formation of twelve pilots who made up the first mission of the 49th Fighter Squadron: six of these young men would not survive the war.

Many years later, Greg would reflect on preparing for combat. *The only way to get prepared is to get in combat. You have to do your best, and if you survive the first few missions, your chances actually improve. You learn fast in combat. You want to get (a new pilot) through his first mission.*

Greg's own combat baptism occurred two days later, on May 8, a second anti-shipping sweep in which 24 aircraft of the 49th FS escorted six B-26s, again to the Egadi Island group. In what must have seemed an anticlimactic mission, especially considering the deadly drama two days prior, Greg's formation saw no enemy aircraft, was not targeted by flak, and saw just one German vessel.

Notwithstanding his uneventful first combat mission, the stark risks of aerial combat became apparent early to Greg. *I remember the first mission where I saw tracers coming at me. A 109 was on my tail. And I got to thinking later that I was seeing all these tracers, but there were four times that many rounds that I didn't see. There were tracers coming at me and across the wings, but I managed to get out of that situation—it was an exciting moment for sure.*

Greg would quickly begin to acquire the mental toughness that was a common trait among experienced combat pilots. His early experiences with disappointments and the personal resolve that he had shown in the face of those disappointments prepared him, however slightly, for the tough situations he would face in combat. He had learned that being aggressive was an acquired trait, and as the number of his combat sorties began to climb, he felt confidence in his own abilities growing as well.

I felt really comfortable in the airplane, and I thought I handled the airplane pretty well. I would practice cutting one engine back, seeing if I could control it, and so forth. So I really felt like I could handle that airplane really well. I enjoyed the low missions. We would be so low that we would pick up water from the props.

Base life at Telergma

The 14th Fighter Group and its three squadrons of P-38s advanced to Telergma during the first week of May 1943 and remained for just five weeks. A diarist from the 82nd FG, George Underwood, would later comment that Telergma was a "windy, barren, rocky, cold place with some barren hills to the south. It didn't look like much to us from the air, but it looked like less after we landed. You might think by the name Telergma that there was a town there, but there wasn't—just a little Arab village with a population of about 100.

A more dirty and filthy place you'll never find anywhere in the world. There wasn't anything about Telergma that made you think of an air base except maybe the muddy strip of dirt that we landed on."[8]

Scorpions were abundant and aggressive. In what became a daily ritual, shoes, bedding and personal gear in the tents had to be checked and cleared, and the squadron learned that Algeria was also home to the full range of desert critters, including the Mediterranean recluse spider, the camel spider, and the Egyptian cobra.[9]

It didn't take long for Lt. Gregory to learn that life on the AAF air bases in North Africa would hold little charm. His most acerbic comments related to the food. *Everybody got dysentery, and we lost weight, and the food was just terrible. For one thing (the cooks) weren't trained. They were selected from those who couldn't do anything else.*

After the war, the Air Force really put emphasis on food. They did not during the war, and we really suffered by it. The squadron was set up with a mess tent. A series of tables covered by a tent. They had utensils, but we had to wash them after we used them. I don't think it was sanitary because we all got sick as a result of the food and the unsanitary conditions. You just did not enjoy going to the mess hall.

Greg and his fellow pilots and tent-mates, Bland, Neely, Gregory and DeMoss. (Gregory)

There was little diversion on base. Movies, which would be commonplace later in the war, were never shown during Greg's combat tour. A USO group of American women provided donuts and coffee after flights. The squadron personnel did not get any leave while based at Telergma, but for a change of scenery, the pilots would occasionally get day passes to visit Constantine, 20 miles to the northwest of the base. *The food there was terrible. And cold beer was not to be found anywhere. We just didn't get off base much.*

The 49th Fighter Squadron, Greg's unit, would launch forty-six missions from Telergma during that time, flying two-a-day missions on 10 occasions. Bomber escort assignments predominated (28), but increasingly the group was assigned to dive-bombing missions (15). Twelve of Greg's fellow pilots from the squadron were lost during the short time it was based at Telergma. In the continuing desperate fight for air superiority in the Mediterranean Theater, losses sustained by the "re-started" 49th began to exceed those of the original 49th when it first began combat operations during Operation *Torch*.[10]

Bomber escort

Greg's early assignments were remarkable for their range of mission types, and for their varying intensity: his first eleven missions would include high-altitude escort of B-17 bombers (4), mid-level escort of B-25 and B-26 medium bombers (2), dive-bombing (2) and fighter-bombing sweeps (3).

The Intelligence Section of the 12th AF in early 1943 identified and prior-itized a list of 80 critical Sicilian targets, and with the adoption of NASAF's new strategy for getting and holding air superiority, the destruction of airfields and air force supporting facilities was of utmost importance. Fifteen of the top 20 targets were German or Italian airfields or landing grounds. On May 21 NASAF set in motion an ambitious plan that would send eight of its nine bomber groups in a massive bombing attack against three priority targets (#5 Sciacca, #6 Castelvetrano, and #8 Villacidro) and a lower-priority airfield at Decimomannu. [11]

The North African Strategic Air Force (NASAF) emptied its fighter airfields to escort bombers to these targets: Greg's group would escort B-17s to Castelvetrano (Sicily); the 1st FG would escort B-17 bombers to Sciacca (Sicily); the 82nd would escort B-25 medium bombers to Villacidro (Sardinia); and the 325th would escort B-26 medium bombers to Decimomannu aerodrome (Sardinia). The 82nd and 325th would also undertake dive-bombing missions against German anti-aircraft gun positions on the island of Pantelleria.

Pre-strike reconnaissance photo of Castelvetrano Aerodrome, prior to the attack on May 21, 1943. (National Archives, 342-FH-3A27204-B52325AC)

The missions against German airfields at Castelvetrano and Sciacca would undoubtedly stir the hornets' nest. The Luftwaffe operated six fighter fields in northwest Sicily: NAAF intelligence estimated that there would be approximately 174 single-engine fighters among those airfields.[12]

At this time in the war, the German air defenses of Sicily were the responsibility of Jagdgeschwader 53 (JG 53)—the Luftwaffe's 53rd fighter wing. JG53 was one of the most experienced Luftwaffe units in the Mediterranean Theater, having seen combat in four different theaters and recorded hundreds of aerial victories.[13]

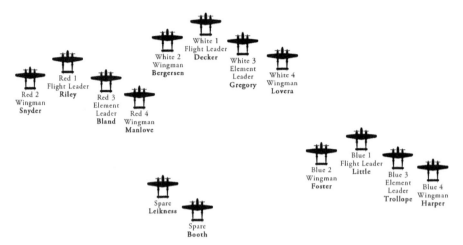

49th Fighter Squadron formation. Mission to Castelvetrano Aerodrome, May 21, 1943. (Samuel Richardson, Yosemite Productions)

The 14th had completed three missions to this sector of Sicily, and on each, the ground fire from large and medium caliber anti-aircraft guns had been intense, while the Luftwaffe pilots had shown great eagerness for combat. The 14th lost four pilots on these three missions.

The mission assigned to the 14th FG on this day required twelve aircraft, with spares, from each of the group's three squadrons. The 49th started the mission with an 0730 takeoff, followed in quick succession by the aircraft of the 37th and 48th. Within 30 minutes, all were airborne and made rendezvous with the B-17s of the 97th and 99th Bomb Groups near the Tunisian coastline.

Greg recalls the mission vividly. The bombers made an accurate drop from 27,000 feet, and mission reports later confirmed that at the time of the attack at least 100 German aircraft were parked on the Castelvetrano aerodrome. As the bombers wheeled away from the target zone and were rejoined by their fighter escort, the Luftwaffe made its first appearance, with upwards of 25 Me-109s and FW-190s attacking the bomber formation on its homeward leg.[18]

On this day the German interceptors were ferociously and persistently aggressive, making repeated attacks against both fighters and bombers, and continuing their attacks beyond Pantelleria and all the way to the Tunisian coastline. The swirling aerial combat over this patch of the Mediterranean involved upwards of sixty aircraft, both German and American. The Flying Fortresses lived up to their billing: the 97th reported shooting down eight of the attacking German aircraft and damaging a ninth, all from the JG53.[14]

Strike photo, Castelvetrano Aerodrome, May 21, 1943. (National Archives, 342-FH-3A27205-B52325AC)

We turned two or three times as a squadron, and then it became sort of an individual thing. All of a sudden we were just all over the sky. When I finally looked around after jogging back and forth a few times, I was all alone. I could see just one P-38 (below me) in a tight circle with four Me-109s. I couldn't see anybody else. Out of all those airplanes, those were the only airplanes I could see. I don't know what happened to all the others, but they were not in my view. You could never imagine. I was at about 15,000 feet, about 5,000 ft. above the circling aircraft. I didn't know who it was, but I kind of thought it might be (Flight Leader) Little. He was no doubt getting fatigued because it is pretty strenuous to pull that plane around for such a long time. He was in a very bad spot.

He had no chance, staying in that circle. It didn't matter—I was going to make a pass at them. The group of five aircraft was in a turn when I first saw them, and they made a couple more turns during my dive toward them. It was a very steep dive, going very fast. I intended to fire at the four 109s, but I wasn't in a position to do an effective shot. But they saw me zoom past, and I was able to get two of them to follow me. I knew not to get into a circle with a 109, but I found out that day that the P-38 could outrun the 109. They both followed me all the way to the coast, but they never got within range to take a shot.

The 109s were so close on him, I don't think anything he could have tried would have succeeded. If he had rolled out, they would have shot him down immediately.

It is now known that Captain Little, with his wingman Second Lieutenant Martin Foster, had broken from the formation in a diving pursuit of two attacking 109s. Foster, unable to stay with Little and undoubtedly going through his own swirling combat action, would later crash land his aircraft on the Tunisian coast near Bizerte. Greg's wingman, Lieutenant Lovera, would eventually rejoin the returning bomber formation, but was forced to land at Bone for refueling.

With the trailing 109s finally giving up the chase, Greg was able to safely return to Telergma, and would learn later in the squadron debriefing that Captain Little was, in fact, the unlucky pilot he had tried to save.

Little had been a flight leader, and with his loss, a new flight leader would have to be designated. The selection of a flight leader was made by the Operations Officer, Captain Decker, and coming so early in the squadron's combat assignment, Decker had little to guide him in the selection process. The "re-start" pilots had all completed flight school at more or less the same time, were equally experienced, and considered themselves to be similarly qualified.

It was kind of strange how Decker handled that, but we all agreed to it and really it was fair. When a flight leader slot came open, he would call in the two most eligible pilots: "OK, we are gonna match for this—heads or tails." It was pretty significant because the day you became a flight leader you began earning captain's pay. It was a fair way to do it, and I thought Decker handled it very well. I lost the coin toss three times, but we had a lot of turnover, so opportunities for promotion came around pretty fast. Eventually, there was no one else to match with, and I became C flight (Blue) commander in late May 1943.

Dive-bombing

In the P-38, NASAF had an aircraft that was well suited for many roles, but it was unsurpassed in dive-bombing. It could carry a 1,000-lb. bomb, and its powerful machine gun and cannon armament made it a formidable ground attack platform. Unlike most other aircraft with wing-mounted armament, the P-38's four .50 caliber machine guns and 20 mm cannon were clustered in the nose of the aircraft. This arrangement permitted a longer range of fire—a Lightning could reliably hit targets up to 1,000 yards distant. The aircraft could bring a tremendous amount of firepower to bear in just seconds.

The pilots of the 49th, like most fighter squadrons, had received no training in dive-bombing during transition training in the P-38—the skills they would need were acquired in North Africa, and Greg's squadron had honed their dive-bombing techniques in practice missions against the dry lake beds near their base.

Greg's first mission involving dive-bombing came on May 24, just two days before becoming Blue flight leader, a day when the North African Strategic Air Force effectively emptied its bases of fighters and bombers in an all-out attack on German and Italian positions on the island of Sardinia. In addition to dive-bombing attacks by all four of NASAF's fighter groups, heavy bombers were sent to attack Terranova and La Maddalena, and medium bombers were assigned missions to Olbia and Alghero.[15]

The all-group assignment had already been scheduled and canceled three times; Greg and the other pilots assigned to the mission were anxious to have it go. Unbeknownst to the pilots, this was the first of what would be a long series of similar assignments. Over the coming 13 days the squadron would complete 15

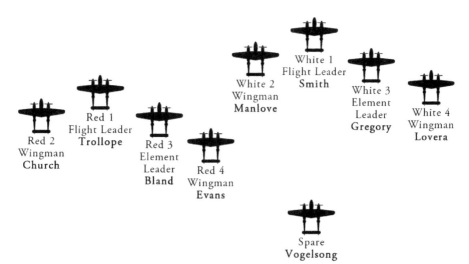

49th Fighter Squadron formation. Mission to Alghero Railyards and Porto Conte, May 24, 1943. (Samuel Richardson, Yosemite Productions)

Alghero and Porto Conte, Sardinia. (Berann)

separate dive-bombing missions. The first mission would inform the squadron and group commanders how well the pilots had absorbed their prior training.

The 14th's mission on May 24 was very much an operational test for its three squadrons. Each squadron was assigned a separate target on the island of Sardinia for a dive-bombing attack—their first combat assignment of this type. The 37th squadron sent a 12-aircraft formation to the Iglesias Zinc and Lead Smelter Works on the southwest corner of Sardinia. Eight P-38s of the 48th squadron attacked the aerodrome at Millis, midway up the west coast of Sardinia,[16] while the 49th squadron sent eight more P-38s to bomb the railyards and factories at Alghero, and the adjoining seaplane base at Porto Conte, 40 miles further up the coast from Millis.

Greg was assigned as element leader to this mission, his eighth combat sortie, again with Lt. Lovera as his wingman.

Alghero and Porto Conte offered a rich mix of targets for the 49th, and the pilots anticipated intense ground fire. Perhaps most troubling for American military planners was the early detection capability that Germany had installed on the island. In order to protect the important aerodromes at Chilvani and

Millis, and the ocean ports at Cagliari and Olbia, Germany had ringed Sardinia with highly effective radar and radio direction finding (RDF) systems. Alghero was itself a site for one of the German radar stations, and the approaching American aircraft would also fall within range of the station at Pula, on the southernmost tip of Sardinia. As was noted in a contemporaneous German report: "Most penetrations (of Sardinian airspace by the Allied air forces) were detected in good time by the 'Pula' station on the southern coast of the island."[17]

For the 14th's pilots, maintaining the element of surprise was critical for a successful mission, but with these early warning systems in place around Sardinia, catching the Axis off guard would be tricky.

The missions were launched when the 49th's aircraft began taking off at 1210, followed at 1220 by the 48th and 1235 by the 37th. In less than two hours the western coastline of Sardinia was in view.

We went out right on the deck—no more than 15 feet above the water. When Captain. Trollope, the flight leader, began to gain altitude, that was the signal for us to move from our standard echelon position into trail position, and to prepare for attack. The city (Alghero) was right on the coast, and the rail line ran right through the city. It was easy to identify and very visible.

We climbed up as high as we could go in a real powered flight—I think I reached about 1,500–2,000 feet. We hadn't practiced that before—this was our first [attempt at this type of attack]. It was just a big zoom. We climbed at a steep angle and then started our dive. We throttled back a bit, 'cause you are going to gain a lot of speed in that dive. We pulled the (bomb drop) handle at about 300 feet. Greg would later describe this as a "reaction-type" experience—knowing where the ground was became almost a subconscious act. At that time, and that speed, there was no time to rely on instruments, or even to refer to them.

The pilots were exceptionally accurate with their bombing runs. The first flight each landed their bomb on the factory complex, and Greg's formation had four accurate hits on the rail yard northeast of town.

We had been briefed that there was a harbor (Porto Conte) adjacent to the rail complex and that if we came out of our dives in good position, we could make a strafing run on any targets. As I pulled out of my dive, I was headed straight toward two large seaplanes. It was late in the afternoon, and they had all been tarped for the night. They were aligned perfectly, and I quickly turned on my gunsight and made a long burst at the first seaplane. I was no more than 15–20 feet above the sea, and it was an easy shot. It broke into flames and looked like it was finished. I started firing at the second seaplane, gave it the same long burst. It too burst into flames and was burning fiercely as I flew overhead. I had just the proper amount of time.

Savoia-Marchetti S.66 Twin Hull Flying Boat. (Wikimedia Commons)

The seaplanes destroyed appeared to be the very large three-engine Savoia Marchetti S66s. The squadron had caught the Axis forces with twelve of the large seaplanes at the base—two others were destroyed by other pilots on the mission.

It was an outstanding mission. We really did not get fired upon at all. We snuck in and dropped our bomb on the rail yard, got that strafing pass in, and got those four big seaplanes. It was really a good mission, and it started us off on a good wave. After that our next bombing was on the island of Pantelleria.

In the succeeding two weeks, the 49th completed another 14 dive-bombing missions, including several to the Axis-held island of Pantelleria, located between Tunisia and Sicily. The unit developed a high degree of proficiency in that type of attack. *We thought we were doing pretty good with our dive-bombing experience and capability.*

Greg flew many missions to the northwestern sector of Sicily, on both dive-bombing and bomber escort missions. His expertise in combat was growing, but also growing was his awareness that on any mission, anything could happen.

The mission of June 4 was a case in point. On this day, the 49th put up twenty-four P-38s to fly as top cover for 30 P-38s from the 1st Fighter Group. The aircraft of the 1st were "bombed up," carrying 1,000-lb. high explosive

(HE) bombs normally used against hardened targets. The objective for the day's mission was the aerodrome at Milo, near Trapani, in the northwest sector of Sicily.[18]

Milo was a major Luftwaffe stronghold in northwestern Sicily. In addition to the ferocious flak and ground fire that would protect the aerodrome, Milo was home to one of the Luftwaffe's most experienced fighter groups—Jagdgeschwader (JG) 27 and its three squadrons, which by early 1942 had been credited with downing over 1,000 Allied aircraft; since withdrawing from Tunisia in April it had downed a further 78.[19,20]

Aircraft of the 1st and 14th FGs rendezvoused near the Tunisian coastline in early evening. Approaching the coastline of Sicily at wave-top height, the formation was within sight of their target by 1745. The dive-bombing P-38s "jumped" to an altitude of 4,500 ft. before rolling into their dive and releasing at 2,500 ft.

In a stroke of luck that might be attributed to the lateness of the hour, and to the stealth of their approach, no German aircraft engaged the formation. Three 109s and one FW-190 were seen above the formation during the bombing but did not engage either the bombing P-38s or the escorts.

This was a really hot area, and when we flew into this area, we could always expect a lot of 109s. There was one squadron of elite 109s that they called the "yellow-nosed squadron." They were really tough and really aggressive. I thought we were going to get a lot of combat that day, but that squadron did not come up, and it didn't happen. Lloyd DeMoss always talked about the yellow-nose squadron that he had seen. We had heard that Goering had somehow distinguished this squadron for the excellent job they had done.

As the P-38s wheeled around for the return to base and began to reform, the 49th suffered a shocking loss.

We were off shore when two of our guys crashed into each other. That was a bad flight, to lose two. It was Green and Bergerson, and I was really upset when I saw them fly into each other. We were in a tight turn, and I saw them crash into each other, and go into the water. We were all at low altitude—3–4,000 feet, and neither of them was able to straighten the airplane out to make a water landing, or to bail out. There was not time for them to get out of the airplane. It was a sad sight. I don't know which one was at fault. I thought it was bad enough that we had 109s shoot a lot of us down, but it was too bad that we lost pilots flying into each other. It was just a bad event.

All the pilots still had limited combat experience. First Lieutenant John Green had joined the squadron just 12 days earlier and was on his third combat mission. Second Lieutenant William Bergersen had joined the squadron on April 11 and was on his fourth mission. Their loss in what can only be attributed to pilot error brought home to the squadron the reality that none were immune from the risks of combat, and that their lives could be ended through no fault of their own, in the blink of an eye.

The attrition of fellow pilots and the accumulating risk in the combat missions became wearing on the squadron. While Greg believes he was able to always have his head in the game, he also recalls detecting combat fatigue in himself at one point. *Combat fatigue is there, and we all had to deal with it. It affected some more than others. You just don't go out, mission after mission, and lose so many friends, without it affecting you. There were times where we were losing so many, you get to wonder how long… I think Knott did a study one time, and he figured that the luckiest of us would have maybe 20 more days, or something like that, at the rate we were going… Of course, it doesn't work that way, because as you gain experience you become a better survivor. But you think about the odds of being killed. You have to because it's real.*

By mid-summer, Greg and his squadron mates had experienced many losses, but for Greg, the toughest came on June 26 when his longtime friend, Lt. William Neely, was killed in a training accident very near the Telergma airfield. Greg had driven Bill to his aircraft on the flight line for the training exercise. Hearing of the crash, Greg had hurried to the crash site just in time to see his friend's body being brought down the hillside. Bill Neely was an excellent combat pilot, had been promoted to Flight Leader sixteen days earlier and had already led his formation on seven missions. Greg and William had attended college together at Middle Tennessee, had joined the Aviation Cadet Program together, had completed all three phases of their flight training together, and had flown at least seven difficult combat missions together. At every point, they had served together. Neely's loss was very hard on Greg, a loss that Greg feels to this day. *But with the press of combat, you just had to move on.*[21]

Neely's death held particular poignancy as it followed so quickly after a successful pilot rescue mission: one that saw Greg recommended for a Distinguished Flying Cross. On June 20 Greg was leading a flight of four P-38s, escorting B-26 bombers to the German airfield at Bo Rizzo. The bombers made a successful drop from 16,000 feet, but facing intense flak, one B-26 was shot down. As the rest of the bomber formation wheeled about to return to base and were rejoined by their P-38 escorts, they were jumped by approximately twenty-five Me-109s and FW-190 aircraft.

The German fighters managed to get in very close on one or two of their passes, and Capt. Decker's plane was hit in the wild melee that ensued. With

Decker's plane badly damaged, Greg made an audacious head-on attack against an attacking Me-109, giving Decker enough time to stabilize his aircraft, feather his props, and descend for a water landing. He escaped the sinking P-38 and deployed his survival dinghy.

As Decker's plane hit the water, the three pilots in his flight circled his location, recorded the coordinates, and provided cover against the superior numbers of German aircraft that were still pressing their attack. Forced to return to base by low fuel, eight of the 49th's pilots, including Gregory, then returned immediately to relocate Decker and provide air cover. They located him, apparently uninjured, just to the west of Egadi Island, and requested a pick-up from the Air-Sea Rescue service.

The lateness of the hour prevented a rescue and a second rescue mission was launched by the 49th the next morning, led by Greg. Decker was again sighted in his dingy at 0745, having spent the night in open water. Food and water were tied to a life vest and dropped to Decker while seven aircraft maintained patrol overhead. A single-engine float plane—a British "Walrus"—was led back to Decker's location, landed, and brought Decker aboard.[22]

Decker's rescuers returned to base at 1510—a 10½-hour mission, and the end of a grueling two days of flying. Decker was checked out at a hospital in Tunis, was found to be in good condition, and returned to the squadron to face some good-natured ribbing. Harper remembered: "Goddamit Decker if I'da been with you I wouldn't have let you done that." Lieutenant Knott saw Decker get shot down and heard Decker's version of the story: "We were in this flight, and my turbo blew up." And Knott said, "Yeah that guy who was right on your tail is the one who blew it up."[23]

Colonel Troy Keith, commander of the 14th Fighter Group, would later recommend Greg for the Distinguished Flying Cross in recognition of his bravery and perseverance:

> William J. Gregory, O659810, Captain, Air Corps, 49th Fighter Squadron.
> For extraordinary achievement while participating in aerial flight in the North African Theater of Operations as pilot of P-38 type aircraft. On 20 June 1943, as flight leader, Captain Gregory was escorting B-26s to Bo Rizzo A/D, Sicily. As the squadron was leaving the target area, they were aggressively attacked by over twenty-five Me 109's and FW 190's. In the violent combat that followed Captain Decker's plane had been shot up and an Me 109 was closing in for the kill on his crippled P-38. Captain Gregory immediately saw this 109 and broke into the enemy aircraft head on, closing to a range of 50 yards, and giving him a burst of machine gun and cannon fire which set the engine on fire and probably destroyed it. By this action Capt. Gregory undoubtedly saved his fellow officer's life because Capt. Decker was later able to crash land his plane safely and was rescued by a plane escorted by P-38s which Capt. Gregory was leading. The flying skill, devotion to a crippled comrade,

and fighting spirit of Capt. Gregory as a combat pilot have reflected great credit to himself and the Armed Forces of the United States.

Keith also recommended two other pilots from that day's mission for DFCs. Of the three nominees, Greg alone did not receive the medal. The recommendation was presumably halted by his squadron commander, whom Greg had previously confronted for a practice with which Greg sharply disagreed.

That squadron commander had a practice of assigning new combat pilots as his wingman for their first combat mission so that he could personally attest to their readiness for combat. In several instances, as the fighter formation neared the target, the commander would peel away from the formation and return to base with his wingman, either determining that the new pilot was not ready for combat, or concluding that taking the "green" pilot to the critical point of attack was sufficient for his first mission.

In either case, Gregory was critical of his commander's policy, reasoning that removing two or more aircraft from the formation threatened the success of the mission, and endangered the lives of the pilots who were forced to continue the mission with a less-than-sufficient force.

When Greg reckoned that his commander had left the formation one too many times, he challenged him on it, and words were exchanged. Greg clearly recalls the dispute, and while no disciplinary action was taken against him, he and his commander remained at odds for the duration of their combat tour.

The 49th advances

As Allied ground forces in North Africa advanced, so too did NASAF's bombers and fighters, relocating to airfields closer to strategic targets. El Bathan was one of fifteen sites in eastern Tunisia under active consideration for a temporary airfield. A "greenfield" site, El Bathan's clay soil was dusty in dry weather and muddy in wet weather, limiting it to "temporary use as a strategic dry weather base for combat aircraft." It would occupy a "footprint" of just less than two square miles, and the Army engineers would build it in just six days. As an advance base intended for short-term use, the airfield would include no barracks, hospital buildings, support buildings, hangars, or workshops. There were no special provisions made for ammunition storage, and it was not equipped for night landings.[24,25]

The 14th Fighter Group was the first unit to occupy the base, and remained there only from July 3 to July 25, 1943. On its departure, the base was used by medium bombers of the 320th Bomb Group (BG) until early November and was then apparently abandoned.[26]

El Bathan would be the exclusive base for the P-38s of the 14th Fighter Group, but the bombers would not be far away: The 17th and 319th Bomber Groups were flying B-26 Marauders out of Djedeida, five miles to the east; the 320th Bomber Group, also flying B-26s, was operating at Massicault, three miles southeast. With a total of 192 B-26s based in such a small area, on a calm morning, the pilots of the 14th would be able to hear the engines of the B-26s warming up as they received their preflight briefing.[27]

The 14th arrived at El Bathan in that miserable summer of 1943 just in time for the sirocco—a hot wind coming out of the Sahara, blowing dust into tents and aircraft, and driving daytime temperatures to 120 degrees. Fred Wolfe with the 82nd Fighter Group talks about coping with the strong Sahara winds: "All we could do was dampen a sheet or towel, lie down, and cover ourselves up with it. When the wind was over we'd get up and dust ourselves off."[28]

The sun was relentless. Men covered their backs with hydraulic oil as protection against sunburn. Aircraft were too hot to touch, and pilots would be wringing wet with sweat before their aircraft got off the ground.

One thing was really strange. It was so hot that summer, but on missions, you lose about three degrees of temperature for every thousand feet that you ascend. We didn't have very good heaters in the P-38s, and when you got up to 30,000 feet our hands would get so cold we'd get frostbit. Even though we wore gloves, why, it was really cold. You were just shivering in the cockpit at those altitudes. We had those leather jackets, which were good. But it was so hot on the ground that you couldn't wear them. You'd just wear a long-sleeved shirt and a flying suit.

Usually, when we left in the morning, we would have the flaps up on the tents to keep it open. One day, I guess I had been shaving early in the morning. I had this mirror—a two-sided mirror—it fell on the ground by the side of my cot. During the day when the sun came up, the sun focused the rays on the cot, and it burned up my cot while I was off on the mission. My tentmates said, "Hey, we had a little fire while you were gone." That really happened. I never knew it would do that, but it sure did. The rays of the sun just focused directly, and of course, the heat was intense.

In the midst of that scorching heat, the ground crews encountered unexpected problems. Crew member Lloyd Guenther recalls: "In this heat and humidity, we had trouble with the guns freezing up on high-altitude bombing escort missions… Sometimes the planes came home, and the guns would be a solid mass of ice and frost from the cold upstairs and the humidity near the ground, condensing on them. We went to a special sperm oil, which kept the guns from freezing."[29]

Temperature was far from the only privation faced by the group. Future Nobel laureate John Steinbeck, serving as a correspondent during the war, filed a report from North Africa just before the invasion of Sicily: "The men suffer from strain. It has been so long applied that they are probably not even conscious of it. It isn't fear, but it is something you can feel, a bubble that grows bigger and bigger in your mid-section. It puffs up against your lungs so that your breathing becomes short. Sitting around is bad."[30]

For the pilots, it was a case of one type of stress being superimposed on another, and then on still another. The business of flying ultra-high performance aircraft, laden with high-octane fuel and a half-ton of explosives, was inherently dangerous, even during routine training operations. Added to this was the strangeness that characterized North Africa at that time, and the frequent change of location to other, more alien airfields. There were worries about parents back home, new wives or newer children. Physical fatigue increased with each passing day, and in some the physical depletion began to have an effect on combat readiness, regardless of the pilot's willingness for combat. Malaria and typhus were endemic. Food was often poor, and rejuvenating sleep rare. Dysentery was common, and all pilots experienced significant weight loss.[31]

Within the squadron, avoiding stress or mitigating the resultant physical and emotional strain was never an option for the combat pilots. As horrific as their previous mission might have been, combat was inexorable, and their next mission was always close at hand.

There were times that I would wake up in the night, dreaming about a mission. It was not a persistent thing with me, just once in a great while. Maybe we had lost somebody, and I couldn't get it off my mind. Of course, the days and nights were so hot during that summer, and we slept on cots with not a very good mattress, so you had to be very tired to sleep under those conditions. Usually, we were.

None of us were all that healthy. We didn't have any recreation really. We didn't even have exercise. No PT and that might have helped too. I think it probably would have helped. We all got dysentery, and we all lost weight. I think I weighed 118–120 lbs., and we had a lot of stomach problems because of food.

The 49th would eventually fly 26 combat missions from El Bathan before being moved again in late July to a new base at Ste. Marie du Zit, south of Tunis.

Fighter sweep

By mid-June, Allied bombing attacks were launched with even greater intensity. Over the succeeding 25 days, NASAF heavy and medium bombers were sent out on 99 bombing missions, primarily targeting German and Italian air force units located on Sicily, Sardinia, and Italy. Sicily—the next objective for the advancing armies—had become the focal point of American bombing raids.

During this lead-up to the invasion of Sicily, the 14th FG flew as fighter escorts on 20 of those 99 bomber missions. Lt. Gregory flew six of these missions, as well as two fighter-bomber missions and two search missions—essentially flying two days out of every three.

The Allied invasion of Sicily—Operation *Husky*—came in the early hours of July 10. All units of the 14th flew missions, and many of the pilots flew two or three sorties. The 14th, along with all other P-38 units in NASAF, were assigned "targets of opportunity" missions, essentially fighter-bomber sweeps attacking any target that came into view. The objective on this day was to isolate the battlefield by interdicting German forces and slowing German reinforcements.

The American amphibious forces landed in an arc along the coastline from the Irminio River in a northwesterly sweep to the city of Gela and continued to Licata. Meanwhile, British forces landed along the southeastern coast of Sicily from Cape Passero northward to Syracuse.

It was anticipated that the Italian coastal defenses would be easily overcome, but that the German army would counterattack vigorously from positions immediately inland from these landing beaches.

German and Italian forces that would likely reinforce their coastal defenses on D-Day were known to be based in the Enna-Caltanissetta region, and it was well known that the reinforcing forces would have to use two main roads leading to the invasion beaches: the southern roads from Canicatti and Piazza Armerina. It was also known that reinforcing and/or retreating forces were likely to use the Vizzini—Caltagirone road, and the road leading to the invasion beaches from Ragusa.

Air Force bomber and fighter missions on D-Day were concentrated in a zone measuring 50 by 70 miles in southeastern Sicily. German defensive units were positioned within that corridor, and it was on the few roads within the area that reinforcements would pass on their way to the beachheads. NASAF's fighter missions would be flown in this zone, against "targets of opportunity": truck convoys, troop columns, tanks, artillery pieces, anti-tank guns, motorcycles, and staff cars.[32]

The 14th FG was assigned seven missions for July 10—each consisting of 12 P-38 aircraft. By the end of this day, NASAF's P-38s would fly 829 sorties.

The 14th's first mission of the day was given to the 37th Fighter Squadron. By the time the mission began, 20 minutes before dawn, an Allied paratroop attack had begun, and American and British troops were beginning to come ashore.

Within hours the Italian defensive forces had mounted a counterattack against the landing force at Gela, soon joined by the Herman Goering Panzer Division.

By 0700, the 37th squadron had overflown the massive Allied invasion flotilla, crossed the Sicilian coastline, and sighted a line of trucks moving south near Cap di San Pietro. The squadron made an effective dive-bombing attack, and on return to base reported large concentrations of truck, tanks and motorcycles moving south toward Comiso Aerodrome below Vizzini: precisely what was expected as the Axis forces moved to the defense.

This large armored column moving south from the area of Vizzini—probably the Herman Goering Panzer Division—was to be targeted repeatedly by the Allied fighter-bombers in many of the missions of July 10.

Lt. Gregory's assignment this day was the 49th's sixth of the day. Their mission: search and destroy targets of opportunity in the area from the coastal town of Licata to the German airfield at Gerbini, in northeastern Sicily.

Taking off at 1450, the mission included the following pilots:

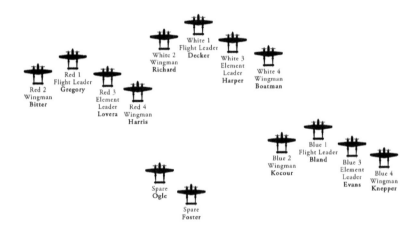

49th Fighter Squadron formation. Fighter sweep—targets of opportunity in southeast Sicily, July 10, 1943. (Samuel Richardson, Yosemite Productions)

When F/O Richard's aircraft developed a mechanical issue just 10 minutes after takeoff, Lt. Foster took his position as wingman to Capt. Decker. The formation included the most competent, most experienced combat pilots NASAF had to offer, flying the most performant combat fighter in the world. Ten of these pilots had together already logged 260 combat missions and were on average halfway through their combat tours. The two new pilots assigned to the mission—Kocour and Knepper—each had a handful of combat missions, and their competence in combat was growing with each mission.

In what must be seen as a failure of the group's intelligence contingent, the pilots' preflight briefing for this mission evidently did not include reference to information recently received from the 37th FS. In two missions earlier in the day, the 37th had reported large concentrations of German armor, vehicles, and troops in the corridor extending south from Vizzini. That intelligence was apparently shared within the 37th: in the last mission of the day, the 37th—taking off shortly after Decker's flight departed—was sent to attack the same concentrations near Vizzini for the third time that day.

A successful interdiction of that German concentration could have had a profound effect on the course of the invasion on D-Day. As events would prove out, subsequent fighter sweeps did not uncover any targets of higher value than those near Vizzini. Certainly, had Capt. Decker known of the location of this concentration of forces, his flight course and mission would have taken a much different direction, and probably had a much different outcome.

In fairness, it must also be said that that Decker's mission may have been sent as far as Catania in order to intercept reinforcing troops potentially moving south from Catania or Messina—a second Italian reserve division was known to be in the area south of Catania, and it was not known whether this force would be sent against the American landing forces at Gela, or against the British forces near Syracuse. It was known that roughly one third of the Herman Goering Division was located in the vicinity of Catania, and it is plausible that Decker's mission was to seek out and attack that concentration.

Decker led his formation "on the deck" as it crossed the Mediterranean and neared the coastline of Sicily. As it reached the Sicilian coastline at Gela, just before overflying the invasion armada, it increased altitude and continued on a generally northeastern course over Ponte Oliva, to and beyond the landing complex at Gerbini, and continuing to the port city of Catania. This course took them slightly to the west of the region in which the German Army was staging its decisive counterattack against the American landing at Gela. Not finding targets at any point on their outbound leg, Decker wheeled the formation back around, and continued their visual search for targets on a southwestern track, intending to fly over Vizzini and Comiso before returning to base.

Greg, flight leader for Blue flight, notes: *We flew over the coastline of Sicily at altitude. And there were all these ships lined up for what seemed like 50 miles. When we flew over these ships on the way in we were about 10,000 ft. Maybe 7,500. We had been briefed that they (the US Navy) might shoot at us, but they shouldn't since we were P-38s and they probably would have identified us. But they sure did. Fortunately, no one got hit, and we didn't lose anyone from that. That is why we were so high when we went in. We went all the way to Mt. Etna inland, then we turned around 180 degrees and were coming back. It seemed like there was no war on for most of that mission. Of course, our own ships shot at us, but we did not receive any ground fire going over from the Germans.*

The formation had flown across most of the southeastern part of Sicily without having encountered any enemy aircraft, without receiving any enemy ground fire, and without spotting any suitable targets for their 500-lb bombs. All the while the largest amphibious operation in the history of warfare was underway just a short distance to the south.

Decker's squadron continued in the direction of the beachhead at Gela, and within a few minutes his formation would have exited Sicilian airspace. Still intent on finding a useful target to attack, Decker "jumped down" low on a course that took them in the direction of Vizzini—the exact location where the Herman Goering Division had just retreated following their mauling by the US Army and Navy at the Gela beachhead earlier in the afternoon.

At this point in the mission, the aircraft were still in formation, flying at 3,000 ft. altitude, and spanning a distance of roughly a quarter mile from the far left to the far right of the formation. *And that is where, near the coastline, the Germans had this heavy concentration—in this kind of valley, as I recall. There were a lot of trees in that area—could have been an olive grove.*

We didn't see all of this going in.

The squadron was fast approaching a concealed column of 20 German tanks and 25 trucks on the road northwest of Vizzini, and was taken completely by surprise. The Germans were on high alert, having just been beaten back at the Gela beachhead. They were experienced gunners, equipped with fearsome armament, and were ready to release a barrage of antiaircraft fire. Flying in close formation, at a low altitude, the P-38s were enormous targets.

The ground fire erupted in a seeming wall of flak. The P-38s immediately dove, strafing as they neared the vehicles, the pilots hurrying to release their bombs.

There was no signal from the flight leader. It was not a typical dive-bombing run. It was more of a strafing run, but we dropped our bombs as we were approaching. A few trucks, tanks, and other vehicles were spotted, and they were attacked successfully.

Quickly glancing to his right, Greg saw his good friend Wallace Bland and his formation taking heavy fire, strafing as they dove into the formation.

The German ground fire concentrated on the center and right four-plane flights in the formation—Decker and Bland's flights. According to official reports, six aircraft were damaged by flak, and two pilots—Lt. Harold Harper and Lt. Herman Kocour—had one engine shot out and had to nurse their aircraft back to base on the remaining engine. Greg saw Harper feather his engine, and moved his formation over to escort him back to base.

Flying on Harper's left, Greg remembers: *The concentration of the fire—this was all very quick. We flew over at a very fast speed. Bland and Knepper got the concentration of fire. It was a matter of placement of the aircraft. I saw Bland get hit, and if I had been leading B flight, as Bland was, I would have gotten hit. He was pretty low when I saw him.*

According to Lt. Lovera, flying just behind Bland: "I saw Lt. Bland's plane going down, and the left engine was smoking. He called over the radio that the airplane was out of control and about that time the left engine caught fire and the plane peeled off and did a wing-over to the left and blew up. As the plane started over, I saw an object go past the tail assembly, but I did not see a parachute open."

Lt. Evans, also flying just behind Bland, reported: "I saw Lt. Bland's left engine smoking and tried to call him on the radio and tell him about it, but he didn't reply. Then he called and said he was going to bail out. His plane turned over and started down. I saw him bail out but his parachute didn't open, and I saw him hit the ground."[33]

And flying in fourth position in Bland's formation, Lt. Allan Knepper was also pouring cannon fire into the German armored column when he was hit by their ground fire. His plane peeled up, made a half roll, and crashed straight into the ground.[34]

Base life at Ste. Marie du Zit

In late July the group were moved to a new base. *Of the three bases that we occupied, Ste. Marie du Zit (SMdZ) was the best. It was a more desirable location than the other two. It was located about 30 miles south of Tunis and was a little higher in elevation, which made it a little bit more enjoyable. I got a couple of days of rest leave. We were very close to the seashore, and I'd go for a day or two. It was a break that we never had before, being close to the beach. There was a nice restaurant down there. The attraction really was the restaurant where we could get a good meal.*

The Germans had used that field before we did, and they left some of their explosives around in the airplane parking area. We cleaned up the area a little bit to avoid stepping on one of the presents they had left behind. But SMdZ was the preferred place that we had occupied. I remember making several flights from

Ste. Marie du Zit. I always enjoyed taking off from this base because it was a much better base.

The 49th escorted its sister squadron, the 37th, on August 11, providing high cover for a dive-bombing mission to a rail and highway complex on the toe of Italy. It returned just in time to welcome a visiting USO troupe. Bob Hope, accompanied by singer Frances Langford, Jack Pepper, Tony Romano, and Jerry Colonna gave the airmen a great show and were in return treated to a flight in a "piggy-back" P-38.

As the War Diary of the 49th Fighter Squadron reports: "A huge truck trailer was the stage and a P-38 the background. Miss Langford again charmed her listeners, many of whom remembered her from her performances at March Field (Calif). Hope, impromptu, was at his best and was roundly enjoyed by most of the members of the 14th Group since nearly everyone was able to attend. The only women present besides Miss Langford were three Army nurses as spectators. Hope reported that people in the States were eating horse meat and that Bing Crosby was making a fortune selling it."[35]

And, in attendance, Capt. William Gregory. *Everyone really enjoyed Bob Hope and his troupe—Frances Langford and all the others. It was really uplifting to have them come to entertain us. I have great respect for Bob Hope and what he did for the military during his lifetime.*

When we moved to SMdZ, it was a time for me to reflect on our losses during the previous period. It seemed that we had taken a big hit from the Luftwaffe. We had lost 19 pilots at this time. If I remember correctly, when we started we had a total of 27 new pilots. Counting up all the losses, it seemed like 19 was a big loss.

On the other hand, I really had the feeling that our position had changed. We now really had the upper hand. By this point, we began to have the feeling that we could defeat the Luftwaffe in that area. And actually, the statistics at that time had us very much to the advantage, including all of our losses and all the Luftwaffe losses. They were suffering greatly at this point. I had this good feeling at this point that we were going to be successful in our efforts, and even though we had lost 19 good men, we were on the rise, and I thought we would be able to handle it pretty well to the end.

Closing his combat service

Greg would witness the surrender of German forces in Sicily on August 17. He had been a part of the air offensive against Sicily from day one, and in that period the Allied air forces had lost some 400 airplanes and pilots. The Axis forces lost 1,850—of those, 1,100 had been destroyed on the ground. The fearsome NASAF bomber force of B-17s, B-25s, and B26s, in combination with a ground attack by light bombers and fighter-bombers, had delivered a blow to the Luftwaffe from which it would never recover. Reich Marshall Galland would later write: "Our pilots were exhausted to a terrifying degree. The Luftwaffe was burning up in the southern theater of the war."[36]

Greg would fly nine more missions from the 14th's new base at Ste. Marie du Zit, his final combat assignment coming on August 21. His tour ended as it had begun, escorting B-17 bombers, this time a five-hour mission to Aversa, Italy.[37] During his combat tour, Greg flew combat missions, on average, every other day, never having more than three days off between missions.

Greg completed all fifty missions in the same aircraft—P-38 number 55—officially P-38 number 43-2534. It was his aircraft, his and his flight crew's—no other pilot would mount no. 55 during Greg's combat tour. *It carried me throughout the combat tour, and I hated leaving that airplane and that crew—it was a wonderful crew. And yet I knew that the plane would need to fly every mission it could.*

No. 55 was scheduled to fly the very next mission, on August 25, a massive 200-aircraft combined fighter sweep that included 24 P-38s from the 14th fighter group. The target was the huge aerodrome complex at Foggia, Italy, and the American aircraft planned to attack from a low altitude in line abreast formation, hoping to catch the Luftwaffe unawares in a broad strafing attack.

No. 55 would be flown by Lieutenant Hester, in his first mission with the squadron since reporting four days earlier. The mission entailed the longest flight the squadron had made on a strafing mission, and was terrifically successful, destroying many German aircraft on the ground. Lt. Hester was seen at the commencement of the attack but was not seen later when his squadron reformed for the flight back to base. It was later confirmed that his aircraft had been downed by ground fire and that he had been killed.[38]

They were going to do a strafing mission on Foggia on the next mission, and I kinda would have liked to have done that mission. But I really did not have a choice. I had flown plane 55 throughout my 50 missions, and I was still there when it flew the next mission, and unfortunately, it did not return on the very next mission. I think if I'd have been there it would have returned. As far as I know, I don't think they permitted anyone to go beyond their 50 missions.

Over the course of Greg's 86 days of combat, his squadron had lost 14 of the original "start-up" pilots with whom he had trained and entered combat, including his closest friend, Lt. William Neely. Five replacement pilots were also lost, several during a mission in which Greg was also assigned: an attrition rate of 57 percent.

The pilots had been posted to North Africa to restart the original 49th squadron that had suffered such severe attrition during the early days of America's fight in North Africa. In fact, the losses to Greg's group exceeded those of the earlier group—the greatest difference was that in the earliest days of the 14th's combat campaign, the pipeline of replacement planes and pilots did not permit the group to maintain strength. By the time Greg and his fellow pilots arrived in North Africa in the spring of 1943, there was no shortage of either aircraft or new pilots, so even with its appalling losses the 14th was able to maintain its combat effectiveness.

Greg earned his first Air Medal on May 13 and by the time he had completed his final mission he had earned eight Oak Leaf Clusters to accompany the Air Medal. While his group commander recommended that Greg be awarded the Distinguished Flying Cross for extraordinary achievement during his mission on June 20 over Bo Rizzo, Sicily, Greg was never awarded the medal—possibly the only surviving pilot in the original 49th fighter squadron "re-start" group who did not receive the DFC.

Throughout his combat tour, and despite the wretched conditions on the ground, Greg never missed a flight due to a malfunctioning aircraft, nor to illness, and never aborted a mission for any reason.

Greg had mixed emotions about ending his combat tour. With his fellow pilot Lloyd DeMoss, he spent a few days at a base south of Ste. Marie du Zit, on the Mediterranean coast, waiting for a flight home. *We would go to the beach there every day, and soon met two French girls who also used that beach. I think I had the cutest girl—she was very nice and very young—about 18—and she had a very nice figure. I also met her mother, who was very attractive as well. That helped us pass the time until we got a flight home.*

Greg's orders arrived on September 26, 1943. They directed him, together with 26 other members of the 14th Fighter group, including his CO, Major Trollope, and the Operations Officer, Maj. Decker, who Greg had helped save after ditching in the Mediterranean, to debark from North Africa to the United States, "by military or commercial aircraft, surface vessel, belligerent or otherwise, and/or rail." They were authorized up to 15 days to report for re-assignment, and most of the men, including Greg, would use this time to visit family and friends back home.[39]

CHAPTER 5

Coming Home—Endings and Beginnings

When air transport became available, the flight home took several days. Greg landed at Bar Harbor, Maine on October 4, 1943.[1]

One of the first things I wanted was a milkshake, 'cause I hadn't had one in such a long time. But it made me sick—it was something I had not had in my stomach for such a long time. I finally got home, and I was very happy to be home and to greet my family and neighbors. I stayed home for about a month, and it was a great time to be at home and to relax.

I was home for about a month, and during that time Lloyd DeMoss called me to announce his engagement to Helen Dwire, one of his classmates at Centenary College in Shreveport. I had seen her picture at Ste. Marie du Zit and had fussed at him for not courting her more. I told him "boy you are crazy not to go with that girl." It was the most beautiful picture I had ever seen. I guess he did when he got back. He was sort of a hero back in Shreveport and had asked her to marry him, and she said yes. I was kind of proud of him for that, 'cause I thought she was a beautiful girl.

I visited Bill Neely's family. They lived in Smyrna, TN, not far from Hartsville. I spent most of the time with his father. Bill had a really nice pistol that he treasured very much, and I had brought it back to give to the family. I told his father that Bill had liked this gun very much, and I wanted to give it to him. Surprisingly, he didn't want it. He said no, I would prefer that you keep it, which I did. I also learned that there was an airfield built near Smyrna that could have been named Neely Field, both because of Bill's death in the war and because the Neelys owned the land that the base was built on. But his father didn't want that either.

As his home leave was ending, Greg received orders to report to the Army Air Corps Redistribution Station #2 in Miami where he remained for two weeks of further recuperation and for final processing of his service records and payment, and to undergo evaluations.

Capt. William Gregory, with Sam Jones Gregory, during home leave at Hartsville, October 1943. (Gregory)

It was kind of a reward for crews that had completed their fifty combat missions, or twenty-five for bomber pilots. There weren't too many bomber crews there at that time. So many of them got shot down during that time that they were not very successful in getting twenty-five missions, particularly in England. It was a long time before the first one—it may have been the Memphis Belle—made their twenty-five missions.

All returning fliers who completed their mission got two weeks at the famous and palatial Cadillac Hotel. It was nothing but food and relaxing and having a good time. We had a lot of pilots who finished their mission who were there at that time.

After two weeks in Miami, Greg returned home for another two-week visit, and while there received orders to report to the 337th Fighter Squadron (329th FG) at Glendale, CA. He bought an old car and drove it to California. On arrival, he and Lloyd DeMoss were sent to the North Island Naval Air Station in San Diego, where the 337th was then based.[2]

After being checked out again for P-38 aircraft, and following a few days of flying, Greg and Lloyd learned that their squadron commander had received a requirement for two pilots to report to the Dallas Ferry Command to ferry P-38s from Dallas to Newark, New Jersey where they were dismantled, loaded on waiting freighters, and delivered to England for combat service. Citing the fact that they were both new to the squadron, and both bachelors—the AAF was making an effort to reduce the amount of time newly-returned combat veterans would be separated from wives and children—their commander gave them the assignment.

They reported to Dallas in December and ferried three aircraft before receiving further orders to return to the 329th FG which had recently been reassigned to the Ontario Army Air Field, just east of Los Angeles.

The 329th Fighter Group functioned as a Replacement Training Unit, to which newly commissioned pilots were assigned for P-38 transition training followed by several months of further intensive instruction before being assigned to a combat unit. Greg was assigned as flight leader in the group's 337th squadron; Lloyd as flight leader in the 331st squadron. As flight leaders, they supervised a team of instructors and were also assigned three or four trainees themselves. They found themselves in very much the same situation they'd been in when they were themselves undergoing transition training, but in this case, it was their students who were experiencing the high-performance P-38s for the first time. By this point in the war, the AAF had fine-tuned transition training for new pilots. Pilots received at least five hours of cockpit time before ever taking off, and eight hours of transition flying in the P-38 before intensive flight instruction began.

Many of the flight instructors were, like Greg, combat veterans who delivered instruction in acrobatics, aerial bombing, gunnery exercises, and simulated individual combat. Navigation missions, instrument flying, and night flying were also prescribed. After 1943, training emphasis was on high-altitude operations and on the development of combat vigilance and aggressiveness.

Accidents, often fatal, were a weekly event. In the month preceding Greg's arrival in Ontario, five P-38s had been involved in accidents, mostly landing or ground accidents, but one involving an engine failure that required the pilot to bail out. In their first month as instructors, one of the students in DeMoss' squadron crashed his aircraft during a belly-landing, and three in Greg's squadron crashed, killing two of the new transition pilots. Flying in very intense combat simulations, seemingly every conceivable form of mechanical failure or pilot error occurred.[3]

On February 11 Greg received the terrible news that his good friend Lloyd DeMoss had been killed in a training accident at the airfield. Lloyd had been a superb pilot. He originally named his P-38 fighter in North Africa "The Gentleman"—the moniker of the sports teams at Centenary College. But it was renamed "Bad Penny" by his crew because it had made so many dangerous sorties over enemy territory and had always returned safely. Having served through harrowing combat in North Africa, Lloyd's death was a special tragedy for Greg. He and Lloyd had trained in the P-38 together at San Francisco, had embarked for North Africa together, and were tentmates at every base they flew from in North Africa. They were together on their first combat mission, and flew together in 17 of their 50 combat missions in the Mediterranean Theater. When their departure orders finally arrived, they left North Africa together.

Throughout his combat tour in North Africa, Greg's closest friends had been his tentmates and fellow 49th squadron pilots, and now three of the four had been killed within eight months of each other: Lt. Bland on a combat mission, and Lts. Neely and DeMoss in training accidents. Only Wayne Manlove, also a flight instructor with the 440th Base Unit at Santa Maria AFB, remained.

DeMoss' death underscores the widespread losses among pilots—veterans and training cadets alike—during this period of the war. With so much flight instruction occurring, and with the intensity of that instruction, losses were often stunning. In the same month that Lloyd DeMoss lost his life, 161 other pilots also lost theirs in flight accidents within the continental United States alone.[4]

On the day of DeMoss' death, Greg had been on a short hop to March Field. On landing back at Ontario, he was given the bad news. *Since I had been with him in the 49th, I was selected to escort Lloyd's body on the two-day train ride from Ontario to Shreveport, LA. When I arrived there, Lloyd's family, and his fiancée Helen, were waiting at the station. I stayed with the DeMoss family during my three-day stay in Shreveport, and attended his burial. I found Helen very distraught with her loss.* Greg consoled Lloyd's family, and Helen, as best he could, in return being consoled by them.

Helen and Lloyd had been engaged for just three months. At the time of DeMoss' death, she was just short of 21 years of age.

Greg and Helen got to know each other in those three days, and when he asked if he could write to her, she agreed. Greg returned to California to continue his duties as a flight instructor, and he and Helen corresponded through the months following.

Helen Lillian Dwire had been born June 6, 1922 in the Fort Worth area, and moved with her family to Shreveport at the age of four. The oldest of four, Helen grew to be an alert, engaging, and artistic young woman.

At Bryd High School, Helen edited the school newspaper and made excellent grades. She had become an accomplished vocalist and competed in the high school's first talent competition in 1937. Her beau, "Weenie" Bynum, was the school's star running back.[5]

She entered Centenary College in Shreveport, and throughout her college years created a wake wherever she went. One fraternity named her "Sweetheart" two years running, and in 1939 she was chosen Miss Centenary by the college's boys. Helen was a guest vocalist at many Shreveport events, and participated in the Centenary-sponsored "Kollege Kapers," a variety show that toured four area towns and featured a 15-piece swing orchestra, tap dancers, piano teams, several other vocalists, and a play in which she starred.[6] She continued to excel academically, and represented her sorority, Alpha Xi Delta, in the Girls Honorary group, the Maroon Jackets.[7]

In any epoch, Helen would be a stunning beauty. In the September 16, 1938 edition of *Centenary Conglomerate*, her college newsletter, she was described as "a scrumptious blinker-full," and in 1942 she was described as "a college beauty" in the hometown newspaper. How she acquired the nickname "Bobo"—an epithet that would endure for much of her life—is an enduring bafflement.

Helen was, like all youth in America in the early 1940s, deeply affected by the ever-present ominous war news. Glancing around her college classrooms, she would know that every life in the room would be altered by the war. Most of the young men would be in the service, some would be killed, and all would come back changed. And she would know that the lives of her young female classmates would also be shaped by the war years to come. Their boyfriends and brothers would leave for overseas duty, and they themselves would very likely take a hand in the country-wide mobilization that was then gathering momentum. The future became less focused for them; the immediate of greater import.

Helen graduated from Centenary College in 1942 with a Bachelor of Arts in History. After graduation, she taught at an elementary school in a

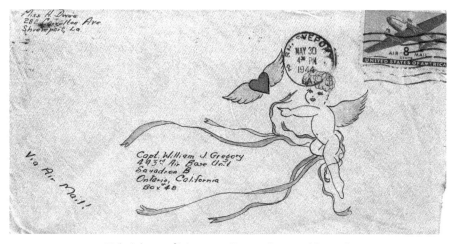

Helen's letter of May 30 to Greg at Ontario. (Gregory)

small Louisiana town before returning to Shreveport where she found work as a draftsman. Her graphic skills are evident in the lyrical illustrations that grace the envelopes of the many letters she wrote to Greg while they were apart. She clearly felt an immediate closeness to Greg—in March alone she wrote to him twice weekly, and in the months following, at least once a week.

Today Helen would be described as a very creative graphic artist. In 1943, she would more likely be termed an exceptionally clever cartoonist. Her artful letters to Greg attest to the great attention to detail that would characterize her life: a life of style and creativity.

In May, one of Greg's pilots was preparing to embark overseas. His wife and two small daughters needed transport from Ontario to Shreveport, and Greg offered to escort them. By this time, he and Helen had been in frequent correspondence for 10 weeks, and the two were becoming close.

I volunteered for that long trip 'cause I wanted to see Helen again. My days with Helen were very special. We did a lot of talking, and a lot of planning. Finally, toward the end of the trip—it was a wonderful evening—I proposed to her, and she accepted. We set November 25 as the date for our wedding.

Greg returned to Ontario to continue flying and instructing. A few days before the scheduled wedding, he requested an airplane to fly to Shreveport and was given a Douglas A-24 Banshee two-place dive-bomber. A friend planned to accompany him to visit his own family near Shreveport, and would then fly the aircraft back to Ontario while Greg and Helen returned by car.

The flights to Shreveport were weather-challenged. *I had not planned on the weather turning against us, and leaving Tucson, we ran into really bad weather. For the next four days, it was the worst rainy season I had seen for a long time.* Flying mostly on instruments, they made it as far as Big Springs, TX, before abandoning any further travel

Capt. and Mrs. William J. Gregory. (Gregory)

by plane—the weather was just too severe. Helen's brother, Jeff, collected them there and delivered Greg to Shreveport.

The drenching rain continued, right up until the hour of their wedding, when the clouds broke and the sun came out brightly. They married at 2:00 p.m. on November 25 at Broadmoor Baptist Church, with Greg's father, Sam Jones Gregory, serving as best man, with a reception following at Helen's home. The newlyweds started late for Dallas, with Jeff and friends giving chase for quite a few miles.

Helen had never ventured farther than Fort Worth and in the coming days she would receive many cultural sensitivity lessons, including one when she and Greg stopped to visit some popular caves in West Texas. Arriving at the caves, and joining a crowd of 40 others, Helen remarked: "Listen to all those funny accents…" Greg responded, "You know, if they heard you talk, they would say that YOU have a funny accent," to which she retorted, "Oh, I don't. I don't have an accent at all." *But of course, she did have a lovely Louisianan accent and would receive quite a bit of good-natured teasing later in California.*

Arriving at Ontario after five or six days, Greg and Helen settled into his garage-loft apartment. His unit flew continuously, seven days a week, with instructors scheduled in 24-hour shifts—noon to noon—followed by 24 hours off. *It was a busy time, but a really wonderful time. We lived in Pomona, in the southern foothills of the Sierra Nevada, and it was only about 30 miles to Los Angeles and Hollywood—a short drive in those days. At that time, we had a lot of things to see in those two cities. We had lots of tickets to shows, and we danced to a lot of bands. It was just a wonderful time to be there, and we enjoyed those years very much. She was a wonderful wife—the only woman in my life that I really thought about marrying.*

Greg and Helen made new friends at Ontario and reunited with some of Greg's former friends. Greg had gone all through flight training

Greg's favorite photo. With Helen on a California beach. (Gregory)

with Frank Mullinax, who was also stationed at Ontario,[8] and two of Greg's former squadron mates in North Africa, Fred Bitter and Beryl Boatman, were also instructors there.[9]

He became a Flight Commander in charge of 15 instructors and 30 trainees. Flying both day and night training missions, Greg's team showed the transition pilots what they had learned in their own combat tours, especially the tactics to use to be successful in combat.

Greg continued to lose friends, even after their combat tours were complete. John Harris, also then a flight instructor, and a pilot with whom Greg had flown many combat missions, was killed in May when his P-38 lost an engine on takeoff. And Greg's last remaining tentmate from his combat tour in North Africa, Wayne Manlove, was killed in a crash at the Point Sal Gunnery Range on August 22.[10]

Manlove, Bland, Neely, and DeMoss. All shared the tight bond that comes from combat. All had flown together on their very first combat mission in North Africa in May of 1943. And now all gone. Greg's attitude was characteristic of him: *You just have to go on.* But listening to Greg's wistful recollection of those friends decades later is evidence of his heartfelt and enduring loss.

Neither was Greg's hometown of Hartsville spared: by war's end 18 Trousdale County men would lose their lives in the fighting, many of them familiar to Greg.[11]

In December his commanding officer recommended Greg for promotion to Major, making particular mention of Greg's "devotion to duty" and noting the "excellent and highly efficient manner in which he served as leader and handler of members of his flight."[12]

Like many veteran pilots, Greg was eager to have his wife join him on a flight, and the base commander permitted spouses to join their husbands once a year. In this, though, Greg would be disappointed: *Helen did not like small planes—I flew her just once in a trainer airplane, an AT-6 or something similar.*

At the time, the airfield at Ontario was equipped with a relatively wide range of aircraft, P-38s, Navy SB-2C and SBD bombers, Vultee trainers, and two P-59s—America's very first jet airplane, built by Bell Aviation. Greg was eager to fly the P-59 and arranged for a fellow pilot who had himself flown the P-59 just once before to explain the instrumentation and engine-start procedures. His introduction to the P-59 was reminiscent of his first flight in the P-38. In that aircraft and others he would fly later in his career, his first flight was a solo.

Normally before you would fly a really different airplane you would have a lot of schooling. But I had no schooling at all. I started the engine, closed the canopy and taxied away. I had been told to be careful not to overheat the engines, so I took things slowly. I lined up on the runway and pushed the throttles forward, and as I reached flying speed lifted the aircraft off the ground. It was a strange sensation lifting off with no props.

The P-38's propellers pulled the aircraft through the air; in the P-59 the propulsion came from the rear of the engines, pushing the aircraft forward. The propellers of the P-38 had always been a symbol of security to Greg, a visible manifestation of the power of the aircraft. *I didn't have that same feeling with the jet aircraft.*

Greg's first flight in the P-59 lasted about two hours—the maximum flight time for that aircraft. *It was an easy plane to take off and land and was not hard to fly at all. I flew it two or three times, and it was always a different sensation flying this jet and no props. I was going through the air real smoothly, but it was different not having props.*

The Gregorys planned a trip to Tennessee in late July 1945 with Frank Mullinax and his family. It was to be Helen's first visit to Hartsville. Frank dropped Greg and Helen at Hartsville before continuing to his nearby hometown of Watertown. For the return, Greg and Helen would train to Shreveport, and the Mullinaxes would collect them there for the final drive back to Ontario. The Gregorys and Mullinaxes pooled their gas ration coupons for the round trip and made the long drive in Frank's Chevrolet Coupe. Reaching Hartsville, they remained for about 10 days, and then traveled to Shreveport to visit Helen's family. A few days after arriving in Shreveport, the second atomic bomb was dropped on Nagasaki, and the war was ended. Greg, Helen, and the Mullinax family returned immediately to Ontario. *We didn't need any more coupon tickets for gas after that.*

On reporting back to his unit, Greg learned that his job had changed. Instead of providing flight instruction, he would now be ferrying P-38s to Kingman, Arizona to be destroyed. *We had a lot of P-38s, and they were going out of the Air Force inventory. By that time we had the P-59 and F-80 fighter jets, and there was no plan to use the P-38s any longer. We flew some brand new P-38s to Kingman where they were cut up for scrap metal. We didn't like to see that, but the P-38 was no longer going to be an airplane for the future—its job had been done.*

Greg had flown the P-38 from May 1942 through 1945, and in that time logged about 1,000 flight hours in the aircraft—an impressive record in such a relatively short period.

When that was finished, the base at Ontario closed, and those of us who were there were moved to March Field, 30 miles to the southeast near Riverside. It was chaos at that time—so many were getting out of the service.

Greg decided to remain in the service a bit longer, hoping that he might be assigned to a tactical unit. He held a staff position, did some teaching, and was involved in Air Force planning as units began to be eliminated. He did manage to do some flying at March Field and was checked out in the B-25 bomber. *The Air Force had modified some of the B-25s to create more space in the rear for passengers. At the time, many Air Force personnel were being sent to schools around the country, and it was our job to deliver the students using the B-25s. I recall one flight in which we left March Field for New York. We delivered some students to Denver, others to Kansas City, and still others to Illinois, picking up other students along the way, before completing the outbound leg to New York. We returned to March, making similar stops on the way to our home base.*

But by the summer of 1947, he had not been able to secure a position with a tactical unit, and it began to appear that there would not be much of a future for him in the Air Force. *We were not doing much flying, I didn't have a very promising job, and the personnel had been cut back so much that it didn't seem like there would be many opportunities. So I requested separation and left the active Air Force at that time.*

Greg's active duty ended on June 13, 1947, when he received his appointment to the Officers Reserve Corps, Army of the United States.

Civilian life

Greg and Helen relocated back to Shreveport, where, harkening back to his summer as a book salesman in Louisiana, Greg took a sales position with Proctor and Gamble. He also enrolled part-time at Centenary College, Helen's Alma Mater, taking night classes and working toward his baccalaureate degree in Business Administration. They had expected their first child two years earlier, but when Helen suffered a miscarriage, they began to doubt whether they would be able to have children. But the arrival of their daughter, Gretchen Dollye Gregory, on January 4, 1949, put those doubts to rest, and the Gregory family settled into their first home on Victory Drive.[13]

While working and studying, Greg remained in the AF Reserve and was assigned to the reserve unit at Barksdale AFB. Since 1946, the Air Force Training Command had been based at Barksdale, and with the rapid demobilization that was occurring across the country, had become the main training organization for the postwar USAAF. *The Reserve was at Barksdale and a bunch of us old World War II guys would go out to the base on weekends and would fly whatever was available—we always had AT-6s out there. We didn't receive any pay for it, but it was enough that we could keep our hand in flying.*[14,15]

At the time, Greg's reserve unit was the 392nd Bomb Group (Reserve). Greg, then a Major, had been assigned as its Operations Officer.

Maj. William Gregory, Operations Officer, 392nd Bomb Group. (*Shreveport Journal*, Friday, September 17, 1948)

A big change for Barksdale came in late 1949 when the Strategic Air Command unseated the Air Force Training Command, installed the Second Air Force, and began moving bombers "capable of atomic delivery" to the base.[16] In a development that would have a profound effect on Greg's future service, by the end of the year Barksdale had become home to 91st Strategic Reconnaissance Wing and the 301st Bombardment Wing, flying B-29 Superfortresses.

I really wanted to get back in fighters, but Barksdale was a bomber base and they wanted me to fly B-29s.

Post-war, the 301st flew standard B-29 very heavy bombers until June 1949, and just before moving to Barksdale the Group began receiving atomic-capable B-29s. The 353rd Bomb Squadron Historian records the modifications that were necessary to accommodate atomic weapons: all but the tail guns were removed to lighten the aircraft; the forward bomb bay was modified to accommodate the five-ton atomic weapon, and the rear bomb bay was fitted with a fuel tank. Importantly, the aircraft were modified for air-to-air refueling and redesignated B-29MR ("Receiver" aircraft).[17] Concurrently, other B-29s were modified to operate as air refueling tankers and were designated KB-29M.

The deepening Cold War

By the time the last shot was fired in World War II, the United States and the Soviet Union were rapidly settling into mutually exclusive and intractable positions regarding the future shape of global geopolitics. The Soviets had committed themselves to a Marxist-Leninist based communism, and in the immediate postwar years began to extend control over the Eastern Bloc countries. The US was equally committed to the process of democratization among all countries of the world, and with the adoption of the Truman Doctrine in the spring of 1947, the US pledged to support the economies and militaries of countries threatened by Soviet communism.

At the time, the two geopolitical philosophies appeared to be completely incompatible, and the two superpowers became locked in a deadly and unnegotiable zero-sum game—viewed in the US as a contest between free peoples and totalitarian regimes. Stalin fueled world tensions when, in his first radio address after the end of the war, declared that another war was inevitable because of the "capitalist development of the world economy, and that the USSR would need to concentrate on national defense in advance of a war with the Western nations."[18]

The Cold War manifested itself in many costly and dangerous policies. Both countries would soon adopt a nuclear strategy of mutually assured destruction, wherein an attack by one side would result in a devastating, unrecoverable response from the other. Nuclear arsenals began to grow.

The US and the Soviet Union each deployed conventional military forces globally, and supported proxy wars. Psychological warfare, propaganda campaigns, and espionage were all part of each country's response and counter-response. The US promulgated the Marshall Plan for rebuilding European economies; the Soviets responded with their own Molotov Plan. Technological competition heightened, culminating in the Race for Space, and the military advantage to be derived from securing the ultimate "highest ground." Even international sporting events began to reflect the two distinct nationalisms.

Recall to active duty

In the spring of 1951, Greg graduated from Centenary College—the first in his family to earn a college degree. Working at Proctor & Gamble, attending college classes and helping to raise a family left Greg with little free time, but his respite after graduation would be short-lived. The Korean War had started in June of 1950, and on August 27, 1951 the Korean War mobilization led to Greg's recall to active duty, and the reactivation of fifteen B-29 SAC bomber wings, including Greg's, and four B-29 reconnaissance wings.

With the increase in Air Force activity brought on by the Korean War, and by new missions assigned to the atomic-equipped units, B-29 accidents occurred with stark regularity.

In the seven months following Greg's reactivation, a total of 47 separate accidents involving B-29s occurred at US air force bases, thirteen of which involved fatalities. And with the large crews aboard the B-29s, multiple fatalities often resulted. In one incident at Greg's home base of Barksdale just before his reactivation, a plane experiencing multiple system problems successfully crash-landed after seven of the crew bailed out. And in August, a B-29 crashed while attempting an engine-out landing at Barksdale, destroying the aircraft and killing all eight crewmen. Greg had flown with that aircraft and crew previously on a long and tedious mission and had concerns about the crew's performance. *I recommended that the standardization board give the crew a check flight, but it didn't happen before the crash.*

These incidents were stark reminders to the entire Shreveport community and especially to all the personnel and families at the base that they were involved in a dangerous pursuit.[19]

The B-29 Superfortress

The Boeing-designed B-29's maiden flight came in late September 1942. Designed as a high-altitude strategic bomber, the aircraft was larger and more performant than the other "heavy" bomber in wide usage during World War II—the B-17 Flying Fortress. The B-29 was fast and could operate at very high altitudes. Over short distances and at low altitude, it could carry a 20,000-lb bomb load.

Specifications: Boeing B-29 Superfortress[20]

Powerplant: 4, Wright turbosupercharged radial engines, 2,200 hp each.
Crew: 11 (Pilot, Co-pilot, Bombardier, Flight Engineer, Navigator, Radio Operator, Radar Observer, Right Gunner, Left Gunner, Central Fire Control, Tail Gunner)

Boeing B-29 *Superfortress*. (Wikimedia Commons)

Max Speed: 357 mph.
Service Ceiling: 31,850 ft.
Range: 3,250 miles
Empty Weight: 74,500 lbs.
Wing Span: 141 ft. 3 in.
Length: 99 ft.
Height: 27 ft. 9 in.
First Produced: 1941
Production: over 3,000

The aircraft's innovative design included a fully pressurized cabin, tricycle-style landing gear, radar-based bombing and navigational system, and a rudimentary but effective analog computer-controlled fire-control system for its ten .50 caliber Browning machine guns. Its advanced design, coupled with a flurry of modification requests that began almost immediately, combined to cause early manufacturing challenges and production delays. Originally planned to be deployed to Egypt, with Germany as its primary target, the B-29 was eventually based only in the Pacific Theater, and flew its first combat mission against Japan in mid-1944. Bases for the bombers were established on the islands of Tinian, Saipan, and Guam, each within striking range of Tokyo, and from these bases and others in the region, the Army Air Force launched devastating attacks against military and industrial targets on the Japanese homeland, sometimes numbering over 1,000 bombers in a single attack. In three years of production, over 3,000 B-29s were manufactured, and two, the Enola Gay and the Bockscar, dropped the atomic bombs that led to the war's end.

SAC deployed non-nuclear-capable B-29 groups to its Far East Air Force in 1950, where they conducted strategic bombardment missions over North Korea. However, the B-29's role in Korea soon became limited because of the paucity of suitable strategic targets in North Korea, and its vulnerability to the recently introduced Soviet jet-powered MiG-15.

SAC soon developed an operating practice of deploying bomber forces forward, most frequently to bases in England and French Morocco, bringing the bombers many hours closer to targets in the Soviet Union. B-29 equipped units, including refueling tanker squadrons, rotated regularly to these forward bases.

The Air Force was on the cusp of a significant re-equipping: the B-36 Peacemaker and the B-50 Superfortress heavy bombers began to enter service in 1948. The B-36, a mega-plane irreverently referred to as the "gray overcast," was planned to be SAC's primary nuclear weapons delivery vehicle.

Boeing B-29 dwarfed by the immense Boeing B-36. (Wikimedia Commons)

And while each of the new aircraft being planned for the Strategic Air Command came with new and impressive capabilities, each also shared a common problem—limited range. Even with the forward deployments that would soon become commonplace, it became necessary for the Air Force to consider radically new equipment and techniques to extend the bombers' range.

At this time, SAC planners were of the opinion that a range of 12,500 miles was the minimum requirement for a strategic, atomic-capable bomber. This is about half the globe's circumference at the equator. The estimate was later judged to be extreme and was revised to 8,000 miles—still an impossible distance for the new aircraft.[21]

In the late 1940s, an intense debate was raging between the Air Force and Navy as to which service should be primarily responsible for the U.S's nuclear delivery capability. The Navy had already contracted for a number of "super-carriers," reckoning the Air Forces' bomber fleet lacked the necessary range to conduct nuclear strikes against targets in the Soviet Union.

The debate gave impetus to what had become a continuing investigation of an aerial refueling capability for the Air Forces' bomber fleet. The Air Force had experimented with plane-to-plane refueling for decades, dating back to the first successful aerial refueling in 1923 when two aircraft—linked by hose—transferred seven five-gallon tins of gasoline in a procedure that was described as "You dangle it; I'll grab it." That system proved feasibility, if not practicality.

The British later refined this "high concept, low tech" system with its own hose refueling system, referred to as the "hose and grapnel system," and had conducted sixteen Atlantic crossings in 1938. Army Air Force conducted refueling tests in 1943, using a system derived from the British, with a B-24 refueling a B-17. But the 3,250-mile range of the B-29 very heavy bomber, introduced in the latter years of the war, and the many advance bomber bases in the Pacific, removed the urgency for in-flight refueling during the war.

Post-war, the feasibility of the evolving system was first demonstrated in late March 1948, using two converted B-29 bombers, and in December of that year the Air Force conducted an operational test of what was then called the "looped-hose" system. A B-50A bomber departed Carswell AFB near Fort Worth, flew to Hawaii where it dropped a dummy bomb load, and then returned to Carswell, flying a track of over 7,700 miles, with two refuelings outbound and two inbound. The operational practicality of the aerial refueling was proven beyond debate in late February 1949, when a B-50A bomber undertook a 23,452 mile nonstop flight around the world while being refueled by KB-29Ms using the looped-hose system, a feat that prompted gritty SAC Commander General Curtis LeMay to state that "the Air Force could now deliver an atomic bomb to any place in the world that required one..."[22]

These trials were so successful that the Air Force ordered the conversion of 92 B-29s to serve as tankers using this system (KB-29Ms) and the conversion of another 74 B-29s to receiver aircraft (B-29MRs). New bombers coming online were also equipped to accommodate this looped hose method of aerial refueling.

In 1949 the 301st began receiving the new KB-29Ms and was one of the first Air Force wings to conduct aerial refueling operations. The tanker unit was affectionately called the "Ape Squadron," as the KB-29M's appeared to have tails when they transferred fuel, and all of the tankers had nose art that featured apes as the central figures.[23] The Air Force rapidly became dependent on in-flight refueling. By the end of 1950, the Air Force had created twelve squadrons of the KB-29Ms (126 aircraft); by 1952 it had thirty (502 aircraft), and by 1956, forty squadrons. A growth that prompted one of LeMay's advisors to quip: "We built, and we are continuing to build, our strategy around refueling. As of today, 'the tail is wagging the dog'."[24]

KB-29M tanker

Greg's first assignment in the 301st Bomb Wing at Barksdale was as co-pilot to its 301st Air Refueling Squadron, joining three bomber squadrons. *This was my first experience at the controls of a B-29 after flying many other kinds of aircraft before it. It was the biggest airplane I had flown at that time. It was a little different at first, particularly seated on the left of the cockpit, whereas in a fighter aircraft you are right in the middle of everything. It seemed a little bit strange at first, particularly on landing. But I really didn't have any trouble with it after a couple of flights. I was able to get checked out in the B-29 pretty fast, and I soon got a crew of my own—a crew of ten. It was really different flying solo in a single-seat P-38 and then having 10 crew members on the B-29. I kind of enjoyed all that help. There was a lot of esprit de corps in the tanker squadron, and we had a really good crew. My tanker was called "C'est Si Bon."*

The Air Refueling Squadron had only been instituted in March 1949, and was charged with a function that was very new to the Air Force. The new squadron was given little guidance on how to accomplish the refueling—just a one-half page "manual." Squadron personnel established the transfer procedures, but it required nine months of training and refinement before the first successful hookup was made, and another four before a reasonable level of proficiency was attained.[19]

The unorthodox air-to-air refueling system that was in place upon Greg's introduction to the KB-29M aircraft prompted historian Joseph Baugher to write: "In retrospect, this… system was unbelievably awkward and cumbersome, and it is a wonder that it worked at all. That it was so successful is a testament to the courage and ability of all concerned."[25]

The historian of the 3021st's 353rd squadron was in full agreement: "The original B-29 air-to-air refueling method was far different and much less sophisticated than later procedures. Veterans of the era refer to it as a 'Rube Goldberg' device—an overly complicated, jury-rigged set of equipment to accomplish a simple task."[26]

Greg did not disagree: *It was rather a crude process. It had to be done just right, or you would have problems.*

The refueling operation was undertaken at a relatively low altitude—12,000 to 15,000 ft.—because the reel operator's position in both aircraft was not pressurized. The two aircraft flew in formation, with the tanker positioned slightly above, to the left, and to the rear of the receiver aircraft. The process began when the tanker aircraft deployed a weighted grapnel at the end of a 150-foot cable, an assembly that was heavy enough to hang nearly vertically. The bomber, referred to as the "receiver," extended an unweighted 300-foot cable that was light enough to deploy nearly horizontally. With both lines fully extended, the tanker pilot gently eased the tanker to the right, just aft of the bomber's tail, thus crossing over and snagging the bomber's cable. The tanker's reel operator then hauled in both cables and attached the bomber's cable to a 200-foot long, 2.5-inch diameter fuel hose. The fuel hose was then reeled back into the bomber, attached to its fuel receptacle, and locked into place, after which the fuel was gravity-fed from the tanker to the receiver aircraft, at a rate of about 110 gallons per minute.[27]

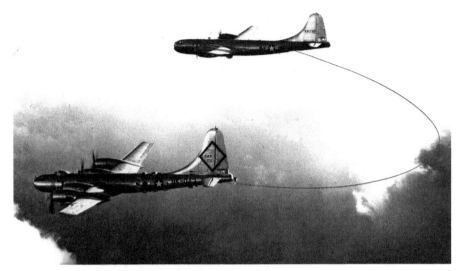

KB-29M tanker refueling a B-50A strategic bomber. (Wikimedia Commons)

The hookup procedure required about fifteen minutes and the fuel transfer just over 20 minutes, during which time the two aircraft flew in very close formation, tethered via a 200-foot hose. After fuel transfer, the procedure was reversed to retract the hose into the tanker and the bomber cable back into the bomber.

The tanker had to do a crossover, getting very close to the tail of the receiver B-29. The props were very close to the tail of the receiver—a few feet. We never clipped a tail, but you had to get pretty close. After the fuel had moved to the bomber—2,300 gallons were transferred usually—the bomber would release the hose which we recovered back into the tanker. Once that was done, we released the bomber's line, and the refueling was complete. This was close formation flying all the time. You had to be close to the bomber, and had to be steady so as not to put too much stress on the hose. It was quite an interesting operation—you had to do a crossover with these cables and hoses, and it was rather exciting.

This hose and grapnel system was not only slow and difficult but was only of use in planes with large crews to assist in handling the refueling hoses. The procedure required considerable skill on the part of the pilot and reel operator, and there were frequent equipment malfunctions, severed hoses, and lost weights. The hose system was replaced after a few years with the "flying boom" refueling system developed by Boeing.[28]

The USAF now had the ability to strike any target on the globe, and settled the argument as to whether the USAF or US Navy should be charged with the US's nuclear delivery capability. SAC underwent a massive expansion, while the Navy, which had planned for the construction of nine "supercarriers," each costing in the neighborhood of $200 million, canceled the contracts before construction began, and did not build any additional carriers until the USS *Forrestal* was built in late 1955.[29]

Overseas deployments continue

The 301st took a position in regular overseas temporary duty rotations (TDY), with its next deployment coming in January 1950—a three-week exercise to Goose Bay, Labrador to acquaint the aircrews with cold-weather operations. Greg's refueling squadron did not deploy, but was used extensively in support of the bomber's training missions.

In May of 1950 the 301st made its first overseas deployment to the United Kingdom, which included all three atomic-capable bomb squadrons, Headquarters and the Air Refueling Squadron—nearly 1,400 officers and enlisted men, 60 aircraft, and tons of gear. The wing was somewhat dispersed, with one bomb squadron, the refueling squadron, and headquarters at Lakenheath, and two bomb squadrons stationed at Sculthorpe. The outbound leg included the tragic loss of sixteen airmen when a KB-29M tanker crashed during an attempted landing at Lajes, Azores.

This deployment, initially scheduled for 90 days, was extended indefinitely, much to the detriment of morale of both the men in England and their families in Louisiana. Living conditions were "marginal." Personnel arrived in England with summer-weight clothing which proved inadequate as the cold and rainy British fall and winter approached. The squadron historian reports: "Apparently things were a bit out of hand at the bases when the local women showed up in the showers and there was general rowdiness."[30] It was probably a relief to all parties when the 301st ended its deployment to England in mid-December, 1950.

A further full-wing deployment came in April 1952 with a 90-day TDY back to Great Britain. On this deployment, which also included the air refueling squadron, the wing received a special reception, as recorded in the squadron records:

> As the Unit had earned a less-than-exemplary reputation during its 1950 stay in England, shortly after their arrival, General John McConnell, Commander of Seventh Air Force, called in the Unit's Commander and read him the "riot act"; in short, the shenanigans of the last trip were unacceptable. Colonel Wade got the word across to the troops in small discrete meetings, but in no uncertain terms. There were no problems.[31]

Greg deployed again with the 301st in a 90-day TDY to England in December 1952, basing out of three British airfields: Upper Heyford, Brize Norton—both about 70 miles west of London—and Lakenheath, 80 miles to the north. The timing of the deployment was unlucky.

On the morning of December 5, Londoners stoked their coal fireplaces against the chill of a winter cold snap. Concurrently, a high-pressure weather system stalled over all of southern England, resulting in a temperature inversion, with the warmer air above stagnating colder air at ground level. The sulfurous coal soot continued to build, and with no air movement, ground visibility was reduced to near-zero, and toxic levels of pollution soon developed. Transportation halted, schools were cancelled, and greasy grime covered exposed surfaces. The weather system finally broke four days later, leaving a death toll estimated at 12,000 people.[32]

Just ahead of this calamity flew the 301st. The initial aircraft departed Barksdale on December 3, and encountered the same disastrous weather system that would settle on London two days later. The aircraft of the 32nd BS, accompanied by fifteen refueling tankers, were scheduled to leave Barksdale first. It was intended that the 32nd's standard B-29s would land and refuel at Bermuda, while those bombers equipped for aerial refueling would be refueled aloft and continue nonstop to England. After refueling the B-29s, the tankers would land at Bermuda to support the rest of the wing as it moved to England. Such was the plan, but in the end, only one bomber made it to England nonstop. Another landed in the Azores, and the balance recovered in Bermuda. The 10-day weather delay in Bermuda included Greg and his crew.

The next day eight bombers left Bermuda for England, but due to the bad weather, SAC Headquarters diverted them into Sidi Slimane, Morocco, where they remained until December 11. SAC also delayed the departure of the other two squadrons from Barksdale until December 10 and 11.

Greg remembers the flight well. *That was a terrible trip. We made it to the island of Bermuda. The big London Fog was in effect at that time, and the weather was really bad over there. We stayed in Bermuda waiting for the weather to clear. We finally got clearance to go, took off right after dark, and had icing all the way across the Atlantic—it was a terrible night. We were at about 20,000 feet and would hit moist areas where it would freeze. On the B-29 you would lose about 30 knots of airspeed in a matter of seconds when there was a buildup of ice on the leading edge of the wings. Fortunately, we had deicer boots on the airplane, and when we hit the deicer button it would shed the ice and the airspeed would pick up again. We never got out of the icing area—we never flew high enough to get out of the weather that was leading to the icing. We did that deicing procedure all through the night.*

When the bombers reached Lakenheath Air Base, only the first three of the aircraft were able to get in. Greg was fourth to attempt a landing but found himself waved off because the weather was too poor. Directed east, he found a base that was open on the coast, and was able to land at last. *It was night again when we landed, and we had to go into the city to find accommodations—it had been a long flight. The next day we were just able to get into Lakenheath, but it was still a very low ceiling—not more than 300 feet—and I was flying instruments the whole way there. That winter, every time I took off we were in the soup by the end of the runway, and we never saw the ground again till we landed.*

When finally reassembled in England, the 301st acquitted itself well in many respects during this three-month deployment, despite the consistently poor weather, and an epidemic of influenza that more than filled the hospital at Brize Norton in December. Soon after its arrival, the wing participated in the RAF Blind Bombing Competition, with one of its squadrons, the 352nd, finishing in first place.

The weather was bad the whole time we were there—three months. At one point, my flight engineer [Mutt Pucket] told me that the number one engine was not acting right. I tried to get it changed, but they told me that the condition of the engine was not bad enough to warrant a change-out.

So we took two or three flights with it and made it OK. At the end of the deployment, on our trip back to the States in early April I was afraid we might have trouble with that engine, and we did. After we were well out to sea I rendezvoused with our bomber, made contact, and got the hose into the bomber. We had just started refueling when the number one engine quit. It was the left engine, which is the one nearest to the B-29 receiver.

Normally there was no communication between the tanker and the receiving aircraft, and even with Greg's aircraft experiencing a flight emergency, there was still no contact.

A new copilot had been assigned to me who was known to be a troublemaker. I yelled to him to "feather number one." The copilot erroneously tried to hit the number four engine for feathering. I was about to lose two engines! Mutt Pucket slapped his hand away from number four and then feathered number one. Having lost 25% of my propulsion, I added a bit of power on the No. 2 engine in order to keep balance on the aircraft and was able to stay in position with the bomber. We went through the process of refueling and recovering the hose—I thought I could maintain position long enough. The bomber knew I was on three engines, and they throttled back a little bit to make it easier for us. It was a scary time, particularly since I had this copilot that wasn't so sharp and had almost caused us to lose two engines.

I really had my hands full—I had a copilot that was of little help, losing an engine, getting it feathered, maintaining position, and not losing the hose. It all turned out OK, but it was tense for a time.

We then turned back to the bomber's base at England and stayed for three days to get the engine replaced. We tried again, and everything went fine.

The 301st returned to the States in March and was commended by the Second Air Force for the outstanding manner in which it carried out the deployment. And the same officer who had chastised the 301st upon its deployment to England in September commended the unit for its "superior performance in the face of adverse weather, operational difficulties, and maintenance problems."[33,34]

A change ahead for Gregory

Greg's recall to active duty had been for 21 months, so at the end of that time—shortly after his return home from the UK deployment—he could have left the service. However, he had doubts. *I got to thinking that it was not a good thing to be in and out of the service. I had to either be in or be out, one or the other, because the world passes you by otherwise—you either lose out with your competitors in the business world or the Air Force world.*

As the Korean War began to wind down, permanent Air Force assignments came open when other pilots elected to leave at the conclusion of their contracts. Greg let it be known that he would like to remain in the service, and when a slot came open, he took it. It was a significant decision that would keep Greg in the cockpit, would potentially set him on a path to tremendous opportunity, but would shape his and his family's life for years to come. He had not discussed it much with Helen. As a result, his decision, while carefully reasoned, would catch his wife off guard.

One evening while we were at a party at the Officers Club at Barksdale one of the wives commented to Helen, "Congratulations, you are staying in the service." They about got into an argument. Helen wanted to correct her. But she asked me about it, and I said: "Yeah, I guess we will be for a while."

Helen was steamed. Their daughter Gretchen, then not quite five years old, would later comment that for two weeks her mother would only speak to Greg through her. Until hearing of Greg's decision at the cocktail party, Helen believed she and Greg would continue the life they had begun in Shreveport before his reactivation. Sixty years after he made this decision, Greg would relate this story with a self-conscious chuckle in his voice, as if to imply that he is still a bit sheepish about Helen's reaction to this news and really truly wishes he had a do-over on how that decision was made.

CHAPTER 6

SAC Command Pilot

The Air Force's Strategic Air Command (SAC) had been faced with significant changes since its inception, and postwar challenges were expensive and complex. The aging KB-29s were being replaced with the new Boeing KC-97 tanker. And the B-29s that SAC had operated as America's primary post-war deterrent for seven years were being replaced by the Air Force's newest bomber, the vastly more performant B-47.

The B-47 Stratojet

The Boeing-built B-47 Stratojet had its origins as early as 1943 when the Army Air Forces informally prompted aircraft manufacturers to begin research into jet-powered bombers. A formal request-for-proposal ensued, with the Air Force providing an initial set of aircraft specifications that it believed would permit the aircraft to avoid enemy interceptor aircraft: a near-supersonic maximum speed of 550 mph, a cruise speed of 450 mph, a range of 3,500 miles, and a service ceiling of 45,000 feet. Four aviation companies took the bait: North American Aviation, the Convair Corporation, Boeing and the Glenn Martin Company each submitted designs.

That these four companies would respond to the request-for-proposal is unsurprising. Together they were responsible for many of the more important aircraft then being flown by Allied forces in all theaters of the war, including the BT-9 trainer, the B-25 medium bomber, the iconic P-51 fighter, the A-36 ground attack aircraft (North American); the B-24 heavy bomber, the PBY seaplane (Convair); the B-17 and B-29 bombers (Boeing); and the B-26 medium bomber and A-22 light bomber (Martin). The Air Force awarded study contracts to all four companies.

The design Boeing presented to the Air Force included 35-degree swept-back wings—a radical design element at that time in aviation history—and six wing-mounted jet engines. The Air Force saw promise in the design, and in April 1946 ordered two prototypes, designated the XB-47. The aircraft rolled out in mid-September 1947, first flew on December 17, and just over a year later broke all coast-to-coast speed records, posting an average speed of just over 607 mph on the cross-country flight.[1] A second, very successful, prototype followed in July 1948, leading the Air Force to place a small production order, followed by a ramp-up as the aircraft was officially approved. Boeing built the aircraft at its plant in Wichita, where it had built B-29s in years past. But so eager was the Air Force for the B-47 that arrangements were made for the aircraft to also be manufactured by Lockheed (Marietta) and Douglas (Tulsa). By 1951 SAC began equipping its bomb wings with the aircraft, replacing the much less performant, piston-engined B-36 bomber that had been in service since 1948.

The B-47's aircrew consisted of just three crewmen: pilot and co-pilot sat in tandem under a fighter-style bubble canopy, with an "observer" positioned forward in the nose. The crew workload was high: the B-29s and B-36s which

Boeing B-47 Stratojet strategic bomber. (Wikimedia Commons)

it replaced had crews of and 11 and 15, respectively; the B-52 which would succeed the B-47 would have a five-man crew.

Specifications: Boeing B-47 Stratojet[2]

Crew: 3 (Pilot, Co-pilot, Observer)
Powerplant: 6, GE turbojets, turbosupercharged radial engines, 7,200 lbf each.
Max speed: 607 mph.
Service ceiling: 40,500 ft.
Range: 2,013 miles
Empty weight: 79,074 lbs.
Wing span: 116 ft.
Length: 107 ft. 1 in.
Height: 28 ft.
Production: 1,341

The observer position was work-heavy: that individual would have to do what three men (navigator, bombardier, and radar operator) did in the B-29. New equipment made it a different job, as did the B-47's greater performance. SAC anticipated the challenge with its "triple-headed monster" school at Mather AFB, California, where crewmen were trained to perform all three tasks.[3]

The aircraft was as fast as fighter jets then in development, making forward-firing defensive armament unnecessary. A tail turret equipped with twin 20 mm Browning machine guns, fired by the copilot using remotely controlled, radar-directed fire control, was deemed sufficient.

The new aircraft was qualitatively different from the B-29: it was much faster and so aerodynamically clean that it was much more difficult to slow down than its propeller-powered predecessor. Pilots commented that flying the B-47 was like going from "a Model 'T' to a Ferrari."

The B-47's operational profile had an inherently tight "coffin corner," much like the U-2 design that was still many years in the future. Operating the aircraft at 35,000 feet produced the optimum fuel consumption and greatest range at most weights, but resulted in a very slight difference between its maximum Mach speed and its stall speed—just 9.3 km/hr. Operating just below this narrow "window" could result in stall; operating just beyond it could induce excessive stresses in the aircraft. The B-47's autopilot was rudimentary, and at altitude the pilot had to hand-fly the aircraft. On very long trans-oceanic flights, monitoring the airspeed continuously and making necessary throttle adjustments became a taxing issue for the pilots.

Due to the relative inefficiency of their six jet engines, the various models of the B-47 required between 9,100 and 10,400 feet for takeoff, largely dependent on the loaded aircraft weight. Consequently, the B-47 was equipped with Jet-Assist Take-Off (JATO). With JATO, the takeoff distance was reduced to as little as 7,200 feet. The term "jet" is a misnomer—in fact, the JATO thrust was provided by a number of small solid-fuel rockets, making *RATO* more apt. Early B-47s, up to the E model, were equipped with an internal JATO system. Later models used external rocket racks for the boost.

The B-47 was a major part of the US strategic reconnaissance and nuclear strike force, and represented a new and chilling threat to the Soviets: "The aircraft was specifically designed as a high-altitude, high-speed bomber, to either photograph or destroy the Soviets' major infrastructure—factories, rail yards, and airbases. The B-47 was especially feared by our enemies because it gave the United States an unstoppable nuclear strike force."[4]

Boeing would eventually produce over 2,000 B-47s in eight variants, and the Strategic Air Command would equip 28 bombardment wings and five wings of reconnaissance aircraft with the B-47.[5] Pilots generally gave the B-47 high marks: the aircraft handled well in flight, with a "fighter-like" light touch to the controls. The bubble canopy for the pilot and copilot provided good vision and was also quite reminiscent of fighter aircraft.[6]

B-47 with rocket-assist take-off. (Edward Air Force Base media gallery)

The B-47 also posed fresh challenges for the tankers. Historian Richard Smith noted that the aircraft was not wholly compatible with SAC's slower and altitude-limited piston-engine tankers:

"Fully loaded at its 175,000-pound takeoff weight, KC-97G tanker then in use was hard put to reach an altitude of 20,000 feet. But a B-47's cruising altitude was 35,000 feet. For its refueling, a B-47 had to descend to the tanker's altitude, and start refueling around 18,000 feet. While the tanker got lighter, the B-47 became heavier, requiring more speed to stay in the air than a KC-97's engine could match. The result was the 'toboggan' maneuver in which both airplanes entered a shallow dive, a risky descent for two very large airplanes joined by a refueling boom."[7]

Aircrew training for the B-47

Transitioning to the B-47 presented the 301st with both challenges and opportunities. The flight crew of three on the B-47 replaced the crew of 11 on the B-29, leaving the wing commander with a surfeit of trained airmen, and allowing an element of discretion as to whom would move to the new jets. Some of the aircrews went on to the air-refueling squadron that was in the process of re-equipping with KC-97s. Some personnel transferred to other SAC flying assignments, such as B-36s, and still others moved to ground jobs. The pilots chosen for the B-47s would require very extensive transitional training.

Although he had never flown the bomber version of the B-29, Maj. William Gregory was one of the wing's pilots selected to transition to the new B-47. He received orders releasing him from his posting with the 301st and assigning him to transition schools preparatory for duty with a B-47 Wing. With this assignment, he knew that he would remain in SAC, would fly bombers, and would remain on active duty for the foreseeable future.[8]

The Air Force wanted to prepare the crews well for that airplane. The B-29 usually had a crew of 10 or 11. The B-47 was only going to have three people—two pilots and an observer. It was thought that the aircraft commander needed to go back to school to learn bombing and navigation. So I was first sent to a ground school at Ellington AFB near Houston for six months, and at the completion of that school, I would then spend six months at Connelly AFB near Waco for navigator/bombardier training.

We really didn't need all that much training, but it was good to have. At Ellington, Greg flew in the Convair T-29—the "flying classroom," where he received navigation instruction with others while aloft.

When Greg began school in Houston, Helen remained in Shreveport, deeply pregnant with their second child, a daughter who would be born on July 20, 1953—Jamie Helen Gregory, named for both parents. At the time, "Cookie" Bumstead had just been introduced to the Dagwood & Blondie cartoon strip, and older sister Gretchen, apparently seeing a resemblance, gave her new baby sister the same nickname. Henceforth, she was always "Cookie." Ten days after her birth, the family had settled in Houston for the duration of Greg's school.

I completed that nearly year-long training program in the summer of 1954. It was the best ground school I had ever attended for flying an airplane.

At this point, Greg was ready for an assignment to an operating B-47 unit, and he soon received orders for the 19th Bombardment Wing based at Pinecastle, Florida, near the then-sleepy little town of Orlando.

The 19th was one of the most storied aviation units in the American military. It had roots in the Lafayette Escadrille in France during World War I, and was among the first groups to receive the B-17 when it was introduced in 1938. It had been originally posted to the Philippines in a last-minute but futile effort to strengthen American forces in the southwest Pacific in late 1941. Caught up in the Japanese invasion of the Philippines and Java in the weeks following Pearl Harbor, the 19th joined the hard-pressed defensive forces in Australia in 1942. The group would be an essential part of the early American advances against the Japanese and remained in the theater with B-17s until the spring of 1944 when it returned to the US to be refitted with the B-29 very heavy bomber, and by February 1945 the group was back in action against the Japanese.[9]

The Gregory family, having become proficient by this time in moving to new bases, new cities, and new quarters, made the move to Pinecastle later that summer. They settled into temporary quarters just in time to celebrate Cookie's first birthday. It was her third home in her first year.

Flying the B-47 with the 19th Bomb Wing

Shortly after arriving at Orlando and getting the family settled, Greg was made an aircraft commander and sent for further training to Wichita, Kansas. *It was the best school I ever attended. We were there from November to February and then had a two-week course to study the bomb that we were going to be responsible for.*

I had never been so familiar with an airplane as I was with the B-47. It was a great airplane—the prettiest bomber ever built—it has six engines, and swept wings—and was the fastest bomber in the world for several years. It was a slick-looking airplane. It looked fast even when it was sitting on the ground.

The mission of the 19th Bombardment Wing, as established by the Second Air Force, would eventually be to: "(Conduct) strategic bombardment operations on a global scale, either independently or in cooperation with land and sea forces."[10] But in the early months of the 19th's activation, the mission was much different: to provide transition training to its personnel—air and ground crews alike.[11] A Mobile Training Detachment was set up at Pinecastle to provide an introduction to the B-47 for pilots and airmen—the program ran 64 hours for the pilots, and 128 hours for the airmen—a training course intended to broadly familiarize personnel with the B-47 before being reassigned to further, more intensive training in the aircraft.

Transitioning a wing to a different aircraft was a terrifically complicated undertaking. A steady stream of personnel was funneled into 13-week transition training schools at McConnell, Connally, Ellington, Mather, and Amarillo Air Force Bases—a pipeline that would continue for many months. In mid-June 1954, as Greg was completing his transition training for the B-47, the 19th Bombardment Wing had begun the process of converting to the B-47 aircraft at Pinecastle AFB. At that time, the wing included 45 pilots, and by the end of July, this number had increased to 106.

Staffing, equipment, and training challenges repeatedly caused delays in the 19th coming to full combat readiness. June 1955 was initially set as the date by which the 19th should be combat ready with a minimum of 33 trained crews. But the Second Air Force later changed the date to August 1955, and also increased the combat crew target to 40.[12] As the history of the wing records:

> For the 19th Bomb Wing, it was a new twist to the lion and the lamb story, as the year 1954 blew in with a prop wash and blasted out with jet exhaust. The wing underwent a metamorphosis: (*changing*) homes, planes and even commands. B-29s were flown in the spring, and B-47s were in the fall, with the long summer in between a time for the chrysalis to change in its cocoon.[13]

The wing had been without aircraft for six months, and took possession of its first B-47 on November 5, 1954. A milestone was reached at the end of January 1955 when one crew from the 28th BS and one crew from the 30th BS were declared combat ready—the first 19th BW B-47 crews to achieve that status.[14] With the arrival of its aircraft, and with the pipeline of trained crews starting to run full, the 19th Bombardment Wing became operational again, and the primary mission of the wing shifted to flight operations, with the training of personnel relegated to a secondary mission.

The 19th shared Pinecastle with the 321st Bomb Wing. By the end of April 1955 the two wings held upwards of 90 aircraft, and with the full staffing contingents, the base was badly overcrowded. Accordingly, plans were developed to complete the move of the 19th to nearby Homestead AFB sometime in 1956.

Greg was assigned to the wing's 30th Bomb Squadron. During October, while his squadron commander was attending transition training at McConnell AFB, Greg served as acting squadron commander—his first taste of squadron command.

In April 1955, as the flight crews of the 19th began their last phase of training, the wing scheduled a series of training missions designed to simulate combat conditions for the B-47 crews. The first mission was flown on April 7, designated Operation *Free Beer*, with each of the 19th's three squadrons putting up three aircraft on simulated bombing runs against American cities, including Avon Park and Fort Pierce in Florida, Atlanta, Birmingham, Little Rock, and Clarksdale, Missouri. The mission included four bombing runs for each of the aircraft. As it happened, the schedule was a bit too aggressive. Of the nine aircraft, one returned to base with a mechanical issue, and four others had failures of their K-system bombsights.

Nonetheless, in the chilling language of the Cold War Air Force: "In general, the mission was considered to be a success. Based on the assumption that the standard nuclear weapon of 83 kilotons was used, every target would have been extensively damaged. Avon Park would have been almost completely destroyed, and Atlanta would have received extensive damage. The center of Birmingham would have been demolished, while the steel mills, 12 miles southwest of the target area would have been partially damaged but not put out of operation. Little Rock would have been completely wiped out."[15]

After this first mission, the remaining missions in the series were postponed, "until the wing achieved a greater combat capability."[16]

In late June, as Greg was completing his first year with the 19th, the wing flew its first large-scale unit simulated combat mission (USCM) to train and evaluate the aircrews in the performance of flying a "stream-type" bomber mission. On each of three successive days, ten aircraft from each squadron conducted simulated attacks on Atlanta, Little Rock, and Dallas, using in-flight refueling and incorporating fighter interception. Simulated bomb drops were made using both radar bombing and visual drops. The wing commander considered the mission to be highly successful from the point of view of staff familiarization and crew training, though less successful in the bombing portion of the mission: although the "circular errors" of the drops were small enough that the mission, had it been live fire, would have been devastating to the targets.[17]

By the end of July 1955, the 19th Bomb Wing had 38 combat crews operationally ready. A graduation exercise mission—Operation *East Wind*—was scheduled for the first week of August, and the results of that operation would be used to determine the final combat readiness of the 19th Bombardment Wing.

Anticipating a positive result from *East Wind*, and eager to add the B-47 units to America's defense inventory, the Second Air Force directed the 19th to begin planning for its first overseas deployment—Operation *Road Race*—a 10-day exercise in October to Sidi Slimane in French Morocco, for the purpose of a "special weapons exercise." For Greg, it would be a somewhat familiar locale—he had first visited Casablanca, just 135 miles to the southwest of Sidi Slimane, in the spring of 1943 at the start of his combat tour during World War II.

Further anticipating a positive result from *Road Race*, the Second Air Force planned to enter the 19th BW into a regular overseas rotation, commencing in mid-January with a 45-day temporary duty tour to French Morocco.[18]

Much was riding on the results of Operation *East Wind*, which was flown as scheduled in early August. Consisting of a series of simulated atomic bombardment attacks against American target cities, the missions were flown successfully, with the result that the 19th BW, including bomb squadrons and refueling squadrons, were determined to be combat ready. *Road Race*, the 19th's move to Homestead AFB, and its entry into the regular overseas rotation were all on schedule.[19]

Operation *Road Race*, the 19th's first overseas deployment, was a combined training exercise with the 321st BW in which aircraft would depart from Pinecastle in early October, refuel twice while airborne, strike designated practice targets in France and Italy, and then reassemble at Sidi Slimane in French Morocco before making their return to Pinecastle. Thirty-two crews from the 19th participated, and in testament to the complexity of this type of long-range combat mission, just fourteen aircraft were able to make scorable target runs—a result that the wing commander considered to be "very good." With its success in *Road Race*, the unit's first scheduled full deployment back to Sidi Slimane remained on track for January 15, 1956.[20]

The purpose of the TDY to French Morocco was decidedly twofold. It was first to continue the practice of SAC to maintain a forward-positioned strike-ready force in the event of the outbreak of hostilities. Additionally, its purpose was to continue the extensive operational training that the wing had undertaken since its earliest days at Pinecastle and to test the unit's ability to make this type of full deployment while maintaining its deterrent capability.[21]

The deployment of 19th BW personnel and equipment to Sidi Slimane began on January 2, 1956 and included 1,319 airmen and officers from the 19th and Pinecastle's 813th Air Base Group for support. The wing was transported aboard Military Air Transport Service (MATS) C-118 aircraft, with the final delivery of personnel and cargo made on January 15.

The wing's B-47s left Pinecastle on January 7 and SAC, never failing to take advantage of a training opportunity, laid on Operation *Sword Play*—an additional USCM to be conducted during the outbound leg of the deployment. In *Sword Play*, 41 combat crews from the 19th—including William Gregory and his flight crew—sortied from Pinecastle, incorporated two aerial refuelings and a simulated atomic strike on designated targets before terminating at Sidi Slimane, Morocco. The aircraft took off in five separate waves throughout two days, and by the early morning hours of January 11, 41 aircraft were on-station at Sidi Slimane, having completed the training exercise with excellent results.

One day later a wing evaluation mission commenced—Operation *Big Deal*, which entailed a simulated strike against a Moroccan target. Operating on three successive days, the mission included 39 aircrews, and upon completion was judged to have been 84 percent effective.

During these training runs, the aircraft of the 19th did not carry live nuclear munitions. Instead, they loaded a 10,000-lb. dummy bomb. One mission included the release of this dummy bomb on a target sector in the sea—Greg reported the huge effect the release of the heavy load had on the aircraft—it went into a temporary but steep ascent immediately after the drop.

The bomber crews were assigned targets in the Soviet Union, and their assignments were not often changed. Greg's target while deployed to Morocco was the hometown of Josef Stalin—Tbilisi, Georgia, near the easternmost arm of the Baltic Sea, and just 125 miles northeast of NATO ally Turkey. Though Greg never made a practice run at Tbilisi—that was expressly forbidden—he and his crew studied the target extensively, as well as the surrounding terrain. In the event of hostilities, his munition was a single Mark 15, 3.8 megaton bomb, weighing 7,600 lbs. Roughly a yard in diameter and three yards long, it was the first relatively lightweight thermonuclear bomb created by the United States and was considered as a transitional design between fission and thermonuclear weapons. The Mark 15 was 250 times more powerful than the 15 kiloton bomb dropped on Hiroshima.[22]

During missions, the bombers in Greg's squadron took off in rapid sequence, but once airborne the B-47s separated as they made their way to their assigned targets. With the exception of aerial refueling, there was no formation flying in the B-47—each aircraft and aircrew operated as an independent unit. In the event of real hostilities, Greg would have released his bomb from around 45,000 feet, an altitude made possible by the burn-off of fuel in reaching the target. *We trained the whole time we were in England or North Africa. We had a lot of training missions that we flew during that time when we were TDY.*

We deployed to Sidi Slimane in North Africa, 135 miles to the northeast from Casablanca, Morocco, and remained for three months. It was a good program, because normally if we had an alert, or things got bad and we were going to deliver our bomb, we would have to fly all the way from Orlando to our target in the Soviet Union. It was a great thing to put all that distance behind you because we could be over the Soviet Union in much less time from our position in England or Morocco.

For Greg, being on deployment was little different than being at Pinecastle—they did the same types of training exercises in Morocco that they would have done back in the States. The only difference was that they were on alert at the same time.

The deployment to Sidi Slimane was a solid success for the 19th, and it was with some relief that *Sword Play* ended well. The wing resumed normal operations in Morocco—that it to say continued training—on January 16. For the balance of January and February, training was conducted on bombing, navigation, air refueling, gunnery, special weapons, and more. In February, Operation *Joy Ride* was completed over a six-day period to test the unit's recovery bases, and in late February the wing participated in an air-sea rescue exercise, nicknamed *Jumping Bug*. For the month, the 19th would complete almost 2,000 hours of flying, all without even a minor flying accident. The Second Air Force then laid on two more operations for the 19th—Operation *Blue Cross* to be conducted as part of the 19th's deployment in March, and Operation *Devil Fish* in May following its return to Pinecastle.[23]

The deployment to Morocco was not without challenge for the airmen and officers of the 19th. While the maintenance facilities and equipment were considered excellent, the facilities for administrative sections and billets were minimally adequate. Personal were quartered in Dallas huts with minimal heating provided by pot-bellied stoves or oil-fired circulating stoves—a situation that gave rise to frequent respiratory infections. Despite the endemic gastro-enteritis in the region, the Air Force personnel had low rates of infection.

Administrative offices were housed in windowless, poorly heated Quonset huts. One section felt particularly aggrieved, according to the wing history: "The Adjutant's Section was set up in a hall adjacent to two latrines. Practically everyone entering the headquarters passes through the office, thus causing excessive interruptions and distraction in performing the assigned duties."[24]

Redeployment back to their home base Stateside following an overseas TDY was no less complex an operation than the original deployment. The Wing's move back to Pinecastle—*Operation Buckhorn*—commenced on March 31, and was completed on April 21—a move encompassing over 1,100 airmen and officers, and 350,000 lbs. of cargo. And even on the wing's flight home after a challenging deployment, the 19th was further tasked with yet another practice strike mission, targeting Stateside objectives before finally landing back at Pinecastle.

The wing's performance on its first overseas rotation was very strong. *Sword Play* had been rated at 94 percent successful, while *Jumping Bug, Blue Cross* and *Buckhorn* were all scored at 100 percent. The overall performance of the wing was excellent, and morale was at a high level throughout the TDY period.[25]

Foreign deployments would typically involve three or four wings, each wing with three squadrons, and each squadron equipped with 16 aircraft. Normally one or two wings would deploy concurrently to England and Morocco, with close to 300 bombers under deployment. And under the SAC rating system, the wings graded each aircraft crew quarterly.

The deployment was also a solid success for William Gregory and his crew. *We trained constantly when we were deployed to North Africa. Don Todt, my navigator/bombardier, and also my bridge partner, was excellent at scoring high for us on his bomb scores and navigation scores. On this, my first overseas deployment with the 19th, we were rated as number one out of 48 B-47 aircrews in the entire wing on that particular deployment. Although it was not advertised and nobody except us knew about it, we were very pleased to finish the deployment that way.*[26]

When the deployment was over, Greg flew home—a long flight, requiring two night refuelings, on a course that took them near Thule, Greenland, for navigation purposes, and then into Orlando.

Prior to our scheduled takeoff, it looked like the weather was really really bad, and following our briefing I told my crew that we surely wouldn't go on these conditions. We had received the weather briefing, and while there were no alternates given, I was still skeptical that we would go. But we did go, and I thought we might land somewhere en route—the Azores, perhaps, but that didn't happen either. We swung to the north toward Thule, Greenland to receive an aerial refueling, and the tanker planes reported that they had gotten off, and were at an altitude of about 12,000 ft. We were just above the clouds at 39,000 feet, and were preparing to descend to the tanker's altitude.

The standard refueling practice in that situation required the B-47 to descend in a tight circle, and Greg had just started his descent when something went terribly wrong.

Just as we were going to descend to rendezvous with the tanker, all my instruments went blank—I lost all instruments.

Greg had to make the spiraling, high-speed descent using only a needle, ball, and airspeed—the same instruments he used when first learning to fly the 40 horsepower Piper Cub. His copilot also lost his instruments, and was in no position to offer any help whatsoever. *Don [Todt, navigator] had an analog compass and read out the degrees as we spiraled down, letting me know how quickly I was turning.*

This type of spiraling descent was the preferred method for losing altitude prior to taking on fuel. It usually would have taken a couple of minutes to make his descent. *It goes pretty fast. You are going down in a circle, very fast, your nose is way down. It is a good way to do it because you don't cover a lot of area. You are in a tight area.* Greg had done this many times, but always with a full complement of flight instruments.

There was no option for us—I had to have the gas, and we had no chance of reaching any other refueling station. We were somewhere around Greenland, and survival would be a matter of a minute or two if we had to ditch. I broke out of the clouds and lo and behold there was the tanker right in front of me. I got onto the boom of the tanker and did not let go until I had a full load of fuel.

The electrical breaker on Greg's aircraft had tripped. The control panel was located toward the rear of the aircraft, rearward of the copilot's position, and could not be accessed by the copilot while seated. It was impossible for the copilot to attempt to reach the panel with the aircraft in the steep, diving turn. *There was not a thing he could do. When we got down (to the altitude of the tanker), I asked my copilot to get down out of his seat and crawl rearward to a position where he could access the breakers. He was able to do so, and reset the breaker that had popped.*

With the refueling complete, Greg was able to continue to Orlando, landing in the early hours of the next morning.

That was stressful, but I really didn't feel the stress. I think I always had a feel for the airplane: maybe in my seat. Even manually flying this airplane—and we were going down at a high rate of speed—I could feel it starting to burble a little bit. Kind of a high-speed shock. It was the airframe telling me it didn't like what I was doing. So I knew exactly what to do, to roll it out a little bit—I was in too much of a turn, so I had to gently roll it out, and I just did that all the way down. Even going back to the light aircraft, the PT-19 and others, you have feelings when you are doing things right with the aircraft. You would get some feedback from the aircraft.

While he had been deployed to Morocco, Greg's wing had begun making final preparations for the move to Homestead Air Force Base. Some of his fellow pilots had already visited Homestead in order to get a lay of the land, but having just completed a long deployment, a fatiguing nine-hour flight from Morocco, and having survived an equipment failure over the Atlantic that could have easily resulted in the loss of aircraft and crew, Greg decided to delay his visit to Homestead for a week.

I rested that day, and the next day, a Saturday, I got a strange call from the Operations Officer of my unit, the 19th Bomb Wing. He informed me that I had been selected for an interview for a classified program, that an airplane had been dispatched for me, and asked if I could meet the airplane at noon Sunday. I said that I could, and the next morning I put on my uniform and met the airplane for a flight to Turner Air Force Base at Albany, Georgia.

The request left Greg a bit baffled. He knew that his aircrew had placed first for the quarter, but that information was not, in his mind, widely known. He was a pilot, evidently a good pilot, and a careful one. He boarded the specially dispatched airplane at Orlando not knowing the purpose of the interview, or its consequence for him, his career, and his family.

CHAPTER 7

Project Black Knight and the Origins of America's High-Altitude Program

Greg had completed his first, and what would be his last overseas deployment with the 19th Bomb Wing. He, and some 20 other pilots, had been under scrutiny by the Air Force for some time for what would become the US Air Force's first high-altitude surveillance program: Project Black Knight. The unit would be equipped with a limited number of innovative and uber-altitude aircraft, new high-resolution cameras, and the latest in electronic signal-gathering equipment. These pilots would be the first in the Air Force to routinely fly above 65,000 ft. on missions.

Origins of Project Black Knight

Although American leaders had hoped for an extended period of postwar peace and reconstruction based on cooperation with wartime Allies, the Soviet Union and its communist satellites were increasingly hostile toward the nations of the West, in particular, the United States.

Crisis followed crisis in a cascade of stunning communist initiatives and American counter-moves in the years following World War II. In June of 1948, Stalin ordered the Berlin Blockade to prevent deliveries of food, materials, and supplies to West Berlin. The United States, Britain, France, Canada, Australia, New Zealand, and several other countries responded with the massive "Berlin airlift." Within a year communism was entrenched in China when Mao Zedong's People's Liberation Army defeated Chiang Kai-shek's United States-supported Kuomintang (KMT) Nationalist Government. And again within a year, the forces of North Korea, with the support of Mao's China, invaded South Korea.

As historian R. Cargill Hall would note: "The sequence and pace of these events, coupled with available intelligence, prompted American political and military leaders to believe that their Soviet counterparts might well be preparing to occupy Western Europe, coincident with a surprise attack on the United States"[1]

During this time, the USSR had become a "denied" area. Travel within its territory for foreigners was severely limited, and their interaction with Soviet citizens was discouraged. Even city street maps were denied to all, including Russian citizens. Conventional intelligence methods failed to generate reliable information about the country or its military capabilities. "Our intelligence at the time was limited to such sources as German reconnaissance photography from World War II, human intelligence gleaned from the captured Germans and other refugees released from the Soviet Union and Eastern Bloc nations, and the writings of a few dedicated scholars in the West."[2]

In July 1953, the CIA prepared an assessment of the US's foreign intelligence program, and remarked on the difficulties in securing covert intelligence within the Soviet Union: "(It is) more and more apparent that 'black' penetration of denied areas is increasingly hazardous, and because of its illegal nature does not ensure accessibility to strategic targets"[3]

The Soviet penchant for secrecy was well understood by America and its allies. As early as 1939, Winston Churchill had famously referred to Russia as "a riddle, wrapped in a mystery, inside an enigma,"[4] and in May 1945, Churchill further alluded to the secrecy inherent in the Soviet government and military: "An iron curtain is drawn down upon their front. We do not know what is going on behind."[5]

The performance of the American intelligence community, severely degraded by downsizing and budget reductions following the war, was at a low ebb. The Berlin Blockade had not been foreseen, the Soviet's first nuclear detonation in 1949 came a year and a half ahead of US intelligence estimates, and it would later be shown that US intelligence had badly overestimated Soviet progress in rocketry. It was becoming strikingly apparent that the US and its allies needed more and better intelligence than they had been receiving.

Author Michael Peterson, in a recently declassified National Security Agency (NSA) document, writes clearly of how advanced American intelligence would ultimately become, and how rudimentary it was in its beginnings: "In 1945, the Soviet Union might as well have been on Mars. The United States knew little about this vast state that stretched 5,000 miles east to west and 2,000 miles north to south, spanning two continents and almost half of the world's twenty-four time zones. Except for small areas immediately around Moscow, Leningrad, Vladivostok and maybe Murmansk, the military and economic landscape of the Soviet Union was mostly a mystery.

"By the late 80s, the state of American intelligence is vastly different from what was true in the late forties. In intelligence maps today, *every* fighter base, bomber base, ICMB launch site, *every* fixed air defense radar and surface-to-air (SAM) missile site, *every* Army barracks complex and its tank and artillery park, and *every* naval base with their complement of warships, would be identified and fully characterized. *Every* civilian and military wartime command bunker would be highlighted; *every* major factory and industrial complex would be listed, along with what was manufactured and at what annual rate. *Every* nuclear power plant would be identified, and all oil and gas bearing regions would be delineated. Gold mines and other mineral sites would be marked. This wealth of information is taken for granted today, but it was not forty years ago."[6]

In July of 1947, Truman signed enabling legislation that created the Central Intelligence Agency (CIA) and the National Security Council (NSC) and concurrently reorganized the military forces into a unified Department of Defense. At the same time, the newly reorganized US Air Force created the USAF Security Service (USAFSS) to bolster its intelligence capability. With these initiatives, the national leadership acknowledged that, in the Cold War, defense was reliant on intelligence. Together, the CIA, DOD and NSC agencies would direct US defense policy in the Cold War.

The primary purpose of America's military intelligence operation was to characterize the military potential, and possible intentions, of its adversary—the Soviet Union—and to develop plans for potential military action. Several types of intelligence were needed. Air order of battle data could be used to confirm the number, types, and location of deployed aircraft. Information on the command and control and communication structures of opposing forces could be used to understand current or pending operations. Collection of routine communications could reveal training exercises that reflected strengths or weaknesses in operational capabilities or indicate the current order of battle information on both ground and air forces. Troop movements or the deployment of heavy bomber and tanker activity could indicate impending activity. By collecting electronic signals, analysts could characterize the location and technical parameters of Soviet radars supporting a range of air defense functions, including ground-based search, surveillance, and weapons systems radars, aircraft detection and tracking radars, and radars supporting surface-to-air missile systems.[7]

The Air Force faced a deep intelligence void. As it went about planning for potential future hostilities, the American Air Forces knew that a robust strategic bombing capability would be needed, but had very little actionable intelligence on the Soviet military or its infrastructure. It was severely deficient in targeting information, and alarmingly, had almost no effective means to secure the necessary intelligence. The USAF's intelligence community lacked doctrine, processes, procedures, and perhaps most significantly, a suitable aerial platform from which aerial surveillance could be conducted.

By 1950, the Air Force and the CIA missions, and the systems and doctrines they would need to meet those missions continued to evolve. But it had become increasingly clear that in some important aspects, the mission of these two agencies would be closely aligned—even co-dependent—and that much of the intelligence they required could only be obtained, at least in the short term, by high-altitude overflight of the Soviet Union.

Robert Perry, in *A History of Satellite Reconnaissance,* notes: "Overflight, whether covert, overt in the face of Soviet protests, or openly conducted under the sponsorship of some international agency, was by 1955 very nearly an essential of national security for the United States. Like espionage, overflight was a customary, if seldom acknowledged, instrument of peacetime military activity. Literally, hundreds of instances had been recorded starting with French and German penetrations of border defense zones in the pre-1914 period. Aircraft violations of international boundaries were among the most frequent causes of ambassadorial protests and apologies during the late 1930s. Incidents involving both Russian and American aircraft were common to the fringes of both the iron and bamboo curtains during the late 1940s. Neither side ever admitted a deliberate policy of aerial espionage, but its existence was indisputable."[8]

The criticality of aerial surveillance—taking the highest ground

Aerial reconnaissance had its roots 2,000 years ago in China, with the introduction of man-lifting kites to scout enemy defensive positions or determine the best avenue for an attack—both objectives that would come to permanently dominate military planning. As technologies developed, methods of aerial observation became increasingly sophisticated: from tethered balloons through dirigibles to fixed-wing aircraft.

Innovations continued, both in aircraft design and in the science of surveillance. In 1910, a wireless air-to-ground telegraph was successfully tested on a Wright Model A, exponentially increasing the aircraft's value to the Army ground commander. Armed forces around the world quickly adopted the new technology and adapted it for aerial reconnaissance.

The first official US military reconnaissance flight in an airplane came in March 1911 during the American action in the Mexican Revolution. The Italian Air Force first employed fixed-wing, camera-equipped aircraft on a combat mission along the Libyan coastline during the Italo-Turkish War of 1912, and by 1912 the US Army had largely abandoned the dirigible in favor of airplanes. America's first use of aircraft for combat surveillance over foreign territory came in March 1916, when aircraft were used by General Pershing during the Punitive Expedition against Pancho Villa.

In the days leading into World War I, America's intelligence, surveillance and reconnaissance (ISR) capabilities had been nascent. There had been little prewar training, and communications were unreliable. But World War I evolved into a war of artillery, and all combatants became increasingly reliant on the imagery supplied by airborne ISR to provide artillery coordination and damage assessments. Additionally, ISR made huge contributions in identifying orders of battle, weaponry, installations and defensive structure, and for front-line tactical observations. And missions were projected far beyond the front lines to conduct strategic reconnaissance on military and industrial targets.

Throughout the war, aircraft became increasingly performant, permitting operations from increasing altitudes. Camera technology kept pace with very high-resolution imagery along with better reliability at more extreme conditions. Airborne ISR had become an essential component of military preparedness.

The value of airborne ISR would not be in question during the years following the war, although Army ground commanders continued to perceive aerial reconnaissance and artillery observation as the aircraft's main contribution to land warfare, views that would change radically in the interwar years. During those years, the American military leadership assigned highest priority to the development of doctrine and platforms for strategic bombing but were slow in recognizing that the *sine qua non* of strategic bombing was prior target intelligence.

Concurrent with the significant advances in aircraft design and performance, the sciences of electronic data gathering and codebreaking began to gain strength in the interwar years. By the outbreak of World War II "signal intelligence" (SIGINT) had come into the military lexicon, and encompassed both communications intelligence (COMINT) and electronic intelligence (ELINT). SIGINT became a critical adjunct to photographic intelligence (PHOTINT) and to the age-old traditional methods of intelligence gathering—human intelligence (HUMINT).

In the early months of World War II, neither Great Britain nor the United States possessed either suitable reconnaissance aircraft or trained photo interpreters, deficiencies that soon became both apparent and intolerable. In response to enormous demands by all branches of the armed forces, the doctrine of aerial reconnaissance matured quickly, and the tandem demands for photo intelligence and signal intelligence began to attain priority status.

America's first ELINT recon mission was flown in March 1943. In what was to become the core foundation for later USAF intelligence gathering, American air forces flew a specially-equipped RB-24D aircraft—call sign "Ferret-One"—against Japanese radar locations on Kiska Island in the Aleutian Island chain. When the Japanese radars illuminated the incoming bombers, the signal intelligence personnel on board collected specific data on the radar signals, thereby permitting ground interpreters to precisely identify the location of the radar sites. In an early confirmation of the value of signal intelligence, Alaskan-based bombers were then sortied to attack and silence the Japanese radars. By the second half of 1943, similar missions were used widely against German and Italian radar installations in the Mediterranean Theater.

Ferret missions, aptly named from the Latin *furittus*—"little thief," would become routine practice for the Allied intelligence communities, quietly collecting information from an unwitting enemy.

The post-war demand for aerial intelligence

In the "thrust-and-parry" that characterized the Cold War, US Army Air Forces reconnaissance aircraft began flying recon missions along the borders of the Soviet Union and its European satellites as early as 1946. These missions initially flew under the internationally accepted Peacetime Aerial Reconnaissance Program (PARPRO) guidelines which stipulated that reconnaissance missions remain outside of Soviet and Eastern Bloc airspace.[9]

An assortment of World War II-era transports and bombers were used to conduct reconnaissance missions along the periphery of the Soviet-controlled territory. Large aircraft were required because signal collection equipment at the time was based on large, bulky and heavy vacuum tube systems, and only large aircraft could carry the equipment and still provide a long "dwell time" over the target region. The information gathered was useful in characterizing the nature and scope of the air defenses along the Soviet border, but did almost nothing to identify potential military and industrial targets deeper within Soviet territory.

Ferret missions continued into the late forties, with B-17 and B-29 reconnaissance aircraft equipped with the latest intercept, direction finding and radar equipment. B-29s operated in the Alaska, Kuril, and Siberian coastal areas and over the North Pole, and two B-17s operated in Europe, primarily in search of Soviet guided missile activity.[10]

Responding to increasingly strident calls for more and better intelligence, and in a potentially dangerous escalation of surveillance tactics, US Air Force and Naval aviation units began to request approval for overflights of Soviet territory—a clear contravention of international law. The resultant flights, tracked by Soviet air defenses, generated such a vehement response from the Kremlin that they were suspended by 1948, and the US surveillance reverted to PARPRO.

A snapshot of the Air Force's reconnaissance inventory in January of 1950 gives testament to the minimal assets available to the intelligence community. Strategic reconnaissance was organized in three wings, with a total of just 78 aircraft available for mission assignments—most of which were World War II-era B-29s that had been converted for reconnaissance work. None could operate above 33,000 ft., placing them well within the Soviets' air defense capabilities.[11]

For its part, the Soviet Union had by the early 1950s augmented its ground-based defenses with a robust air defense network, effectively ringing the borders of the Soviet Union and Eastern Europe with air defense radar stations and advanced fighter regiments, all coordinated by new command and control systems. The range, azimuth, and altitude of intruding aircraft, and sometimes the aircraft type, could be quickly ascertained by the air defense radars and reported through the command and control systems.

In 1952, the Soviets began converting from high frequency (HF) to very high frequency (VHF) radio transmission, causing a major problem for western intelligence agencies. Unlike HF signals which can be intercepted for thousands of miles, VHF signals were essentially line-of-sight, and were undetectable beyond about 125 miles. Allied ground intercept stations in Europe and Asia were sited outside that listening range.

The Allies soon began establishing new networks of VHF intercept sites, but their limited range prevented signal intercepts from vital areas deeper within the Soviet and Eastern bloc regions. What was needed was *altitude,* giving critical emphasis to the need for airborne communication intelligence reconnaissance.

In the earliest days of the Korean War, President Truman and British Prime Minister Clement Attlee agreed to conduct periodic aerial surveillance of the Soviet Union—Britain overflying the European Soviet Union, and America the Asian region. These overflights were largely strategic in nature, and were intended to generate order of battle information, to surveil nuclear facilities, and most especially to assess the Soviets' long-range air forces. But concurrently, the American leadership began receiving urgent calls for more and better tactical aerial intelligence to aid ground troops in planning and operations.

This decision to authorize overflights, made in secret, established a critical precedent for future high-altitude reconnaissance of denied territory, operations that would lead the United States into increasingly harrowing waters.

The first beneficial intelligence came from Great Britain, when, in mid-April, 1952 it flew three US-manufactured RB-45C aircraft in separate tracks over the Baltic States, Belorussia, and Ukraine. The surveillance aircraft were detected but not intercepted by Soviet fighters and were able to overfly Soviet air bases, missile sites, and other similar targets of strategic importance. The missions resulted in a horde of photographs of hundreds of different intelligence targets and confirmed that there was no immediate threat of a Soviet attack against the West.[12]

Those overflights were defensible under international law because the Soviet Union was continuing to provide war materiel, aircraft and even pilots to Communist China, thus making them "un-announced co-belligerents" in the conflict.

Rarely throughout the Cold War was America in a position of complete confidence regarding its defense against Soviet attack. In later phases of the Cold War, defense agencies worried about land-based and submarine-launched ballistic missiles. But in the mid-50s, the greatest concerns related to Soviet offensive capabilities—bombers—and Soviet defensive capabilities: air defense missiles, radars, anti-aircraft systems, and fighters.

The Soviet Union gave American angst a further boost when it premiered its new Myasishchev M-4 jet bomber during the 1955 Soviet May Day parade. The United States government believed that the bomber was in mass

Soviet Myasishchev M-4 Bison bomber. (Wikimedia Commons)

production, and would soon be deployed in numbers vastly exceeding those in the US Air Force—a belief that took hold within the intelligence community and the general American public: the infamous "Bomber Gap."

By 1953 the Korean War had ended, Khrushchev had succeeded Stalin, Churchill replaced Attlee, and Eisenhower likewise Truman. President Eisenhower brought two important principles to his presidency: a deep-seated understanding of the crucial importance of adequate intelligence for the military; and a commitment to easing Soviet-American tensions in the face of advancing nuclear arms capabilities. Following the Korean Armistice, he knew that the US no longer had a valid justification for incursions over Soviet or Chinese airspace. But both he and British Prime Minister Churchill faced the dilemma posed by intelligence demands—balancing their countries' national interests against further deteriorating Soviet relations, or potentially leading to armed conflict.

Before leaving office, President Truman had directed the NSC to "evaluate the net capabilities of the Soviet Union to inflict direct injury on the United States, up to July 1, 1955."[13] That report, delivered to President Eisenhower in May 1953, made the following disturbing assessment: "America's continental defenses are not adequate to prevent, neutralize, or seriously deter the military or covert attacks which the USSR is capable of launching, nor are they adequate to ensure the continuity of government, the continuity of production, or the protection of the industrial mobilization base and millions of citizens in our great and exposed metropolitan centers. This constitutes an unacceptable risk to our nation's survival."[14] In short, America lay wide open to Soviet attack.

Eisenhower took the exceptional step of adopting Truman's wartime over-flight program in *peacetime* and authorized what would become known as the Sensitive Intelligence (SENSINT) Program—a program to use military aircraft to conduct periodic overflights of denied territory. These overflights involved both the US Air Force and Navy, relied on a range of standard and modified aircraft, and conducted both shallow and deep penetration missions between 1953 and 1956.

Overflights were made of both the European and Asian sectors of the Soviet Union. And while peripheral reconnaissance operations could be undertaken without White House advance clearance, overflights were a different matter. Theater commanders and leaders of the intelligence community requested approval for an overflight mission of a specific target to an Air Force Deputy Chief of Staff, thence to the Chief of Staff, and to the Joint Chiefs of Staff. Next to approve were a "Special Group" consisting of the Special Assistant for National Security Affairs, the Secretaries of State and Defense, the Director of the CIA and the JCS Chair. Only then would the request be delivered, by hand, to the White House for the president's review and decision.[15]

In 1956, President Eisenhower received a report from the RAND Corporation as disturbing as Truman's "net capabilities" analysis. The RAND report, which focused on US strategic air power, concluded, in part: "…the enemy… could destroy two-thirds or more of SAC bomber and reconnaissance aircraft" in a surprise attack.[16] Not addressed in that report were civilian casualties, industrial paralysis, or continuity of government.

The report was alarming for several reasons. The communist-supported invasion of South Korea evidenced a readiness to launch a surprise attack. For Americans this was all too reminiscent of the Japanese attack at Pearl Harbor that led to massive loss of life and treasure in the Pacific. Intelligence planners were cognizant that such a surprise attack, if it incorporated atomic weapons, could be vastly more damaging. And the American leadership was also aware that deficiencies in its intelligence information had been strongly contributory to the Japanese success at Pearl. President Eisenhower and his contemporaries were hyper-aware of the need for better intelligence, and the RAND report gave strong motivation for intensifying reconnaissance of the Soviet Union.

The Air Force was precise as to their concerns over the Soviet Arctic: "Critical areas, in so far as Soviet capability for delivering atomic bombs on targets within the United States is concerned, are the Chukotskiy Peninsula area and the Murmansk area. We have repeatedly emphasized the importance of these two areas, but positive intelligence on both areas is lacking."[17]

The greatest threat to the United States was from a trans-polar bomber attack from bases in the Soviet Union's northern reaches. In its National Intelligence Estimate (NIE) of 1955,[18] the CIA projected that the Soviets were then-capable of launching as many as 330 nuclear bombers in a surprise attack, and that 250 would reach their targets. In the NIE of 1956,[19] the projections were far worse: analysts expected that all four types of Soviet nuclear bombers expected to be operational by 1959 would be capable of reaching virtually any point in the continental United States. Attacking in 1959, the Soviets could launch 815 nuclear bombers, with the expectation that 640 would reach their assigned target area.[20]

Responding to demands from the military and intelligence communities, Eisenhower approved an unprecedented and aggressive overflight program— Project Home Run—under which Strategic Air Command RB-47 surveillance aircraft would overfly and chart nearly the entire Soviet Arctic, a 3,500-mile swath from the Kola Peninsula to the Bering Strait. Operating between March and May 1956 from the ice-covered runways at Thule AFB in Greenland,

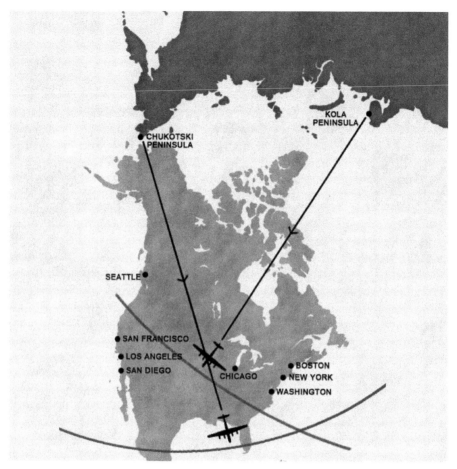

Probable Soviet nuclear bomber first-strike capability as of mid-1955 relying principally on Tu-4 bombers on unrefuelled (one way) missions. (Samuel Richardson, Yosemite Productions)

without benefit of hangars in the sub-zero weather, and under complete radio silence at all times, the aircraft successfully reconnoitered the entire northern Soviet frontier. The operation, which ultimately included 156 overflight missions of Soviet territory, required sixteen RB-47E PHOTINT aircraft and five RB-47H ELINT aircraft—practically America's entire inventory—and twenty-eight KC-97 tankers.[21]

Home Run yielded a trove of data, including intelligence identifying gaps in the Soviet radar coverage that was invaluable for planning ingress and egress routes for American bombers should hostilities start between the Soviet Union and the West. The fact that those earliest overflights operated more or less with impunity added to the frustrations of Soviet authorities. "In its aftermath, one can only imagine the frustration, rage, and abrupt ending of careers that beset leaders of the Soviet air defense forces."[22]

Soviet interdiction

The Soviet Union did not hesitate to attack Allied aircraft when the opportunity presented, and during the Cold War all belligerent nations' air defenses were on high alert. Between 1945 and 1965, 195 incidents were reported in which aircraft from a variety of nations were attacked, shot down, or forced down by intercepting aircraft, ground fire or guided missiles from the Soviet Union or its allies. Additionally, commercial airliners were attacked by the Soviets in nine separate incidents during this period, with great loss of life.[23]

As early as 1947—before the USAF had been established—the Army Air Forces was aware of the risks associated with peripheral missions: "This mission is considered a most hazardous one both from the natural peril and capture standpoints. All flight personnel are volunteers and are fully apprised of possible consequences should the plane be forced to land in foreign territory. The crew is warned that in the event of detention in foreign territory repatriation will be attempted but will probably be unsuccessful. For purpose of cover the project is described as a weather mission. Equipment for complete demolition of the plane and its contents has been provided."[24]

The first attack by Soviet air defenses against a US reconnaissance aircraft took place over the Sea of Japan in October 1949. That unsuccessful attack was the precursor to thirty documented attacks by the Soviets against US aircraft, and dozens more against Allied aircraft, between 1949 and 1972. Between April 1950 and March 1964, thirteen US reconnaissance aircraft were shot down by Soviet air defenses.

Most of these attacks occurred in North Asia, reflecting the tension the region was experiencing with Soviet developments in the Kamchatka Peninsula, and events in China and Korea.

But the locations of these aircraft losses testify to the wide geographic scope of the reconnaissance efforts that were undertaken by America: downed aircraft had taken off from airfields in Alaska, England, France, Germany, Pakistan, and Turkey. And air losses were not limited to Air Force aircraft: both the Navy and the Army were deeply involved in their own SIGINT programs. Three of the 13 shootdowns were naval aircraft.[25]

As noted earlier, the American Air Force and CIA intelligence community was hardly blameless in these incidents. While most intelligence missions were peripheral and did not violate Soviet airspace, many did. While obtaining complete statistics on Soviet claims of border crossings is very difficult, in 1995 and 1996, the Russian magazine *Aviation World* (*Mir Aviatsiyi*), published a series of articles titled "Hot Skies," which cited 113 border-crossings by US aircraft between 1953 and 1956. The series described in some detail twenty-one Soviet intercepts against more than thirty-seven aircraft.[26]

The USAF steadfastly maintained that its missions were for reasons other than military intelligence gathering. For example, when in March 1953 a MiG-15 attempted a shootdown of a SAC RB-50 bomber, the Air Force claimed the aircraft was on "weather recon" in international airspace. Actually, it had been engaged in a highly sensitive electronic intelligence (ferret) recon mission.

In that instance, the Air Force "doubled down" on its cover by demanding that the US State Department issue a protest, which they did, "vigorously" protesting the incident to the Soviet Foreign Office. The protest note said the US "expects to be informed at an early date of the disciplinary action taken with regard to the Soviet personnel responsible for the attack."[27]

Senator Ralph Flanders of Vermont was not buying it and charged that the Air Force was "waging psychological warfare on the people of the United States" and that its claim that the RB-50 was engaged in a routine weather recon flight was preposterous. The Senator also noted: "That recon bomber was not there on weather business. It may nevertheless have been engaged on a useful mission."[28]

Aircraft development—finding the right platform

By the mid-1950s, the frequency and ease with which the Soviets intercepted US aircraft made it clear that the aircraft being used for intelligence gathering were inadequate to the task and could not conduct high-altitude reconnaissance safely. Given the time required for new aircraft development, the Air Force began to consider other platforms that could be readily adapted for reconnaissance. A solution to this strategic problem arose from tactical demands in Korea.

With the Korean War in full cry, the Army needed a night attack bomber to interdict enemy supply lines. It requested proposals for an aircraft that could reach 40,000 feet, with a range of 1,150 miles and a top speed of 630 mph. Importantly, the request included both domestic and foreign aircraft manufacturers, and reflecting the Air Force's urgent need for an improved bomber in Korea, it further expedited the process by considering only proposals based on existing aircraft.

Despite the unmatched track record of the American aerospace industry, the British aviation industry had made significant advances in jet engine design that resulted in greater thrust and durability than those of US jets. The design proposed by English Electric for its Canberra twin-engine medium bomber was the leading candidate from the outset. Following a fly-off of the five competing aircraft, the Air Force confirmed its selection of the Canberra.[29]

In order to hasten delivery, the aircraft was built by the Glenn L. Martin Company under license from English Electric. Production went forward at lightning speed despite a host of production delays, and the aircraft now designated the B-57 made its first flight in July 1953—just 28 months after Martin had received the Canberra contract. Deliveries of the B-57 began in July 1954, and by 1957 four bomb groups had been equipped with the new bomber.

Over time, the Canberra design would prove to be an effective replacement for the World War II-vintage B-26 and would remain in the Air Force inventory for over thirty years, including eight years of combat operations in Korea, Vietnam, and elsewhere. While it was in service, the Canberra was the only tactical bomber in the USAF inventory. In a testimony to its highly adaptable design, it would eventually be produced in 18 different variants. "As the immortal DC-3 is the great workhorse of air transports, the Canberra certainly occupies a similar niche in history among combat aircraft."[30]

The Air Force also recognized the new possibilities for reconnaissance presented by the new B-57s. Ten B-57s underwent special modifications to sharply reduce the aircraft's weight, permitting high operating altitudes. Now designated RB-57A and operating under the codename "Heart Throb," six aircraft were subsequently deployed to Europe, and four to Asia, operating under the SENSINT program to conduct deep penetration flights of the Soviet Union and Eastern Bloc countries. Despite the increase in altitude that the modifications to the RB-57A permitted, however, the aircraft was still vulnerable to interception by the latest Soviet fighters. They simply could not fly high enough.

Even as the new B-57s and RB-57As were coming off the Martin assembly line, the intelligence community—both within the CIA and within elements of the Air Force—recognized that satellite surveillance would represent the ultimate reconnaissance platform. It also realized that those systems were still years in the future. The U-2 spyplane had been in development since 1953, but the Air Force needed one more "stop-gap" platform, an expedient that would at least approach the high-altitude capability then considered necessary, altitudes that were beyond the capabilities of the RB-57A, and would be beyond the reach of Soviet fighters.

The Air Force began considering existing airframes that could with modification meet the operating requirements for a high-altitude overflight aircraft. It naturally turned to the B-57—now its most performant bomber—to become the platform for its aerial reconnaissance program, recognizing that the aircraft would create a "bridge" to the U-2, which itself would "bridge" to satellite systems. The resultant aircraft, after having received extensive modifications, was designated the RB-57D. Very much a bespoke aircraft, only twenty were built, in three distinct variants. Thirteen of them, designated RB-57D-0, were single-pilot aircraft equipped with K-38 and KC-1 cameras for high-altitude photography. Of these, seven were configured for inflight refueling. One aircraft, designated RB-57D-1, also a single-pilot aircraft, was built for radar mapping, and was equipped with AN/APQ-56 Side Looking Radar (SLR). The other six aircraft, designated the RB-57D-2, were built for electronic intelligence, and were also equipped for inflight refueling. With the heavy crew workload, this aircraft operated with a two-man crew.

Outwardly the differences in these three models were not significant, but all were designed for specific missions, in specific regions of the world.

In the new aircraft, the wings were stretched to an impressive 106 ft., nearly twice the length of the original B-57, and incorporated an internal wing structure design based on an innovative honeycomb configuration. The

RB-57D aircraft with standard B-57. (Wikimedia Commons)

engine nacelles were enlarged to permit installation of the new 10,000-lbs. thrust J57 engines. Since the aircraft would be used exclusively for unarmed reconnaissance, the bomb bay doors were skinned over to reduce weight, wing spoilers were installed to augment the stubby aileron, and wing flaps and "speed boards" were eliminated to further reduce weight. With all the weight reductions made, the empty weight of the new, much larger B-57D was roughly the same as that of the B-57.

The resulting aircraft was considered "an overpowered glider," and with a capability of reaching 70,000 ft., it could not be intercepted by the MiG-15 Soviet fighter, the primary threat at that time.[31]

Specifications: Martin RB-57D Canberra[32]

Powerplant: 2 Pratt & Whitney J57 turbojets, 10,000 lbs. thrust
Crew: 1 or 2 depending on variant.
Max speed: 600 mph.
Cruise altitude: 65,000 ft.
Range: 2,000 miles
Wing span: 106 ft.
Takeoff weight: 59,000 lbs.
Wing span: 106 ft.
Length: 66 ft.
Height: 15 ft. 7 in.

The innovative wing design would later require modification: the honeycomb wing structure designed by Martin engineers was light and strong, but it was vulnerable to water seepage and wing stress. Further, the wing spars and some of the skin panels were prone to cracking—several of the aircraft were retired after their wings separated following landing.[33]

In early May 1956 SAC activated a new wing, the 4080th, and tasked it with managing the new high-altitude reconnaissance aircraft. Two squadrons were assigned to it: the 4025th, which would be equipped with the new RB-57D aircraft and within which the Black Knight Project would operate; and the 4028th, which would later be equipped with the U-2, and within which Project Dragon Lady would operate. Initially based at Turner AFB, the wing and its component squadrons would move to Laughlin AFB, near Del Rio, TX, in April 1957, under the command of Colonel Hubert Zemke.

Both the 57s and the U-2s would be used to support the overall mission of the 4080th, specifically: To conduct strategic reconnaissance operations on a global scale, either independently or in cooperation with other air force units; to maintain a state of readiness to permit immediate deployments; to train reconnaissance and refueling crews, and to standardize tactics and procedures for strategic reconnaissance operations.[34]

Deliveries of the RB-57s to the squadron began almost immediately: U-2s were delivered to the 4028th about a year later. By the end of May 1956, the 4025th had received three RB-57Ds from the Glenn L. Martin factory in Baltimore, but the deliveries were not coming fast enough to satisfy the squadron commander: "Aircraft delivery to date has been very unreliable," and the delayed deliveries were creating problems for acquiring and training aircrews, for maintenance scheduling, and for flight operations.[35]

The newest Black Knight

Still weary from his recent TDY to Morocco with the 19th Bomb Wing and Operation *Buckhorn*, Greg was understandably, and keenly, curious as to the purpose of the interview that had been arranged for him. In Turner AFB near Albany, GA, where Project Black Knight was being developed, he learned that he was being interviewed for a highly classified assignment, as both an aircraft commander and also a detachment commander responsible for 100 people.

I figured I would not be selected because at that time as a B-47 pilot I was supervising a total of two people. I was told that we would go TDY for three months to a remote location, anywhere in the world, and I would conduct flight operations. I felt sure that I would not be selected. This organization had all the priority it needed to select anybody for this position. They could have chosen someone who had strong flight experience as well as experience in managing deployments. I would not have selected me. The person they should have hired was an operations officer. I had no experience managing maintenance people.

Greg was told that he would hear the result of his interview in a few days. And so it proved: around a week later he received the surprising instruction to proceed to the Dave Clark Brassiere Factory in Worchester, MA.

I flew to Worchester, where Dave Clark met me and one other pilot at the airport, took us to his factory and gave us a short tour. He showed us a room where there must have been 250 women at individual sewing machines making beautiful garments for women. His company had lots of experience making tight-fitting garments for ladies. He also had a very small section that made tailored pressure suits. That was a brand new thing.

Lockheed and Dave Clark were experimenting with fully pressurized "Mission Complete" suits that would allow the pilot on a high altitude mission to continue flying in the event of depressurization. But the cockpits in the RB-57D and the U-2 were too small for those bulky suits, and pilots were instead equipped with so-called "Get Me Down" partial pressure suits that would protect the pilot during an emergency depressurization while guiding the aircraft to a lower altitude. Loss of cabin pressure was always a "mission abort" situation for the pilot, since the lower altitudes would bring the aircraft within range of enemy fighters or ground fire.

Clark's MC-3 suit used capstans on the arms and legs—molded, cold-resist-ant neoprene tubes inside a cloth sheath. During decompression, the capstans inflated, tensioning the cloth encircling the extremity. The suit also incorporated an inflatable bladder that surrounding the torso, hips and upper thighs. When actuated, the suit would prevent the pilot's body from swelling under the sud-denly reduced cabin pressure. The model MA-2 helmet used in the RB-57D and the U-2 was made by the International Latex Corporation, and it provided constant pressure and oxygen to the pilot's head with a tight-fitting liner and seal covered by a rigid shell. Separate nylon gloves were pressurized, but pilots wore standard flight boots and often wore a lightweight flight suit over the pressure suit to prevent the suit from snagging on the cockpit controls.[36]

The suits could be further adjusted with lacings that extended up the inner thigh, across the chest and small of the back. Zippers were sewn at the ankles, wrists, back and across the chest, and a shoulder zipper made the suit easier to put on and remove.

After the initial fitting, Greg returned to Worcester for a final fitting, and then reported to the Firewel Corporation in Buffalo. Firewel had supplied the cabin pressurization system for the RB-57D and U-2, and made its high-alti-tude chamber available for testing Clark's suits. Two test practices were followed: a slow decrease in pressure to confirm the suits' functionality and mobility, and a second sudden decompression test to simulate an actual emergency.[37]

The qualification process required that we be able to ascend to 65,000 feet in an unpressurized chamber and remain there for 30 minutes. When I was tested, the capstans inflated, and I could not believe how difficult it was to exhale against the pressure in the face mask or even move. Our doctors stressed that we could not survive more than 15 seconds without pressure suits.

Pilots often found the suit uncomfortable. "After a six- or seven-hour mission it was not unusual to have black and blue marks over your body where there might have been a wrinkle in the fabric that persisted for the entire mission. That was especially bad if the suit had been inflated for a while, because you might end up with a fold in your skin that matched the fold in the suit that would not go away for days."[38]

RB-57 Canberra on start-up. (Wikimedia Commons)

Greg stepped into America's high-altitude program just as Project Home Run was hitting its stride, and just as the first RB-57Ds were being delivered to the 4025th. The intelligence community had every right to feel good about its prospects: Home Run was yielding exceptional data, even though the aircraft being employed were less suited to high-altitude reconnaissance than the RB-57Ds that would soon be operational.

To begin with, Greg would fly the B-57C, an airplane with a unique system for starting the engines. It used an electrically ignited single-shot starter cartridge. When fired, the cartridge burned for 10 seconds, directing its force against a starter turbine, which then brought the engine up to starting speed. This system eliminated reliance on powered start carts and made it possible to operate from unfamiliar airfields during combat operations. In the starting process, early cartridges emitted a dense black smoke—making it appear that the airplane was on fire.

While on a flight through Detroit, when I was ready to start the airplane again, this huge smoke arose from the starting cartridge. The firetrucks started to come, and I told them that we were just starting the engines up, and they went back to their shed.

He soon moved on to the RB-57D. *It was the first airplane that would fly to 67,000 ft. and there was no trouble getting to that altitude. We really didn't know what to expect when we reached that altitude because no one had flown that high before.* Greg and his fellow pilots became the first "Stratonauts." They began flying the RB-57Ds at Turner AFB, Albany, in May 1956 and spent a year there before transferring to Laughlin AFB at Del Rio.

Organization

The Black Knight Program was conducted within a single squadron—the 4025th Strategic Reconnaissance Squadron—and its initial commander was Colonel Dan Maloney. *A colonel for a squadron was unheard of—no squadron was commanded by a full colonel up to that time. Frank Wyman was the deputy commander. Both were very capable. The RB-57D-0 photo planes were first out of production, and shortly after I arrived at the squadron, they had me scheduled to take the first overseas deployment to Japan.*

Greg had returned from his deployment to Morocco with the 19th Bomb Wing on April 21, hustled to Albany for the Black Knight selection interview, and was then dispatched to New York for a pressure suit fitting. On June 1, 1956, just six weeks after completing his TDY in Morocco, he was officially assigned to the 4025th and started becoming familiar with the B-57Ds, the first of which had just been delivered to the squadron. Everything was happening at a breakneck clip.

Greg was immediately tapped to head a deployment of the RB-57D-0s to Japan. *I had been doing a lot of TDY, so shortly after I arrived at the squadron I talked to Col. Maloney and told him that I had just returned from a long TDY, asking to be excused from the first deployment but saying that I would be happy to go on the second deployment.* His commander didn't take too kindly to that, but reluctantly agreed, and as a result, Greg became attached instead to the D-2 model and was put in charge of the D-2 detachment.[39]

I was new to the airplane and to the organization. The airplane was easy to fly; it was getting to know the organization that was the harder part. In order to manage a deployment, I really needed time to get to know the organization. I think I had used the fact that I had just returned from TDY as a reason for not wanting to immediately re-deploy, but it really was more than that. I felt like I was too new in the unit.

By the end of June, the 4080th Wing's inventory had increased to eight RB-57Ds and by the end of August to 11, enough to commence tactical operations. The nine remaining aircraft to be supplied to the wing would trickle in over the following six months.

Training for Black Knight began to heat up in August 1956. By this time, nine aircrews had completed transition training into the RB-57D, and 20 more aircrews were in the transition process.

Deployment

The RB-57D-0s were designed for overflights to gather photo intelligence. Within four months of receiving their aircraft, the squadron's first deployment occurred with Operation *Sea Lion* when a detachment of RB-57D-0s was sent to Yokota Air Base, Japan to conduct photo reconnaissance over sensitive areas of the Far East.

This unit, Detachment 1, deployed on September 1, 1956 with seven RB-57D-0s (PHOTINT), and included sufficient aircrews, equipment, and maintenance personnel for a six-month deployment. The unit lost one aircraft due to a landing accident en route, and flights were delayed by a typhoon. But by September 17 all remaining units of the detachment were at fully operational status in Japan.

Shortly after Detachment 1 reported itself fit for operations, Detachment 2 was dispatched to Eielson AFB in Alaska for a 90-day deployment to conduct extended cold-weather testing of aircraft and component systems. That detachment, which included 4 RB-57D-0 (PHOTINT) aircraft, was abruptly suspended on October 10, after 10 days in Alaska.

These two deployments constituted the Air Force's next phase of evaluations for the RB-57 weapons system—field tests to determine if small deployments could operate effectively and relatively independently.

The year 1956 was seminal in Air Force intelligence-gathering history. In January and February Operation *Genetrix* launched over 500 high-altitude balloons to take aerial photographs and collect intelligence over China, Eastern Europe and the Soviet Union. Project Home Run's stunning intelligence yield came in March–May. And Eisenhower approved U-2 overflights of the Soviet Union—including the first two missions that overflew both Leningrad and Moscow—in July.

The Soviet response to these intelligence initiatives was predictable. Following the storm of protests that ensued, Ike became very concerned that the overflights would adversely affect any chances of improved relations with the Soviets.[40]

Despite his concerns, the president approved a three-aircraft overflight of the eastern Soviet region using the 4025th's RB-57D-0s then on deployment to Japan. That mission, flown in December 1956, provided marginally useful photo intelligence on the Soviet Pacific Fleet, but the three aircraft were detected, tracked, and identified by Soviet air defenses—making it impossible for the United States to deny the existence and purpose of the overflights.

In the face of yet another diplomatic furor, the president ordered the immediate stoppage of the overflight programs. And this decision gave great impetus to the ELINT-equipped RB-57D-2s, which operated peripherally, and were not intended to overly the Soviet Union.

As was proven by the initial deployment, the D-0 was a loser. It did not have a suitable camera for an aircraft that would be taking photos at 65,000 feet. I really thought the D-2 had more potential. It had excellent equipment for electronic intelligence gathering and was a good airplane, and I thought this would be a really good place to be. So I concentrated on the D-2, and it proved to be the real success story of the Black Knight program. The ELINT equipment on the D-2 was better than the photo equipment that was installed on the D-0s.

Proving the weapons system

The RB-57D-2 platform used for ELINT missions was equipped with a new and very complex system for the collection and integration of electronic signals. Termed the "320-SAFE" system (Semi-Automatic Ferret Equipment), the Martin-built equipment collected a variety of electronic signals from several "radomes" located on the fuselage, and fed the resultant "take" into a magnetic tape recorder.

The operation of the complicated electronic intelligence-gathering equipment was altogether too demanding for a single pilot to manage, and a second cockpit was added to accommodate an Electronic Countermeasure (ECM) officer. Both pilot and ECM operator cockpits were crammed with control panels and indicator instrumentation for each of the signal intercept systems, creating a heavy workload for the flight crews during ELINT missions.

The novelty of the system related to the tape recorder. Previously, for example on earlier RB-47 reconnaissance aircraft, a radar operator would record signal characteristics in a handwritten log. The new, semi-automatic system incorporated in the RB-57D-2 would record the data on tape at the press of a button by the operator.

It was estimated that this new system would "increase the traffic-handling capability of manned ferrets by a factor of three to five."[41]

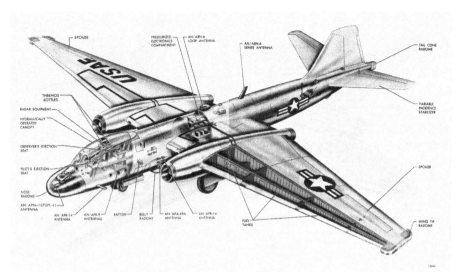

RB-57D Schematic, indicating multiple radomes and sensors. (Table of Organization, 1B-57D-2-7, courtesy of John Sheehan, Canberra SIG)

These sophisticated electronics were unproven. A Weapons System Phase Group was created, and Project Blue Tail Fly was initiated with Greg named Project Officer.

This plane was really ahead of its time, especially with regard to ELINT. It was equipped with the new 320-SAFE system, the latest in ELINT collection equipment. I didn't know much about it, but I found some people in the squadron who had been working with it since it had first been delivered. So I got to working with them and really bore down on them to learn everything that I could about that system. We were working toward being able to go overseas with that airplane, and the 320-SAFE system was critical for success.

During the testing period, an unforeseen event thrust Greg into a new and more challenging role with the squadron.

My close friend and neighbor Frank Wyman had succeeded Dan Maloney as squadron commander and was a very dedicated officer. He would fly you all day and all night if you didn't complain. He did not know when to quit. I was once on a cross-country with him to Offutt Field near Omaha. We had gotten up about 5 a.m. that morning and had gone to Waco to select some pilots, and from there we flew up to Offutt. It was well after dark when we got to Omaha. We went to dinner and got back about 10 p.m. Frank suggested we go into the bar and have a drink. I said, no not for me, I've had enough for the day. He was that kind of guy.

In mid-September 1958 Frank had a trip planned to Andrews AFB at Washington DC, and the weather was reported to be very bad there. *I had become the Deputy Commander about a year earlier, and I cautioned him to be careful. He took off about 7 p.m. from Del Rio and flew into Andrews, and the weather was still very bad. They made one pass at the base, and could not see the ground. The pass was too low, and they flew into trees at the end of the runway, and Frank and his copilot were killed.*

We lived across the street from the Wymans at Del Rio, and our families were pretty close. Their only daughter, Gail, was 11 or 12 years old at the time. The next morning I went with the new Group commander, General Russell, to tell Frank's wife, Jane, what had happened.[42,43]

At that time I became the commander of the 4025th squadron, and remained in that post for four years, which was the expected life of the program.

During the period of May 19 to August 31, 1959, the final test phase of the RB-57D-2 aircraft took place. Greg was directed to plan and conduct a 90-day exercise to confirm the feasibility of the aircraft's deployment. He personally monitored the testing of the aircraft and its ELINT equipment, and established an extensive training program for the aircrews. Problems arose and were dealt with, and in some cases, the corrective actions resulted in system modifications: the 320-SAFE system underwent twelve separate modifications as a result of Gregory's exercise. At the end of this performance study, Air Force Headquarters dispatched General Vinn to Laughlin to make an assessment of the trial program, and to decide whether the RB-57D-2s could be advanced to the next phase—overseas deployment.

SAC did not think this aircraft would ever go overseas. But when we finished this 90-day test, the General said: "I didn't think y'all were going to make it, but I wish you well." In fairly short order, the word was delivered to the 4080th Wing that deployment could proceed to England—Operation Border Town.

CHAPTER 8

Operation *Border Town*—Anatomy of a Deployment

On January 9, 1959 the 4080th Strategic Reconnaissance Wing received Operations Order 33-59A that detailed Operation *Border Town*, a planned four-month program to sweep the western perimeter of the Soviet Union, specifically the East German/Soviet border and the Baltic region, collecting signal intelligence on the Soviet air defenses with the with ELINT-quipped RB-57D-2 aircraft.[1]

Authors Tart and Keefe, in their book *The Price of Vigilance*, explain the importance of the D-2 for electronic and signal intelligence gathering:

> Early on, Allied engineers and intelligence analysts developed defensive measures against enemy radar systems by exploiting the characteristics of deployed radars. Each radar has a signature (set of parameters) that could be intercepted and measured by sensitive receivers and recorded on tape and other media for later analysis. Significant parameters include frequency, pulse repetition frequency, pulse repetition interval, pulse length or duration, and beam width. A radar's signature determines its purpose: early warning, search, acquisition, or fire control, for example. Understanding enemy radar's signature permits one to develop countermeasures, including electronic countermeasures. In fact, simply knowing where specific types of ground-based radars are located (electronic order of battle) is the first step in planning both offensive and defensive military operations.[2]

Even though Greg and his team had successfully completed the 90-day "proving" trial of the D-2s, it was clear to all that the future of the Black Knight program hinged on a successful result from *Border Town*.

This deployment order came just three months after the Soviets had shot down a USAAF C-130A that strayed into Armenian airspace during a perimeter ELINT mission along the border. In response to the shootdown, and the loss of life that resulted, the CIA's Director of Intelligence temporarily halted further intelligence-gathering missions pending the results of an assessment of the program, with the intent of determining if the data obtained during collection missions around the periphery of the USSR was worth the risks to aircraft and crew. The results of the study did nothing to slow the deployment of reconnaissance aircraft; rather, quite the reverse: "The study showed that intercept productivity (by aircraft) was far higher than at fixed sites (ground stations). The intercept was deemed of high intelligence value, and the missions were resumed."[3] Balancing risk and reward, the Air Force deployed the 4025th with full knowledge of the hazards involved.

Operation *Border Town* required the deployment of three RB-57D-2 aircraft and four crews, together with necessary personnel and equipment. The deployed unit, designated 4080th SRW Detachment 7, relocated from Laughlin AFB to Brize Norton Air Base, England, and was in place by January 16, 1959.[4]

The 4080th Wing had its hands full. Concurrent with *Border Town*, the 4028th squadron—now equipped with U-2 aircraft—had two detachments on foreign assignment, and one in Alaska. Detachment 3 was deployed to Ramey AFB, Puerto Rico, with three U-2 units doing collection of upper air samples and weather data for Armed Forces Special Weapons Project and Armed Forces Office of Atomic Testing. Detachment 4 was based in Ezeiza Airport, Buenos Aires, Arg, with three U-2 units, doing similar missions under Project Crow Flight. Detachment 5, consisting of three U-2 aircraft and crews, was in place at Eielson AFB Alaska on Projects Toy Soldier III and Fortune Finder, conducting particulate and gaseous sampling of the upper atmosphere in the Alaskan region.[5]

The 4025th's deployment would be under the command of Lt. Col. William Gregory, who had assumed command of the 4025th squadron just three months earlier. A deployment of this size, involving state-of-the-art intelligence gathering equipment, was a complex undertaking. Greg, in collaboration with the officer charged with the detachment's maintenance activities, selected personnel for the team and appointed a team NCOIC (Noncommissioned officer in charge), who would help ensure that all personnel were adequately trained.

The operations order for *Border Town* called for an advance team of ten officers, 20 airmen, and one civilian to depart Laughlin on January 16. The main body of one officer and 61 airmen would depart Laughlin on January 20, and the aircraft with crews would leave on January 24. The deployment required careful coordination with several USAF units: the Military Air Transport Service (MATS) provided the airlift for personnel and equipment and Air Rescue coverage for air routes flown by deployed aircraft to and from

Lt. Col. William Gregory, Commander, 4025th Strategic Reconnaissance Squadron. (Gregory)

England. En-route services, including air refueling, were provided by the Eighth Air Force; additional support was provided by Lajes Air Base in the Azores, and Harmon Air Base in Newfoundland. The 7th Air Division provided base facilities and support at Brize Norton. A support team that included one complete aircrew and 17 airmen departed Laughlin on January 22 and was positioned at Harmon to provide support in the event of mechanical or fuel issues for the RB-57D-2s while en route. That team was equipped with 28,000 lbs. of cargo, including two J-57 replacement engines. In contrast, the full deployment would require 46 tons of supplies and equipment.[6]

While the presence of RB-57D aircraft at Laughlin was well known to the Del Rio community, *Border Town* would be a top-secret program. All messages to and from the aircraft, and all in-flight course or altitude requests by the pilots identified the aircraft as B-47s, not RB-57D-2s. The ruse was maintained in all Wing reports which indicated that the aircraft originated from and would return to Kelly AFB, TX. In fact, they originated from Laughlin AFB at Del Rio, TX.

Col. Gregory and the advance cohort arrived at Brize Norton on a cold and rainy English winter day, January 19. The main detachment arrived two days

Detachment 7—*Border Town.*

later. The evening of their arrival, Col. Gregory and his team completed an inspection of the Detachment 7 facilities, and the following morning conferenced with the RAF's 3920 Combat Support Group, which would be providing ground support for the Detachment. By the time the main Detachment body arrived on the 21st, all housing, transportation, messing, and hangar facilities had been secured. Everyone was looking forward to the arrival of the cargo support and, last but certainly not least, the arrival of the tactical aircraft.

In a summary report for January 1959, detailing the status of operations and set-up, Greg noted: *It was very gratifying to observe the speed and thoroughness in moving into our Temporary Duty Site and getting set up to operate. The base support has been excellent, the fast response given our requests to Laughlin has been very helpful, and there are no serious supply problems. The choice of personnel selected for this deployment by the various squadrons at the home station appears to have been very good. All sections are well-organized and are functioning in a satisfactory manner. I am well pleased with the officers and airmen which make up this detachment and am of the opinion that they represent a highly qualified capability for proving this weapons system.*[7]

On the 21st, Col. Gregory and Captain Wood, Detachment Intelligence Officer, received a series of briefings at the Seventh Air Division Headquarters, during which they were apprised of the mission assigned to Detachment 7— codenamed *Pied Piper Gypsy*. As reported in the unit history: "It was gratifying to learn of the keen interest shown toward the capability of the RB-57D-2."[8]

The pilots of the RB-57Ds had received a final weather briefing at Laughlin just before midnight on January 23, and by 0100 on the 24th the formation of three was airborne, following a precisely defined course to Brize Norton that included two midair refuelings. The first refueling was canceled due to bad weather, but fuel consumption confirmed that the aircraft could make it to the second refueling rendezvous over Newfoundland. That refueling was successfully completed, but with a touch of drama occasioned by an incorrect warning on one aircraft that indicated its fuel receptacle had not opened. And in a further ominous start to operations, that same aircraft lost its oxygen supply after it had passed the point of no return on the outbound leg. It made a rapid descent, which resulted in excessive fuel consumption. A tanker on cockpit alert was immediately dispatched to refuel the '57, but it soon suffered its own equipment problems when its UHF radio failed, preventing proximity communications with the '57. Despite the loss of radio, the rendezvous was made near Lands End, England, fuel transferred, and the flight to Brize Norton was continued.[9]

The two on-schedule aircraft made their landing approach to Brize Norton just after noon on January 24, 11½ hours after leaving Texas, followed 30 minutes later by the third aircraft. As the Brits at Brize Norton got their first look at the American RB-57D-2s, the control tower operator remarked, "Blimey, it's a Canberra with extended wings," not realizing that he had precisely described the incoming aircraft.

By midnight on January 25, all aircraft assigned to the detachment—the '57s and MATS C-124 cargo aircraft—were safely on the ground in England. Within four days of its arrival at Brize Norton, the detachment was mission-ready.[10]

In a departure from standard procedures, each tactical aircraft was assigned a crew chief with two assistants, an Electronic Counter Measure (ECM) chief with assistants, and a radar chief with one assistant. Additionally, an eight-man team was assigned for servicing, maintaining, launching, and receiving each aircraft, and each aircraft was assigned a civilian representative of Martin Air.

The unit was top-heavy with service personnel, but during the TDY period—including all orientation flights, ELINT missions, and test flights—there was only one ground abort and one delayed takeoff. As Gregory would later note: *The assigning of a complete maintenance crew to each aircraft paid off in many ways, as the RB-57D aircraft had never been in better shape, with each crew trying to outdo the other maintenance crews. The crews never failed to deliver a mission-ready aircraft.*

Material, supplies, and equipment for the detachment were delivered to England using a fleet of five C-124 aircraft provided by MATS. During the deployment of the detachment, numerous delays were experienced by all the C-124 support aircraft, and improper loading of the cargo aircraft had become a problem: the keys needed to unlock some of the equipment arrived well after the equipment itself.

Greg's characteristic directness can be heard in the wing's unit history, in which he made the following scalding assessment: "The support rendered by MATS in transporting the main body of personnel would have been improved if the crews and MATS transport control had been more highly motivated to accomplish the move with a minimum of delay."[11]

Gregory, in his first deployment command, urged a closer liaison between the 4080th SRW logistics team and MATS to avoid the snarl-ups that plagued the initial support flights. The missions of the 4025th required detailed navigation plans, and therefore takeoffs timed to the second. Greg was intolerant of air units that could not follow a schedule. He pointedly recommended that MATS be required to adhere to specified flight schedules, doubtlessly referring to the fact that the launch of *Border Town* (i.e., the departure of the advance cohort) was delayed by 12 hours due to "unavailability of MATS aircraft." He also noted that support for the detachment would have been improved if a survey trip had been made by the 3920th Combat Support Group prior to deployment.[12]

Gregory also commented on the high volume of secret communications: "The administrative workload during the TDY period was much heavier than expected. Approximately 700 incoming or outgoing messages were processed each day, and a high percentage of those messages were classified and required careful logging and filing. There were also numerous reports and routine correspondence that created a relatively heavy administrative workload."[13]

Of great importance was the Physiological Support Section, which when operational included six pre-breathing lounge chairs, facilities to feed two crews, two refrigerators and a stove, drying cabinets and lockers. To purge their tissues of nitrogen, pilots pre-breathed pure oxygen for at least one hour before flight. So efficiently did this section operate that by the end of the deployment, the RAF personnel at Brize Norton had requested the 4025th SRS's help in reorganizing the RAF base's physiological support section.

The balance of January was devoted to settling into quarters, establishing operations centers, and receiving operational and intelligence briefings. The officers and men of Detachment 7 were carefully briefed on the intelligence requirements for the *Pied Piper Gypsy* missions they would be flying, and on the need for tight security for these top-secret flights.

Three orientation flights, codename *Half Breed*, were conducted on the last day of January 1959 to provide an opportunity for familiarization of communication facilities and procedures, and "letdowns" at selected SAC bases in the UK.

In February, a heavy flight schedule commenced, with thirteen sorties, among which were eight tactical missions.[14] The first operational mission occurred on February 3, 1959 and the second just after midnight on the 4th. Eight missions were attempted in February, six of which were successfully completed. All the missions flown were electronic ferret missions using the 320-SAFE (Semi-Automatic Ferret Equipment) system. The long-standing practice for ferret missions had required the ECM officer to write detected signals in a log. In the 320-SAFE system, digital computers were attached to conventional ferret receivers, analyzers and direction-finding equipment and output the "take" on magnetic tape. The ECM officer operated the ferret equipment as previously but could initiate recording at the touch of a button.

Date (1959)	Aircraft #	Type of mission
1 February	968	Test Flight
2 February	964	Test Flight
2 February	965	Test Flight
3 February	968	Tulsa/Skunk
4 February	964	Tulsa/Deer
12 February	965	UK Orientation
12 February	964	Tulsa/Antelope
14 February	965	Tulsa/Fox (abort)
14 February	968	Test Flight
19 February	964	Tulsa/Weasel
22 February	965	Tulsa/Beaver
25 February	964	Tulsa/Bear
26 February	968	Tulsa/Ermine (abort)

Most significantly, two missions did not yield useable intelligence—Tulsa/Skunk and Tulsa/Antelope—due to failures in the all-important 320-SAFE system.

Those failed missions sent a jolt through the detachment. The 320-SAFE system was the primary means by which electronic signals were recorded. Despite the overall success to date of the deployment, if it did not advance the state of intelligence the entire future of the RB-57D-2 weapons system was in serious doubt.

In fact, even as the 4025th was engaged in these *Pied Piper Gypsy* missions, the Air Force was looking hard at the RB-57D platform.

Following the problems associated with the deployment of RB-57D-0 aircraft to Japan, the Air Force continued to view the Black Knight project as unproven. A conference was arranged to discuss the possible phase-out of the photo-equipped D-0s, and Air Force headquarters was awaiting the results of *Pied Piper Gypsy* to determine whether the D-2 aircraft would be retained in the SAC inventory. In addition to considering the deployment itself, the Air Force was evaluating whether the 4080th could deploy a detachment of at least two aircraft on overseas TDY on a continuous basis, and whether the wing had enough pilots to provide a TDY frequency of three months every eighteen months per combat crew.[15]

Indications that *Border Town*'s initial results were less than fully reliable were particularly ominous considering the Air Force's close scrutiny of the Black Knight program. The problems associated with the 320-SAFE system in the early days of this deployment are textbook examples of the truthfulness of Murphy's Law: "If it can go wrong, it will."

The 320-SAFE system recorded electronic signals on a magnetic tape. On the failed missions, it was found that the tape had not passed the magnetic head of the recorder and was binding up on the take-up spool. Maintenance teams could not duplicate the failure on the ground, but on two test flights, the problem recurred.[16]

In what was a "drop everything" condition, the detachment went to considerable lengths to identify and resolve the problem. A case history was dispatched to the States, and two specialists in England were called in for consultation. The on-site representative from Martin Air, developer of the SAFE system, was also involved in the investigation.

After much effort, it was learned that the signal capture system was working fine. Rather, the metal screws holding the cover to the unit were too long and were binding the take-up spool. Shorter screws were installed, and the problem was solved and never recurred.[13]

With the tape system fix in place, the missions recommenced. *The 320-SAFE tapes were offloaded from the aircraft immediately after landing and delivered to one of the buildings where the team would begin the process of downloading all of the "take" from the mission. Computer cards were generated, and on the basis of those cards, the experts could quickly confirm whether the information on the card represented a new signal not previously heard.*

And at the same time we were flying our missions, the 55th Strategic Reconnaissance Wing, also on deployment, would send B-47 ELINT aircraft with us, at lower altitude, flying the same course. Both aircraft were searching for air order-of-battle information on specific Russian radars: the Spoon Rest, Fan Song, and Tall King radars. Missions were flown at night following a route from the UK north up the Baltic Sea as far as Finland, thence east all along the East German border. Both aircraft would pick up electronic signals, and using this tandem approach the Soviets energized more equipment than we could make them use before.[17]

Given the Soviet propensity for shooting down surveillance aircraft, skirting the borders of the Soviet Union required the most careful of navigation. Flying too far away from the border could result in missing important order-of-battle signals; flying too close could put the aircraft within range of fighters or ground fire.

Aerial navigation in the late 50s was not remotely as accurate as that of today. In fact, much of the flying, including the "Tulsa" missions flown during Operation *Border Town*, was done by "pilotage" using an aeronautical chart or topographic map to obtain a fix of the aircraft's position with respect to a desired course or location. These were "peripheral" missions, designed to fly close to the Soviet border, but Greg was specifically enjoined not to overfly Soviet territory. Nevertheless, Greg reports that on one mission a Black Knight pilot did make an inadvertent overflight, though it appears that the Soviets did not attempt an intercept.

The Wing report for February records very encouraging, if preliminary, results for the Detachment 7 deployment: "It is still too early for a full intelligence evaluation of the mission 'take' but indications from partial evaluations by 4080th Intelligence and Seventh Air Division indicates that the results thus far have been excellent..."[18]

Later, Greg would rate the detachment's performance with a bit more enthusiasm: *It was a big success.*

The high-altitude operations that were possible with the RB-57D-2s paid dividends for the signals collection. By operating higher than other ELINT-gathering aircraft, and hence with a more distant signal horizon, the Detachment 7 aircraft were able to excite Soviet radar and other electronic signals that had not previously been detected. Lower-flying aircraft could not elicit signals from the more distantly located Soviet installations.

By early March the aircrews and support personnel of Detachment 7 had begun to function with Swiss precision. From March 3 to 18, the detachment conducted preflight briefings, missions, debriefings, and mission read-outs. No problems, no equipment malfunctions, and no personnel issues. As the deployment entered its second month, its strength stood at 80 airmen, 19 officers, and 11 civilians.

The detachment had received orders for redeployment back to the States upon completion of its final assigned mission on March 17. By the time that mission had concluded, the stand-down was already well underway with the various sub-units already 75–90 percent packed and ready for loading. *The usual tear down, crating, and normal preparation for the arrival of the first support aircraft was initiated. All that was needed was the arrival of the MATS C-124 aircraft to transport the detachment back to Laughlin. However, 35 hours from the scheduled departure of the first two support aircraft, a delay message was received with instructions to "maintain capability."*

With the redeployment already well advanced, the new mission commitment created many problems for the unit. The supply pipeline from the US had to be re-established, the armament and electronics shop and maintenance facilities at Brize Norton had to be re-opened, and the Military Air Transport (MATS) had to be rescheduled. Given the uncertainties of these operations—potential weather delays, equipment failures, etc.—a new departure date could only be estimated, and subsequent deferrals further stressed all the support systems.

On March 19 Gregory received the new mission requirements from the Seventh Air Division—it was to be an all-unit ELINT collection effort in which the three RB-57D-2 aircraft from Detachment 7 would operate in conjunction with four other aircraft from other reconnaissance units.

An attempt was made to fly the mission on March 25, but it was aborted due to a failure of the radar navigation system on one aircraft. The mission was again attempted the following day but was also aborted when the detachment's pilots could not locate another flight of aircraft operating on the same mission.

A third and successful attempt was made on March 27, and with the completion of that mission, the unit again began the redeployment process. On April 1 the first support MATS C-124 arrived to load the detachment's equipment, and by April 3 the detachment was completely airborne for the return trip. By late Sunday, April 5 1959, all of the Detachment 7 equipment and personnel had returned to Laughlin AFB, with all the families there to meet the returning "Knights."

In his summary report at the conclusion of the *Border Town* deployment, Greg noted that the flying commitments of the detachment did not justify the need for three aircraft, as the general rule had been about one flight per individual aircraft every eight days. It was his opinion that too long a ground time was not desirable and that no matter how much attention was given to the aircraft by maintenance personnel, the aircraft and aircrews would benefit from operational checks and flying proficiency sorties. In his view, a three- or four-day downtime for each aircraft was optimum.

He noted that because of the high priority placed upon the successful completion of the mission, the detachment was heavily manned to preclude any possibility of failure due to lack of qualified personnel. Before the end of the operations of this detachment, eight airmen and two civilians returned to the United States early because their services were in excess of need. Greg recommended that future deployments with similar requirements could be reduced by 50 percent without sacrificing the capability of the unit.[19]

Border Town results

It had become apparent to the Air Force and to the American intelligence community that the intelligence yield from *Border Town* was significant. After the initial glitch in the 320-SAFE housing, it was found that "the system could be relied on to perform as specified. And the ability of the aircraft to operate at 'base altitude' resulted in a much larger area of search that extended far beyond that of any other ferret aircraft, resulting in heretofore unknown Soviet sites being incorporated into the Electronic Order of Battle."[20]

The reliability of the equipment of the RB-57D-2 weapons system during Operation *Border Town* far exceeded the collection results of previous ELINT missions by other reconnaissance units. For each mission the 4025th flew, the electronic "take" was carefully analyzed locally, within the capability of available facilities. It was found that "logical information" was obtained on approximately 95 percent of all signals analyzed using a manual readout of the cards produced from the 320-SAFE system. In contrast, the automatic readout used by the 544th Reconnaissance Technical Squadron would produce solutions on only approximately 66 percent of the analysis.[21]

Performing these manual readouts was time-consuming: one intelligence officer and one airman worked six hours after each mission on the analysis. But the increase in what was termed "solutions," i.e., signals intelligence that potentially identified the new order-of-battle units on the Soviet side, clearly justified the effort.

With the completion of *Border Town*, Greg's reputation for being able to plan and implement a complex foreign reconnaissance deployment was well established, and as evidenced by his next deployment, the Air Force was intent on making full use of his leadership capabilities.

Little time was wasted by the Air Force brass in continuing the successes of Detachment 7. In a deployment that both resembled Operation *Border Town* and differed in ways that were informed by the experiences of *Border Town*, on July 10 two RB-57D-2 aircraft were deployed from Laughlin to Eielson AFB in Alaska on Operation *Sand Shark*. The deployment included two aircraft and three flight crews plus necessary equipment and support personnel to participate in "higher headquarters directed missions" over a 45-day deployment.[22]

Greg accompanied the 4025th in the *Sand Shark* operation, during which the squadron made an important discovery. It was in Alaska that they ran into warm weather at altitude—an inversion. *We learned something there—we lost about 5,000 feet in altitude because of this heat inversion—we could only attain about 60,000 feet, and passing through the mid-40s we sometimes had problems losing an engine. We tried boosting more power, and it just wouldn't do it. We finally relaxed because we figured the enemy would have the same problem. We learned that around 40,000–45,000 feet, there is a change in the temperature regime. The outside temp is at the very coldest at that altitude—above that, it gets a little warmer.* This operational nugget would later prove of great value to U-2 operations, particularly with reference to Chinese overflights.

Greg and his team would have experience an episode of déjà vu during *Sand Shark*—an experience that harkened back to the difficulty with the 320-SAFE system during *Border Town*. Just as an improper screw had caused the failure of two *Border Town* missions, during *Sand Shark* one of the D-2 aircraft experienced a pressurization problem during the outbound leg: a problem that was attributed to "failure to replace a large number of screws in the nose flight control hatch, allowing the seal to slip out, thus losing pressure."[23]

The wing dispatched a final deployment of D-2 aircraft, this time to Incirlik, Turkey, near Adana. It was the unit's third deployment in a year—a lot of activity for a relatively small Air Force squadron.

Greg, with his 23-man advance team and 10 tons of cargo, left on MATS C-124s on Operation *Dip Stick* on January 12, 1960. Within a week, the entire detachment was on the ground in Turkey, rapidly preparing for flight operations. A total of eight missions were planned over a 20-day period—a rate that would challenge the team. Adding to the workload of the ground crews was the fact that the aircraft were collecting data on Soviet atmospheric nuclear tests; therefore considerable emphasis was placed on radiation detection and sanitizing the aircraft on this deployment.

Dip Stick again included three RB-57D-2 aircraft and four crews. Gregory selected the same three aircraft for this deployment as had been used on *Border Town*.

In late January, all four aircrews completed familiarization flights around Incirlik, with Col. Gregory himself taking a flight on the 30th. Fourteen operation check flights were conducted during February, with Greg assigning himself to three. Six operational missions were flown in February. Following standard security procedures, as detachment commander, Greg could not assign himself to these missions.

Amidst the swirl of deployment operations, Greg found time to visit the site of the first Christian church at Antioch, not far from Incirlik. In entering what was essentially a deep cavern that provided a safe haven for early Christians, for Greg this meant walking in the footsteps of Apostle Paul who taught the gospel to the first-century church. Much of Greg's prior overseas duty had been to non-Christian parts of the world, so visiting a Christian church for Sunday services was not normally available to Greg. Very early in his career, when first posted to England as a fighter pilot with the 49th Fighter Squadron, Greg and two friends visited a church near their base at Goxhill. For reasons perhaps having to do with the flood of GIs to the area, they did not feel welcomed by the congregation and afterward, Greg was reluctant to try again elsewhere.

By the end of February, it was clear that the weather conditions in Turkey would cause unacceptable mission delays, and on March 7 the entire detachment was redeployed back to Brize Norton for the completion of the assignment.

We had C-119s airlifting us from Incirlik back to England. These were large, two-engine transports first introduced into the Air Force in 1949. On one flight the pilot lost an engine and began losing altitude while flying over the Mediterranean. As he neared the coast of Italy, he made one pass to allow the twenty-three people on board to bail out. One of them, a Chinese kid, dropped through a roof and ended up in a restroom, causing the local Italians to observe that "it's raining Chinese people." The only injury was to another passenger, a captain, who hit a roof, rolled off, and badly injured his back. With all passengers out, the pilot was able to come around again to land on the beach, probably in the water. It was a pretty good job: he was able to save all the passengers, himself, and a lot of equipment.

After flying thee more operational missions from the UK base, the detachment redeployed back to Del Rio during the first week of April. Greg's service to the 4025th and to the RB-57D-2 weapons system was at that point recognized by the Air Force. Citing his exemplary work during the *Border Town* deployment, as well as his valuable contribution to the initial qualification of the weapons system during the 90-day trial at Laughlin, the Air Force awarded Greg the Legion of Merit. Lt. Col. Gregory was just 39 years of age at the time.

The Legion of Merit is a military award of the US Armed Forces given for exceptionally meritorious conduct in the performance of outstanding services and achievements. It is generally awarded to general officers and colonels, and only rarely to lieutenant colonels. For Air Force officers, the LOM is more highly valued than the Distinguished Flying Cross.

Greg's citation, slightly abridged, includes:

> Lieutenant Colonel Gregory distinguished himself as Project Officer for the R-57D-2 Test Group, and as Commander of Detachment 7. Due to Lt. Col. Gregory's leadership and knowledge of the RB-57D-2 weapons system, the fleet was prepared to assume its role as a recognized tool of the United States Air Force one month earlier than its anticipated commitment schedule. As Commander of Detachment 7, Lt. Col. Gregory distinguished himself by his leadership, ingenuity, and his organizational ability. Upon completion of the deployment, Lt. Col. Gregory had provided the USAF with a new proven weapons system which has taken its place as a recognized integral part of the aerial force and an instrument which will foster preservations of peace. Through his aggressive action and perseverance, and through his professional managerial ability, Lt. Col. Gregory's actions have reflected great credit upon himself, his organizations, and the United States Air Force.[24]

Dip Stick was to be the last deployment for Gregory and for the RB-57D-2s. Always intended to be an interim solution to the need for high-altitude reconnaissance, after four years of deployments to Alaska, England and Turkey the RB-57D-2 was by 1960 approaching its planned retirement. It would be succeeded by the latest product from Kelly Johnson's Skunk Works at Lockheed—the U-2, which had itself entered development within a few months of the RB-57D coming online.

By May 1960, all RB-57Ds, including the D-2 ELINT aircraft, had been removed from the 4080th inventory, and on June 15, 1960, the 4025th SRS was deactivated. The D-2 aircraft had deployed three times under Greg's command. He had either directed the deployment, as in *Border Town* and *Dip Stick*, or been on-site, as in *Sand Shark*. Occurring over a period of 16 months, the deployments had resulted in Greg's absence for over 28 weeks.

I was in Incirlik, Turkey, on my last assignment with the 4025th when I got a message to report to CIA headquarters in Washington for a new assignment.

Helen, Gretchen (10) and Cookie (5) welcoming Greg home from deployment. (*Air Force Times*, April 1959)

CHAPTER 9

The CIA and Early U-2 Operations

By the early 1950s the United States and the Soviet Union were settling into their respective Cold War positions: the Soviets intent on expanding the communist ideology and strenuously resisting American attempts at intelligence gathering; the United States, equally committed to the support of free postwar societies, and fearful of Soviet capacities and intents, equally committed to a strenuous surveillance program.

Given the vast breadth of the Soviet Union, and the technical limitations of peripheral ground- and air-based intelligence gathering systems, deeper intrusions into Soviet airspace were critical. President Eisenhower, like President Truman before him, was deeply concerned about a potential surprise attack by a nuclear-armed Soviet Union. On taking office, Ike was familiar with Soviet nuclear arms developments, and cognizant of long-range bomber development. Like his military and his intelligence experts, Ike was essentially blind to Soviet capabilities or intent.[1]

Recognizing the criticality of overhead surveillance, and also keenly aware that reconnaissance overflights of sovereign territory during peacetime were clearly in violation of international law, shortly after taking office President Eisenhower quietly authorized clandestine high-altitude photoreconnaissance of the Soviet Union and the Eastern Bloc.

U-2 program roots

The American intelligence community, including the CIA and those within the military services, actively considered a range of overflight reconnaissance options, each with its own unique set of technical requirements, system limitations, costs, and timelines. The two most encouraging options were high-altitude fixed-wing aircraft—the short-term best option—and satellite reconnaissance platforms, the preferred long-term option.

The aircraft option—initially undertaken through the RB-57D Black Knight Program—was much less costly, and could be delivered much quicker than the satellite option. But it carried the greatest risk, given the Soviet propensity for attempting and often succeeding in shooting down reconnaissance aircraft, even those not intruding into Soviet airspace.

The satellite option was vastly more expensive, with a development timeline of a decade or more. But it appeared to offer a long-term and invulnerable platform for surveillance.

Proponents of aircraft surveillance had to address the twin issues of detection and tracking. Aircraft *detected* over Soviet airspace had already caused many diplomatic furors, putting the US diplomatic corps in the position of explaining what those aircraft were doing over sovereign Soviet territory. But being *tracked* by radar raised the ante, because it increased the risk of the aircraft being downed. If a US spyplane were shot down, and its intelligence collection equipment discovered, it would be impossible for the US to continue to assert that the aircraft was conducting weather missions. America would suffer a significant loss of credibility at home and abroad.

For the fixed-wing system, it was believed that the solution to both detection and tracking lay in altitude, a belief that was based on the assumption that the Soviets were, in the early 1950s, still using the same American-built radar equipment that had been supplied under Lend-Lease during World War II. According to an internal CIA document, "Although the (Soviet) target-tracking radar could track targets up to 90,000 feet, its high power consumption burned out a key component quickly, so this radar was normally not turned on until an early warning radar had detected a target." But the early warning radar was effective to just 40,000 feet. As a result, experts believe that "an aircraft that could ascend to 65,000 feet before entering an area being swept by the early warning radar would go undetected, because the target-tracking radars would not be activated."[3]

Thus, the earliest discussions related to high-altitude aircraft operated under the critical, and what would be persistent, assumption that the aircraft would be neither detected nor tracked.

Programs to develop high-altitude aircraft and satellite systems commenced nearly contemporaneously, although the manner of their development, the costs, and the time required to field an effective program varied considerably between the two options. Significantly, both development projects were primarily designed, evaluated, approved, and administered by the same individuals, organizations, administrators, and ultimately, presidents. And as will be seen, the fact that these systems employed the latest in very specialized technologies (flight, camera, systems control, communications, security, etc.)

meant that a small coterie of contractors was qualified to participate in the development programs. The field of overhead surveillance had evolved into a relatively small club.

Fixed-wing surveillance

In 1952, as a result of the growing concern over Soviet intentions and capabilities, the Air Force had reconfigured the B-47s for reconnaissance, believing that aircraft operating at an altitude of 40,000 feet would certainly be detected, but would be out of range of Soviet fighters. And they were correct, insofar as the MiG-15 was concerned. But when flown within range of MiG-17 bases, the outcome was much different.

By 1954, the Air Force had been successfully flying RB-47 peripheral and overflight missions of the Soviet Union for two years, which appeared to reflect an acceptance by the military and civilian leaders that Soviet detection, though problematic, could be dealt with through diplomatic channels so long as the spyplane remained safe from Soviet fighters. But in May of that year, an overflight mission was intercepted by MiG-17s. Though damaged, the aircraft was able to return to its English base. Subsequent RB-47 missions would not end as well—within a year an RB-47 was shot down by Soviet fighters while on a reconnaissance mission over the Kamchatka Peninsula.

After losing three or four different planes, it was clear that the existing US inventory of planes was not capable of overflying Soviet territory.

In July 1954, President Eisenhower had commissioned a sweeping analysis of the nation's offensive, defensive, and intelligence capabilities, an analysis that would characterize America's ability to detect and defend against a surprise attack by the Soviet Union. The assessment would be conducted by a small but highly experienced team of experts under the guidance of the Technological Capabilities Panel (TCP).

The comprehensive TCP report recommended "a vigorous program for the extensive use of the most advanced knowledge in science and technology," and resulted in a number of critical changes to US defense capabilities.[4] Its recommendation included accelerating procurement of American ICBMs (intercontinental ballistic missiles) and intermediate-range ballistic missiles; speeding up construction of the Distant Early Warning (DEW) Line in the Arctic; and developing a sea-launched ballistic missile.

Addressing the foundational issue of the TCP analysis, a potential surprise attack by the Soviets, the report also proposed methods to acquire and use "strategic pre-hostilities intelligence."[5] More specifically the Panel noted that—at least in the short term—the solution to the nation's intelligence problem was a reconnaissance airplane that could operate at altitudes above those of military aircraft and Soviet air defenses. A technological fix to take the highest ground.

Close on the heels of the TCP report came a separate report from General James Doolittle, also commissioned by the president, to assess the organization and covert operations of the CIA. That report was sharply critical of the CIA's intelligence-gathering capability, chastening the agency for its failure to develop and implement the latest scientific and technological systems for intelligence gathering—including overhead reconnaissance.

With the Soviets showing no reluctance to interdict and destroy American surveillance aircraft, with the tally of lost reconnaissance aircraft continuing to grow, and with the prospects of adequate satellite surveillance still some way off, the Air Force and the CIA lent a high degree of urgency to developing the fixed-wing surveillance platform that would give high-quality surveillance information, while at the same time being impervious to Soviet air defenses. As valuable as the ELINT information collected under *Border Town* and other 4025th deployments had been, the greater need for the intelligence services was photo intelligence. They required a platform that would do what the RB-57D-0s could not do: a platform that would operate higher, and with a better camera.

The Air Force's development team at Wright AFB had begun in late 1952 to consider the feasibility of marrying the new generation of turbojet engines with an innovative airfoil design to produce an aircraft capable of reaching very high altitudes—a platform well suited to reconnaissance, and one which would make detection and interception very difficult. Within six months, these early studies had coalesced into a set of specifications that called for an aircraft that could operate at an altitude of 70,000 ft., with a range of at least 1,700 miles. The main USAF surveillance aircraft at that time—the RB-47—was yielding excellent SIGINT and PHOTINT data from peripheral missions, but it was clear that the aircraft could not attain the operating parameters identified by the Air Force as necessary to avoid Soviet interception. And neither would the soon-to-be-deployed RB-57Ds.

Consequently, in 1953 the Air Force solicited study proposals under Project Bald Eagle for a subsonic aircraft that could meet the altitude and range specification while carrying a payload of up to 700 lbs. Three aircraft designers—Bell, Martin, and Fairchild—responded with proposals for the new aircraft. Lockheed, not included in the RFP but catching wind of the Air Force project through back channels, also issued a proposal that was based on its XF-104 fighter, but with longer, slender wings and a shortened fuselage, an aircraft designated as the CL-282, but later renamed the U-2.[6]

The fixed-wing platform that was the subject of these design studies was a continuation of the Air Force's decision to employ limited-duration "stop-gap measures" to provide the critically needed aerial reconnaissance as quickly as possible. As Robert Perry notes, "Most contemporary defense department opinion was that satellite reconnaissance was only theoretically feasible, and at best could not be of practical use before the mid-1960s." With all the pressure generated by perceptions of bomber gaps and later missile gaps, US defense and intelligence communities could not wait the ten years or more that might be required for those systems to be perfected.[7]

That same group of intelligence planners also recognized that the service life of the resultant high-altitude aircraft would be limited. According to Peter Merlin in *Unlimited Horizons, Design and Development of the U-2*, CIA Director Allen Dulles was advised in late 1954: "The opportunity for safe overflight may last only a few years because the Russians will develop radars and interceptors or guided missile defenses for the 70,000-foot region."[8]

Although Lockheed's design, essentially a jet-powered glider, could meet the proposed specifications, it was rejected by the Air Force in favor of the Bell X-16 and a modified Martin B-57—both twin-engine aircraft in contrast to the single-engine Lockheed and Fairchild designs. General Curtis LeMay, the commander of the Air Force's Strategic Air Command, the organization for which the new surveillance aircraft would operate, famously discounted the U-2, saying he was "not interested in an airplane without wheels or guns."[9]

The US Central Intelligence Agency (CIA) had been fully aware of the Air Force's Project Bald Eagle and was equally cognizant that the proposed Bell and Martin aircraft would not reach the altitudes necessary for safe, that is, undetected or untrackable surveillance of the Soviet Union. It, together with civilian experts, continued to promote the CL-282 design to the Air Force and the American intelligence community. In November 1954, President Eisenhower, having been briefed on the new platform and its capabilities and benefits, gave approval for a joint USAF-CIA project; significantly, the first instance of the CIA engaging in sophisticated aerial technology.[10]

The CIA assigned the cryptonym "Aquatone" for their side of the joint project: "Oilstone" was the USAF codename.

Within eight months, the terms of the CIA-USAF partnership had been defined. The CIA and USAF jointly directed and controlled the Aquatone/Oilstone project, although the headquarters was led by a CIA appointee. The Air Force provided the necessary ground support, including engines, ground support equipment, maintenance and training personnel, and air traffic control. Airframes and cameras were purchased through the CIA's budget, and the Agency was responsible for developing the necessary security protocols. The CIA controlled operational planning, and controlled operations when overflights commenced.[11,12]

In December 1954, using covert CIA funding sources, Lockheed was issued a contract to produce 20 aircraft, with a July 1956 completion date for the first unit—an incredibly short date-to-delivery. Initial flight tests were conducted in August 1955, by which time the aircraft had become known as the U-2, heralding "the beginning of an aeronautical technology program that spanned more than two decades and showcased innovative aircraft design and manufacturing techniques."[13] Within a month the aircraft had reached an operating altitude of 65,000 ft.

Lockheed met that initial deliverable, and the remaining 19 aircraft, on time and at less than $1 million per aircraft. By June 1, 1956, the U-2 had been equipped with the new J57-P-31 engine, and had reached an altitude of 74,500 feet – over 14 miles. On the basis of this astonishing success, the USAF overcame its initial reluctance to the U-2, and in January 1956 awarded a contract to Lockheed for an additional 29 U-2s, to be delivered to the Strategic Air Command (SAC).[14]

Initial flight testing for the U-2 was conducted at a site in southern Nevada that was, at the time, referred to as Groom Lake, and which would subsequently become known as "Watertown," "The Ranch," and more cryptically,

Lockheed U-2 aircraft. (Wikimedia Commons)

by 1958 as "Area 51." For purposes of flight testing, Groom Lake was perfect, but not without challenges.

Most particularly, Groom Lake was located within the Las Vegas Bombing and Gunnery Range, just 12 miles from the Atomic Energy Commission (AEC) nuclear proving ground at Yucca Flat. Some in the U-2 development team were opposed to the site, since Groom Lake was directly downwind of the radioactive fallout clouds that emanated from Yucca Flats. And while the extra security that was afforded by AEC and military restrictions on the surrounding area was advantageous, the frequent atmospheric testing of nuclear weapons so close by, and the resultant radioactive fallout, became serious problems for the U-2 program.

Prior to the airfield development at Groom Lake there had been 32 atmospheric nuclear tests at Yucca Flats. In 1955 and 1956 there were 14 more, and with prevailing winds to the northeast, the radioactive plume usually deposited fallout on the Groom Lake area and resulted in the evacuation of personnel and the interruption of flight test and crew training operations.

By mid-1957, U-2 flight testing and pilot training were essentially complete. The U-2 test operation moved to Edwards AFB, California, and the operational U-2 aircraft were assigned to the 4028th Strategic Reconnaissance Squadron at Laughlin, Texas. This was just as well: within a month of their departure, the most powerful airburst ever detonated within the continental United States was exploded just 14 miles southwest of Groom Lake. Five times more powerful

Groom Lake, Nevada. Home of Area 51/The Ranch/Watertown. (Wikimedia Commons)

than the bomb dropped on Hiroshima, the blast caused widespread damage at Watertown, and left significant amounts of radiation fallout.[15]

Atmospheric testing of nuclear weapons ended in the United States with the enactment of the Above Ground Test Ban Treaty between the US and USSR in March 1963.

The Air Force had not only passed on the U-2 design but actively resisted its development. Its own independently developed RB-57D platform was scheduled to take its first test flight within a few months of the U-2's first flight, and there was concern within the Air Force that the U-2 development program could threaten the introduction of the RB-57D. But the early delivery and exceptional performance of the U-2 so impressed the Air Force that it soon purchased 29 of its own U-2s through the CIA, in a program codenamed Project Dragon Lady, thereby giving the aircraft the nickname that would persist. In what must have seemed an abundance of riches, the Air Force would operate both platforms, each with the potential of changing the US Cold War posture vis-à-vis the Soviets completely, and each with an estimated service life—four years—that would pave the way toward effective satellite reconnaissance. So great was the Air Force's enthusiasm for the U-2 that it attempted to take over control of the CIA-managed covert U-2 program, an attempt that was rebuffed by President Eisenhower. For at least the next five years the CIA would maintain majority control over the project.[16]

A new camera was a necessity for the U-2 as the camera lens would be positioned 13 miles from the object being photographed. Jim Baker, a celebrated lens designer, and Edward Land, who pioneered the Polaroid camera, together built an incredibly high-resolution camera which produced an 18 × 18-inch negative. Because of the camera's excellent resolution, photo interpreters had no trouble identifying objects as small as 2½ feet. On a typical overflight mission, 4,000 images would be taken. Greg, who was to become extremely well versed in U-2s and their capabilities, confirms that the U-2s at that time were also equipped with ELINT equipment and that it was always used. *It was not a primary part of the mission, but we always used it, and would always send in our "take." But the big four-engine jets did a really good job of ELINT, and were better equipped than we were, and could get better electronic intelligence than we could from the U-2s.*

With the introduction of the U-2, and with the continued operation of the RB-57D Black Knight Program, and other reconnaissance programs, the United States was well equipped to provide a continuous stream of overhead intelligence for the critical few years ahead until satellite reconnaissance systems came online.

Technologically equipped for the challenge, the intelligence community was also keenly cognizant that peripheral and overflight missions were intensely provocative. The challenge for all was to develop a practice that would provide the needed intelligence without further roiling international relations. A technological fix and an operating practice that would provide the intelligence needed for the short term, until satellite surveillance became a reality.

Satellite reconnaissance*

Millennia before flight, military strategists recognized the value of holding the highest ground on a battlefield. By the mid-20th century, highest ground was reckoned at somewhere beyond the stratosphere. An orbiting camera would be much more difficult to disable than cameras carried in balloons and aircraft.

The idea of using satellites for overflight reconnaissance had its roots in a RAND Corporation study that gained limited traction within the Air Force when it was issued in 1946. But in 1953 the Air Force confirmed that it was feasible to produce relatively small and lightweight thermonuclear warheads. "As a result, the Atlas ICBM program was accorded the highest priority in the Air Force. Since the propulsion required to place a satellite in orbit is of the same general order of magnitude as that required to launch an ICBM, the achievement of this level of propulsion made it possible to begin thinking seriously of launching orbital satellites."[17] Subsequent RAND studies and associated developments within the Air Force culminated in a RAND recommendation in March 1954 that the Air Force undertake "the earliest possible completion and use of an efficient satellite reconnaissance vehicle" as a matter of "vital strategic interest to the United States."[18] This report was issued almost concurrently with the awarding of the U-2 contract to Lockheed. On the basis of this thinktank recommendation, the Air Forces Air Research and Development Command officially proposed a satellite development program in November 1954—roughly the same time that the joint CIA-USAF U-2 Aquatone/Oilstone program and the Black Knight program had been launched. The 1950s was developing into a hotbed of development for the nation's reconnaissance programs.

The American development plan proposed full operational capability by mid-1963, but even that nine-year timeline seemed at times to be unreasonably short. The program continued with varying levels of interest, fluctuating support, and technical setbacks.

---

* For more detail on the Corona program, see Appendix 2 on page 259.

And then, in October 1957: Sputnik. The Soviets' success in being the first to occupy the "highest ground" sent a shock wave through the American populace and provided a tremendous impetus for advancing America's space program.[19]

Collectively, Sputnik I and II had a "Pearl Harbor" effect on public opinion, and introduced into space affairs the issues of national pride and international prestige—along with fear over the potential militarization of space.

By the end of 1957 the satellite-based reconnaissance concept was generally accepted by the Air Force, CIA, and significantly, the White House, at which time it was agreed that the US's satellite systems would operate covertly. Satellite surveillance was "going black," and the CIA assigned the code title Corona to the covert program.[20]

Since the Corona program would require many missile launches, events impossible to shield from the public, the press, or the Soviets, a cover story was developed and promulgated that announced that the SAMOS photo reconnaissance portion of the WS-117L program, a DOD program well known by the Soviets and the American public, was being discontinued, and was being replaced by a program for scientific collection and research. That cover story would permit the intelligence community to develop, launch, and test a space-based reconnaissance system completely in the dark, under the cloak of scientific research. As conceived by the CIA, "the key element was to be a very tight security wrap around the reconnaissance phase and a concurrent, highly-publicized scientific satellite effort based on the Thor-Hustler rocket combination."[21]

The "open" scientific research aspect of this project would be termed the Discoverer project, an elaborate façade covering the development and initial operation of the Corona reconnaissance satellite. Discoverer missions would feature prominently in the media for many years to follow, a public confirmation that the United States was effectively dealing with the Soviet advances in space technology.

Once underway, Discoverer made a fast start. The first launch, Discoverer I, came on February 28, 1959 and both it and the second launch, Discoverer II in April, established usable orbits. From this encouraging beginning, the next 10 Discoverer launches in the ensuing 12 months were marked by frequent and sometimes spectacular failures, due to a wide range of system malfunctions: on six flights the second stage failed; on four the failure was due to camera problems, the orbiting vehicle, or the reentry system.

By the end of 1959, the CIA and the intelligence community, fervently hoping that Corona would yield clarifying photographic reconnaissance data, had become alarmed. Eight Thor-Agena rocket combinations, and five very costly cameras, had been expended without yielding any intelligence data.

No less alarmed was the president, who anticipated that this intelligence would shape important decisions on national defense, most especially, what to do about the latest fear gripping the media and the American public: the "missile gap."

The American perception at that time was that the Soviet Union, as evidenced by its successful Sputnik launch, had stolen the march to space. Chillingly, in late 1957 Soviet Premier Khrushchev fueled the American angst by asserting that important advances in missile technology had resulted in a Soviet missile that could reach any point on the globe.[22] A month later a member of the Soviet Foreign Ministry privately asserted that: "Soviet ICBMs

Discovery/Corona Satellite Imagery. Mys Shmidta Air Field, USSR. August 18, 1960. (National Reconnaissance Office)

are at present in mass production."[23] By that point in time, America had not only failed to develop a sound ICBM system but was still having difficulty with its medium-range ballistic missile.

The American intelligence estimates of the actual count of Soviet ICBMs varied widely. One Air Force report projected that the Soviets would have 700 operational ICBMs by mid-1963—an order of magnitude more than the United States could hope to deploy. In order to determine the proper American response, the president needed to know if Khrushchev was lying, and that would best be determined through photo intelligence.

While the American public watched, and the intelligence community waited, testing of the launch vehicles doggedly continued, as did testing of the various onboard control systems, communications, and cameras. To everyone's relief, the first major success in the program came with Discoverer XIII on August 10, 1960. That launch, essentially a diagnostic flight designed to assess the performance of the flight systems, attained the correct orbit and correctly jettisoned its payload capsule, which was then successfully recovered. In this diagnostic flight, no camera was involved in the mission. But for the Air Force and the CIA, this was what success looked like.

Discoverer XIII dovetailed beautifully with the Air Force and CIA fixed-wing programs. During the period 1956–1960, a period of frantic development of the Corona satellite, the U-2 was a godsend for the American intelligence community and for the American president. Without the U-2, the nation's leadership would have either been blind to Soviet military developments or would have been required to send lower-altitude RB-57 missions on overflights that would have been increasingly fatal, and which could have brought Russia and the United States closer to war. The U-2 was the short-term but critical bridge to space reconnaissance.

U-2 pilot selection and training

Pilots for the initial U-2 program were selected from the current Air Force reserve ranks, but the covert nature of the operation required that the pilots be willing to resign from the Air Force and assume civilian status—a process that came to be known as "sheep-dipping." The CIA offered handsome salaries for those willing to make the move, and the Air Force promised to return the candidate to his unit at the end of his two-year CIA contract, with no loss of eligible promotion during the period.

U-2 pilots were selected from Air Force pilots, mostly first lieutenants and second lieutenants, and they were told that they would be flying a secret airplane, were to *sign a contract for two years and would make $25,000 a year. It doesn't sound like much now, but they were making $6,000 a year at that time in the Air Force, so it was four times what they were making. But it was a high-risk type of operation. The selected pilots trained at the secret base in Nevada, like the SR71 did later.*

"Because of the strain involved in flying at extreme altitude for long periods of time, painstaking efforts were made to exclude all pilots who might be nervous or unstable in any way," according to the Lovelace Foundation for Medical Education and Research under contract to the CIA. The Air Force and the CIA operated parallel recruitment operations, each with its own criteria for pilot selection. "The CIA's insistence on more stringent physical and mental examinations than those used by the Air Force to select pilots for its U-2 fleet resulted in a higher rejection rate of candidates. The Agency's selection criteria remained high throughout its manned overflight program and resulted in a much lower accident rate for CIA U-2 pilots than for their counterparts in the Air Force program."[24]

In the unique partnership that characterized the Aquatone/Oilstone U-2 program, the USAF—specifically the Strategic Air Command—was responsible for pilot training. Lockheed test pilots first trained a cadre of six USAF pilots, who upon qualification then trained the incoming cohort of "sheep-dipped" candidates. Typical training for contract pilots would include 130 hours or more of flight time and include 60 or more landings. New pilots, most of who were operating in a novel, top-secret environment, learned that the aircraft was both delicate in construction, and required unique and complex flight piloting.

About the U-2

The description of the U-2 as a jet-powered glider is indeed apt. The high-aspect wings designed by Lockheed resulted in a glide ratio of 23:1—comparable to the best gliders of the time. And like gliders, it was a lightly built aircraft. Weight was sacrificed in the quest for altitude. A reduction of one pound in weight would result in another foot of altitude. And the light weight of the aircraft permitted it to carry a high fuel load, which allowed very long flights.

Engine thrust is, in part, a function of altitude: at altitudes above 60,000 ft., the U-2's engine generated just 6 percent of the thrust attainable at sea level, and that required that the airframe design generate an unprecedented amount of lift.

Minimizing the aircraft weight influenced its durability. The relatively frail design was a key reason the USAF had been initially uninterested in the aircraft: design specifications at that time for USAF aircraft required that the aircraft be able to function in combat operations, and meeting that specification required the addition of weaponry and armor plating. The added weight would have meant that the aircraft could never have attained the desired altitude, making it vulnerable to opposing fighters and ground fire. Gregory recalls: *When they built the very first ones, they were pretty flimsy by design, and they didn't think it was going to last more than about two or three flights, but it's still flying today after all these years.*

Everything about the aircraft seemed designed to challenge the pilot. The U-2's flight controls were much like those used in the P-38 fifteen years earlier. Cables and pulleys activated the ailerons and rudder—nothing was hydromechanically boosted. And since it operated for much of each mission at very high altitudes, the pilot controls were geared for high altitude. Light control inputs were sufficient at altitude, but at lower altitudes, control inputs had to be extreme. As a result, the aircraft was equipped with a control yoke, just like the P-38 fighter, that permitted the pilot to apply more force to the control surfaces. Pilot Martin Knutson described the U-2 as "the highest workload airplane I believe ever designed and built… you're wrestling with the airplane and operating the camera systems at all times," leaving no time to "worry about whether you're over Russia or you're flying over southern California." [25] Francis Gary Powers agreed. "Having to navigate, compute ATAs and ETA, turn on the switches as the designated points, pay constant attention to the instruments to keep from exceeding the Mach limitation on the high side and stall the aircraft on the low side, and with the variance in speed also affecting fuel consumption—my work was cut out." [26]

Like the RB-57D, but to a greater degree, the U-2's unique design made it susceptible to both high-altitude stalls, and to high-altitude buffeting. Stalls resulted from too low an airspeed and inadequate lift on the wings. The flat spins that followed a stall could tear the aircraft asunder. In contrast, high-altitude buffeting, or Mach buffeting, resulted from operating the aircraft at too high a speed. The U-2 was designed with a critical not-to-exceed speed, or Mach number, which was determined by altitude. Exceeding that speed causes a shock wave to form as the air flows over the wings' upper surface, and the resultant turbulence causes a flutter of the control surfaces and wings, which could also result in the aircraft coming apart.

With stall speed and Mach speed varying with altitude, the pilots were challenged to operate the aircraft fast enough to prevent a stall, but slowly enough to prevent buffeting. In modern jets, the margin between stall speed and Mach speed is wide. But at the ultra-high altitudes in which the U-2 operated, the stall speed and the Mach speeds approached the same number. In fact, if a pilot turned too sharply, the inside wing could be in "stall buffet" (going too slowly) while the outside wing could be in "Mach buffet" (too fast).[27] In the majority of missions, the pilots had a very narrow window in which to maintain safe operations; as little as five knots when at altitude. Pilots were dependent on the aircraft's much-improved autopilot to keep in the correct flight configuration, and detailed flight profiles were provided to the pilots for each mission, advising them precisely how to operate.

The tremendous lift off the U-2's wings resulted in short takeoffs and low takeoff speeds. But the same lift that made it possible for the U-2 to take off quickly and attain unprecedented altitudes also made it exceptionally difficult to land the aircraft. Nearing the ground, the aircraft would begin to feel ground effects, causing it to "float" over the tarmac. A bounce that might result from a too-rough landing could easily send the aircraft back into flight.

The aircraft had an astonishing climb rate—15,000 feet per minute of sustained flight. It climbed so rapidly through the vertical that icing was never a problem; it flew through moisture-laden cells so quickly that ice did not accumulate.

The aircraft's landing gear was also problematic. To reduce weight, traditional landing gear designs were discarded in favor of a bicycle configuration that consisted of a main set of tandem wheels located just aft of the cockpit, and an in-line set of smaller wheels at the tail. Since this design did not allow the aircraft to taxi in balance, a set of supplemental supports called "pogos" were affixed to each wing, which then dropped to the ground immediately after takeoff.

Landing was also unconventional. As the wheels touched down and the aircraft slowed, one of the wings would settle to the ground, riding on sacrificial skids until the aircraft came to a stop.

It's not all that fast, cruising at about Mach .72, but it's very air-worthy, and it handles OK once you get it in the air. But the worst part of it, it's difficult to land. It's kind of like a kite—it wants to continue to fly.

Specifications: Lockheed U-2S[28]

Powerplant: 1, GE Turbofan, 17,000 lbs. thrust
Crew: 1
Max speed: 500 mph.
Service ceiling: 70,000 + ft.
Range: 6,405 miles
Takeoff weight: 40,000 lbs.
Wing span: 103 ft.

Length: 63 ft.
Height: 16 ft.
Production: 104

While U-2 pilots were outfitted with pressure suits as a precaution against a sudden cabin depressurization, decompression sickness (DCS) remained a significant and persistent hazard for U-2 pilots. A potentially fatal condition, DCS is caused by the formation of nitrogen bubbles in the blood and tissue following a decrease in air pressure. Also common in scuba divers, symptoms of DCS vary widely and range from mild joint pain to serious neurological symptoms, including worsening concentration, confusion, fatigue, and headache.

U-2 pilots were significantly at risk because of the long duration of their flights at extreme altitude—up to nine hours at over 70,000 feet. The aircraft's cabin was pressurized, but only to an equivalent altitude of 35,000 feet. Though well supplied with oxygen in flight, the U-2 pilots operated in a pressure environment equivalent to standing atop Mt. Everest.

Precautions such as the pre-breathing lounge chairs prevented deaths or serious injury to U-2 pilots for over five decades of the aircraft's operational life, but that is not to say the pilots were immune to DCS: 70 percent of pilots reported at least one episode of DCS during their service, and of those, nearly 13 percent were severe enough to require a change in mission or to cause a mission-abort.[29]

Initial flight testing and early U-2 operations had been perilous. By the end of 1956 three accidents had occurred in which pilots were killed, along with other non-fatal accidents. By 1960, the initial 20-aircraft fleet of CIA aircraft had been reduced by five. By 1966, sixteen of those original twenty would crash or disintegrate in flight, with ten pilots killed.

U-2 operations

There was an element of perfection in USAF and CIA plans to operate effective high-altitude surveillance over the Soviet Union. In the RB-57D and U-2 aircraft, they possessed platforms that were made operational in short order, and which they expected would be impervious to Soviet interdiction for at least two years. And while those systems were deployed and generating solid intelligence, the Air Force and CIA continued to shepherd their ultimate system—satellite surveillance—through the myriad administrative, managerial and technical issues on the way to an effective system.

Like the CIA's Corona satellite program, the covert U-2 program was given a cover story for the aircraft and its missions in the event an aircraft were lost

U-2 at Groom Lake, NV. Note the NACA tail markings. (NSA archives)

over hostile territory. With the concurrence of the director of the National Advisory Committee for Aeronautics (NACA), the precursor to NASA, the CIA promulgated the fiction that the U-2 was intended to be used by NACA for high-altitude weather research. And in support of that story, U-2s several times took weather photographs that appeared in the press.

This approach was not agreeable to two of the U-2's earliest and most influential supporters, civilian advisers Edwin Land and James Killian. They advised that in case of an aircraft loss, the United States forthrightly acknowledge its use of U-2 overflights "to guard against surprise attack." Their advice unheeded, the weather cover story contributed to the diplomatic disaster that would soon overtake the U-2 program.[30,31]

This ruse required that the aircraft, ostensibly operating as Air Force aircraft and flying from Air Force bases, would need to fit within the AF organization. Accordingly, within the Air Force, the U-2 operating units were designated as "Weather Reconnaissance Squadrons, Provisional." The provisional designation meant that the detachments did not have to report to higher headquarters, and lent greater security to the U-2 detachments. Within the CIA, these operating units were designated as "detachments," with the first two being designated simply Detachment A and Detachment B.

Initial detachments

President Eisenhower reserved for himself the approval of Soviet or Soviet bloc overflights, and his decisions always involved an excruciating analysis of the balance between risk and reward. Overflights were approved only with great reluctance.

In the mid-1950s, while the U-2 was still under development, Eisenhower continued to hope for a way to acquire the information his intelligence organizations required, but within the framework of accepted international law—that is to say, without violating Soviet airspace with overflight missions. At the 1955 Geneva Summit, with the first U-2 test flight just one month ahead, the president proposed to Soviet Premier Nikolai Bulganin and General Secretary Nikita Khrushchev that the Soviet Union and the United States agree to permit overt surveillance overflights of each other's territory—"mutual aerial observation"—to prove that neither country was preparing for a surprise attack. Khrushchev, believing that the overture was intended primarily to identify potential targets in the Soviet Union, rejected this "Open Skies" proposal.[32]

Eisenhower's Defense Liaison Officer, General Goodpaster, noted that Khrushchev's somewhat characteristically earthy response to the proposal was a repeated "Nyet," accompanied with a wagging finger, and the roughly translated comment, "You're simply trying to look into our bedrooms."[33]

Following this diplomatic setback, Eisenhower and his intelligence experts were left with limited options. The RB-47 and other surveillance aircraft could conduct peripheral and, rarely, overflight missions but in doing so could easily be detected, tracked, and occasionally shot down. All awaited the U-2, which would undergo its first test hop on August 1, 1955.

And in the interim, President Eisenhower continued to receive assurances from some advisors that the U-2 could neither be detected nor tracked.

The CIA's Detachment A—Weather Reconnaissance Squadron, Provisional (WRSP-1)—received deployment orders on May 1, 1956—less than a year after the U-2's first test flight, and almost to the day that Greg reported for duty with the 4025th Reconnaissance Squadron and its contingent of RB-57D Black Knight aircraft. Two U-2s were dispatched to Lakenheath, England, but by June the unit had moved to bases in Germany. The orders referred to the 95-man detachment, ranging from GS-7s to GS-14s, as "Department of Air Force Civilians."[34,35]

At the same time, the Turkish government had granted permission for the CIA to use the airfield at Incirlik, near Adana, and Detachment B (WRSP-2) deployed to that base in late August, 1956. The detachment's first operational mission came in November, with CIA contract pilot Francis Gary Powers at the controls.

Detachment C (WRSP-3) was the third and last group of American pilots to receive training for the CIA. It was activated in July 1956, received its first aircraft in August, and deployed to Atsugi, Japan in March 1957.

Initial Soviet overflights

Initial overflights from Germany of Eastern Bloc countries came on June 20 and July 2, 1956, and were essentially a dress rehearsal for overflights of the Soviet Union. The U-2s were equipped with ELINT systems, much like those used on the RB-57 peripheral missions, which would indicate to the pilots if their aircraft had been detected or were being tracked by Soviet ground-based radar signals.

In what would be an unexpected development and bitter disappointment to many, and a source of great embarrassment to others, Eastern European radars were successful in detecting these first missions. It became apparent that the Soviets had improved their early warning radars. Soviet Premier Nikita Khrushchev further fueled tensions when he advised visiting U.S. diplomats in mid-1956 to "Stop sending intruders into our airspace. We will shoot down uninvited guests. We will get all of your Canberras. They are flying coffins." He was obviously angered by the overflights, and though unaware of the U-2, his sentiments were nonetheless clear.[36]

On the very first U-2 flight, the US knew that the Soviet radars were detecting and sometimes tracking ("painting") the U-2s. We also knew that the Soviets were determined to get that airplane. They were sending up MiGs on every flight to shoot the U-2. The Soviet MiGS would try high speed to zoom up, but they were not successful at all. But we had forecast that at some point we were going to lose one.

Though detected, the missions were considered a success, and yielded good photographic intelligence, giving the starving intelligence community a taste of what was possible with the new system. The CIA began pressing President Eisenhower for authority to begin Soviet overflights, but Eisenhower demurred. As historian Gregory Pedlow notes, "The President was obviously concerned that the CIA estimates that the U-2 could fly virtually undetected were proving false. One of the reasons why he had approved the overflight program was the CIA's assurance that the Soviet Union would remain unaware of the flights or—at the very worst—receive only occasional, vague indications."[37]

Recognizing that the U-2 could not operate undetected, the issue for Eisenhower then became whether it could be tracked. Successfully tracking the spyplane meant that Soviet air defenses could be brought to bear, and increased the likelihood that the plane could be shot down. For assurances on this point, the president had to rely on the same people who had earlier promised it would not be detected.

Despite this unsettling dilemma, President Eisenhower approved an aggressive 10-mission series of Soviet overflights, commencing with a July 4 overflight of Leningrad followed one day later by an overflight of Moscow itself. By July 10, a total of five overflights had been conducted, and to the consternation of all, it was confirmed that "the Soviet air defense system was able to *track* U-2s well enough to attempt interception, but that the fighter aircraft then available to the Soviet Union in 1956 could not bring down a U-2 at operational altitude."[38]

The Soviets responded with a strong protest, stating that the flights could only be "intentional and conducted for the purpose of intelligence."[39] These were exceedingly harrowing times for the White House. Events were moving quickly, and the president could get no consensus from his advisors regarding the risks of these missions.

By mid-July 1956, Ike's alarm deepened over the ability of the Soviets to track the U-2s, and he ordered a halt to overflights. In the complex matrix of international diplomacy, domestic policy, and national defense, the president was ultimately concerned about the violation of international law that the U-2 missions represented, citing "Soviet protests were one thing, any loss of confidence by our own people would be quite another."[40]

The CIA immediately began to develop systems to reduce the U-2's radar cross-section in Project Rainbow, but these early efforts at stealth technology were not successful.

The quality of intelligence provided by the five Soviet overflight missions conducted in mid-1956 was stunning. These U-2 missions photographed nine Soviet bomber bases, as well as the manufacturing plant near Moscow where the bombers were built. None of the new M-4 bombers were seen at any of the nine Soviet long-range bomber bases, disproving the Air Force estimate that the Soviets were already in possession of almost 100, and effectively dispelling the persistent "bomber gap" worry. This was critical information that permitted the president to eliminate the enormously expensive requests for additional B-52 bombers by the Air Force.

In the four years to follow, the American defense leadership—included elected, civilian and military, adopted a pattern of on-again/off-again overflights. Eisenhower approved a December 1956 overflight of Vladivostok by RB-57D (Black Knight) aircraft, on the assurance that the high-speed '57s would not be detected. In fact, they were detected, and the vigorous Soviet protest that resulted caused the president to again forbid overflights of communist territory. His decision brought an end to the military's four-year-old SENSINT program, and henceforth the intelligence community would rely exclusively on the U-2 for overflight imagery.

In May 1957, Eisenhower again authorized limited Soviet overflights, which would yield a trove of intelligence data, including photographs of Soviet nuclear and missile test sites, and the discovery of the never-before-seen Baikonur Cosmodrome. Then, following an overflight in March 1958 that Eisenhower had approved, but which drew an especially vigorous Soviet protest, the president ordered a stand-down for the U-2 that was to continue for 16 months.

National concern over a perceived "missile gap" caused Eisenhower to change his mind again. In early July 1959, the president authorized a single overflight, which yielded excellent photographs of the Soviet missile launch facilities at Tyuratam. No further overflights were made during 1959.

By 1960 the Defense Department and CIA were no longer blind. Although overflights had become a rarity, peripheral missions were being conducted regularly, and the state of intelligence had improved immeasurably. Still, the intelligence community was increasingly alarmed at their inability to prove or disprove the specter of Soviet ICBM missiles. CIA Director Dulles is reported to have been "determined to obtain permission for more overflights in order to settle the missile-gap question once and for all and end the debate within the intelligence community.[41]

Concurrently, the president was equally intent on reaching a diplomatic accord that would lessen the Soviet-American Cold War strains. The pace of technological developments by both sides had reached fever pitch, with rhetoric becoming increasingly strident, and threats overt. Preparing for the Paris Summit in mid-May 1960, with its primary focus on nuclear disarmament, Eisenhower hoped for a de-escalation of tensions.

Cognizant of the delicacy of the upcoming negotiations, but facing increasingly sharp requests from his intelligence community, Eisenhower approved two additional overflights with the provision that they must be completed by May 1.

As will be seen, the first of these two flights occurred on April 9 and was completed without problems. The second mission was scheduled for May 1 and was to have a profound effect on American-Soviet relations and on the American intelligence community. And it would absolutely determine the future career of Lt. Col. William Gregory.

CHAPTER 10

U-2 Shootdown

By 1960, overflights of the Soviet Union had been occurring intermittently for four years, always detected and tracked, always with a Soviet interception attempted but never succeeding. All involved in U-2 operations, including pilots, were aware that overflights had become much riskier. Soviet improvements to their surface-to-air missiles had steadily increased the danger for these missions, and led the CIA to conclude internally in March that Soviet SAMS had "a high probability of a successful intercept at 70,000 feet (21,300 m) providing that detection is made in sufficient time to alert the site."[1]

Gregory recalls: *The CIA was trying to determine how long they would be able to continue these overflights. In mid-1956 they initially thought that it would be safe for at least two years. By 1960 they had been flying over three years, and still had not been shot down.*

Offsetting this risk was the indispensable nature of the intelligence that was generated by the U-2s: by this time, it was the most significant source of covert intelligence on the Soviet Union. Vast swaths of the Soviet Union had been photographed in close resolution, and nearly 5,500 separate intelligence reports had been generated. Twenty-two overflights had already been completed by February 1960, with two more scheduled in the final days before Eisenhower's crucial meetings at the Paris Summit.[2]

The overflight risks were mounting, but the president was intent on receiving as much data as possible on Soviet ICBM deployments before negotiations began at the Paris conference. Now more than ever, intelligence equated to strength.

At this most critical juncture, the Corona satellite system was on the verge of operational status. But intelligence planners had no way of knowing the first solid intelligence from Corona would come later in the year, in August, with the Discoverer XIV mission. They were reluctant to shelve a proven reconnaissance platform on the basis of positive expectations for future Corona flights, and they could ill afford to wait.

To this point, the intelligence community, and therefore the president, continued to be plagued with uncertainty regarding the speculated "missile gap" with the Soviet Union. One ICBM site was known to exist at Yurya, in the north. Another probable site was at Plesetsk. It was anticipated that a further site, so far undetected, would be found in the south.

The first of the missions approved by President Eisenhower was flown on April 9 by CIA pilot Bob Ericson. Flying from Peshawar, Pakistan, Ericson's course took him in a northward direction, bisecting Kazakhstan, then eastward to the region above Mongolia before wheeling back through Kazakhstan, over the Soviet nuclear missile site at Tyuratam and then returning to Peshawar. Ericson's mission was the fourth in a series of overflights originating from Peshawar, all with Tyuratam as a primary surveillance target. Like all previous flights, Ericson's mission was completed successfully.

The second mission, piloted by Francis Gary Powers, the CIA's most experienced pilot with 27 prior U-2 missions to his credit, was more ambitious.[3] Ericson's previous flight had been, like all prior U-2 missions over the Soviet Union, a "there-and-back" mission, overflying a relatively small sector of Soviet territory. In contrast, Powers' mission, codename *Grand Slam*, would transit the entire Soviet Union from south to north, originating at Peshawar and ending at Bodo, Norway. The mission intended to first overfly the Tyuratam Missile Test Range. Then, knowing that the Soviet ICBMs were closely dependent on the rail system, the CIA directed Powers to photograph railroad networks in the north-central region of the Soviet Union, generating information the CIA could use to locate and characterize new Soviet SS-6 ICBM nuclear sites.

The CIA had carefully considered other flight paths to accomplish this mission—codenames *Sun Spot*, *Square Deal*, and *Time Step*. But in opting against *Time Step*, CIA planners had noted: "We can assume with a 90 percent probability of being correct, that (the aircraft) will be detected upon entry, tracked accurately throughout the period of denied territory, and will evoke a strong Soviet air defense reaction. This flight plan would permit alerting of SAM sites and preposition of missile-equipped fighters thus enhancing the possibility of a successful intercept."[4]

Time Step, judged too risky by the CIA, would involve overflight of denied territory for a period of four hours: *Grand Slam* would be nine. If the Soviets were able to track Powers' aircraft early in the mission, it would place him in great jeopardy.

And that is precisely what happened. Powers' U-2 lifted off from Peshawar in the early morning hours of May 1, 1960; Soviet radar began tracking him when he was still 15 miles south of the Soviet-Afghan border and continued to do so as he flew across the Central Asian republics.

Four hours into the mission, with Powers deep into Soviet airspace, his autopilot began to malfunction. *Normally this would have been an abort situation, but Powers was already far into the mission. He did everything he could to get the autopilot working again, while continuing to hand-fly the airplane, and was intent on completing the mission with or without the autopilot.*

Thirty minutes later, a Soviet SA-2 surface-to-air missile detonated just behind Powers' aircraft, knocking off its tail at 70,500 ft.[5]

Following the first mission flown by Ericson we learned later that the Soviets had developed a new MiG that could have shot down Ericson's U-2 on his mission, but it didn't. For some reason they didn't find him, so the MiG ran low on fuel and had to land. Otherwise, we could have lost the U-2 on the first mission, instead of the second mission.

With great difficulty, Powers was able to extricate himself from the damaged aircraft and successfully made the 12-mile parachute descent. Captured by local farmers, Powers would eventually be tried, convicted, and sentenced to 10 years in confinement for espionage. After two years' imprisonment, Powers was exchanged for a Soviet spy and returned to the United States.

The international furor over the downing of a U-2 created a diplomatic windfall for Khrushchev and was a disaster for America's international standing, and for its intelligence community. The president's advisors had by this time abandoned any hope that the aircraft would avoid detection, but counseled the president that the pilot could not have survived the shootdown or the descent from 70,000 feet.

At first the mission directors didn't know what had happened to him. They didn't know if he had been killed or not and put out the erroneous message that he had been flying along the border and he had a compass error and inadvertently strayed inside the Soviet Union. It was a terrible story, and they shouldn't have done this. Powers was several hundred miles inside the Soviet Union when he was shot down. Khrushchev hadn't said anything for the next three days, but then produced a healthy Gary Powers and pictures of the aircraft wreckage.

So we really got a black eye for this. What they should've done is just simply told the truth. There was utter chaos in Washington as a result.

Greg is not alone in his criticism of how the crisis was managed. Former White House Defense Liaison Officer General Goodpaster later reflected: "I have to tell you that the handling of that critical international situation, and it was critical, was about as clumsy in my opinion as anything our government has ever done. I can say that because I had a hand in that business. We had absolutely failed to consider the many "what ifs" of the U-2 overflights in a thorough, realistic, and searching manner."[6]

The president would have been angry and distressed at the lack of preparedness for this loss. As early as 1952, when he was being asked to approve Soviet over-flights, his Air Force liaison advised the Joint Chiefs: "The President expressed concern at the possibility of loss of the B-47 type aircraft to the Soviets and the consequent compromising of our latest equipment. He wished to make sure that the Joint Chiefs had considered this aspect of the problem as an added element of risk."[7] His concern was certainly justified: eight years later, with a different aircraft involved, and despite many assurances, his fears had come to pass.

Eisenhower's much anticipated Paris Summit ended almost as soon as it had begun, with the Soviets demanding an apology, and Eisenhower refusing to give one.

Almost concurrently, NASA elected to end its support of the cover story that the U-2s were conducting weather research under the NASA aegis, stating internally that the agency "would be well advised to disengage from the U-2 program as rapidly as possible."[8]

The combined effect of these developments effectively paralyzed the US fixed-wing reconnaissance community, forced immediate changes in policy, procedures and security protocols, and brought an end to U-2 operations from foreign bases. Historian Robert Cargill Hall comments: "With that loss, the imagery intelligence produced by America's overhead aerial assets went dark—and prom-ised to stay that way until a reconnaissance satellite could be made to work."[9]

In August, the decision was made by the CIA to bring both U-2 units back from Incirlik and Atsugi, along with all personnel and equipment, for relocation to the ultra-secure Edwards Air Force Base in California. Both Detachments B and C were dissolved. HQ decided to release some of its long-serving drivers back to the Air Force. Others were retained out of necessity: it was simply too difficult to obtain and train new pilots. A new unit—Detachment G—would become the CIA's sole functioning U-2 unit and would be staffed with just eight pilots from Detachment B, and three from C, plus a handful of U-2 aircraft, some partially dismantled. With the U-2 now in the public eye, Lockheed's Kelly Johnson no longer saw the need for maintaining an expensive covert contingent at the Edwards North Base, and moved the inspection and repair program for the Air Force U-2 fleet to the Lockheed plant in Burbank.

The Powers aftermath

These final two U-2 overflight missions—the 23rd and 24th—had been conducted by Detachment B from the U-2 base at Incirlik, Turkey. At the same time in Incirlik, Lt. Col. Gregory's unit—the 4025th, equipped with RB-57D-2 ELINT aircraft under the Black Knight Program—was conducting reconnaissance missions along the Soviet border from the hangar adjacent to the U-2s of Detachment B. The Black Knight Program had been designed as a four-year, stop-gap program, and was scheduled to be terminated after Operation *Dip Stick* was complete. In the days leading to the Powers overflight, Greg believed that the 4025th's missions of March and April 1960 would be its last. And they were.

While I was deployed to Incirlik, in April, I got a message that I was to report to CIA headquarters, to be interviewed for an assignment. So I left Incirlik, spent three days at Langley, and then was returned to Laughlin AFB at Del Rio, Texas which was our station at that time. In about a week I got notice that I had been selected for Operations Officer at the U-2 unit at Atsugi, in Japan—Detachment C, the Asian counterpart to the unit at Incirlik. I was going to get to take my wife and two daughters overseas for the first time.

Greg was a natural selection for this assignment: he already had long experience in the high-altitude program and had effectively managed reconnaissance deployments. He did not think that the new assignment would represent any significant changes for him. His new assignment to the Agency involved changes in only two respects: he would now fly a different aircraft and would operate under a different security regime.

Greg was fairly well familiar with the U-2 at this point. The Air Force was operating U-2s in the 4028th Squadron at the same time Greg was flying RB-57s with the 4025th Squadron, both being within the 4080th Wing. The facility used by the 4025th at Incirlik was immediately adjacent to that used for the U-2s, and further, while at Laughlin with the 4025th Greg regularly attended staff meetings called by the wing commander and would hear the reports of the 4028th.

For the Gregorys, the move to a new job, at a new location, would be routine—a seamless transition for an experienced Air Force family. *By the first of May we had gotten our shots and inoculations, and our passports were ready. We had already sent our household baggage to Japan, and were waiting for travel confirmation. When we heard that Powers had been shot down, we knew that everything had changed. It was a terrible mess. It seemed like no one knew what to do, after they had bungled that announcement. And it really put President Eisenhower in a terrible situation.*

Still at Del Rio, Greg finally received orders in late August. By this time, he and Helen had attended several "Sayonara" parties, and the entire family had undergone the standard series of immunizations in preparation for their assignment in Japan. The children received multiple smaller doses, requiring a total of fifteen shots. *That was a lot for a six-year-old to endure.*

So it was embarrassing to receive orders, not to Atsugi as they had hoped, but to the North Base at Edwards Air Force Base, adjacent to the Air Force's Flight Test Center: a satellite World War II base that had been used very little since then.

Detachment G

By the spring of 1957, increased aboveground atomic testing near the Groom Lake U-2 site had created difficulties for the Aquatone project, and led the Air Force to relocate its now fully operational U-2 fleet to Laughlin AFB. Follow-on testing of the U-2 would continue at Edwards Air Force Base (North). The Edwards unit was designated the Weather Reconnaissance Squadron, Provisional (IV), and became operational on June 20 under the command of Lieutenant Colonel Roland Perkins, who had previously served as Operations Officer of Detachment B at Incirlik, Turkey.

From 1957 to 1960, the years immediately preceding Powers' shootdown and Greg's assignment to Detachment G, the Edwards unit conducted a range of tests on the U-2 platform, including systems to reduce the radar profile of the U-2—Project Rainbow—the evaluation of camouflage paint for the U-2, the use of slipper tanks for adding range, camera systems, and a new dual oxygen system.

The Gregorys arrive at Edwards

Instead of Japan, the family's next stop was the Mojave Desert, Edwards AFB. *When we arrived Edwards looked like the end of the earth, and it was in fact in the middle of nowhere: 35 miles from the nearest town, while the nearest Air Force unit was 10 miles away.*

Helen was disappointed to miss the opportunity to live in Japan, but she had lived in Pomona while Greg was posted to Ontario AAF, and had found that living in the pleasant California climate, amidst citrus orchards and near the Pacific Ocean, was very much to her liking.

On the drive to Edwards, seeing fewer and fewer citrus orchards, then less and less foliage of any sort, with the terrain giving way to arid desert, Helen began to be alarmed. Passing through the barren approaches to Edwards, Helen turned to Greg and asked: "It does get better than this, doesn't it?" She began to cry when he replied, "No, this is as good as it gets." When she had recovered a bit, she asked: "What did you do to deserve being assigned here?"[10]

The news that the family would be headed for the Mojave Desert gave rise to a vivid image for Greg's daughter Cookie: "I remember well the image of cartoon characters scratching the sand of the desert floor in search of water. That was all I could think of… that we were being sent to the end of the world, where we would be permanently thirsty. It turns out that that mental picture was 100 percent accurate, as we left the tiny town of Lancaster, California to drive 45 minutes straight into the Mojave Desert until arriving at the front gate of Edwards AFB for the first time."[11]

For those in aviation, there were very exciting things taking place on the base. Chuck Yeager, the first man to break the sound barrier, was head of the Flight Test Center, the X-15 was being tested, and many future astronauts were neighbors. Our daughter Cookie's Sunday School teachers were future astronaut Frank Borman and his wife. Gretchen and the Yeager kids were classmates.

Greg's eldest, Gretchen, recalls: "It turns out that everyone at Edwards at that time was doing something on the cusp. The father of one of my classmates flew the mothership for the X-15, and another flew the X-15 itself." From time to time Cookie would be barked at by a "crabby old Colonel" who disagreed with her short-cut along his six-foot cinderblock fence—that was Chuck Yeager. "My second-grade class was filled with children whose fathers, like mine, were spending every day doing something extraordinary—we just didn't know it then."

Cookie would later recall: "And while pretty much everyone seemed to know what everyone else was doing out at Edwards, no one seemed to know what my father was doing. I remember my playmates' fathers "interviewing" me on occasion as if digging for information. Nothing too overt—'So Cookie, your father is Commander of North Base, right?'—but these were the times I remember being aware that I was being asked for information I didn't have."

During the period in which Greg was in command of Detachment G, his pilot cohort included 13 pilots: himself, Albert J. Rand, Edwin K. Jones, James W. Cherbonneaux, Eugene "Buster" Edens, Barry H. Baker, James A. Barnes, Martin A. Knutson, Jacob Kratt, Jr., Glendon K. Dunaway, Robert J. Ericson, Bedford Schmarr and William W. Hall. Eleven of these were among the 30 pilots initially recruited to the CIA's U-2 program four years earlier. All had served in one or more of U-2 Detachments A, B or C prior to their arrival at Edwards and reassignment to Detachment G.

Greg relied heavily on seven of these pilots: Rand, Cherbonneaux, Edens, Baker, Barnes, Knutson and Ericson accounted for 111 of the 125 missions flown during Greg's command.

The commanders of Detachments B and C, all holding the rank of full colonel, had been reassigned after having served almost four years in their posts. When originally ordered to Atsugi, Greg would have assumed the position of Operations Officer—a position suitable for his rank of lieutenant colonel. Reassigned to Detachment G, when he arrived at Edwards he was the senior officer, and took over as acting commander.

Greg's mission as commander of Detachment G was twofold: to develop and maintain an operational capability for the U-2s; and to continue supporting the development and testing activities that the detachment had been conducting prior to his arrival.[12]

But by this time, I was the senior officer among this group, and although I had not yet attained the rank of full colonel, I was named the acting commander of the unit there, which had all the planes they had been flying in both units, plus most of the fliers. Greg's reassignment came as a surprise—at Atsugi, he would not have been in charge of Detachment C. His posting to Edwards did not include a promotion, but did include a higher order of responsibilities.

Project Aquatone had received the new codename "Chalice" in June 1958 when a small Royal Air Force contingent was integrated into Detachment B at Adana. As Commander of Detachment G, Greg reported to the Director of Operations for the U-2 program, Colonel Stan Beerli. Beerli was deeply steeped in the overhead program: he had commanded both Detachments B and C before moving to his current post in August 1959.

Security within Detachment G would be wholly distinct from what Greg had experienced with the Black Knight Program in the 4025th Strategic Reconnaissance Squadron. Flying RB-57Ds out of Laughlin AFB, no effort was made to keep missions a secret. The entire neighboring community was aware of the flight operations at Laughlin, both RB-57Ds and U-2s, and the private civilian publication *Laughlin RECON* was exceptionally well informed about squadron operations. At the time the 4025th reached the end of its service in the spring of 1960, the *RECON* said farewell with an above-the-fold salute to the squadron, including a listing of all the squadron officers, their ranks, and their photographs, with Greg's picture at the top of the page.

Things were much different at Edwards. The CIA had developed an entirely new "compartmented" system to manage the "take" from U-2 missions. "To achieve maximum security, the U-2 program developed its own contract management, administration, financial, logistics, communications, and security personnel, and thus did not need to turn on a day-to-day basis to the Agency directorates for assistance. To reduce the chance of a security breach, the Agency always referred to the aircraft as 'articles.' Similarly, pilots were always called 'drivers.'"[13]

Among other aspects of security, Greg was given a new name for use when the situation warranted: Bill Gray. He was required to send monthly letters to fictional close friends in Mansfield, Louisiana, John and Barbara Smith and their two children, a ruse that he maintained for the many subsequent years when he held a Top Secret security clearance. Messages to his friend were always in code, and the complicated code cypher was based on a short poem: "Nothing else disturbed the gentle dusk that settled down upon the mountain top like a blanket laid quietly over a sleeping child."

Each month Greg would laboriously craft a coded message to his supposed friend, which to the unwitting reader would appear to be a lighthearted note between good friends, but which when decoded would confirm Greg's competence in using the code, as well as his location and status. This fiction would have allowed Greg to get a message back to the CIA in the event he was ever downed or captured in denied territory; thankfully a situation that never developed.

When I arrived, the North Base was a mess. It had been neglected and was very dilapidated. I always thought that if you were head of an organization, it was better to keep folks busy, rather than have them sitting around. One of the first things I thought we should do was to clean the place up a bit, and we got busy in doing that. I also wanted to keep the organization functioning. It is not good for an organization to be idle. So we started flying the airplanes just to keep everything functioning as a unit, keeping the organization active.

President Eisenhower had announced that there would be no more overflights, and the prospects for the future of the program looked bleak. Greg assumed that his job was going to be to deactivate the unit. *We had about 10 U-2s and a squadron that was one of a kind. It included Air Force officers, NCOs and enlisted personnel, CIA specialists for communications and security, civilian pilots, Lockheed civilians serving as mechanics, thirty other specialists who maintained the high-tech cameras, radios, ELINT collection systems, and autopilots, plus four British officers, a flight planner and flight surgeon, and eventually a Navy Lt. Commander.* Within the authorized contingent of 181 personnel, Greg had more civilians that military personnel.[14]

When I first saw this group, I didn't know what to expect as I was accustomed to military personnel looking sharp in uniforms, but it became one of the best organizations I was ever associated with. I was so impressed with the mission-focus of the civilians, as they worked just as hard to insure there were no failures.

Greg had never flown the aircraft that now equipped his command, and it became necessary for him to arrange for himself a short period of transition to the new, rather difficult-to-fly airplane. And like his introduction to the P-38 many years before, his first flight in the U-2 would also be a solo. He used the pilots under him to provide training in the U-2, and with his deep flight experience, he soon qualified in the U-2. As will be seen, Detachment G was sent on many deployments, both within the Zone of the Interior (ZI) and abroad. Greg would go on each deployment, and would always fly the U-2 during each deployment.

It was rare, but not unheard of, for there to be two concurrent U-2 deployments, such as occurred on February 21, 1962, when one contingent was overflying Cuba at the same time a different contingent was operating over Vietnam. With Greg accompanying each deployment, in his absence the remaining team at Edwards was administered by Greg's deputy, and one of the CIA people on staff.

With the Corona satellite system still in its infancy, the CIA was eager to get its reconnaissance function back in action following the Gary Powers incident and was considering other methods of operating the U-2 fleet. Eisenhower's approval or disapproval of proposed U-2 overflights had been heavily influenced by the often intense diplomatic rows that these flights generated, and he was now weathering the storm of controversy surrounding the Powers shootdown. But the value of the overflight function was irrefutable. Historian R. Cargill Hall, noting the costs and benefits from these missions, wrote: "But if overhead reconnaissance efforts eventually prompted an international furor and scuttled a summit conference—they also succeeded spectacularly; they would illuminate the course over which the Cold War would play for the next thirty years."[15]

In late September—just a month after first being assigned to Detachment G—Greg got a call from Washington to advise they were sending a seven-man team out to the Edwards North Base to observe an exercise devised to simulate deploying a U-2 unit overseas, taking two or three aircraft, and conducting three reconnaissance missions with no resupply. This was a significant departure from prior U-2 foreign operations, which had relied for several years on fixed, and well equipped, bases in Japan and Turkey.

Greg and his team developed a plan that would be put into action 24 hours before each mission's takeoff. It provided an uninterrupted block of time for each section to complete their tasks: fueling, sensors, loading the camera, and the all-important navigation plan. Pilots were given a paper copy of the navigation plan, which included specific turn points, altitudes, and target coordinates, and times to camera-on. Carefully timed, the navigation plan was easier to follow when the aircraft took off at the scheduled time because in doing so the pilot would always be in sync with the navigation plan. *It was a good plan that served us well for the next five years, and allowed our sorties to take off on time, which was of great importance in terms of following the navigation plan that was developed during that 24-hour period.*

The pilot had to be a pretty good navigator and had to do [celestial] check points along the way. But there was no pilotage—we had quite a staff of navigators—they did the navigation plan for him, and he just had to follow it.[16] He couldn't do his own detailed navigating on top of everything else. Once he left, there was no communicating back to base, and he did not know anything about the quality of the pictures he was taking. He only knew if the camera was operating or not. And neither did we know. After he landed, we always had a plane to fly the film to DC where it was processed and evaluated.

The inspection team wanted to see three missions during the week-long evaluation, each flight one day apart. During that week all three flights were completed, each mission was off on time, the target tracks were covered very well, and all systems worked perfectly, with no malfunctions. The inspection team commander said that he would report that we had passed.[17]

This evaluation was critical to the continued life of the U-2 program. The positive results indicated that it was no longer necessary for U-2s to be based abroad, that they could be deployed as needed to provide overhead intelligence over whatever hot spot or troublesome action developed, on just 24 hours' notice. Even with its primary mission no longer feasible—overflights of the Soviet Union—the U-2s could still provide critically important overhead intelligence anywhere in the world. Marking this milestone in U-2 operations, the cryptonym for the Agency's U-2 program was changed from "Chalice" to "Idealist."

I was pleased that we had passed this little exercise, though I didn't think it would lead to anything. But in October, just five months after the Powers incident, I received a call from Washington stating that we would deploy a detachment to Laughlin AFB the next day and begin the first overflights of Cuba.

Greg was well familiar with Laughlin and Del Rio, having been commander of the 4025th squadron there. Detachment G would frequently stage out of Laughlin in coming years and on those deployments would share the airfield with the USAF U-2s based there with the 4080th SRW.[18]

Kick Off and *Green Eyes*—prelude to the Bay of Pigs

During late summer of 1960, the CIA was planning a counterrevolutionary invasion of Cuba for the following year, a covert plan to oust Fidel Castro. Like all military, or in this case, paramilitary operations, the first requirement was intelligence, and high-altitude reconnaissance would be a key part of the intelligence-gathering effort.

Detachment G's first operational deployment—the CIA's return to high-altitude reconnaissance following Powers' shootdown—came little more than a month after the unit had been "re-certified" to conduct operations. Two overflights—codename Operation *Kick Off*—were approved by the Joint Chiefs of Staff to obtain intelligence on the order of battle for Cuban air and ground units and to collect geographic data to be used for choosing an invasion site.

With Gary Powers settling into his cell at Vladimir Prison and preparing for the public spectacle that would be his trial, the CIA forged ahead with its intelligence mission and the application of its best asset—the U-2.

Kick Off required that Greg's Detachment G deploy to Laughlin AFB at Del Rio, TX with a relatively Spartan team which included, in addition to Greg, a navigator, weather officer, medical officer, a five-man maintenance team, three technicians for the cameras and sextants, a two-man security team , two drivers and two aircraft. No hangar space would be provided—all maintenance and pilot pre-breathing tasks were to be conducted from within the accompanying C-54 aircraft.

Logistics planning was critical. As a self-supported mission, everything needed was included in the "Go kit," down to #2 pencils and a coffee pot, encompassing 3,500 lbs. of cargo.

The cover story for *Kick Off* was that the Agency U-2s were conducting an operational readiness test at a simulated staging base. Even deployed forward to Del Rio, the flights would be long—over-nine-hour missions covering 4,100 miles. For these missions, all markings were removed from the aircraft, and the pilots were required to remove all personal identification. Phone calls and letters were not permitted. The missions were flown on October 26 and 27, 1960 (Mission Nos. 3001 and 3002, both piloted by Rand) and while the overflights were operationally successful the photo "take" yielded poor photo results due to heavy cloud cover over Cuba.[19]

As the American presidency transitioned from Eisenhower to Kennedy, planning for the Bay of Pigs invasion moved forward. Greg's unit would continue with Cuban overflights, and three additional missions were laid on, codenamed

Operation *Green Eyes*. Greg and his team again deployed to Laughlin and completed the overflights on November 27 and December 5 and 11, 1960 (pilots Jones, Cherbonneaux and Edens), this time with good results. *We pretty well mapped the place, completing several successful flights from the west to east and back again to the western end of the island. We knew where everything was.*

Polecat—prelude to Vietnam

The CIA was entering a phase in which its attention would be increasingly focused on two widely disparate locations: Cuba and Vietnam. And with concerns over political developments in both countries, the CIA began ordering overflight missions—all of which had to be conducted by the CIA's sole remaining unit, Greg's Detachment G.

Southeast Asia had been very much in the CIA's field of focus for some time. As early as 1957, the CIA had been supplying arms to a group of dissident army colonels in support of a coup attempt on Indonesia's then-President Sukarno. In March 1958, the CIA's U-2 Detachment C had moved temporarily from Japan to Cubi Point Naval Air Station in the Philippines to conduct reconnaissance overflights, completing 30 missions by June. Despite the significant commitment of US arms and aircraft, the coup failed.[20]

Later in 1958 and continuing right up to the May 1960 Powers incident, Detachment C made multiple overflights of China, Tibet, and much of Southeast Asia, and regularly flew missions to collect high-altitude air samples seeking evidence of Soviet nuclear tests. With the detachment's withdrawal and dissolution, further overflights in Asia fell to Detachment G at Edwards.

Greg's unit had completed their series of overflights of Cuba in mid-December, 1960. *I was pleased with the timing, as I would be home for Christmas. But two days later I received a call that I was to proceed as quickly as possible to Cubi Point Naval Air Station, adjacent to the big US Naval Base at Subic Bay in the Philippines.* The Agency wanted to conduct overflights of Vietnam and Laos and wanted the first mission flown in early January. Greg would miss Christmas with the family, as it was necessary for him to leave immediately to begin preparing the base for the arrival of his detachment.

We had a hangar at Cubi Point base, and the Navy was a very good host, and never interfered in any way. I tried to keep them informed of what we were doing. There wasn't much to do there—but we were right on the coast, and a lot of the guys liked to swim and snorkel. There was a golf course there available to us, and sometimes we would take a trip to Manila for an overnight stay. It was a very scenic area. We had a luau one time, with a large hog that had been prepared for our group.

The area was subject to severe weather, but the typhoons that appeared to be headed for the base usually turned away in time. On one deployment, though, there was an exception. *The wind blew hard for 24 hours, then about 2 a.m. it got really still. I was asleep but woke up because the noise had changed from very loud rustling of the wind to complete silence. The typhoon had passed right over us. In about 30 minutes, it started blowing in the other direction even harder than it had before. It did a lot of damage, but our airplanes were safe in the hangar, which withstood the high winds. It was a terrible storm—high winds and heavy rains.*

The deployment, Operation *Polecat*, had been ordered by the Eisenhower administration because of the collapse of the neutralist Laotian government in late December, the supply of Soviet arms to leftist antigovernment forces, and the concern over a potential invasion of Laos from North Vietnam and possibly Communist China. Concurrently, a new U-2 unit had been authorized—Detachment H—to be based on Taiwan as a joint operation with the Nationalist Chinese. The detachment received its first two aircraft on December 14, 1960: one was painted with the Nationalist Chinese insignia; the other was left unmarked so that it could be used by Detachment G pilots as needed. Commencing in February, pilots from Greg's detachment used the unmarked U-2s to complete seven overflights of North Vietnam during the first half of the year.

I flew commercial and got there Christmas Eve. The fleet was in at that time, and the Air Station Commander, a Navy Captain, invited me to a Christmas party in the evening. It was just a small affair, but there were two or three admirals there. One, in particular, was very curious as to why I was sent to the Philippines immediately before Christmas. He was curious about what was going on. Of course, I couldn't tell him. This was a fairly common situation for Greg, and he would often deflect these inquiries with, "You know the government; they do these kinds of things."

Prior to this overseas deployment, which would be Detachment G's first, Greg went over the detachment "Go kit" with his staff. *I told them we are gonna be over there by ourselves, and you have to be sure that we have all the material that we will need for the duration. We could, and did, order small stuff [from its Stateside supply service]. But the team did really well in preparing these kits—a conglomerate of all the stuff we would need. Usually about three months' duration. It worked pretty well.*

Greg's deployment would also include an aircraft dedicated to delivery of the photographic and ELINT "take" for processing in Washington. On landing, the U-2's film was quickly offloaded onto the transfer aircraft for immediate takeoff. There was also a tanker for refueling operations that doubled as transport for some of the detachment personnel. Other personnel and equipment were delivered using C124 cargo aircraft.

In early January 1961, just eight months following Gary Powers' shootdown, the detachment began the first overflights of Vietnam, four years prior to the big military buildup in 1965. By this time, Detachment G was becoming a seasoned unit, having already completed a prior (Stateside) deployment to Del Rio for the Cuban overflights.[21]

Detachment G had become a highly efficient asset for the intelligence community, a fact that was readily attested to by the CIA: "In addition to carrying out the operational mission, Detachment G has served as a test unit for new developments, tactics, and techniques in both equipment employment and personnel management. All key project replacement personnel receive initial and familiarization training at Detachment G prior to further assignment at field units.[22]

All flights were performed routinely, and the "take" delivered to the newly-established National Photographic Interpretation Center (NPIC) in Washington. However, unbeknownst to Greg or his team, the film and ELINT records for the final two missions of that deployment—January 16 and 18—were in for an adventure, one that would constitute a potentially major security breach.

The material had been processed at the Eastman Kodak plant in Rochester, NY and was then being forwarded on an Agency C-47 to Washington for analysis. During the flight one of the aircraft's two engines failed, and in order to keep the aircraft aloft the crew jettisoned 43 boxes of highly classified film over mountainous terrain around Williamsport, Pennsylvania. After making an emergency landing at the Scranton-Wilkes-Barre Airport, the pilot alerted CIA Headquarters, who immediately contacted the Pennsylvania State Police. With the wooded area secured, an Agency security team eventually located all 43 containers; not one had broken.[23]

Greg's detachment flew seven overflights of Vietnam and Laos, all while based at Cubi Point NAS. The overflights concentrated on the lines of communication leading into Laos and scanned North Vietnamese airfields searching for Soviet aircraft. By the end of January, the invasion scare had been debunked, and Detachment G returned to Edwards in early February.[24]

After several successful missions, we returned to Edwards in mid-February. When I returned home, I found that my wife Helen and daughters Cookie and Gretchen had left the decorated Christmas tree and presents in place since December. When I walked in Christmas music was playing—it was really a festive time. A short time later a delivery man rang the doorbell, and when he saw the celebration, he asked "Are y'all early or late with your celebration?" and we told him that we celebrated whenever we got the opportunity—which was true in those years.

By mid-March, Detachment G was again deployed to Laughlin for Operation *Long Green*—two overflights scheduled for March 19 and 21,

1961 to photograph Cuba in final preparation for the invasion. They were back to Laughlin in early April for Operation *Flip Top*, and between April 6 and April 29, 1961, the detachment would make 15 overflights of Cuba to provide photographic intelligence of the actual invasion, which came on April 17, and its disastrous aftermath.[25]

The CIA-directed invasion of Cuba at the Bay of Pigs quickly became a complete debacle, a source of great embarrassment for the Kennedy administration, and a significant diplomatic setback for America with allies and foes alike. *This was another dumb, dumb decision. I just could not understand why somebody on Kennedy's staff didn't stop him. It was obvious that it was going to fail, particularly when they were not going to support the landing, it was destined to fail.*

Detachment G operations

Following the U-2 shootdown over the Soviet Union, a Committee on Overhead Reconnaissance (COMOR) was formed to "coordinate development of foreign intelligence requirements for overhead reconnaissance projects over denied areas."[26] COMOR approved all overhead reconnaissance, by U-2 and satellite, by photographic, ELINT, COMINT, infrared, RADINT or other data gathering means. Intelligence target requirements were vetted by COMOR, and those selected for execution were forwarded to the US Intelligence Board and the CIA's Office of Special Activities (OSA). Once OSA approved the mission, the implementation mechanism was set in motion.

The first step was to carefully assess weather over the target area to determine on which date an overflight would be most likely to capture good data. Once this date was set, Detachment G was alerted.

OSA's alert came not less than (but often not more than) 24 hours prior to take-off for the mission. Greg was given a few key parameters on which to base the deployment. This included the required takeoff time for the deployment, the general area of operation, equipment requirements and any instructions specific to this deployment.

Twelve hours before the required takeoff, a detailed mission plan was provided by OSA to Greg, including altitudes, headings, targets and camera flight lines. Also included were emergency instructions, authorized emergency landing bases, and special information related to survival, cover and friendly forces. Hostile air radar locations and other threat information were also provided in advance of the pilot briefing.

OSA would make a final weather check over the target area, and advise a Go-no-go not less than two hours before the required take-off. Concurrently

CIA headquarters would confirm that late-breaking developments on the domestic or political scene would not prevent the mission.[27]

A standard practice soon developed for Detachment G deployments: normally Greg would dispatch two or three aircraft, and four pilots. Greg always flew during those deployments, in orientation and check flights, but did not fly actual missions. *Due to security concerns, the commanders were never permitted to participate in the overflights. They directed the flights but did not fly.*

Mission alerts came to Greg by the secure phone line from CIA/Washington and were somewhat informal. *The phone would ring, and Jack Ledford would be on the end of the line, on a secured connection. Jack would tell me what we needed to do, and he would say "Can you be ready tomorrow?" and I would say "Oh sure, we can do that."*[28]

That one call was all the notification Greg would get. By the time Ledford made the call, the decision about the deployment had already been confirmed through all necessary channels in Washington. *When they called, we went right to work. I called a staff meeting immediately and told our guys to get everything ready for a deployment. Normally I would take about 80 people, plus equipment. At that time, the clock was already started. The staff was on call all the time, and following the briefing, the wives would all be told, "I'm gonna be gone tomorrow…" And they all realized that we had this type of operation. I never had any trouble at all, or with people complaining about it. It was just the business we were in.*

If someone was on leave, he would normally not be recalled, but someone else in the group would be found to do the job. There was a lot of cross-training in the detachment, and Lockheed's detachment manager would take care of all personnel requirements.

Most missions required overseas deployments, and Greg would be told to deploy to a particular place, but would not be given specific missions and tasks until after the unit arrived at its foreign destination. Greg's communications team would get to work immediately to set up secure connections with CIA, and when Greg reported the detachment in position and at full readiness—normally one or two days after their arrival at the foreign staging base—the particulars about the individual sorties would be sent by Ledford's group. *They would send us the routes by secure communications (i.e. Teletype), which we could receive anywhere overseas. The system was pretty good—they could contact us wherever we were.*

Each deployment normally consisted of a number of sorties, sometimes as many as ten, and occasionally two-a-days. Generally, deployments were expected to last for up to three months, and the detachment never had more than one full deployment underway at any one time, although on rare occasions missions would be flown from widely separated locations.

When on deployment, the civilian staff and contract employees in the command, administration, and support teams often outnumbered the CIA personnel: for example, the aircraft engines, photographic and navigation equipment were maintained by contract employees, and as many as 12 Lockheed Aircraft Company employees would accompany each deployment to assist in the maintenance of the aircraft.

Greg would normally be assisted by a Deputy Commander who functioned as Senior Operations Officer, and by a four-person section for administration, finance and clerical support. His Operations Section would include a Deputy Ops Officer, two navigators who functioned as flight planners, an Intelligence Officer, two weather personnel, and two clerks. A flight surgeon accompanied all deployments.

Security was provided by a 17-man team that included CIA and General Service personnel, Air Force enlisted personnel, and civilian contract guards. The Communication Section would also include a combination of CIA, GS, USAF and contractor personnel, totaling 19. The Materials Section would be responsible for preparing and managing the "Fly kits" of maintenance and materials supply and would number seven. Assigned to fly the deployed U-2s were four to five pilots.[29]

Edwards AFB, North Base, *c.* 1960. (Wikimedia Commons)

At this point in his career, Greg had completed thirteen deployments. By his own estimate, he was away from home two-thirds of the time he commanded Detachment G, and his absences carried a cost for Greg and his family. *Our cover story in Detachment G was that we were operating as Weather Detachment #4. Helen and the children knew that I was flying U-2 aircraft, but they accepted the cover story that I was doing weather-related surveillance flights. On my deployments, they never knew where I was going, or when I would return.*

By this time the U-2 had been flying for five years, but the learning curve for this hard-to-fly aircraft never let up. We learned some things in the high-altitude program, early on, that were not generally known. For example, we had learned earlier, while flying B-57Ds in the Black Knight program that a temperature inversion would often occur between 40–45,000 feet. That was a critical point, as it was at that altitude where we would sometimes lose the engine. When that happened, the aircraft would normally glide down to 30,000 feet, and at that altitude, you could usually "get a light"—restart the engine.

At that time, the CIA had a U-2 squadron based in Taipei, flown by Taiwanese pilots, who were having a lot of trouble with engine flame-outs at 40–45,000 feet. At that altitude on their missions, they would be well over China when that would occur, putting them in great danger. A descent to 30,000 feet for an engine restart would put them well within range of Chinese ground fire and antiaircraft missiles.

I was asked to go with a team to Taipei to help them correct whatever they were doing wrong. We remained in Taipei for a few days, and in observing their flight operations, we learned that they had been maintaining the same rate of climb from takeoff to mission altitude. We asked them to lower the rate of climb as they approached 40,000 feet, and maintain that lower rate through 45,000 feet. They adopted this flight change and were successful in eliminating engine flameouts—that was all the adjustment that was needed to correct the problem. The unexpected thermodynamics at that particular altitude and the necessary changes required for our aircraft operations were important things for us to understand.[30]

Following the very long flights made over Cuba and Southeast Asia, the CIA determined that the U-2's range had to be increased. By June 1961 Lockheed had begun modifications to turn six CIA aircraft into the aerial refueling-capable U-2F model in 1961, permitting some Cuba missions to originate from Edwards, and Greg reports some 12-hour missions. All Agency pilots were trained in the techniques of in-flight refueling.

Greg and his pilots were all well familiar with aerial refueling, a routine but exacting task. But with the U-2s, it became a very delicate operation. The relatively frail U-2s had to avoid the vortexes coming off the wingtips of the KC-135 tankers, as well as the turbulent air caused by the tankers' four large jet engines.

During the first few years of refueling operations, two [USAF] U-2s crashed after their wings broke off as they crossed into the turbulent area behind the tankers.[31]

Having gone through the aircraft modifications and pilot training for aerial refueling, Greg learned that although operationally feasible, inflight refueling of the U-2s did not dramatically extend the mission length. In the words of OSA: "The introduction of inflight refueling allowed an increase in range up to the limit of the pilot's physical endurance." The longest flight involving IFR was staged from Takhli on 10 Nov 1963 (#3238) with air refueling over India, coverage of the Northeast Frontier, and return to Takhli. "Because of the physical condition of the pilot [Driver Al Rand] on landing after more than 12 hours flying, it was concluded that no flights of more than 10 hours would be planned in the future."[32] Greg notes: *But today, they can do 12-hour missions without refueling—the engines are so much more efficient.*

On his long flights, Greg was constantly busy in the cockpit. In the U-2s, and in earlier aircraft in which Greg flew with a copilot, there was plenty to do. *We were not just sitting there waiting for something to happen. If I was flying the airplane, even on autopilot, I never dozed. And even with the co-pilot at the controls, I was always alert.*

Greg reports a final coda to the Gary Powers story, once Powers had been returned to the US. *My boss called me and said CIA Director McCone had requested that I fly with Powers. I thought it was a waste of time, but the Director had formed the opinion that Powers had violated his contract with the Agency, and was looking for a reason to punish him.*

This check ride would be the first time Powers flew since being shot down. The goal of the flight was to establish his readiness to return to flying status. He was a good pilot—I knew that before I ever flew with him. He had a lot of time in the U-2 and had flown fighters before that. But Powers was happy to get back in the airplane and came out to North Base at Edwards. I flew with him twice in a T-33 airplane—it was the only two-seat aircraft we had at Edwards at that time. He checked out fine. He was a good pilot who had an unlucky day.

In a secret CIA interview in 1992, Security Officer Joe Murphy offered this assessment of Powers: "Most detachment personnel held him and the other drivers in awe and great respect, realizing that they were putting their lives on the line each time they flew a mission. During operational missions, everyone tensely awaited the pilot's safe return." Referring to what he termed "the vastly uninformed and misinformed American public and press," Murphy said that "those officials who knew the man and his orders gave him an unqualified 'well done.'"[33]

Cuban Missile Crisis

The Cuban Revolution of 1959 and Fidel Castro's subsequent economic *entente* with the Soviet Union led to increasing concerns among the American leadership about the possibly unfavorable political direction Castro's government might take. This concern prompted President Eisenhower in 1960 to direct the CIA to plan Castro's overthrow, a mission that coalesced under the new Kennedy administration into an invasion of Cuba by CIA-supported Cuban exiles at the Bay of Pigs in April 1961. Within three days, the invasion became a disaster, causing further loss of international prestige to Kennedy and the United States, making Castro a national hero, and resulting in even stronger relations between Cuba and the Soviet Union.

The failed coup came just as the United States had begun deployment of its first nuclear-tipped medium-range ballistic missile (MRBM), the PGM-19 Jupiter, to advanced bases in Italy and Turkey. These 60-foot missiles carried a 1.45 megaton thermonuclear warhead with a range of 1,500 miles and an accuracy of ½ mile. Deployed on the southern flank of NATO, these missiles sharply upset the nuclear balance in the region, and were greatly unsettling to the Russian military.

These two events added gravity to Russia's consideration of its own increasingly vulnerable position with regard to nuclear weapons, and to its relations with Castro's Cuba. The Bay of Pigs debacle led Russian leadership to recalculate the potential diplomatic and military windfalls that might result.

Regarding long-range strategic weapons, the Soviet Union was at that time in a position of great vulnerability: it possessed only 20 intercontinental ballistic missiles capable of reaching the United States from the Soviet Union, with sharp concerns about their accuracy and reliability. The Soviets were much better equipped with medium-range ballistic missiles, which were capable of targeting American allies and Alaska, but not the contiguous United States.[1]

Authors Graham Allison and Philip Zelikow explain that: "The Soviet Union could not right the nuclear imbalance by deploying new ICBMs on its own soil. In order to meet the threat it faced in 1962, 1963 and 1964, it had very few options. Moving existing nuclear weapons to locations from which they could reach American targets was one."[2]

Cuba was just such a location, and Khrushchev seized the opportunity for an "instant strategic adjustment"[3]—an adjustment that would put the Soviet Union on a nearly equal basis versus the United States in terms of nuclear deterrence. And Khrushchev did not require long-range nuclear weaponry—medium-range ballistic missiles would deliver the desired diplomatic or military impact.

Negotiations for the installation of nuclear missiles in Cuba began in early 1962, and an agreement between the Soviets and Castro was reached in May. The Soviet military proposed a force of twenty-four medium-range ballistic missile (MRBM) launchers and sixteen intermediate-range (IRBM) launchers. Each of the launchers would be equipped with two missiles (one serving as a spare) and a single nuclear warhead. It was also proposed that the defensive and support contingent in Cuba include four elite combat regiments, twenty-four advanced SA-2 surface-to-air (SAM) missile batteries, forty-two MiG-21 interceptors, forty-two IL-28 medium-range bombers, twelve Komar-class missile boats, and coastal defense cruise missiles.[4] The commander of the Soviet operations in Cuba arrived on July 10, followed two days later by a contingent of 67 specialists in missile site construction, in what had become codenamed in Moscow "Operation *Anadyr*."[5]

Cuba remained a vexation for the United States, and the demand for high-altitude reconnaissance remained at a high level. Not long after the failure at the Bay of Pigs the CIA authorized monthly CIA overflights by Detachment G in Project Nimbus, and following reports of increased Soviet activity on the island, by the spring of 1962 the Agency ordered overflights increased to twice monthly.

Our next overflights of Cuba were made on May 23, 1961. We flew from Edwards, refueled over Corpus Christi, conducted the overflight, and then returned to Laughlin AFB near Del Rio, Texas. We flew four overflights and saw a lot of suspicious buildups. We photographed 35 MiG-15s and -17s, and 12 MiG19s, plus a lot of anti-aircraft guns.

Over the next 16 months Detachment G would fly twenty-eight overflights of Cuba—459 flight hours. Some launched from Laughlin, requiring a short-term deployment for Greg and his team. Other missions during the spring of 1962 were, like the flight on May 23, flown from Edwards using mid-air refueling.

Between the start of Nimbus on May 23, 1961 until mid-September, 1962, Detachment G would fly at least 39 missions, the majority of which were over Cuba, although eight were made over Vietnam.[6] The CIA's attention was clearly bifurcated, and Detachment G was severely challenged to keep up with the intelligence demands. Cuba and Vietnam are nearly antipodal: Cuba is 2,300 miles east of Edwards AFB; Vietnam is 8,100 miles to the west. Cuba and Vietnam are therefore separated by a distance of 10,000 miles.

Soviet construction was well underway at several sites in Cuba during the summer of '62, but was undetected by the U-2s, despite the fact that these exploratory missions covered the entire length of the island, and nearly the entire breadth. In a mission flown on August 5, the extensive militarization of Cuba was evident in the mission photos, and a new urgency was felt within the Agency and Detachment G. A quick follow-up mission was scheduled for August 8 but was repeatedly delayed by weather for three critical weeks. The mission was finally flown on August 29 (Mission 3088) with Bob Ericson at the controls—the same man who had flown the last successful overflight of the Soviet Union one month before Gary Powers' shootdown. Ericson successfully overflew the western end of Cuba, then continued to the east. He covered the entire island and then repeated the

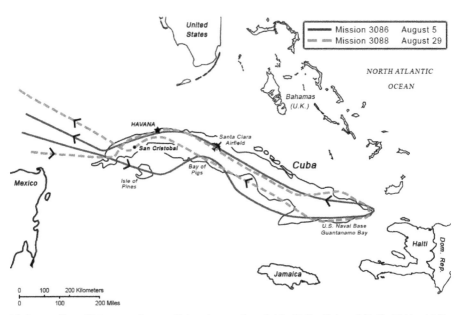

Flight profiles of U-2 aircraft over Cuba, August 5 and 29, 1962. Cuban Missile Crisis, 1962. (Samuel Richardson, Yosemite Productions)

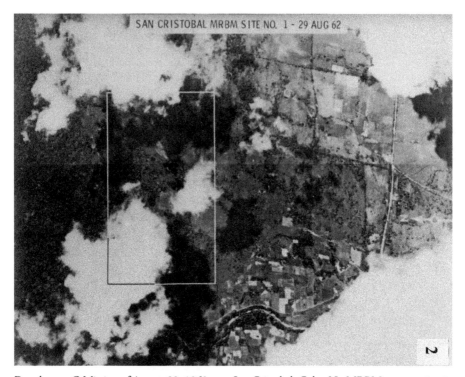

SAN CRISTOBAL MRBM SITE NO. 1 - 29 AUG 62

Detachment G Mission of August 29, 1962 over San Cristobal, Cuba. No MRBM construction in evidence. (NSA archives)

coverage of the western end of the island. It was a long flight, nine hours, terminating back at Laughlin AFB.

The film was quickly processed and then rushed to the photo interpreters in Washington, who clearly identified eight SA-2 surface-to-air missile sites. A ninth was discovered the next day, along with six guided missile patrol boats, and crates indicating many more MiG-21s—irrefutable evidence of the nature of the Soviet buildup in Cuba.

Sometimes the photos did not give the CIA what they wanted, normally due to cloud cover. On the August 29 flight, I got a call about the mission… right after Ericson landed, asking me what I thought. I said it looked pretty good. We knew we were going to have trouble on the eastern part of the island, but in fact, it was a little more open than we expected. Actually, the eastern part of the island was not the serious part anyway, the western part was.

Minutes after the film was placed on a light table in Washington, a photo interpreter reportedly shouted "I've got a SAM site!" *The next day I got a call from CIA, and was told "this is the most important mission you will have ever flown."*

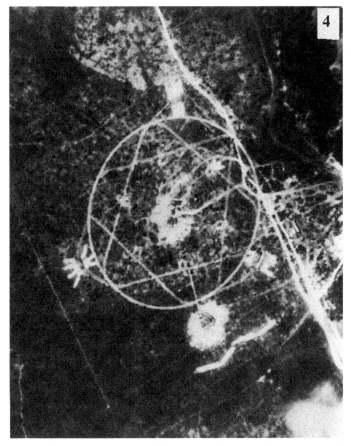

CIA U-2 mission of August 29, 1962 confirming Soviet SA-2 Surface to Air missile site at La Coloma, Cuba. (NSA archives)

The discovery of SAM sites was sobering to all. It meant that the CIA would not be able to overly Cuba with impunity. CIA Director McCone reportedly observed: "They're not putting them in to protect the cane cutters. They're putting them in to blind our reconnaissance eye." Using U-2s for reconnaissance had become problematic, and senior administration officials became cautious.[7]

Adding to the challenges for Detachment G, on September 4 Greg's direct report at the Agency changed: Col. Beerli was reassigned back to the Air Force, and was replaced by Colonel Jack Ledford who occupied the newly created position as Acting Director of Special Activities.

We stepped up the tempo again, and on September 5 (3089) we found three more SAM sites, plus a MiG-21 at Santa Clara Air Base in Cuba—the most advanced airplane of the Soviet Union. There were a lot of crates there indicating many more MiG-21s. The photo interpreters knew that Soviet ballistic missiles were normally protected by surface-to-air missiles deployed in a protective circle and that the U-2's detection of these SAM sites strongly suggested that a ballistic missile would be somewhere nearby. American intelligence knew, or thought they knew, that very soon we would find this ballistic missile.

The SA-2 missile sites were worrisome to the Agency as it planned for future U-2 missions over Cuba—memories of the Powers disaster were still fresh. His plane had been shot down by the same type of missile.

Tensions within the Agency were further heightened as a result of an Air Force U-2 overflight in the Soviet Far East that was intended to be peripheral, but which actually overflew Soviet territory. Then, just three days after Greg's Detachment G pilots discovered the second set of SAM sites on Cuba, a U-2 flown by a Nationalist Chinese pilot out of Taiwan was shot down over mainland China. The CIA was on tenterhooks.[8]

The first SS-4 medium-range ballistic missiles arrived on September 8. Nuclear warheads began arriving on October 4.

At this most critical juncture, bad weather and a temporary stand-down of CIA U-2s in response to the Chinese shootdown impeded U-2 operations over Cuba, and the next mission, conducted September 17 (3091) yielded no useable images due to heavy clouds over Cuba. Poor weather continued until finally, on September 26—nearly a month after the initial SAM sites had been spotted—Detachment G overflew eastern Cuba in mission 3093 and discovered three additional SAM sites. A follow-up mission was flown on September 29, and found still another SAM site, plus evidence of a costal defense cruise missile site.

Exercising great restraint in the face of the new SAM threats, the CIA's overflights continued into October. Flying peripheral missions on October 5 and 7 that avoided known SAM sites, Detachment G pilots discovered a total of 19 SAM sites, but found no evidence of the construction of medium-range ballistic missile sites. Greg is convinced that, absent those delays, the pilots of Detachment G would have located the MRBM sites. The circle of defensive SAM sites was well documented, and somewhere within that 20-mile perimeter, an area of little more than 300 square miles, would be the site.

By this time, intelligence agents on the ground in Cuba had reported sightings of what appeared to be SS-4 medium-range ballistic missiles, and the CIA pushed strongly for greatly expanded overhead surveillance. As the SAM sites neared operational readiness, the risk to reconnaissance aircraft intensified: Greg's new boss at the CIA, Colonel Jack Ledford, estimated the odds of losing a U-2 over Cuba at one in six.

It was clear that the U-2 overflights would intensify and there was some concern about Detachment G's ability to meet the demand: Greg's squadron had 10 U-2 pilots based at Edwards in California; the Air Force had 36 operating out of Laughlin AFB in Texas. It was also expected that the next flight would discover the ballistic missile sites and that the public would very soon be aware of the situation.

Attempts were made to photograph Cuba with satellites, but the satellites' normal orbits placed them over Cuba too late in the day—after clouds had formed. Further, only the U-2s could provide the high-resolution images that photo interpreters needed to discern accurately what was being done at the missile sites.

Up to this point—October 9—the CIA's cover story, in the event of a shootdown or other mishap, was that the aircraft was being flown by Lockheed pilots on a routine ferry flight to Puerto Rico. The Air Force proposed a different cover story—that the overflight was a routine Air Force peripheral surveillance mission that had gone off course. It was generally agreed that the Air Force ruse was stronger, but adopting that cover story would mean that the overflights would have to be made using Air Force pilots—the CIA's unit would have to stand down, a decision that led to a series of robust arguments from within the Agency.

Col. Jack Ledford, newly assigned to the Agency, noted that the Air Force U-2s were more vulnerable than the Agency's aircraft, and broached the compromise solution of using the Agency's more performant U-2s with USAF pilots. The suggestion was not well received by the Acting CIA Director Marshall Carter, who argued: "To put in a brand-new green pilot just because he happens to have on a blue suit and to completely disrupt the command and control and communication and ground support system on 72 hours' notice to me doesn't make a God damn bit of sense, Mr. Secretary."[9] President Kennedy decided after long discussions and many heated arguments with the CIA that the Air Force would fly all future reconnaissance missions, with the shadow of the failure of Bay of Pigs impacting his decision to move from the covert/CIA direction back to the US Air Force. Should anything go wrong, it was determined it would be preferable for the pilot to be a member of the US Air Force.

The 4080th Wing at Laughlin selected the two pilots from the 4028th squadron for the mission—Majors Steve Heyser and Rudolph Anderson, both of whom I knew well from my duty with the 4025th while a Black Knight.[10]

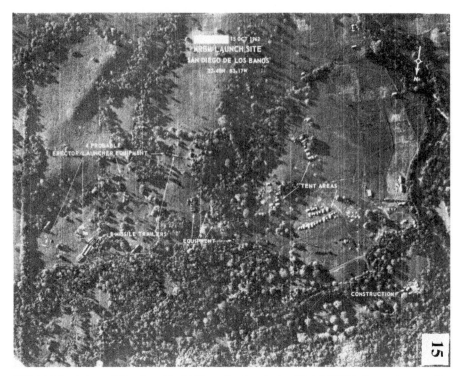

USAF U-2 mission of October 15, 1962 confirming Soviet SS-4 MRBM site at site near San Cristobal. (NSA archives)

A large contingent of Air Force personnel from Laughlin AFB, together with three generals from the Strategic Air Command HQ, and the two assigned Air Force pilots, arrived at the North Base on October 11. The familiarization would be hasty—the next overflight of Cuba was scheduled for October 14.

Issues of organizational control aside, the CIA's U-2s were more performant than those operated by SAC—being equipped with superior electronic countermeasures, a better engine, and a higher maximum altitude. *It was decided that the next two missions would be conducted using my squadron's U-2s, which were equipped with the new and more powerful J-75 engine, allowing the U-2s to operate 3,500 feet higher than the Air Force's aircraft, which mounted the older J-57 engine.* It was also agreed that the Air Force pilots would receive familiarization training from Detachment G.

General Compton, SAC Director of Operations, requested that my people prepare the airplane; my camera technicians loaded the camera, my mechanics

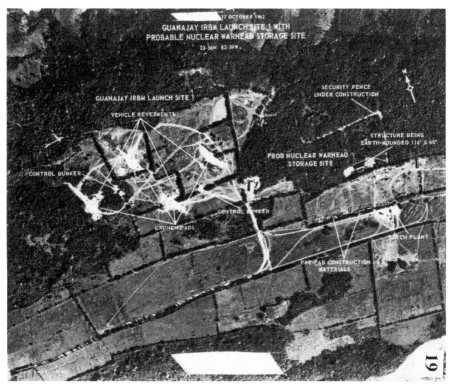

USAF U-2 mission of October 17, 1962 confirming Soviet Intermediate-Range Ballistic Missile (IRBM) at Guanjay, Cuba. (NSA archives)

prepared the plane, and all preparations were conducted by my team. Compton asked me to certify the plane's readiness to fly a successful mission. That evening, as my team was diligently working to prepare the aircraft for flight, Helen and I hosted Heyser and Anderson to a home-cooked meal.

Shortly after midnight on the 15th, Steve Heyser took off in the pitch-dark night, meeting the sun over the Gulf of Mexico. He flew near the Yucatan peninsula before turning north towards Cuba. Flying at 72,500 feet, he crossed directly over the western end of Cuba where Greg's unit had found the SAM sites, and completed his overflight in six minutes, taking 928 photographs in the process.[11]. After landing at McCoy AFB near Orlando, Heyser's film was immediately processed and revealed the installation of the medium-range ballistic missile site at San Cristobal, where Greg's team had found the first SAMs.[12] The offensive missiles had been discovered, over a month after they had first arrived in Cuba.

US Navy low-altitude images taken October 23, 1962, of Soviet medium-range ballistic missile (MRBM) installations at San Cristobal, Cuba. (NSA archives)

While the CIA did not fly these important missions, the CIA's Deputy Director—the same man who argued so vehemently in favor of keeping the overflights a CIA operation—had the satisfaction of personally briefing President Kennedy on the discovery of the missile sites.

SAC U-2s, augmented by Detachment G's U-2s, were approved for as many overflights as were needed to cover Cuba completely, without further consultation with the Special Group, and would eventually fly 82 overflights in the succeeding two months. In the week that followed, Air Force pilots flew multiple missions each day from a deployment based at McCoy, and confirmed that in just a few short weeks the Soviets had managed to install 24 clusters of SAM missiles, four medium-range nuclear missile sites each equipped with four launchers, 39 of the latest MiG fighters, and four 1,200-man battle groups equipped with tanks and battlefield missiles. Also found were intermediate-range ballistic missile sites under construction. All only a few miles from America's border.

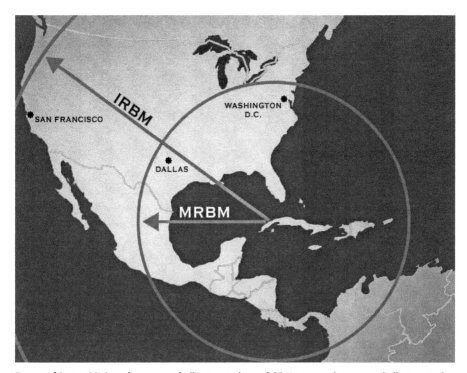

Range of Soviet SS-4 medium-range ballistic missiles and SS-5 intermediate-range ballistic missiles, if launched from Cuba. (Samuel Richardson, Yosemite Productions)

Low-altitude tactical reconnaissance missions were also flown. *The tactical units really got involved after that point when the president wanted more information. They used RF-8As over Cuba, at a low level, to see if the missiles were plugged in. They made a camera run right over the missiles—it must have been pretty exciting, and it must have really woke up the Russian guys. The plane would have been on afterburner, going at a very high speed, because if the SAM sites were plugged in they would have taken a shot at the RF-8As.[13]*

When the news broke that the Soviet Union had installed SS-4 medium-range ballistic missiles (MRBM) in Cuba, with a range of 1,100 miles that put most US cities in peril, the public was shocked: there was no public knowledge of the prior 10 months of secret surveillance of Cuba.

Seven messages were exchanged between Kennedy and Khrushchev during the week following. The UN was in session during that period, and a dramatic moment occurred at a UN meeting when Ambassador Adelai Stevenson urged the Soviet ambassador to admit the presence of Soviet missiles in Cuba. He continued to deny it, just as Khrushchev had done. But in a tense and exciting moment, Ambassador Stevenson showed the world the U-2 photographic evidence of the existence of missiles in Cuba. It seemed like every day we were going to war. This was a very exciting moment in history that I remember very well.

On October 22, about a week later, President Kennedy established a naval blockade of Cuba. It was only seven days, but it seemed like a month because everything was so tense at that time. There were several Soviet ships inbound toward Cuba. For another day or two, it was really tense because President Kennedy said that any ship that crossed this line would be sunk. For two days the ships continued to sail closer to the line before they finally stopped on October 24. On October 28 Khrushchev finally agreed to remove the missiles, the Soviet airplanes, and personnel.

Khrushchev's concession was made in response to a secret agreement that the United States would also withdraw its PGM-19 Jupiter missiles from both Italy and Turkey. By November 9, all 42 SS-4 missiles had been shipped out of Cuba.

Few people realized at the time how close we had come to going war. President Kennedy's staff was almost equally divided between trying diplomacy and destroying the missiles before they could become operational. The Air Force, Army, Navy, and Marines were at a high state of readiness. Several wings of fighter planes had been deployed to air bases in Florida. It would have been easy to knock out the missiles, however had we done that, the Soviets would have responded likewise.

Greg and his team were well pleased with their unit's performance during this most critical time in America's history. But it is also true that Greg's unit consisted of top-performing aviation professionals in all positions—both in the pilots' ranks, among technicians, and within the maintenance staffs. Having discovered the SAM sites, Detachment G badly wanted to locate and photograph the medium- and intermediate-range ballistic missile sites. President Kennedy's decision to have the final missile discovery missions flown by Air Force personnel—even though they were flying Agency aircraft that had been prepared by Agency personnel—was a big disappointment to the men of Detachment G.

And it was particularly hard for Greg: the USAF pilots who took over the Cuban overflights were from the 4028th Strategic Reconnaissance Squadron—pilots well known to Greg from his time flying RB-57D-2s with the 4025th SRS. He may even have known some of these same pilots from his time piloting B-47s, or even earlier, as pilot of the KB-29 aerial tankers. *But bad weather and bad luck and a little in-fighting between the CIA and the Air Force delayed our next flight, or we would have found the first missile in Cuba.*

Greg's citation

After the crisis, there was some discussion of who found the missiles first. Of course we found the first surface-to-air missiles and the Air Force found the others. The Air Force received a lot of deserved credit because they did a really good job on this, and a lot of publicity and they got a lot of rewards, and of course, my group received no publicity at all, and we couldn't because of who we were working for.

Greg's unit, the Weather Reconnaissance Squadron, Provisional No. 4, was awarded the Air Force Outstanding Unit Award. The somewhat cryptic citation reads "For exceptionally meritorious achievement in support of military operations from 1 Aug 62 to 3 Nov 62," and was signed by Curtis LeMay, Chief of Staff to the Secretary of the Air Force.[14]

The CIA Director, Lt. General Marshall Carter, presented me with the CIA's Medal of Merit, with this commendation:

> For his meritorious contributions to the national intelligence effort. As leader of a small group engaged in operations of great importance and sensitivity, Colonel Gregory demonstrated professional abilities and leadership qualities of the highest order. His dedicated performance meets the highest standards of service to our Nation.[15]

General Carter also presented me with a personal letter from President Kennedy expressing his appreciation to me for the work of my squadron, and regret that the information would never become part of history.[16] I was permitted to share the contents of this letter with my squadron, and my pilots each received the CIA Star Medal. Immediately following the ceremony, the medal and letter were taken from me and kept at CIA HQ in Langley. I did not expect to see them again.

In October of 1962, the whole country learned about the Cuban Missile Crisis. I think every family in the US knew about it, including my mother and father. But they never knew that I had a small role in it. They never knew that I was involved in it at all. I just never talked about it. Even after, it was such a secret for so long, that even after it was declassified, I still didn't talk about it. It just didn't seem right.

In what may have been the CIA's finest hour in the Cold War, the essence of its overflight of Cuba was its timeliness. The schedule of overflights that the CIA had been conducting for the 10 months prior to the initial discovery of SAM sites created a baseline of data against which Soviet missile construction activity and deployment could be judged. Had the CIA been less vigilant, the Soviets could have advanced much further in the development and installation of both offensive and defensive systems—both conventional and nuclear. When the actual nuclear missile sites were discovered, the Soviets had already deployed 42,000 Soviet military personnel to Cuba, along with 150 nuclear warheads, and were already far advanced in making them fully operational.[17]

A delay of just a few weeks would have allowed the Soviets all the time they needed to create a force on Cuba that would have required a huge American military effort to disable, at a horrific cost that carried global implications for the survival of mankind.

In Greg's words: *The CIA have made more than their fair share of mistakes, but deserve credit for their role in the Cuban Missile Crisis. My small squadron at Edwards North Base was successful in discovering the SA-2 missiles and building the collection of photographic evidence of Soviet buildup in Cuba. The CIA brought together unique talents that made possible what no other group would have had the collective skills to accomplish. Without this capability and early detection, it is likely that the Soviet Union would have been successful in deploying even larger numbers of missiles and forces in Cuba without detection.*

In 1975, 13 years later, my squadron's role in the Cuban Missile Crisis (to my great surprise) was declassified …and the CIA medal and President Kennedy's letter were returned me, allowing my children to learn about this chapter in their own lives and mine for the first time. On October 16, 1962, a time sometimes referred to as "The Missiles of October," it is highly likely that nearly every family in America became aware of the Cuban Missile Crisis… every family…except my own mother and father… who never learned about my involvement.

CHAPTER 12

Puerto Rico, Southeast Asia, and Whale Tale

With the world still composing itself following the nearly apocalyptic Cuban Missile Crisis, Greg and Detachment G next deployed to Ramey AFB, Puerto Rico in Operation *Seafoam* in early December 1962. Their mission there was driven by CIA concern over guerilla activities along the Venezuelan border by pro-Castro forces. After completing six overflights the Detachment redeployed to Edwards on December 22.

Over the next two years, Agency U-2s would complete 36 photographic missions over North and South Vietnam. With the passage of the Gulf of Tonkin Resolution in August 1964, the Strategic Air Command of the USAF assumed responsibility for all U-2 missions over Indochina, a decision that harkened back to the Cuban Missile Crisis, when the CIA similarly passed the reins over to SAC. And as before, the Air Force unit that took over responsibility for overflights was Greg's former unit, the 4080th SRW at Laughlin.[1]

When deployed, Greg was first and foremost a manager of people. *When we went overseas, we had so many different categories of people, from different organizations, each of which had their own personnel contract, and they were treated different by their organizations. CIA people, AF people, factory people, etc. There would be occasional gripes: "This guy is getting more per diem than we are," etc. I told them we all have a contract with our government, and if you don't like your contract, you can apply to his company. They wanted to give me something to worry about, and I just refused to worry about that. The truth was we all had a contract that we had to live by. They just wanted to complain—people do that. They didn't get very far with that.*

On balance, Greg was well pleased with his team. The Air Force was not involved in maintenance on the aircraft: everything from the engines and airframe to avionics was handled by civilian personnel. Lockheed's team normally consisted of a dozen people, working under a team leader who reported to Greg. *I really appreciated the civilians. They went to not-very-good places, like Takhli, and yet there were never serious complaints. They worked very hard to make sure the mission was a success, and they did not want their part of the mission to be the cause of failure. Everybody knew what they were responsible for. They did their very best to make sure that everything that they were responsible for worked. It was just that kind of attitude. We kind of used that sort of an incentive for everybody to do their very best. And they were good—it was really a rag-tag bunch. I had less military people than the civilian group or CIA group.*

First operations in India

Just a month after the Cuban Missile Crisis, China staged a series of massive attacks against India's western provinces—the start of the Sino-Indian War (Oct–Nov 1962) and with the concurrence of Indian Prime Minister Nehru, the CIA began conducting overflight reconnaissance missions of the Chinese-Indian border area. But beyond lending assistance to an ally, the CIA was witting to other benefits that might develop from aiding India in the conflict. The intelligence gathered on these border overflights would also be retained by American intelligence, but perhaps of greater importance, this support could sway India into permitting a U-2 staging base in India. Such a base would allow the CIA to conduct overflight missions over regions of the Soviet Union and China that were out or reach of U-2s operated by Detachment H in Taiwan.

Greg's deployment of a 30-man team and one U-2 aircraft was in position at Takhli, Thailand by the end of November, 1962. Previously Detachment G had based out of Cubi Point Naval Air Station on the shores of Subic Bay in the Philippines. But Takhli, 144 miles northwest of Bangkok, was much closer to the target region.

It was a very busy time for us. Just a month after the Cuban Missile Crisis, the Chinese-India situation blew up, so in December we deployed to Takhli Royal Air Force Base in Thailand and started overflying the Chinese border, completing a total of seven missions.

The first two overflights of Tibet were completed on December 5 and 10 and in both missions the U-2s experienced serious problems with fuel icing. Further flights were halted until the problem could be investigated. OAS headquarters contacted both Kelly Johnson at Lockheed and Greg in deployment and requested an immediate investigation, to include test flights at both Edwards and Takhli. Seventeen days passed before it was found that a Phillips fuel additive was a safe fix for the icing problem. U-2 missions continued on December 17 and all seven were completed by January 22, 1963.[2]

Greg and his team would return to Takhli six weeks after the Tibetan overflights to conduct a series of 17 overflight missions, targeting Southeast Asia, North Vietnam, Laos, China, Tibet and the Northeast Frontier region of India, and the Burma border. While Detachment G began flying missions from Takhli, headquarters continued negotiations with India that would permit use of an Indian air force base—if only for refueling post-strike. Between March 1 and August 10, Greg's pilots flew eight overflights of North Vietnam, Laos, and China.[3]

The intelligence agencies in the US were taking an increasing interest in politics and events in the Far East, and both Detachments G and H became very active in mid-1963. Of particular interest were China's nuclear facilities, its missile test range, and other targets in northern China, Manchuria, and west-central China.

With overflights of Russia prohibited, but with no reluctance to overfly China, the U-2s were increasingly exposed to risks of shootdown by SA-2 missiles. To counter this risk, Greg's unit had by 1965 been equipped with a host of electronic countermeasures (ECM), including a device that alerted the pilot that an SA-2 missile had been launched against him. The device was nicknamed the "Oscar-Sierra" unit, which was the acronym for the expletive U-2 pilots used when they learned that a missile was inbound: "Oh, shit." Also included was a device that produced false-angle returns to the homing radar aboard the approaching missile to steer it away from the U-2.[4]

Operations out of Takhli

The Royal Thai Air Force Base at Takhli was an ideal place for Detachment G to conduct secret operations. They shared the base with only a few RTAF fighter jets which flew very little, probably because of budget constraints, and never at night. The base was divided in half by the runway, with the Thai operation on one side and the Americans on the other.

A US Air Force facility at Okinawa maintained our portion of the base. A different CIA operation came in and out of there occasionally. They flew airplanes that landed on short runways, and they were doing a different operation for the CIA. We didn't talk to them, nor did they talk to us. That operation had been going for some time, and it was still going on when we left after our final visit.

Greg found the barracks at Takhli adequate rather than comfortable, but the food stood out. *We could choose either American-style or Thai food. The Thai food was very hot—lots of peppers. I often ate the Thai food, but I had to be careful because some was too hot for me. We had a large group of elite Thai paratroopers that ate their meals in the same facility. They watched me eat the Thai food, and were waiting to laugh at me if I ate something that was too hot.*

Later on one of my trips, I was given a big bottle of hot peppers, which I took home at the end of our deployment. My wife Helen liked hot seasoning also, but she found that the peppers I brought back were too hot for her, and we eventually got rid of it.

Greg was always receptive to morale-building opportunities for the personnel under his charge during deployments. *The U-2 deployments always included an amphibious airplane with six assigned paratroopers, to be used in case an aircraft went down over water during a mission.* On one deployment to Takhli, Greg was asked by the paratroopers for permission to use the airplane to make practice jumps over Takhli.

I said, "Yes, sure, you can do that." At this time we used the old chutes with very little directional control, not like the ones today. The paratroopers would put out a blanket, and make their jump from their amphibious airplane with the man landing closest to the blanket winning their private bets. These were well trained paratroopers and had gone through a lot of training to be fit for this job, to be able to rescue pilots that had gotten shot down. Fortunately, we never had to use them in that role, but it was good to have them in that capacity.

At other times, Greg readily granted permission for his pilots to bring hand-controlled model airplanes on deployments. *The space on the airplanes was really at a premium, but I authorized that. They put on a pretty good show, flying and dogfighting the small planes. As with the paratroop jump, large crowds of locals would gather to watch the flight demonstrations.*

At Takhli there were a lot of days we didn't fly. So I planned things to do when we weren't flying and usually planned a trip into Bangkok so that everyone would have at least one visit there.

One time I was preparing for a deployment back to Takhli, in Thailand. The commander there had two little daughters, and I suggested to Helen and my girls that they might prepare a gift for them. They put something together, and I delivered it to the commander's family shortly thereafter. They had a great time opening the package. We had put in some English-language comic books, and the girls' mother read those comics seriously like she was learning English.

Every few months the Thai officers from the other side of the base would have a get-together, and Greg was always invited. He found that the event followed a particular routine every time. *I would drive over to their side of the field at the appointed time, usually about 6.30 p.m. There would be about 30 Thai officers, including Colonel Boncha, the base commander. The men would gather on the right side of the room, and after about 30 minutes the wives would arrive and sit on the other side of the room. The men and women never mixed, and I always left shortly after the women left, explaining that I had work to do. I only wanted to be there a short time to show my respects.*

If I was going to be involved in flying the next day, I would beg off from having a drink. But if not I would usually have one drink with them. Then would begin a long evening. At an appointed time, after a couple of hours, the wives would leave, I would make my excuses, and the men were free to do whatever they wanted to do. A lieutenant general joined them for one of their parties that I also attended. He was short, a three-star general, and he liked to party as well as the rest of them. I didn't know it at the time, but things got pretty wild. The general jumped off of a platform, and I think broke his leg. But that didn't stop him. He stayed with them till 2 o'clock in the morning.

Col. Boncha was highly respected by his own personnel and by the Americans. Anytime he was in sight by any of his people, they would make an effort to salute him—sometimes from a half a mile away. He had a jeep that was easily recognized, and they would salute the jeep as long as they could see it.

Greg recalls that he was always very respectful of what Detachment G were doing, and never inquired into any of their activities. He accepted that what they were doing was necessary, and never interfered in any way nor suggested that anything be done differently. *He was a great host and gave us free rein of our side of the base. He could be very strict, and didn't want his people to do anything that might cause embarrassment to him or to others—he once summarily executed one of his men for theft. He might have been considered almost a tyrant at times—he was very strict. But he was very helpful to us and never bothered us at all. It was a great place for us to be for several trips.*

Later, after Detachment G had left the area, the base was used extensively by the US Air Force for operations during the Vietnam War.

While at Takhli, Greg saw a report come across the CIA communications that he had been promoted to Colonel. At the time Greg was 43 years of age, and the promotion came three years ahead of when he would normally be eligible for the rank. He hadn't a clue up to that point that he was being considered for promotion. *Jack (Ledford) had something to do with that. He called Helen to let her know. There was a celebratory party at Takhli.*

The CIA's willingness to provide intelligence to India was based on its interest in developing better information on the disputed area. But additionally, it was hoped that India would eventually agree to provide a permanent staging base for both Detachments G and H operations, a base from which ELINT and photo missions could be launched into the further reaches of the Soviet Union and China. *The Indian government was very sensitive about giving us permission*

CIA U-2 Commander Col. William Gregory at the time of his promotion. (Gregory)

to land there, but in 1963 they finally did and offered us the unused base at Charbatia. I was ordered to fly August 2 from Edwards to Washington where I was joined by two more people from the CIA, and we flew on Pan Am 1, first class, to Delhi.

The inspection was disquieting. "[The inspection team] found runways not yet usable, the hangar not yet completed, barracks and mess not completed, no medical facilities available and no ground equipment. A readiness date of November 15 [1963] was forecast by the Indians but was considered optimistic by the visiting team."[5] Greg had other views, perhaps colored by his prior deployments to bases that had been problematic for U-2 operations: *The Indian Air Force flew us down to Charbatia, and I was pleased to find that it was a good base. I was really pleased at the condition of the base, and I told them right off that the base was even more than adequate.*

Greg made the most of his opportunity to fly commercial, first class no less. On August 13 I flew back up to Delhi, then on Pan Am 1 again all the way back to the west coast—all the way around the world.

OSA was successful in receiving authorization from the Indian government for the use of Charbatia for refueling, and Detachment G's U-2s at Takhli launched four additional overflights of Tibet between September 29 and November 10. At the request of Thailand's Prime Minister, Greg's team then flew a series of three additional missions over Burma, Laos, and North Vietnam on November 14, 15 and 17, after which it redeployed back to Edwards.

South American operations

While Greg's detachment was conducting operations in Southeast Asia, the CIA was growing concerned over events in Venezuela. It appeared that an anti-government movement—the FALN—was planning to interfere with free national elections, to discredit the US.-friendly government, and to attempt to bring Venezuela into Castro's orbit. And it appeared that Cuban and possibly

Soviet support for the guerrilla activity was infiltrating across the border from neighboring British Guiana.[6]

Detachment G was again deployed, this time to Ramey Air Force Base in Puerto Rico. Greg took pilots Barnes, Ericson, and Edens on this deployment, each flying two missions over Venezuela and Guiana between December 3 and 19, 1963. The overflights were conducted with good results, and Greg and the Detachment G team returned to Edwards just in time for Christmas, 1963.

After roughly a week at home, Detachment G again deployed to Takhli for two missions on December 29 and 30. Pilot Rand continued to Tao Yuan, Taiwan to complete a single mission over Southeast Asia, North and South Vietnam, Laos and Cambodia.

A further major deployment came in late February, again to Tao Yuan. Pilots Baker and Knutson completed four missions over the same regions Rand had covered in January. The detachment redeployed to Edwards, and a new, very long deployment was launched almost immediately—back to Takhli for a series of overflights that eventually numbered fourteen. The detachment's most seasoned pilots—Ericson, Knutson, and Edens—blanketed Southeast Asia, North Vietnam, China, Cambodia and Laos before returning to the States after a 45-day deployment. This deployment would be Greg's last to Takhli, though he would lead Detachment G on subsequent deployments to India.

Project Whale Tale

The shootdown of Gary Powers' aircraft over the Soviet Union in 1960 and the immediate return of all U-2 overseas deployments to Edwards had led to deep consternation within the Agency, and within NATO members. While America's allies recognized the critical importance of the intelligence made possible by U-2 overflights, none was willing to endure the political pressures inherent in providing bases for the aircraft. Ultra-long U-2 flights, using aerial refueling, were technically possible, but the cockpit hours exceeded the pilot's endurance. Even as Detachment G was successfully completing overseas deployments with the U-2s, the CIA and Air Force continued, without success, to secure suitable overseas bases for the U-2s. In May of 1963, still considering its options, the CIA returned to a proposal that was first broached during the Eisenhower administration—launching U-2s from aircraft carriers. When, in August of 1957, Lockheed's Kelly Johnson was queried about the concept's technical feasibility of U-2 carrier operations, he had identified three "must-haves" in order to make the U-2 safe for carrier operations: strengthening the main and tail gear for the higher loads; installing an arresting hook and associated structure; and providing a fuel dump system to permit jettisoning fuel before landing in the event of an aborted mission. The modifications were estimated to weigh 227 lbs., a weight increase that would reduce the operating ceiling of the U-2 by 1,000 feet.

At the time, Johnson also observed: "A quick glance at the map indicates operations from the North Sea, Mediterranean, Pacific, and Indian oceans could yield coverage of all but the upper central third of denied area." He also observed that: "Carrier qualifications may be troublesome and time-consuming. It would mean extensive training of either present (U-2) pilots in carrier operations, or carrier-qualified pilots in U-2 handling."[7]

At that time, with a surfeit of foreign land bases open to U-2 operations, the proposal gained no traction, and neither did other attempts by the Navy to interest the CIA and Air Force in its carriers between 1957 and 1960.

But current conditions gave the proposal new life. Developing a carrier-launch capability was of great interest to General Marshall Carter, then Deputy Director of the CIA, and soon to be made Director of the National Security Agency (NSA). Carter was cognizant of upcoming French nuclear testing in the Pacific, and knew that there would be a continuing requirement for overflights of Southeast Asia in the coming years. He was also aware that reconnaissance flights over Yemen and the United Arab Republic would soon become critically important to the intelligence community. Carter ordered a comprehensive study of the concept, which started with a clear statement of purpose: "The basic question is whether or not this aircraft can be economically adapted to work from carriers with an acceptable margin of safety in flight operations, and... operate with frequency varying from occasional to repeated, without affecting the Navy's disposition of forces." And which concluded: "Present engineering analyses confirm that the aircraft can be so operated theoretically as to produce a viable carrier capability for reconnaissance purposes."[8] The study would be undertaken by Col. Jack Ledford, Assistant Director of the Office of Special Activities (OSA) and his deputy, James A. Cunningham, and their staffs.[9]

With Lockheed's confirmation that the U-2 would require only slight modifications to permit carrier operations, a detailed investigation by the CIA confirmed the technical feasibility of operating the U-2 from carriers and held in abeyance the question of economic feasibility. It approved a trial project under the codename "Whale Tale." The principal concerns identified early in the process related to landing: the normal "tail-high" attitude of the aircraft on landing, combined with normal down- and up-drafts present aft of carriers, required, in the words of the CIA, "adjustments to technique."

Additionally, Lockheed was asked to develop special slings and fuselage carts to facilitate loading and moving the long-winged U-2 in the limited aircraft hangar deck and elevators.

At the time, Detachment G was operating the U-2F variant, and in late July 1963, Lockheed received the green light for modification to two of the aircraft, resulting in the U-2G variant. Concurrently a pilot training program was started which would include suitability tests aboard a carrier.

Catapult assists for the U-2 were out of the question—it was simply too fragile an aircraft. Consequently, the U-2 would take off from the carrier under its own power, using the long axial carrier deck.

Additional operational changes were also required. Normal landings on carriers are made with an approach 3–4 degrees from horizontal. The U-2 would have to approach much flatter—at 1.5–2 degrees—in order to engage the arresting cables. Landings would be made on the angled deck: takeoffs would be made on the straight deck.[10]

The carefully crafted U-2 carrier trials would proceed in three phases. Phase I consisted of takeoff and land approach trials by Lockheed pilots using the carrier USS *Kitty Hawk*. In the first stage of Phase II, Detachment G personnel would undergo preflight and orientation training in carrier operations. The second stage involved actual carrier landings using Navy aircraft. The final stage involved carrier-type approaches and landings in the modified U-2G at Edwards AFB.

Phase III also included three parts, the first of which consisted of takeoffs and captured landings by Lockheed pilots, using the modified U-2G. The second stage consisted of takeoffs and captured landings by Detachment G pilots. The final stage was an actual deployment for Detachment G aboard a carrier.

On August 2, 1963, Project Whale Tale commenced when a conventional (unmodified) U-2 was flown to San Diego under cover of darkness. After midnight, it was loaded aboard the carrier USS *Kitty Hawk*, and with exacting care was stowed below decks in the hangar bay. Greg, his Detachment G team, and eleven Lockheed employees, including Kelly Johnson, had gone to San Diego and joined the test group aboard the ship when the carrier put out to sea the next morning. The aircraft carried the letters "ONR" on its vertical stabilizer in support of the cover story that the aircraft was operating under the auspices of the Office of Naval Research.

The *Kitty Hawk*, operating with a minimum crew for reasons of security, took up station on August 5, 1963, 50 miles off the coast of California, beyond the sight of land. It was expected that the trial could be conducted in a single day and that the *Kitty Hawk* would be back at North Island by 1400 hours.

The aircraft was positioned carefully at the end of the carrier's straight deck. Selecting the takeoff point was critical, and was influenced strongly by fuel load. The operating manual warns: "Careful consideration was given to clearance of island superstructure and other obstacles. The line-up point is critical due to the flow of air around the 'island, and takeoffs can be very hazardous unless extreme care is exercised in selecting the TO point."[11]

Underway at 20 knots and with a 10-knot headwind, the deck crews had some difficulty in holding the U-2 on deck, even before the engines had been advanced. On launch, the 16,000 lbs. of thrust produced by the J-75 engines had Lockheed test pilot Bob Schumacher airborne in just 321 feet—about one third of the available flight deck. Clearing the bow, the U-2 was already 1,000 feet above the carrier—a spectacle never before seen by the Navy personnel on deck.

With the takeoff trial a success, the aircraft made a number of simulated landing approaches. On his final approach, Schumacher touched down briefly before powering up and flying back to Burbank—no arrested landings were attempted in this first proof-of-concept trial.[12]

On returning to the Lockheed plant at Burbank, the U-2 underwent modifications to strengthen the landing gear to accommodate the sharp deceleration associated with carrier landings, to install an arresting hook at the rear of the fuselage, and to fit mechanical "spoilers" onto the trailing edges of the wings to allow the pilot to almost instantly stall the wings upon touchdown. A fuel dump system was also installed in the event an aircraft was forced to return early after launching from the carrier deck.

With Whale Tale I complete, the concept of U-2 carrier operations was considered operationally feasible, if only on a provisional basis. On September 4, 1963, Greg met with the key members of the Whale Tale team—including James Cunningham and James Cherbonneaux of the Agency, James Barnes, one of Greg's U-2 pilots at Edwards, and three Navy representatives—to develop a plan for U-2 carrier pilot training under the designation Project Whale Tale II.[13]

Since Whale Tale was a covert CIA undertaking, it became a Detachment G operation, and Greg was asked to nominate two cohorts of pilots to go through the carrier qualification program. The Navy transferred a Landing Signal Officer (LSO), Lieutenant Commander John Huber, to Detachment G for the duration of the program.[14]

The three-stage training program commenced in mid-November 1963 when an initial group of four pilots arrived at the Monterey Naval Air Station in civilian clothes and booked rooms at the Motel 6 on Fremont Street. While these pilots were beginning their carrier training, three of their fellow pilots—and Greg—were deployed to Takhli, conducting overflights of China, the Northeast Frontier area, Southeast Asia, Burma, Laos and Vietnam.[15]

Stage one of the pilots' training was conducted at the LeMoore Naval Air Station, in which they were first checked out in the Navy's T-2A training jets supplied by the Monterey Naval Air Station, and subsequently trained in carrier-type approaches and landings. This two-seat jet was considered by the Navy to be an intermediate training aircraft, and from the late 1950s until 2004, virtually every jet-qualified naval aviator and flight officer received training in the T-2A. This initial cohort required just four days to complete this phase of training.

The second cohort of pilots had been scheduled to begin stage one training at Monterey immediately after the first cohort departed for Pensacola, originally estimated to be some time in December. But Detachment G was at the time deployed to Takhli, Thailand, and was involved in overflights of northern and west-central China and Mongolia. Pilots slotted for the second group of training were not available until early January. Greg, also part of the Takhli deployment, had requested one of the training slots in the second cohort for himself, a request that was quickly granted. Also included in Greg's cohort was Bob Schumacher, long-time Lockheed test pilot who had flown the U-2 in the earlier feasibility trials, and was slated to conduct the first carrier flights following training.

Greg's cohort began stage one of the training on January 5, 1964, and completed it on February 15. Greg had just one check-out flight, and thereafter all his flights on the T-2A were solo. He and his group completed over 100 simulated landings at Edwards, and by mid-February Cmdr. Huber was satisfied that the team was ready for the next phase of training—carrier landings of the T-2A.

Stage two of the pilot training involved additional carrier-type landings and approaches at the Naval Air Station in Pensacola, to be followed by actual T-2A landings and qualifications aboard the aircraft carrier USS *Lexington* in the Gulf of Mexico.

Just before takeoff for our first carrier landing attempts, the Navy required us to view a 30-minute training film of terrible, unsuccessful carrier landings. I don't know if it was much of a confidence builder, but apparently, all the pilots who went through the training program at that time got a dose of that. They had every kind of landing you can imagine. They flew into the aft end of the ship, off the side, just an unbelievable number of crashes—there was not a good landing in that film.

The legendary USS Lexington *carrier was waiting for our arrival a few miles offshore. We were at 5,000 feet or so, and the deck looked very short as I approached the carrier, but after getting into the landing pattern, it began to look more normal, and all the good training came back.* Commander Huber was positioned near the touchdown spot on the deck and gave instructions as needed.

We were trained to immediately go to full throttle the instant the tires hit the deck so that if our tail hook missed the arresting cable, we would be able to re-launch and be safely airborne. This was fortunate because on my first landing the tail hook didn't engage—it bounced over the arresting cables and I had to go around for a second attempt. Huber called and said don't worry about that, you made a good approach and good landing, and it will probably behave the next time. And so it did—the next landing was OK.

The T-2As required a boost from the steam catapult, and that together with normal engine run-up made for a lot of cockpit noise during takeoff. On Greg's first takeoff, he found that once he had cleared the carrier deck, everything went very quiet. *I thought one of the engines had quit, but everything was just fine. I had just gotten clear of the deafening catapult. I think they should have briefed us on that—"don't worry about the noise and the quiet after that"—it was a bit of a surprise. I enjoyed the takeoffs and had no trouble with the landings. All six of us made six landings each.*

The lieutenant commander who controlled the flights on the carrier was surprised to observe that Greg was a full colonel. He said, "Sir, carrier training is for younger pilots, so why in the world are you doing this at this point in your career?" Greg retorted that this was the first opportunity he'd had. *He sort of got a kick out of that. We celebrated that night after we had passed the air qual program.*

The third phase of pilot training commenced on February 29, 1964 when the first U-2G was delivered to Edwards AFB. Each pilot continued to refine the carrier-type approaches and landings first learned in the T-2A, but now in the significantly different U-2G aircraft, until the LSO considered each pilot ready to land the U-2 aboard ship.

The Detachment G pilots had developed a profound respect for Commander Huber's judgement and experience in carrier operations. When Huber declared the pilots operationally ready and Whale Tale II was successfully concluded, each pilot felt confident of his ability to undertake the arrested landings.

The final phase of the carrier qualification, designated Whale Tale III, would consist initially of U-2G landings and takeoffs aboard the USS *Ranger* by a Lockheed test pilot, followed by similar qualification of all the Detachment G pilots. In the final phase of the project, Detachment G would conduct an exercise to test the operational capability and effectiveness of the carrier-launched reconnaissance aircraft.

The carrier qualification program moved quickly. As Detachment G personnel were completing final U-2G landing training at Edwards, Lockheed pilots and Detachment G pilots from the first training cohort loaded aboard the *Ranger* and were en route to the test area off San Diego. On February 29, with Lockheed test pilot Bob Schumacher again at the controls, the U-2G (designation Article 362) successfully completed a series of touch-and-go landings, but on Schumacher's first arresting-hook landing attempt,

U-2 take-off from the USS *Ranger*, March 1964. (Lockheed Martin)

the aircraft bounced, with the hook engaging the arresting wire while the aircraft was in the air, and causing the aircraft to slam back onto the deck. Minor damage resulted to the nose section of the aircraft. *The CIA people who were on the ship thought that might be the end of the program, but Kelly Johnson knew he could fix the problem, and he did. He was such a remarkable person—I think he was the greatest aeronautical engineer of our time.* The damage was quickly repaired below decks by Lockheed people aboard the ship, and the U-2G was flown to Burbank in order for its onboard instruments to be read out and analyzed. On March 2, Schumacher returned to the *Ranger* with a different aircraft, Article 348, and successfully completed four arrested landings. Later that day, Lockheed turned the aircraft over to Detachment G, and pilot Robert Ericson made several touch-and-go landings but was not able to complete any arrested landings. Running short of fuel, the pilot returned to the North Island NAS.

On March 3, a second Agency pilot, Jim Barnes, flew Article 348 from North Island to the *Ranger*, and on making his first touch-and-go landing, allowed the right wing of the aircraft to drop. The right wing skid caught on an arresting cable and was torn off, and his plane's right aileron was damaged. Only able to turn in one direction, Barnes opted not to ditch the aircraft, but instead managed to fly it to Edwards for repairs. *He did a marvelous job of saving that airplane. It could have spun the aircraft around. We learned something from that.*[16]

With both U-2Gs now damaged, a week was allotted for repairs to be made. This delay was advantageous for all. The pilots refined their approach techniques by applying the experience gained from the March 3 tests by the Agency pilots.

Detachment G recommended landing qualification efforts on March 9, 1964, and within two days all pilots qualified in the U-2 without further incident, with each pilot, including Greg, making six takeoffs and six landings. At this point, Whale Tale III was successfully concluded; Detachment G was operationally ready for carrier deployments, the first of which was already laid on.

Operation *Fish Hawk*

Two years earlier, France had designated Moruroa and its sister atoll Fangataufa in French Polynesia as sites for its nuclear test programs, and had recently announced plans to detonate a hydrogen bomb over the Moruroa Atoll on July 2, 1966—codename Aldebaran. The intelligence community was eager to understand France's nuclear capabilities and authorized a U-2 photo reconnaissance overflight, codename *Fish Hawk*, to overfly the French nuclear test area in order to "ascertain the imminence of actual nuclear tests."[17]

In early May 1964, I selected detachment personnel and a staging kit which Lockheed flew to Alameda on the SF Bay, where we again loaded aboard the USS Ranger, *sailing under the Golden Gate Bridge as we departed. Also included in the team was a photo interpreter who would use the ship's photo lab to provide a rapid look at the photographic "take" to confirm that it met the requirements for resolution and quality. Two U-2s were flown to Hickam Air Force Base, Hawaii—Articles 348 and 362, the same aircraft flown on initial carrier qualifications in March—and on May 12 they ferried to the* Ranger, *200 miles away, where the pilots underwent refresher training in carrier landings. The Navy insisted that the entire exercise be completed in secret, which meant radio silence for the carrier and its destroyer escort.* But Greg's detachment had a continuous communication link with OAS headquarters via a clandestine net.

This project was unique for the Agency: it was the first time that the detachment commander—Col. Gregory—would plan and launch an operational mission. And it was also the first time most of the detachment personnel would cross the equator aboard ship—qualifying them for induction into the Shellback Clan. *The day we crossed the equator, in Navy tradition, we celebrated King Neptune coming aboard with a ceremony that qualified all of us as Shellbacks.*

On May 19, as we approached a point 800 miles from Moruroa in the Tuamoto Archipelago in the far reaches of the South Pacific, we began our preparation for the mission. The U-2 was moved up to the flight deck and prepped for the mission, the pilot was briefed, and the takeoff was made, again using only a third of the length of the deck. The missions required coverage of five targets, with one considered primary and four secondary. The mission went well, and all of the targets were covered, and the pilot safely returned to the Ranger.

As detachment commander, and as the individual who crafted the detailed operational and logistical plan for *Fish Hawk*, it fell to Greg to prepare a summary report for OSA headquarters. In it, Greg noted the importance of timing: like all Detachment G missions, the navigation plan for the two missions was developed with great care and precision, and required the pilot to fly the aircraft at specified speeds and altitudes, making turns according to an exacting timetable. No navigation was done by the pilot—he was simply too busy attending to other cockpit tasks. A late takeoff would create huge problems for both the pilot and the navigators aboard ship, and could even result in failure of the mission. Detachment G pilot James Barnes—a pilot who had previously served in Detachments C and B, who had flown 14 prior U-2 missions for the detachment—would fly the mission on May 19, 1964.

The preparations proceeded without any hitches and takeoff went almost exactly as planned. Despite a tropical deluge drenching the ship and aircraft about 45 minutes beforehand, the takeoff was made at precisely 0700 as scheduled. Barnes' aircraft disappeared from the ship's radar at the 300-mile point, precisely on course. It subsequently reappeared at the precise location estimated by the navigator and radar operator, materializing below the thick overcast at 4,000 feet after a smooth descent and no course corrections.

The mission's photographic "take" was aboard the aircraft—no data transmission to a ground station was possible at that time in the U-2's service history. So a safe landing was critical for the survival of the pilot, the recovery of the mission photos, and for the continued feasibility of U-2 carrier launches.

We were concerned over the landing, for the sea had gone to an unpredicted state 4 with 6–8 feet swells and occasionally 10–12 feet. The pilot made a nice approach and good landing, trapping the number 1 wire. The ships personnel were amazed that the landing was made within 30 seconds of the predicted time given to them prior to takeoff.

The photo intelligence was considered excellent, although two of the target areas were obscured by cloud cover. The U-2's onboard telemetry system sent a data report to the carrier at 30-minute intervals, and reported that all 30 of the critical components of the aircraft were operating nominally.[18]

The film was immediately offloaded, developed, and analyzed, and the CIA's onboard photo expert confirmed to Greg that the material met the necessary standards. *I reported to CIA headquarters that it looked like everything went well and in the meanwhile Captain William E. Lemos, commander of the ship, had turned the ship toward the States again. About 30 minutes later I got the message that they (CIA) would like one more sortie over the target area. So I had to go and talk to Captain Lemos to turn the ship around again for that second mission.*

The second mission was flown on May 22 by contract pilot Buster Edens to confirm the positive results of the first mission, and to overfly the two targets that had been obscured in the first. Though he had no way of knowing at the time, this would be Edens' final operational mission for the detachment.

The second mission was also completed successfully, with all five targets again photographed. *Weather covered approximately 90 percent of the entire area but surprisingly all four targets were open and good coverage was obtained on all of them. On landing, an unpredicted sea state 4 existed and the deck was pitching a good 6–8 feet. But the pilot made a very fine level approach averaging out the ups and downs of the unstabilized "meat ball" and made a perfect trap on the number 3 wire.*

CIA headquarters later told Greg that the results of this extraordinary excursion were highly successful. The commanding officer of the USS *Ranger,*

Captain Lemos, noted in his report that: "The precision with which the whole U-2 operation was planned and executed was outstanding in all respects." The Fleet Commander endorsed Lemos' findings, saying: "That the operation was concluded successfully attests to the suitability and reliability of a CVA (aircraft carrier) as a launch platform for this type of operation". The CIA's Directorate for Science and Technology would later report: "From an operational and security standpoint this was one of the most successful operations of this nature ever conducted by the United States." Greg and his team had clearly demonstrated the operational feasibility of carrier-launched missions.[19]

The deployment was completed on May 28 when the *Ranger* returned to Alameda. As with all other deployments, Greg was with the contingent but did not fly operational missions—company policy.[20]

I am still impressed that this mission was conducted in total secrecy and zero publicity. With about 4,500 carrier personnel plus the destroyer escort on the mission, it was a tribute to the military's capability to keep secrets... then. It was done in total secrecy, and no one ever knew about this until it was declassified several years later. It is really a credit to the Navy to have done it that way.

The technical and operational feasibility of carrier-launched U-2 missions had been clearly demonstrated, but economic and diplomatic considerations determined future carrier operations. In September 1964, and again in March 1965, a joint American-British plan was developed for carrier-based U-2 overflights of crisis areas in the Mediterranean, notably Cyprus. But the diplomatic risks and financial costs involved in operating a carrier, with its attendant flotilla of defensive vessels and service ships, were simply too high to justify the intelligence yield of this and other possible carrier-based missions. And operationally, the long time required to assemble the vessels, and the difficulty associated with maintaining secrecy, sharply limited the usefulness for U-2s. Additionally, high-resolution space-based reconnaissance imagery from the Corona system was showing such promise that the refinement of U-2 operations off carriers was no longer supportable. The U-2Gs were never again used off carriers; in 1969, the much larger U-2R was flown from the carrier USS *America* in what is believed to be the last carrier-launched mission for the U-2.[21]

Indian operations

By the end of 1962, it was clear that Detachment G would soon be overtaxed by demand for intelligence missions, and it became evident that it required more than the single staging capability at Edwards. By the end of 1963 the detachment acquired two additional contract pilots, and Edwards underwent a substantial and much-needed facelift. A new office building, two warehouses, an avionics building, fitness center and mess hall were constructed, the hangars were remodeled, new fuel storage tanks were installed, and the runway was resurfaced. Detachment G's contract pilot cohort included Hall, Barnes, Schmarr, Baker, Knutson, Ericson, Edens, Rand, and Gregory.

In the spring of 1964 the Air Forces Strategic Air Command was given the responsibility for tactical coverage of Southeast Asian targets in support of the Vietnamese military command. This decision "relieved Detachment G's thinly stretched resources," and by 1965 Takhli had become a semi-permanent station for Detachment G's U-2 operations in support of both the Air Forces' U-2 operations and those of Detachment H based in Taiwan.

I took a detachment to that new base, Charbatia, west of Calcutta, and prepared for our first mission from India in late May 1964. The Indian government sent their number one intelligence guy down to supervise what was going on. His name was Rumgee Singh. I got to know him very well. He liked to invite me over to his room in the evening, and we would talk for a while. He asked me if I had been to see the Taj Mahal, and I said I had not, though I knew it was one of the wonders of the world. He said, "I will just fly you up there"—it was about 700 miles.

Detachment G's sole mission on that deployment to Charbatia came on May 24, 1964—a sortie by pilot Ericson over Tibet and the Sino-Indian Border that yielded good results. The detachment returned to Charbatia in late December, bringing their own water purification plant, to find the runway resurfaced and the hangar improved. Three missions were flown over the same regions that Ericson had covered in May, and the detachment redeployed back to the States by the end of the year. *All the missions went well, and the night before we were to leave, Singh called a meeting to thank us for our help to them, and for the success of all the flights. He told the group that he had promised to fly me to the Taj Mahal, but that it didn't happen. And then he gave me a replica of the Taj Mahal, which I have cherished to this day, and which is still in my apartment.*

Singh would later request that I return to India for a six-month period to help with its Air Force planning, but the Air Force would not allow it.

Greg's tolerance for the conditions at Charbatia was not shared by others on the deployment. The blistering heat prevented outside activity during midday hours. Gastroenteritis was widespread. Equipment supplied locally was in poor condition, and the drenching rain and high winds made operations in the open-ended hangars difficult.

For Detachment G, the return from Charbatia marked the beginning of a long hiatus. No missions were flown between January and October 1965—a remarkably long period considering the frenetic pace that the unit had been maintaining since the summer of 1960.

Detachment G testing program

In addition to conducting operational reconnaissance missions, Detachment G was also heavily engaged in U-2 research and development projects. For example, Detachment G worked on the development and testing of the U-2's electronic systems along with OSA technicians and private contractors. And significantly, Greg's unit was centrally involved in the conversion of U-2 aircraft engines to the more performant J-75 Pratt & Whitney engines.[22]

To this point, Detachment G had a sterling record for safe operations. Quite contrary to earlier U-2 operations, the CIA's U-2s had operated without a fatal accident for nearly 10 years, a record that Greg's unit maintained until April 26, 1965, shortly before Greg was scheduled to be relieved of command. Thirty-five-year-old Eugene "Buster" Edens, one of the original U-2 pilots—a man who had flown with Detachments B and C before his assignment to G, and who had flown 17 missions with Detachment G—was making his final approach to the runway at Edwards following a routine mission. When he began experiencing a problem with one of his aircraft's wings, he applied power and climbed away from the airfield. But on reaching 3,000 feet, the aircraft began a spiraling descent from which it could not recover. Edens ejected at 400 feet, too low for his parachute to deploy fully, and was killed when he hit the ground.

Edens' aircraft, Article 382, was one of those modified for the carrier landings trial. *We had flown it in the morning, and the pilot said that it was not flying right. Edens' fatal crash occurred on the afternoon flight. Kelly Johnson of Lockheed came to Edwards to evaluate the crash site, but the cause was never determined.* Edens at the time was a civilian pilot under contract to the CIA. Prior to Greg's appointment as detachment commander, while flying with Detachment B, Edens had completed at least one Soviet overflight and was the first to photograph the major Soviet space launch facility at Tyuratam.[23]

On reflection, and despite Edens' loss, Greg is well pleased with the overall performance of the detachment during his tenure. *A pretty good record to lose just one aircraft, considering all the flying they did all over the world. We had a group of really good pilots.* Greg equally praises the maintenance team of the detachment, noting that in all those years under his command, the U-2 never lost an engine on takeoff.

CHAPTER 13

The A-12 Archangel and a Turning Point

Even as the U-2 spyplane became operational in 1956, the intelligence community believed that it would be able to safely operate on Soviet overflight missions for a maximum of two years. It also knew that the date on which effective satellite surveillance would be fully operational was indeterminate. Just as the U-2 served as a necessary follow-on to the RB-57Ds, one further fixed-wing platform was needed to safely bridge the gap between the U-2's expected obsolescence, and the advent of satellite reconnaissance. In this context, "safely" now meant a system that could operate undetected, was untrackable, or was impervious to shootdown.

The CIA's earliest investigations into that platform—Project Gusto—envisioned a program that would operate covertly, would be developed "in profound secrecy," and would extend the CIA's capabilities in high-altitude PHOTINT reconnaissance, a mission that it had come to relish.[1]

CIA-sponsored operational analysis had concluded that the combined effects of supersonic speed, a very low radar cross-section (RCS), new radar-absorbing technologies, and ultra-high altitudes would greatly reduce the chances of detection and tracking by the increasingly advanced Soviet radars, and also significantly lessen the potential for interception by surface-to-air missiles.[2]

Lockheed's Kelly Johnson would later recount an April 1958 conversation with CIA Deputy Director Richard Bissell: "We agreed that there should be one more round (of aircraft) before satellites would make aircraft reconnaissance obsolete for cover reconnaissance."[3]

By late 1958, after reviewing a number of conceptual designs submitted by industry and the military—including some best described as outlandish—a high-level CIA panel of experts concluded that developing the new platform would indeed be possible, and urged further design studies and testing into what would later be termed "stealth technologies." By June 1959 advanced feasibility studies had received presidential approval.

The CIA solicited proposals from two aerospace companies for the requisite aircraft: Lockheed, which was well familiar with high-altitude aircraft, and Convair, which was then building the B-58 supersonic Hustler bomber for the Air Force. Both responded in August 1959 with design proposals for aircraft far in advance of anything then flying, proposals subsequently given close scrutiny by a review panel composed of the Department of Defense, the US Air Force, and the CIA.

Lockheed's final proposal was designated the "A-12," its twelfth design iteration, the previous eleven designs having been presented to the CIA and rejected. The long, slim A-12 included two huge jet engines, twin tails, and small back-swept wings from which projected a long, sharp nose. The design was sleek and arresting.

While on paper the Convair design promised better overall performance, it was considered to be "technologically riskier" than the Lockheed design. It was determined that the Lockheed design offered the better overall combination of speed, altitude, size, and range, and further to its advantage, Lockheed had a long history of high-altitude aircraft development, careful budgetary controls, and the development of highly secret projects. In February 1960, it was the Lockheed design that was selected for production.

With that selection, Gusto came to an end and Lockheed received a contract for 12 A-12s.[4,5] The CIA perversely assigned the codename "Oxcart" to the project as it moved into the production and operation phase. Lockheed's own internal cryptonym for the aircraft was "Archangel."

As with the U-2 development, Lockheed would design and build the aircraft, and incorporate critical systems supplied by others: Pratt & Whitney would provide the engines; Perkin-Elmer Corp. would design and build a new, highly advanced camera system; Honeywell Corp. would design both the inertial navigation and automatic flight control systems; and Firewel and the David Clark Company would provide pilot equipment and life support hardware.

By October 1960, the CIA and the USAF had outlined an agreement for the organization and delineation of responsibilities for Oxcart, which would generally follow the same arrangements that had marked the successful U-2 program. The agreement, approved by both parties in February 1961, confirmed that the CIA would be responsible for the continuing R&D for the project, for operational planning, and for the direction and control of activities in the final operation phase of the project during overflight launches. The USAF would contribute funding and would provide a wide spectrum of support for the project activities, including refueling tankers and other support aircraft, and site security.

The tightly-controlled Groom Lake facility in the Nevada desert—the same location that supported the U-2 program—was selected as the site for flight testing. Groom Lake was within the Atomic Energy Commissions nuclear test site, which ostensibly managed the facility. The initial cover story promulgated by AEC in press releases prepared by the CIA was that the site would be used for Air Force-sponsored radar studies. It was planned that the covert A-12 detachment, when fully operational, would continue to operate from Groom Lake.[6]

At Groom Lake, project management would closely resemble that of Detachment G at Edwards North Base. Air Force Col. Robert Holbury commanded the newly-instituted 1129th Special Activities Squadron (SAS), with a CIA staffer as his deputy. Their mission: to develop and maintain an operational ready unit capable of executing missions as directed by the CIA project HQ.[7] And like Detachment G, the team at Groom Lake would be composed of USAF personnel, civilian staff, and contract personnel from Lockheed and other technical systems suppliers.

The new aircraft was unimaginably advanced. It would operate at Mach 3.2 (2400 mph), 900 mph faster than the then-current fastest airplane. It would reach an altitude of 90,000 feet (17 miles) or more, closely approaching the then-current record for fixed wing aircraft. The high speed would expose the aircraft to temperatures of over 550 degrees Fahrenheit, requiring Lockheed to construct the aircraft from a titanium alloy, a metal having high strength, light weight and good resistance to high temperatures, but which was also an exceedingly difficult metal to use in fabrication. The continuously curving airframe design, a forebody with tightly slanted edges called chines, engines housing located mid-wing, canted rudders, and nonmetallic composites in the wings, chines and tails all acted to decrease the RCS to levels acceptable to the CIA.[8]

Production was rife with problems, and each A-12 that came off the Burbank manufacturing line was essentially handcrafted: hardly a desirable condition. Issues of titanium fabrication, lubricants, engines, fuel, navigation, flight control, ECM, radar stealth, and pilot life-support systems all required innovative solutions from Lockheed, and it was later observed by Thomas McIninch that "Lockheed's solutions constituted the greatest single technological achievement of the entire enterprise."[9,10]

The Lockheed A-12 Archangel. (Wikimedia Commons)

And it was expensive. By January 1960 production price of the 12 aircraft was nearly $104 million. By November 1961, the price tag had increased to $165 for a reduced production of just 10 A-12s.

The A-12 was manufactured and ground tested under the highest security conditions at Lockheed's plant at Burbank. Owing to its covert status, the completed airframes could not be flown to Groom Lake and they were too large to be carried on cargo aircraft. Instead, completed airframes were disassembled and loaded into two Lockheed-designed trailers. One large, 35 x 105 ft. carriage box contained the fuselage, riding on its own landing gear. The second trailer carried a smaller carriage box that contained the wings, rudders, and forward fuselage section.

The first A-12 airframe (Article 121) was delivered to Groom Lake on February 28, 1962 and made its first official flight on April 30, 1962—two and a half years after the awarding of the contract to Lockheed, and one year later than promised. Six months later, the A-12 program became more urgent when an Agency U-2 was downed by a surface-to-air missile at the height of the Cuban Missile Crisis, strengthening doubts within the intelligence community about the sustainability of the U-2, and giving enormous impetus to the Oxcart program.

By the end of 1962, five A-12s were delivered to Groom Lake.

Specifications: Lockheed A-12 Archangel[11, 12]

Powerplant: 2, Pratt & Whitney
Turbojets, 34,000 lbs. thrust each (on afterburner)
Crew: 1
Max speed: 2,524 mph
Service ceiling: 90,000 ft.
Range: 3,000 miles

In-flight weight (max): 120,000 lbs.
Wing span: 55 ft. 5 in.
Length: 101 ft. 9 in.
Height: 18 ft. 6 in.
Production: 15

The challenging and time-consuming flight testing of the aircraft and its systems began, with very encouraging early results. In the aircraft's second official flight, it broke the sound barrier, reaching Mach 1.1. By November, 1962, the aircraft had achieved a speed of over Mach 2, and an altitude of 60,000 feet. Eight months later Mach 3 was reached, and the first sustained flight that attained full operational conditions—Mach 3.2 at 83,000 feet—was made in February 1964. By the end of 1964, eleven A-12s were in inventory at Groom Lake, four used for testing and seven assigned to the detachment, including one two-seat trainer variant. Flight testing continued as the platform slowly worked its way to a condition where an operational deployment could be made.[13]

The performance of the A-12 platform generated considerable interest from others in the intelligence community, who viewed the aircraft not as an end in itself, but rather as the starting point for further innovative defense and reconnaissance projects. Three new platforms emerged in the early 1960s that were slightly modified clones of the A-12: the Air Force's prototype YF-12A high-speed interceptor; the unusual M21/D21 drone reconnaissance system; and most spectacularly, the SR-71 high-altitude Air Force reconnaissance aircraft.

Deploying the Archangel

The original objective for the A-12—overhead reconnaissance of the Soviet Union—had been obviated well before the aircraft had completed flight testing. Soviet air defenses had evolved apace, and were capable of tracking even the high flying, uber-fast A-12. Additionally, President Kennedy had announced that no further Soviet overflights would be made, a policy continued by the Johnson administration, and by the time deployment could be made it was expected that satellite reconnaissance would provide the Soviet overhead intelligence requirements.

But China was a different matter. The PRC had successfully tested a nuclear device in October 1964—a development that demanded close surveillance. Developments in Southeast Asia had increasingly drawn the CIA's attention, leading to further requests within the intelligence community for overhead reconnaissance.

And just as Greg and Detachment G, in the months following the Powers' shootdown, had undergone an operational test in order to confirm its readiness, the CIA intended to task the A-12 unit with a simulated operational mission as a final evaluation prior to deployment.

Operation *Silver Javelin* was slated for January 1965—a series of long-range, high-speed, high-altitude proving flights. The results of this operation would determine whether the A-12 was ready for its first mission, most likely an overflight of Communist China, or a mission over Southeast Asia, or both.

In mid-1964, anticipating a positive result from *Silver Javelin* and a fully operational A-12 detachment, OSA chief Jack Ledford began considering the composition of his command team. Ledford was aware that the A-12 had not yet attained its design range, and could not be tasked with missions originating from its base at Groom Lake, as was first intended. The earliest missions would have to be launched from a deployed location outside the United States. And while the Agency had a solid four-year history of forward deployments of its U-2 unit at Edwards, the A-12 was a vastly more complicated aircraft, and its deployment would be a much more complex undertaking. It would require more planning, more personnel, more equipment, and much more support. It was especially clear that Ledford's command team would need experience in forward deployments.

At this critical juncture, Ledford knew that Col. Holbury, commander of the A-12 detachment at Groom Lake, was due for reassignment, probably before the unit's first deployment. He reasoned that Holbury's Operations Officer, Col. Hugh Slater, formerly commander of the CIA's U-2 Detachment H in Taiwan, would be a competent replacement as unit commander. What Ledford needed was a new Operations Officer. The roster of candidate officers would have been quite short, but Ledford knew exactly who was at the top of the list, and in May booked a flight to Edwards.[14]

At the Edwards North Base, Col. Gregory's assignment to Detachment G was scheduled to come to an end within a year, and he had begun to wonder what his next posting would be. In particular, would it be to another unit within the Agency? Or would he revert to the Air Force, and if so, to what post and with what duties?

When Ledford arrived at Edwards, he told Greg he wanted them to take a trip north to Groom Lake. They made the short flight in the detachment's two-seat T-33, with Greg at the controls.

I was aware of the area, and Jack wanted to show me around all the facilities. It was a great place for secrecy. That was when I had my first look at the A-12 aircraft—they had two or three parked on the ramp there—and got in one. They were already flying them, but it was real early in the program.

Ledford told Greg: "You see what is here, and I would like you to move up here and take up the Operations part of the program."

Jack Ledford and Greg had worked together for four years in the U-2 program: Jack at the CIA's Office of Special Activities in Washington leading the program, and Greg at Edwards in command of the U-2 squadron. The meeting at the Ranch came just a couple of years after the Cuban Missile Crisis. Ledford was fully aware of the role Greg's Detachment G had played in the resolution of that crisis, and of Greg's earlier command of the 4025th SRS and his exemplary performance during its overseas deployments. Ledford made the offer in the full confidence that Greg could transition easily from Edwards to Groom Lake, and from the U-2 to the A-12. He knew that whatever further challenges might lay ahead for the Archangel, he would not have to worry about the competence of the command staff.

It was an astonishing offer. As Operations Officer, Greg would have flown the A-12 himself as part of his duties at Groom Lake, and would have been in charge of all the training and operational deployments later. He would coax the aircraft to its final design range, to higher speeds and greater altitudes, and would have been tasked with completing the air refueling capability for the detachment. He would fly an aircraft that was nearly 5 times faster than the U-2, to altitudes three miles higher, touching the edge of space. *That airplane was Mach 3, something like 2,100 miles per hour. That was a job that most Air Force officers would have killed for, a job you would really fight for. If things had gone well, I would have made general from that job.*

I had been in the high-altitude program for eight years by this time. I knew this new assignment was going to be another four or five years where I would be away for 70 percent of the time or more and see my family very little, and for the first two years of that period hardly at all. I would surely be on the first operational deployment of the A-12, and when it became operationally ready, I would have been in charge of that as well. I would have had to go up there almost immediately, would have led a team, and would have been in charge of training.

The operation at Groom Lake did not permit resident dependents. Greg reasoned that his family could move from Edwards to Las Vegas, the closest city to Area 51, but that would still put them two and a half hours distant by car. Greg wrestled with how to become more of a family man, and at the same time see the world from 90,000 feet.

Family matters

With her marriage to Greg, Helen had become a wartime bride to a fighter pilot. They seldom discussed the hazards of his flight career, although the continuing loss of good men through aviation accidents at the air field was impossible to ignore. Having lived through the loss of Lt. DeMoss, Helen was keenly aware of the dangers, even Stateside: dangers that persisted even in peacetime. But she was accepting of Greg's love for flying, and of his dedication to the Air Force mission. And she had great trust in his ability. *She always thought I would come back, and I did too.*

When Greg left the service in 1947 and returned to civilian life, Helen would have been pleased to see that he had the skills and dedication to excel in private sector employment. But this was cut short by his reactivation for the Korean War, and any hopes Helen may have had for a civilian career afterwards ended when Greg, feeling the compelling allure of flight, had decided to accept a posting to the 301st Bomb Wing at Barksdale. But she was deeply committed to Greg, and had readily accepted the new challenges that came with Greg's new post, and with his ever-increasing deployments.

Greg's first overseas deployment had come as a KB-29 tanker pilot when his 301st Air Refueling Squadron was posted to Lakenheath, England in May, 1950. Originally set for 90 days, the deployment was extended "indefinitely," and Greg did not return until mid-December. Their first separation in their young marriage, the deployment had left Helen to care for their two-year-old daughter, Gretchen, and to learn to cope with Greg's absence. But other wives were experiencing the same separations, many also for the first time, and there was an element of common cause among them.

Author Robert S. Hopkins notes: "Departures were tough. Sweethearts were left behind. Fathers were gone for Christmas, school plays, or the birth of a child. Wives were forced to cope with traditional 'man-of-the-house' duties like income tax preparation, mowing the lawn, or fixing the clutch in the car all while fulfilling their ubiquitous role as homemaker."[15]

During Greg's early Air Force career, while flying KB-29 tankers or the B-47 strategic bomber, Helen had known to what foreign base he was being deployed. And although that was some comfort, while Greg was on deployment—and his deployment could last as long as six months—he never had direct contact with Helen or spoke to the kids. For both, it was as if Greg had been teleported to a distant planet.

They were both in the Service: both knew that what they were doing made a difference to their country. But it was tough, and Greg would readily admit that the separations were toughest on Helen.

Like every other Air Force wife, Helen made innumerable adaptations to cope with her husband's absence. Among other things, she assumed the role of disciplinarian. In later reflections, daughter Cookie recounts: "My mother decided that our father would never play the role of disciplinarian… ever. If my mother had leaned on the old adage of 'Just wait 'til your father comes home!' I would have waited months for the needed attitude correction. Justice with Helen Dwire Gregory was both swift and thoughtful, and we moved on. Our mother let our father be the source of unmitigated joy in our lives, despite the enormous sacrifices she made and the frustrations and challenges she faced with two children… often absolutely alone and in a remote location."

Cookie describes their home as "exquisitely and efficiently run by my mother" during Greg's many absences. On his return from deployment, he would reintegrate himself into the patterns and rhythms that Helen had established in the household. "Many of the quarters around us went through dark periods when 'Dad came home.' That was not the case for us."

Helen kept the children busy, and on each deployment she would initiate a project that would occupy the family for the two or three months of Greg's absence. Painting the house, creating new needlepoint covers for the dining room tables, making new ornaments for the Christmas tree—something tangible to fill the long nights and empty weekends that lay ahead. Throughout, the children were taught never to ask when their father would return home.

Mail from Greg was rare and censored. In 1963, when Greg was promoted to full colonel—a huge event in the life of a career Air Force officer—the news came to Helen from an office in Washington, DC. Greg was on deployment and could not call to tell her himself.

At Edwards, wives were briefed on their husband's assignment, but the information provided was primarily intended to strengthen the cover story

Helen's graphic art. (Gregory)

for the covert U-2 operations: "WRSP-IV conducts high-altitude research, and … classified research and development studies … for the Department of Defense." Conceding the classified nature of the operations, wives were instructed what they could say about their husband's occupation, and what to do if questioned too closely.[16] Helen was convinced that their house phone was bugged.

Her children recall Helen crying just twice. The first time was on the unexpected death of her mother while Greg was on deployment. The second was on a Christmas Eve when she was attempting without success to assemble a bicycle. Cookie recalls: "Silent crying seemed to me to be the saddest thing I had ever witnessed, but I knew enough to turn around and go back to bed… never mentioning the scene again."

Deployments were always hard on families. Much earlier in Greg's career, immediately following his deployment to Morocco as a B-47 command pilot with the 19th Bomb Wing, many in Greg's wing opted to leave the service. The wing reported: "During (April) the reenlistment rate fell to nine percent. Of 35 personnel discharged only three reenlisted."[17] Perhaps an illustration of the difficulties faced by those deployed, and by those who remained at home.

And the nature of Greg's work with Detachment G would have taken both Greg and Helen by surprise—most particularly, the extent to which he would be deployed.

Prior to his assignment at Edwards, Greg's deployments had been more or less routine for a command pilot in the Air Force: two deployments while flying the KB-29, one with the B-47, and two with the RB-57D-2s, plus other short-term travel and TDY. Families knew about deployments well in advance, and could plan for the separations. It was all part of the job for an Air Force officer, and for his wife.

But command of the CIA's U-2 unit was different, and in unexpected ways. Within two months of his arrival at Edwards, Greg was deployed to Del Rio for overflights of Cuba in Operation *Kick Off*. In the first twelve months after their arrival at Edwards, Greg and the detachment deployed seven times— including two deployments to Cubi Bay in the Philippines for overflights of North Vietnam and Laos.

During that time, Helen settled into an awareness that her marriage to Greg, her relationship to her children, and her life at Edwards would be markedly different from anything she had experienced before. She, like the wives of other men in the detachment, would have no more than 24 hours to prepare for Greg's departure, would not know where in the world he would be, did not know when he would return. And while it may not have been talked about openly, both she and Greg knew that he was engaged in a risky business. When she saw him off on his many departures, she would have displayed a confidence that he would return safely, but would always have the gnawing anxiety that something could go wrong.

Edwards itself was different in many ways from the Gregory's previous homes at Ontario, Del Rio, or Orlando. The Laughlin AFB and the town of Del Rio was the smallest of the base communities to which Greg and Helen had been posted, and until Edwards, was the most isolated. But Del Rio had a population of around 30,000, and Laughlin was home to a large Air Force contingent that included the 4025th and 4028th SRS and the 4080th SRW. This created a large service community that supported the families of men on deployment. At the time of Greg's posting to Edwards, the population of the surrounding census district was only 1,845, and his small unit, the WRSP (IV), was alone at North Base.[18] The nearest town of any size was Lancaster, 30 miles to the southwest, with a population of 26,000 in 1960.[19] And there was little about Greg's work that Helen could share with friends or family.

In the second year of Greg's tenure at Edwards, the rate of deployment increased. Greg deployed nine times in that period, always to Del Rio, and always for overflights of Cuba. Some deployments were brief—a week or less. Others, like the eight-mission deployment that began on August 5, 1962, would last for over a month. By the end of 1964, Greg had completed an estimated 29 deployments since his first deployment with the 301st Bomb Wing five years earlier—surely an Air Force record. And beyond deployments, Greg spent a considerable amount of time away from Edwards on official CIA business. After five years of increasingly frequent deployments at Edwards, Helen began to feel the effects of Greg's separation from family, something that she at long last shared with him.

Following Greg's return in April from his long deployment with the U-2s to Takhli, Thailand, Helen spoke candidly with him about the increasing difficulty she was having with his long absences. *She said, "I don't know how much longer I can take these separations," and she confided that, often without a husband, life was passing her by.* It says much about Helen that she did not talk to him about all the challenges she had to face while he was away, or how hard it was to be effectively a single parent for those long months. It was Greg she missed. It was being separated from him that mattered most.

Greg took pause. Helen had at long last come to the end of her forbearance of Greg's deployments, and another factor in his mind was his two daughters, then in high school. *I really had to think about [Ledford's offer] because I just returned about 10 days previously from another lengthy TDY, and my wife, who didn't know about this offer, had recently told me that our separations were becoming more difficult. Helen was a wonderful person, a good mother, and had always been so supportive of me.*

It was a tremendous offer, and I thought long and hard about it before explaining to Colonel Ledford that I really appreciated the confidence that he had shown in me by this offer, but that I felt like I had to turn it down for these reasons.

Ledford understood. A year earlier he had written a memorandum to the CIA Director reporting (in part): "Since the signing of the original (pilot) contracts in 1956 ... operational requirements have increased, and they have been required to spend more and more time away from their families."[20] During 1962 and 1963, the pilots averaged five months away from home each year. It was worse for Greg: his pilots did not go on every deployment, but he did.

He [Ledford] told me that when my tour was up at Edwards, he would help me get whatever assignment I wanted, within the Agency, the Air Force, or anywhere in the Defense Department.

I didn't discuss the offer or my decision with my wife. If she and I had discussed the job, and if I had shown even the slightest enthusiasm for it, she would have probably said go ahead and do this. But I didn't have that conversation with her, and I think it was the smart thing to do. I really don't have any regrets. It was an enormous opportunity, and I sometimes think about what might have happened if I had taken the job. I would have gotten deeply involved in the operation of the A-12.

And so in mid-1965, at the conclusion of my assignment at Edwards, I told Colonel Ledford that I would like to go to the National War College for a year if there was space.

Command of Detachment G passed to Lieutenant Colonel Miles Doyle. At the time Greg separated from Detachment G, having served five years as its commander, and by special order of the Air Force Chief of Staff, he was awarded his second Air Force Legion of Merit for "exceptionally meritorious conduct in the performance of outstanding service."[21, 22, 23]

Col. William Gregory, Commander, CIA U-2 Detachment G. (USAF)

CHAPTER 14

National War College, the Pentagon, and AFIT

Greg's request for a posting to the National War College (NWC) put Jack Ledford in something of a bind. The selection and admission process for the NWC was long and detailed, and the admission slots for the incoming class would normally have long been committed. Greg could not have deferred to the following year's class because he was already at the maximum age for admission to the College. But a year earlier the CIA had lobbied the National War College for an increase in allotments to agency from three to four slots, and Ledford managed to secure a place for Greg.[1]

Greg's class—the NWC's 20th—would number one hundred thirty-five and would include thirty-three civilians from nine agencies of government in addition to designated service personnel. No foreign observers were included in this class, though they had been in prior classes. All male, the average age of the class was forty-three years, with all military members holding the grade of Lt. Colonel or higher, or Navy equivalent. All students were required to have both "Q" and Top Secret clearance, and all were nominated on the expectation of "outstanding service in the future."[2]

There were only 25 individuals each from the Army, Navy, Air Force and Marines, and about 25 civilians who were accepted each year. Most of the service personnel would have had 15–20 years of experience, and only high achievers were selected for the War College. It was a sort of stepping-stone to make general.

Founded in 1943, and modelled after the Imperial Defence College in London, the school's original intent was twofold: first, to promote greater understanding between the civilian and military components of government in their respective areas of interest and responsibility, and second, to foster a greater understanding among the military services as regards their respective areas of effort, and especially their capabilities and limitations.[3] At the end of the war, the college took on a much broader perspective, most particularly including the role of the military and civilian defense organizations in the development of national and international strategic defense policy.

"The College is concerned with grand strategy and the utilization of the national resources necessary to implement that strategy... (preparing) future leaders of the Armed Forces, State Department and other civilian agencies for high-level policy, command and staff responsibilities... Its graduates will exercise a great influence on the formulation of national and foreign policy in both peace and war."[4,5]

The scope of the carefully designed curriculum included several key areas of study, predictably including an analysis of the nature and interdependence of the US military forces, and the integration of these forces with foreign policy. The United Nations came under scrutiny as a means of avoiding armed conflict between nations, and other "significant" nations were studied with respect to their international relations, areas of disagreements and conflict, and policies designed to prevent war.

The role of the US military in implementing national policy in peace and war was studied, as were strategy, war planning and the theory and practice of war, fundamentals of strategic thinking for national security matters, the impact of science and technology on the armed forces, and the use of joint and combined forces in the implementation of national and/or coalition objectives and policy.

The War College sought to stimulate the intellectual curiosity of its students and to foster independence of thought and the capacity to think objectively. In Greg's enduring opinion, the widely held perception of the National War College as a think tank for the conduct of war might be in error: *I really believe that the name of the NWC is wrong because it really concentrates on peace.*

The ten-month program was divided into ten separate courses designed to meet the mission and scope of the college and culminated in a Defense Strategy Seminar. Interestingly, though the nation was on the cusp of a major military campaign in South Asia, Vietnam was not specifically mentioned in any of the curricula for the courses offered to the class of 1965–6. However, as part of Course Five—The Communist State—a lecture and discussion group was held relating to a document prepared by the Chief of the Strategy Division of the Joint Chiefs of Staff, entitled: "Analysis of US Strategy in Vietnam, July 1965."[6]

The program was conducted using guest lecturers, intensive course readings, daily discussion groups, field trips, and a concluding Individual Research Paper. The guest lecturer program was particularly intense: four lectures were scheduled each week, with the lecturer making a formal presentation, followed by question-and-answers from the audience, and ending with an additional small-group informal meeting.

The college was located at Fort McNair, very close to the capital, and regularly invited eminent foreign visitors and high officials in the US government to address the class on subjects of their own choosing.

It was a really interesting year—with the War College being located in Washington, we had so many great speakers available, including President Nixon, Congressmen, Senators, top bureaucrats, and foreign speakers. Every day we had new speakers of the highest order. Among those speakers were Dean Acheson, Dr. Walter Rostow, General Bernard Schriever, Madame Chiang Kai-shek, Cyrus Vance, and many more.

We didn't study war tactics at all. The value of the college was associating with people from other services and from the state department and the other government civilian services as well.

While commanding U-2 Detachment G, Greg had worked for and within the Central Intelligence Agency but retained his rank as Colonel in the US Air Force. Leaving the Agency and Edwards, Greg was assigned to Detachment 14 (3825th Support Group [Academic Support]), with permanent duty station at the National War College at Fort Leslie J. McNair, Washington DC.

The program start date was August 12, 1965, and he was expected to complete the course of study by June 3, 1966—a program duration of 42 weeks. Additionally, Greg was ordered to report to the Flight Manager at Andrews AFB in Washington to schedule proficiency flying, and for that purpose, he was attached to the 1001 Air Base Wing at Andrews AFB.

Then aged 45, Col. Gregory, wife Helen, and his daughters Gretchen (aged 16) and Jamie ("Cookie", aged 12), moved to Playfield Street in Annandale, Virginia, for what they believed would be a one-year assignment to Washington DC, a prospect viewed favorably by only some of the family.

Greg arrived in Washington with an impressive aviation and command background, and a remarkable set of commendations, including two Legion of Merit awards, the Air Medal with eight Oak Leaf Clusters, and the Air Force Commendation Medal. What his instructors and fellow students would never see was the Medal of Merit he had recently been awarded in secret by the Central Intelligence Agency.

The class was divided into four parts, and we took a month's tour to any region of our choosing. I chose South America. We had an airplane at our disposal, and with the staff, there were probably 40 of us on the airplane.

In my case, we took off from Washington and the tour included Panama, Brasilia—the capital city then in the making in Brazil, Rio de Janiero, Paraguay, Argentina, Chile, Central American and finally Mexico City. It was really a great trip, and we all learned a lot on that trip.

Students were given the option of combining the NWC curriculum with courses at George Washington University (GWU) leading to a master's degree. Thirty or forty participated. *It really made for a busy year because we had to take extra courses at GWU during this time. But all those who participated completed the program and received their Masters in International Relations.*

A thesis was required at both GWU and the NWC. As noted, students at the college were encouraged to develop perspectives on strategic policies that were both national and global in scope and to cast a very broad net in their consideration of what constitutes "security" for the United States. For Col. Gregory, having been a combat fighter pilot, the command pilot of a nuclear-armed SAC bomber, and having spent much of his career in the stratosphere, it might be expected that his thesis would be oriented toward military or space technology, advanced weaponry, or international diplomacy. In fact, he directed his thesis research in a surprising direction. His topic: "Agrarian Reforms and Their Implications for Future Stability of the Mexican Government."

Greg's selection of this topic for what would be a year-long research effort was partially influenced by his Latin American tour, which included a visit and extensive briefings in Mexico. In retrospect, it is reasonable to also assume that his selection of this topic was greatly influenced by his experience as a young man in Tennessee, the son of a desperately-poor sharecropping father who himself felt the same oppressive poverty that Greg observed, 27 years after leaving the farm, among the villagers of Mexico.

Greg's selection of that topic and the recommendations he made at the conclusion of his research are revelatory and reflective of the *terroir* that remained with Greg to that day—his life growing up as the poor son of a Tennessee sharecropper.

In his research, Greg learned that the agrarian reforms that had been taking place in Mexico since the turn of the century had resulted in "tiny farms (of) very limited capability (without) the potential to provide an adequate standard of living." And like tenant farmers and sharecroppers in the southern United States, Mexican farmers who benefited from agrarian reforms still lacked direct ownership of land: "In reality, he is owner of the property only in the sense that he is afforded the opportunity to till the soil and reap its benefits during his lifetime," without enjoying the liberties associated with full ownership: essentially, a tenant farmer for life. He also noted the inadequacy and unfairness associated with the farm credit system in Mexico: "The lack of available farm credit at reasonable rates imposes a hardship on the peasant farmer," and in that he could just as easily have been addressing the harsh banking practices of the 1930s that led to the bankruptcy of his father's very promising Tennessee farm.[7]

One wonders how long Greg had been nurturing the concepts and ideals expressed in his thesis: "It is a common fallacy to think of land reforms only as a method for the redistribution of land. In the ideological concept, they are much more than that. They represent a useful method for improving the social and economic well-being of the farmers. Land reform seeks the advancement of the human resources on the land; the improvement of living conditions for farm families and the opportunities for continued betterment. It has the potential of increasing the contributions of agriculture to the stability and prosperity of the nation."

While the "hacienda" system of huge private agricultural holdings in Mexico paralleled neither the pattern of land ownership in the American South in the first half of the 20th century, nor the micro-farms that resulted from the "Ejidos" system of land redistribution that was adopted later in Mexico, there was a great similarity in the *effects* of legal and financial institutional policies in Mexico and the southern United States. Greg found the hacienda system "objectionable because of the moral, social and economic injustice which it imposed upon the very large portion of the population"—language that could easily have been applied to the conditions in north-central Tennessee in the mid-30s.

Greg also noted the importance of education for Mexico. His thesis includes specific recommendations—something not normally associated with research papers—including: "Increased technical and vocational training is needed to better equip the rural population for work both inside and outside the agricultural field." In that, Greg was surely echoing the strong opinions held by his father, Sam, who insisted that his son stay in school, and consider the possibilities of life outside of the farm system. Greg's thesis was submitted to and accepted by the National War College in January 1966, twenty-eight years after he left his family's farm in Tennessee and hitchhiked to Middle Tennessee State College.

It was a really busy year, with the paper I had to finish and with the work at George Washington toward the master's degree. Also at the end of the year, I had to take some really difficult examinations for the master's degree. But all in all, it was a great year, and I really enjoyed it.

With three months remaining at the National War College, Greg received orders for his next assignment—a highly classified position at the Pentagon. The posting to the Pentagon meant that the Gregory family would remain in Washington for a total of six years, something that was much to everyone's liking. But it also meant that Greg's life in the air was over—while many of the graduates of the NWC had returned to their tactical units, Greg's posting to the Pentagon did not include the requirement that he maintain flight proficiency. He was effectively grounded from the day he left the War College.

While not strictly a taciturn individual, Greg is not one to expand on unpleasant memories or to amplify feelings of regret. About his grounding, he would only say: *Yeah, that was bad. I regretted that.*

At that time, Greg had been outside the Air Force proper for several years. His credibility and reputation were well known within the CIA, but less so within the Air Force. *And that was not a good thing. If I had been working for Air Force people during that time, it would have been better for me for the next assignment. In the Air Force, it helps if you have a sponsor—a general officer—who wants you on his team. I did not exactly have that at the time. The fact that I had been working for the CIA for five years actually worked against me for my next assignment.*

His thoughts were not to be shared with anyone at the NWC—his work with the Agency was still classified. He was in a squeeze there because of his commitment to Detachment G.

Greg was assigned to the Directorate of Reconnaissance and Electronic Warfare, of the office of the Deputy Chief of Staff for Research and Development (R&D), within the Headquarters of the US Air Force at the Pentagon. *I had been in reconnaissance for the past nine years, and it was a logical assignment for me.*

The Pentagon

By the time Greg entered the Pentagon's main gate, he had acquired an aura of uniqueness. At the Pentagon, and in his later postings, Greg would join others with equally diverse experiences, many unique in their own ways. As his career advanced, he became a living singularity—there was simply no one else to whom he, or his service to his country, could be compared.

The Pentagon will forever be an impressive building. The world's largest low-rise office building, it stands just 71 feet high—five floors—and encompasses just over one square mile. It is equipped much like a small city, with food courts, restaurants, and shops and even mini-malls sprinkled throughout. But no elevators.

Greg's unit was housed on the fifth floor in the outer ring of offices, and some time was required for him to understand how to locate other offices and navigate to them. Shortcuts—down one corridor, one staircase down, through a connecting aisle, down another staircase, and so forth—became valuable additions to the knowledge base. *We did a lot of visiting with other elements at the Pentagon, particularly in research, and we got to know the way to other offices. It's a very interesting building—one of a kind.*

In first reporting for duty, Greg was the Chief of the Program Group. His commander was Colonel Roger K. Rhodarmer, who reported to the Deputy Chief of Staff for R&D, and functioned as the Assistant for Reconnaissance.

Rhodarmer's division was responsible for research and development of Air Force reconnaissance, both strategic and tactical. In this capacity, the division reviewed and made recommendations on the many R&D projects funded by the USAF—all of which were aimed at enhancing America's reconnaissance capability. At any one time, Greg's team would have 50 or more separate projects, each in varying stages of development, and each with its own budgets, development team, and of course, problems. Each project was assigned to a project officer within the division who was responsible for knowing everything about the project: its objective, leadership, current status, and whether it was operating within its approved budget.

The division was deep within the Air Force organization. The Deputy Chief of Staff to whom Rhodarmer reported was one of sixteen DCSs that made up the team of the Assistant Vice Chief of Staff. No family tree had more limbs, or was more complex, than the organization of the US Air Force, to say nothing of the larger Department of Defense of which the USAF was one component.

Greg was deeply experienced in the field of strategic reconnaissance, and R&D programs that related to the U-2 or SR-71 were right in his wheel-house. But tactical reconnaissance was new to him, involving differing tactics, missions, and aircraft. Greg's division was also heavily involved in the development of drones, and it was not going well. *We were having so much trouble with the drones. This was in '66. Like all new things, it was full of problems from the start.*

In practice, each month Rhodarmer would convene a review of all the four or five dozen programs currently being funded by the Air Force for reconnaissance. Each program officer would report on his assigned projects, with particular reference to whether the funding allocated to the project was adequate, or whether the approved funding was more than what could be justified for the project.

For example, one of Greg's assignments involved a new R&D program for the Tactical Air Command (TAC). The project involved developing a new system for developing all the film that was being acquired by TAC—much of it coming from the intensified conflict in Vietnam. *The project was being developed by Tracor Corp, and would be laid out in several buildings, and was going to be an expensive program, in part because it would process many different types of films, each with its own set of developing equipment, procedures, and material. I spent a couple of days at Tracor going through what they were proposing to do. It looked to me that they were going to have too much, so on my return to Washington, I proposed that we cut back on that program, which was done.*

We had programs throughout the US, and even some foreign programs. But we always had some programs going on at Wright Patterson. Our project officers would go to Wright regularly. We developed these programs based on the best solutions for the problem we were working on.

During Greg's tenure, he was given new and expanded responsibilities. By late 1969 Greg was Chief of the Reconnaissance Division and Rhodarmer was reassigned to lead the Air Force's F-15 development project, an assignment that led to great success and resulted in Rhodarmer being promoted to Brigadier General. He was replaced by his then-deputy, Colonel Theodor Coberly.

At that time, NATO maintained a Reconnaissance Committee consisting of eight to ten member countries. Greg was designated as the US Air Force delegate to the committee and served as its chair. The committee met twice yearly: the first meeting of the year was to familiarize all members with the current state of reconnaissance and to provide for mutual cooperation in the field of European reconnaissance. In the second meeting of the year, Greg would brief higher-level military commanders on the current state of reconnaissance.

It was a very interesting job, but it wasn't as good as the job I was supposed to get. It sort of destroyed my hopes for making general. But going to Washington had been a life-changing move for all of us. My daughters were exposed to different people, different young people, Gretchen completed college and met her future husband, Gene Davis. If I had taken the -71 job, we would eventually have gone back to Beale AFB in Calif, and neither girl would have been exposed to the people they married. It was life-changing for the whole family.

Greg's posting to the Pentagon would not lead to a general's star, but in recognition of his work the Air Force would award him his third Legion of Merit, an award no doubt initiated by Rhodarmer and Coberly. The citation accompanying the award reads, in part:

> Colonel William J. Gregory distinguished himself in outstanding service while assigned to the Directorate of Reconnaissance and Electronic Warfare. In this important assignment, the leadership, exemplary managerial skill, and ceaseless efforts resulted in highly significant contributions to the operational effectiveness, modernization, and long-range development of reconnaissance and electronic warfare forces of the United States.
>
> The superior initiative, outstanding leadership, and personal endeavor displayed by Colonel Gregory reflect great credit upon himself and the United States Air Force.[8]

It was about this time, 1969, that Helen's brother, Jeff Dwyer, married Virginia Clinton.[9]

Jeff died in 1974, and at his services, Virginia's son Bill Clinton delivered what Greg describes as an eloquent eulogy for Jeff. Greg spent quite a bit of time with the then-twenty-eight-year-old Bill Clinton in the days surrounding Jeff's services. *I asked him what his plans were, and he said that he intended to return to Arkansas, and get into politics.*

Greg would later speculate that, had he been a younger Air Force officer at the time Clinton became president, he might have had the opportunity to serve as a military advisor. But, as he also reflects, *our politics did not go well together!*

The Air Force Institute of Technology

Greg worked at the Pentagon for five years, and then in 1971 took a call from Major General Ernest Pinson, the commandant of the Air Force Institute of Technology (AFIT) at Wright Patterson AFB. Pinson explained that he was looking for a Vice Commandant and Chief of Staff. He wanted someone who had command experience in strategic air command, had reviewed Greg's record and wanted him to consider the job.

On General Pinson's invitation, I went to Wright Patterson and visited AFIT. I met his qualifications but did not think I would be qualified for the job because I had not been in the field of education before. I told him that his job offer was so different from what I had been doing that I didn't think I would be suited for it.

He showed me around the Institute and explained that I would be his chief of staff, would handle all the staff meetings, would be pretty much in charge of whatever was going on, and would be responsible for making sure everything worked smoothly at the Institute.

Greg was impressed with all the things available at AFIT: it offered graduate programs to Air Force students primarily in engineering at the masters and doctorate level and had one of the best post-grad schools in aeronautical engineering in the country. It also included a School of Strategic Force Studies and one of Systems and Logistics, and through the Civilian Institutions Program, AFIT was responsible for thousands of Air Force students who were assigned by AFIT to universities throughout the country for postgraduate degrees.

I accepted General Pinson's offer and would remain at AFIT for four years, It became a really interesting job—very different from what I had done before, but very challenging, and I really liked the job and the people there.

Greg's position was much like a Provost and included important responsibilities for curriculum development, and faculty recruitment and evaluation.

We had a very good staff, including many full colonels. I convened weekly staff meetings that included all department heads, plus the librarian and other key staff. In a typical staff meeting, I would put out all the information that was of general interest to everyone, and would then call on them if they had anything they wanted to talk about.

Greg lunched with General Pinson every day and the close professional relationship that developed contributed to a smooth operation at the Institute. When Pinson retired and was replaced by Major General Frank J. Simokaitis, an equally positive relationship developed. *General Simokaitis was a really fine person. I got to know him really well. He became a good friend and still is today. He had come from the Pentagon, and on arrival, I gave him a thorough briefing of the Institute and our operations. He was very supportive of all I was doing, instructed me to continue the same policies and procedures. He confirmed that I would continue as Chief of Staff, and allowed me to run the staff as I had been doing before. He didn't make any significant changes.*

Greg's Air Force career came to an end while he was at AFIT, and he retired on August 31, 1975, in the grade of Colonel, at the age of 55. *General Simokaitis made my retirement ceremony very special for me. During the ceremony, he revealed to all in attendance, most for the first time, the history of my years commanding the U-2 reconnaissance unit involved in the Cuban missile crisis. I hadn't expected it to be made public that soon, but it had become declassified, and it was on that day that my wife, my family, and friends learned for the first time about this chapter in my life.*

Maintaining such tight security had been a burden for both Greg and his family for many years. *When I would get an order to go out for an assignment, I could not tell them where I was going, or how long I would be gone. Helen always managed very well and would arrange for a project that she and the girls would work on while I was away. It seemed to work out well for them, and when I returned they would often try to guess where I had been, generally inaccurately.*

At his retirement, General Simokaitis presented Greg with his fourth Legion of Merit, and about the same time, Greg was able to take possession of his Intelligence Medal of Merit from the CIA, permanently this time, along with the personal letter from President Kennedy.

In receiving the third Oak Leaf Cluster to his Legion of Merit, Greg joined a very select group of honorees. Since the Legion of Merit was instituted in 1942, and to the present day, only two other Air Force officers have received four Legions of Merit: John Boyd, a combat pilot and military strategist; and General John Paul McConnell, the same man who, as Commander of the Seventh Air Force, had vigorously chastised the 301st Bomb Wing for its rowdy behavior during a 1950 deployment, and who had later commended the 301st for its exception performance in a later deployment. And it was McConnell who had awarded Greg his second Legion of Merit for meritorious service as commander of U-2 Detachment G, and under whom Greg would serve while McConnell was Air Force Chief of Staff.[10]

Greg speaks well of his Air Force career, and expresses a deep gratitude for the opportunities that came his was. *My years in the Air Force were very good. I enjoyed my entire career, and I think I was lucky in many ways. If I had taken the job with the A-12, I probably would have had an opportunity to earn a general's star, but I don't have any regrets at all. I had some great assignments, and I look back on it with pleasure.*

CHAPTER 15

The Colonel is a Civilian

Leaving Dayton, Greg and Helen visited Austin, Texas in the spring of 1975. *Austin is at its best in April. So, we decided to settle down there.* They knew no one, but began settling into their new home, and Helen got busy making friends and joining organizations. Cookie quips that, "Their goal was to meet enough people to have a cocktail party."[1]

I was really not in a hurry to get a job, so I thought I would take a few months off. Cookie and her husband Phil had moved to Spain, so Helen and I visited them for about a month after they were well settled. It was a great trip—they had been there long enough that they knew where all the interesting places were, and they really showed us around during our stay there.

Back in Austin, a friend had been named director of Texas' Workers Compensation Division. Greg became the assistant director in what he thought would be a short-term job. *But I was in that job for 15 years! It was a really interesting second career. It was the insurance company for the 185,000 state employees. We collected all the injury reports and claims from the employees, and had a team of adjusters and safety people. We would usually get 25 claims a day from employees all over the state. It was very similar to what an insurance company would do in processing claims. It was really an interesting job.*

Many of Greg's former squadron mates from the 49th had bought private aircraft after their retirement from Air Force flying, including his good friend and Operations Officer Richard Decker. But that was not on the cards for Greg.

I would have, except that my wife did not like to fly in small planes. That was a real disappointment to me, because I thought we could have had a lot of fun flying out somewhere for breakfast, and taking little cross-countries. Wright Patterson had a flying club and it would have been easy and interesting to fly over some of the towns there in the area. I think I would have enjoyed that, particularly if Helen would have joined me. But Helen would never agree to

William and Helen Gregory, Gretchen and Cookie. (Gregory)

that. There was something in her life that made her uncomfortable in tight places, and I didn't know about it for a long time. Because of that, I never did buy a plane, and regretted that very much.

It was about this time, the late 1980s, that Greg was released from certain restrictions and obligations under which he had lived since first becoming associated with the CIA. Among other things, he was no longer required to correspond monthly with his fictional friends, the "Smiths," in Louisiana. This came to Helen's attention in an unusual way. Cookie was visiting and helping Helen in the kitchen. "Dad was back in his study watching football, and Mom asked me to remind him that he might take this opportunity to finish the handful of Christmas cards he wrote each year, Mom having to write dozens more. When I delivered the message, Dad gave me a wry smile and said, 'Tell your mother the John Smith family never existed.' Mom's response was, 'Well that's just silly. John's wife is Barbara, they live in Mansfield, Louisiana, and they have two kids, and we've been writing them for over 20 years…' Dad explained: 'For the past 20 years I've been writing to the address in Louisiana to provide evidence that I was still competent in the use of code. They just released me from this requirement… there never was a John and Barbara Smith.' My mother was speechless."[2]

In 1981 I had a new doctor and after a thorough physical he asked me if I smoked, and I said yes I do. He asked me if I wanted to quit, and I said no. At that time I was smoking a pipe. Previously I had smoked cigars, but at that time I was really enjoying smoking a pipe. He told me, "You probably couldn't quit unless I helped you." So I got to thinking about that and talked to Helen about it. "He said I couldn't quit without his help but I am going to do it anyway," and I told Helen I wanted her to quit smoking with me. She smoked cigarettes. She said she would try.

So Greg quit the next day, but Helen continued. In 1988 she began to suffer from what was diagnosed as rheumatoid arthritis. She underwent treatment for

Greg with Cookie and Gretchen. (Gregory)

it for a couple of years, but finally, they suspected it had to be something besides rheumatoid arthritis because her health was worsening. *So finally we got x-rays, and she was badly infected by cancer. She died on November 9, 1990. She was a really great loss. We were married for 46 years. She had been so supportive of me through all the years, and I really miss her. She could never quit smoking, although she tried. She was a casualty of smoking.*

I wanted to quit work when she was suffering somewhat, but she insisted that I stay on. So I did, I stayed on for two more years and retired after turning 72 in 1992. Greg looked forward to taking care of his home, volunteering, playing bridge, travel, and meeting new people.

For Christmas of 1994, at a time of life when many children would be shopping for walkers for their parents, Greg's daughters bought him a bicycle. He took to cycling with enthusiasm and would ride for at least an hour five times a week in the hilly Northwest Hills area of Austin.

I had heard that people would tour Europe on bicycles. I got the name of a New England company that organized these tours and decided to take a two-week trip to France along the Loire valley, passing many 14th-century castles along the way. It was a great way to see a country. There were 23 of us, and we were strung out along the highways. We would do about 300 miles on these trips during the two-week tour, stopping whenever we wanted.

On this and other cycling tours Greg would join, he always arrived into the city where the tour would begin two or three days early or would depart two or three days after the tour ended. These extra days gave him the opportunity to explore the cities in depth, and to better get to know the country he was visiting.

I did a total of eight of these trips to Europe to various countries: France, two in Austria, Denmark, England, Germany, the Netherlands, and Belgium.

As Greg entered his late seventies his life had lost none of its richness. He was deeply involved in cycling, playing bridge with friends, participating in church activities, and volunteering with local organizations. One evening Greg had been invited to play bridge at the Austin Club and during the evening met and played cards with Marion DeFord. They hit it off and began playing bridge when the opportunity arose.

To Greg's great surprise, Marion decided to join him on his foreign cycling tours, starting with one he had planned for Denmark. In testimony to her resolve, she bought a new bike, rode the Northwest Hills, and got into condition for the tour. *I didn't think she would be ready to go; she had not ridden for a long time. So I discouraged her about the trip to Denmark. I didn't think she would be ready for it. But she went, and lo and behold, during the tour she did OK. Marion later joined me for tours of Germany and Belgium. These were really fun to do.*

Several years after meeting Greg and becoming close friends, Marion sold her large house and moved to a new home in Northwest Hills, about a mile from Greg's home.

In later years we did a lot of travelling together, and enjoyed our time together. We took a lot of trips on cruise ships, including one to Singapore with stops at Canary Islands, Gibraltar, Barcelona, Cairo and Alexandria, through the Suez Canal to the Red Sea, around to the Gulf of Aden and then to Dubai, India and on to Singapore. On another interesting trip we took, we flew to Odessa on the Black Sea, and boarded a riverboat there, and traveled all the way back to Germany on the river system, through Romania, Bulgaria, Serbia, Hungary, Austria, and southern Germany. Marion and I also had a great trip to New Zealand, which I then followed up with a biking trip in Germany.

Over the years, Greg kept current on the affairs at what has now become Middle Tennessee University (MTSU), and in particular its Aviation Program, which has become a signature department at MTSU. Greg created a scholarship there for students from Trousdale, Smith or Macon Counties. Remembering his own situation while a student there, Greg stipulated that the scholarship must be reserved for students experiencing financial need. *After I retired I felt like I owed something to Middle Tennessee State, having gotten my start there even though I didn't graduate. I'm just proud that they have continued the program from a really tiny little program that we had back then—to something that is really significant. They have a great program.* While Greg did not graduate from Middle Tennessee, he was named an honorary "Blue Raider," and was the subject of the Feature Story in its January 2014 edition of the MTSU Alumni News.[3]

This would not be the first college scholarship Greg created. After Helen's passing, Greg established the Helen "Bobo" Dwire Gregory Annual Scholarship for voice studies students in good academic standing with leadership potential.

In order to meet new people after he had retired from the State of Texas, Greg joined an organization sponsored by the University of Texas called LAMP—Learning Activities for Mature People—a program "where curious adults can enjoy classes in a relaxed community of friends among leading scholars and experts who share interest in exploring fascinating areas of knowledge and traditional disciplines."[4] Greg developed deep and enduring friendships in the LAMP program, and eventually served as chair. The man who, as an impoverished farm kid, started college on a shoestring, later spearheaded an endowed scholarship program within LAMP that to date has awarded 64 separate scholarships of $2500 to students studying to become teachers.

The first director of the LAMP program, Dean Thomas Hatfield, remembered Greg this way: "In my mind's eye, he is relatively small of stature, soft-spoken and so courteous and unassuming that he seemed shy and reticent—and maybe he was. With his intelligence, insightfulness, and self-confidence, he easily gained the confidence of others without asserting obvious effort. Imperturbable and ever the proper gentleman, he personified the cliché 'cool, calm, and collected.' In no way panicky or impulsive, he was just the kind of person you would want to have his hand on the trigger."

Greg's life now revolves around his friends, exercise, bridge, Longhorn football, a weekly route with Meals on Wheels, and careful—and successful—management of his investments.

Greg's Christian faith has endured since his epiphany as a young man in Tennessee, and his character has long reflected the essential teaching of Jesus to love one another. Just as his early life was marked by a harsh unfairness brought on by poverty, so too has his later life been marked by helping others in need, especially with regard to education.

It must certainly be true that Greg is the only pilot to have flown P-38s in combat, B-47s in the Cold War, and both B-57D-2s and U-2s in the US High Altitude Program. Add aircraft carrier qualifications, and surely Greg is one of a kind—unsurpassed in courage, dedication, pilot ability and depth of experience. He had, for many years, been demonstrating the right stuff before it ever became a national cachet.

Greg's list of awards and citations is beyond impressive, and includes four Legions of Merit, the CIA's Intelligence Medal of Merit, an Air Force Commendation, and the Air Medal with eight Oak Leaf Clusters. (For full details, see Appendix 6.)

Shortly after celebrating his 90th birthday in 2010, Greg was invited by his good friends Gordon, Tony, and Taylor Stevenson to join them for a flight in their T-6 Texan two-place trainer. Greg had flown that aircraft 69 years earlier during his Advanced Flight Training at Moore Field. Designated the AT-6 by the Air Force, the aircraft was used to train pilots in specific combat aeronautics, and to sharpen their skills in navigation and formation flying.

Greg has become a devoted grandfather to his daughter's children. "They look to his wise counsel in many of their life decisions, particularly those involving investing. He never misses a graduation or celebration. In order to share his love of travel as each grandchild has graduated from college Dad has given them a trip to Europe, an experience that they will long remember."[5]

Greg at 99

Greg's life has been marked throughout with a sort of intentionality. Cookie recalls his counsel following a particularly challenging day. Greg reminded her: "It's your choice in each day to be happy. As the day goes on things will happen that may not go your way, but as each new day begins again, you have the power to decide to be happy. It is not a gift to a few... it's a conscious decision."

Reviewing my life from start to finish, I have been so blessed throughout my life. I have been to every state in the United States, and pretty much all over the world. I have traveled around the world twice. I have been to South America, North America, Canada, most of the European nations, including Russia. North Africa, South Africa, East Africa, India, Australia, New Zealand, the South Sea Islands.

Even during the poor years, we did a lot of things we thoroughly enjoyed. We didn't have any money, but we enjoyed being together, and that is so valuable in family experiences to be close to each other.

Also, my religious experience was very important to me throughout my life. I thank God every day now for all that he has done for me, and for giving me such a good life and such a great family.

And I am still enjoying all the things I do. I enjoy where I am living now at Westminster—it is a great place to be at this stage in life, and I have made so many good friends here, and I will always treasure this.

My advice to anyone is to thank God every day for all the blessings that we receive each day that we live.

Greg at 98.

APPENDIX I

Standardized Flight Formation

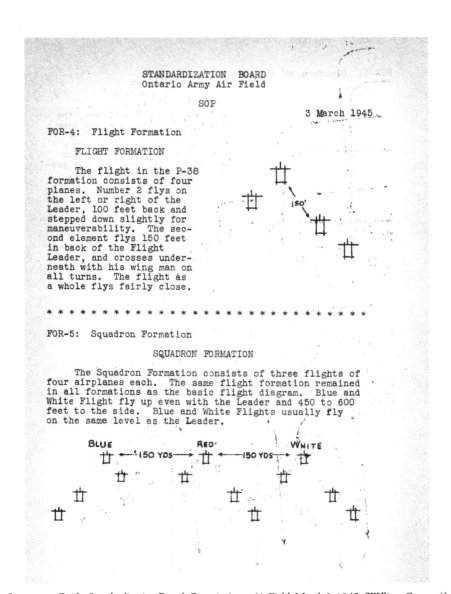

STANDARDIZATION BOARD
Ontario Army Air Field

SOP

3 March 1945

FOR-4: Flight Formation

FLIGHT FORMATION

The flight in the P-38 formation consists of four planes. Number 2 flys on the left or right of the Leader, 100 feet back and stepped down slightly for maneuverability. The second element flys 150 feet in back of the Flight Leader, and crosses underneath with his wing man on all turns. The flight as a whole flys fairly close.

* *

FOR-5: Squadron Formation

SQUADRON FORMATION

The Squadron Formation consists of three flights of four airplanes each. The same flight formation remained in all formations as the basic flight diagram. Blue and White Flight fly up even with the Leader and 450 to 600 feet to the side. Blue and White Flights usually fly on the same level as the Leader.

BLUE ← 150 YDS → RED ← 150 YDS → WHITE

Instructors Guide, Standardization Board, Ontario Army Air Field, March 3, 1945. (William Gregory)]

The Corona Satellite Reconnaissance Program

Satellite reconnaissance

The Air Forces Air Research and Development Command officially proposed a satellite reconnaissance development program in November 1954—roughly the same time that the joint CIA-USAF U-2 Aquatone/Oilstone program and the Black Knight program had been launched.

As with the U-2 and all other advanced aviation systems, the design and manufacture of an effective satellite system was not within the technical scope of the Air Force, and proposals for design studies were solicited in late 1954 from private aerospace corporations: Lockheed, Bell, Martin, and RCA. Lockheed's proposal was accepted, and following a delay that would come to typify early space programs, seven months would pass before Lockheed received a letter contract for the satellite reconnaissance system that was known as Weapons System (WS) 117L on November 5 1956. There were indications that not all were on-board with the concept of satellite reconnaissance: sharp budgetary reductions, bureaucratic delays, competing satellite proposals, concerns for "white" versus "black" projects, and concerns over the legitimacy of conducting overflight given current international law were all responsible for delays to the program.

Over the next two years, WS 117L would evolve into an ambitious program, encompassing a range of missions, and requiring multiple satellites. Principal elements of the system would include the Satellite and Missile Observation System (SAMOS), which would take low-resolution pictures, transmitted electronically back to ground stations. A variation of the SAMOS photo system would be tasked with the collection of electronic intelligence on Soviet radars, also transmitting the "take" to ground receiving stations. Another critical element was the Missile Detection Alarm System (MIDAS), designed to provide early warning of the launch of Soviet missiles headed to the US by looking for the infrared plume of hot rocket exhaust.[1]

Occasionally lost in the fog of these technological developments was a principle of great interest to President Eisenhower—freedom of space. The president intended that international acceptance of the principle of freedom of space would also lead to an acceptance of unimpeded overflight of sovereign territory—thus clearing the way for the overhead intelligence his country craved without fear of Soviet resistance. Almost contemporaneously, the Soviet Union announced their intention of placing scientific satellites in orbit, indicating that photographic equipment could be included in the onboard systems.

The American development plan proposed full operational capability by mid-1963, but in October 1957, the Soviets astounded the world with the launch of Sputnik.

With these developments, the mission of the WS 117L changed. Initially, the photo reconnaissance was linked to Strategic Air Command nuclear strike planning and was intended to provide the "post-strike bomb damage assessment" needed to retarget Soviet objectives that had been missed in a putative American nuclear strike. That system required a resolution of around 100 feet, sufficient for locating bomb craters, but not sufficient for the new task at hand, locating Soviet ICBM launch sites and nuclear-equipped bombers. Importantly, the system had been developed in full public view, and the public had become accustomed to military satellite launches.

With the WS program showing only slow progress, and with the intelligence community pressing hard for overhead reconnaissance, by December 1957 it was decided that those portions of the WS-117L offering the best prospects of early success would be separated from WS-117L, and would be operated covertly under a joint CIA–Air Force management team. Operating under the cryptonym "Corona," the program would be directed by the same team that was, in parallel, directing the U-2 operation. And like Aquatone, the Corona system would incorporate on-board cameras and film; unlike Aquatone, the film would not be flown back to base, but rather a film capsule would be jettisoned from space and recovered in mid-air during a parachute descent. Final project approval for Corona/Discoverer was given by President Eisenhower on April 16, 1958. By July 26, the various systems designs had been reviewed and "frozen." By early April 1958 a technical approach, cost estimates, and an operating plan were in existence, all having received the president's endorsement. The result was a complex organizational and development arrangement that was compartmentalized as follows:

- The CIA set program objectives and was responsible for security, liaison with Department of State, and covert hardware development. It also was charged with ensuring that covert and overt technologies were compatible.
- The Advanced Research Projects Agency (ARPA), a recently instituted "super agency" charged with controlling the various military space system developments and easing interservice rivalries, would provide funding, interface with the Navy, and keep the Department of Defense (DOD) informed.
- The Air Forces Ballistic Missile Division (BMD) developed and provided all hardware, facilities, and personnel for launch and track operations.
- Lockheed Missile Systems Division served as technical director of all equipment excepting camera, payload capsule and support equipment and developed the upper missile stage.
- Itek developed the camera system, Fairchild built it, and GE was subcontracted for the recovery capsule.
- Douglas furnished the Thor boosters that would be used for launch.
- The Navy provided sea recovery of the return capsule.

The manner in which the American satellite system was to be developed could not have been more different than the U-2 spyplane. The U-2 system was primarily developed by one contractor, Lockheed, with one primary customer, the CIA. As Corona moved forward, practically the only things it had in common with Aquatone were that it was developed in secret, and had the same overall objectives.

Ultimately, the Corona technology suite would include the Thor intermediate-range ballistic missile as the first-stage launch vehicle—a system that had been in development since early 1956, was supplied by Douglas and was considered to be a highly reliable platform. A second stage orbital-insertion system from which the satellites would be released consisted of a modified WS 117L upper stages later referred to as the "Agena." The third stage was a 300-lb. satellite which would achieve a nominal 150-mile orbit, and which would contain the primarily intelligence-gathering systems and an occasional scientific research package.

A year would be consumed in settling managerial problems among contracts, squelching competing projects, and resolving turf wars within and among the intelligence communities and military services. Historian Robert Perry comments, "By mid-1959, Corona has been established, its technology applied to actual equipment, its cover perfected, and its tenure extended into the future."[2]

Proving the technical and operational feasibility of the critical systems—establishing a stable orbit, proving the capsule recovery system, and analysis of satellite imagery—would occupy the next 18 months. The project was already considerably behind what must be considered as an extremely optimistic initial timeline.

The introduction of the Corona/Discoverer system would be in three initial phases: engineering flights (to prove systems); biomedical flights (to establish cover); and advanced engineering tests (to perfect the onboard systems). In actuality, cameras would be carried in all of the advanced engineering satellites and some of the biomedical test vehicles. The American public was told that initial missions were research and development flights intended to investigate the feasibility of orbiting, operating, and recovering several vaguely identified scientific payloads. The intelligence community most sincerely hoped that the Soviet Union also believed that fable.

The earliest Discoverer launches established usable orbits and inspired optimism, but subsequently the program became bogged down in a wide range of problems. By the end of 1959, the CIA and the intelligence community, fervently hoping that Corona would yield clarifying photographic reconnaissance data, had become alarmed. In desperate need of information about Soviet missile capability, they had been relying on Corona's readiness to resolve the "missile gap" conundrum.

While the American public watched, and the intelligence community waited, testing of the launch vehicles doggedly continued, as did testing of the various onboard control systems, communications, and cameras. To everyone's relief, the first major success in the program came with Discoverer XIII on August 10, 1960. That launch, essentially a diagnostic flight designed to assess the performance of the flight systems, attained the correct orbit and correctly jettisoned its payload capsule, which was then successfully recovered. In this diagnostic flight, no camera was involved in the mission. But for the Air Force and the CIA, this was what success looked like.

The launch of Discoverer XIV came just eight days after Discoverer XIII had effectively proven that the flight and recovery aspects of the program, but more importantly the Corona camera aboard Discoverer XIV worked perfectly, generating a significant quantity of photographs that were successfully jettisoned and recovered—the first successful recovery of image intelligence from space. The reaction to the process film was "unbridled jubilation." The satellite had completed eight north-south passes over the Soviet Union, including Soviet satellite countries, Yugoslavia, and portions of China. The photographs were of a very high quality, and included coverage of over 1.6 million square miles of the Soviet Union—more than all the previous U-2 overflights combined. Major items of intelligence significance included the Kasputin Yar Mission Test Range, twenty new S-2 surface-to-air missile sites, six more probable SA-2 sites under construction, the Sarova Nuclear Weapons Research and Development Center, several new airfields, and numerous urban complexes. The average ground resolution was 20–30 feet—adequate to suit the purposes of the program, and detailed enough to dispel the then-persistent legend that the United States was lagging behind the Soviet Union in launch-ready ICBMs. The "missile gap" was a myth. Within a year, American intelligence was able to confirm that the Soviets possessed no more than 25 ICBMs, and was also able to precisely characterize the Soviet deployment of medium-range ballistic missiles—information of great interest to NATO.[3]

Supported by additional data from the subsequent Discoverer XVIII mission in December, that fact alone paid for the expensive systems, since it meant that the United States did not have to embark on a hyper-expensive ICBM development program. It "dispelled all residual concern about a Soviet lead in the deployment of intercontinental missiles, and provided the basic hard intelligence around which incoming President JFK and his defense secretary constructed their massive overhaul of US defense priorities, goals, structures, and management processes."[4]

Then President Johnson reflected in 1967:

> We've spent $35 or $40 billion on the space program. And if nothing else had come out of it except the knowledge that we gained from space photography, it would be worth ten times what the whole program has cost. Because tonight we know how many missiles the enemy has and, it turned out, our guesses were way off. We were doing things we didn't need to do. We were building things we didn't need to build. We were harboring fears we didn't need to harbor.[5]

Crowning two years to progress from first flight to useful intelligence, with this "catch" the technical feasibility of all Corona systems had been proven.

The initial Discoverer flights were intended to test and perfect the launch vehicles, onboard systems, and recovery. Once those systems had been debugged, and successful missions became the rule rather than the exception, it became increasingly difficult to maintain the fiction that Discoverer was a scientific satellite. The scientific community wanted to know when and in what form the biological and astrophysical data being collected through Discoverer missions would be available, and began queuing up for payload space for science experiments.

By late 1963, continuing to portray Discoverer as a scientific program had become burdensome to the CIA, and the cover story was abandoned. The

APPENDIX 3

Colonel Gregory's Mission Checklist

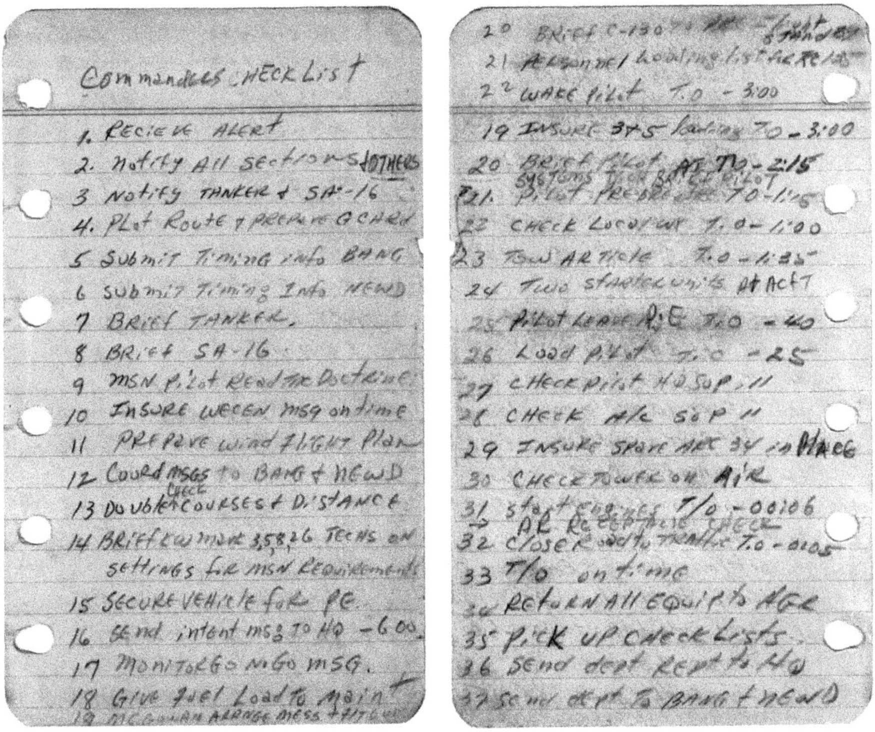

Commanders CHECK List

1. RECIEVE ALERT
2. notify All sections & OTHERS
3 notify TANKER & SA-16
4. PLot Route & PREPARE CHART
5 Submit Timing info BANG
6 Submit Timing Info NEWD
7 BRIEF TANKER.
8 BRIEF SA-16
9 MSN Pilot Read the Doctrine
10 INSURE WECEN MSG on time
11 PREPARE wind FLIGHT Plan
12 Courd MSGS to BANG & NEWD
13 Double check COURSES & DISTANCE
14 BRIEF EW MAN 3,5,8,26 TECHS on settings for MSN Requirements
15 SECURE VEHicle for PE.
16 SEnd intent msg TO HQ -6:00.
17 MONITOR GO NoGo MSG.
18 Give fuel Load to Maint
19 MC GOWAN ARRANGE MESS + FIT LUNCH

20 BRIEF C-130
21 Personnel loading list
22 WAKE Pilot T.O - 3:00
19 INSURE 3 + 5 loading T.O - 3:00
20 BRIEF Pilot AT T.O - 2:15
SYSTEMS TECH BRIEF PILOT
21. Pilot PREBREATHE T.O - 1:15
22 CHECK LOCATION T.O - 1:00
23 TOW ARTICLE T.O - 1:25
24 Two starter units at ACFT
25 Pilot LEAVE P.E T.O - 40
26 Load Pilot T.O - 25
27 CHECK Pilot HQ SOP
28 CHECK A/C SOP
29 INSURE SPARE ACFT 34 in Place
30 CHECK TOWER ON AIR
31 start engines T/O - 00:06
AR RECEPTACLE CHECK
32 CLOSE Road to traffic T.O - 00:05
33 T/O on time
34 Return All Equip to AGE
35 Pick UP CHECK Lists.
36 SEnd dept Rept to HQ
37 Send dept To BANG & NEWD

Commo stand by on SSB
SA-16 T/O RTB to HQ New York
38. Recovery Teamatic at
    KC-135 T/O — : 45
39. Tanker off on Time
40. Report to HQ NEW BANS
41. Meet SA-16 Coordinate
    servicing & send report
42. SA-16 depart on end T/O
43. Receive strike & send msg
    to HQ
44. Mobile & maint REG #5 today
    Landing MINUS : 30.
45. GCA & D7 mm on the air
46. Recover article
47. Debrief pilot
48. Send out arrival
    Rept to HQ Bong recvd
49. Tape record mission debriefing
50. Check on System operation
51. Hump I probe overlays

52. Send out HB jetty
53. Snd out p. I exp't
54. package material
55. make up a craft
56. Snd out msg on dept C-130
57. prepare cut summary

✓

Detachment G's U-2 Missions[1]

TOP SECRET

DETACHMENT G MISSIONS

Date	No.	Pilot	Base	Coverage	Results
26 Oct 1960	3001	Rand	Del Rio, Texas	Cuba	Poor
27 Oct 1960	3002	Rand	Del Rio, Texas	Cuba	Poor
27 Nov 1960	3003	Jones	Del Rio, Texas	Cuba	Good
5 Dec 1960	3011	Cherbonneaux	Del Rio, Texas	Cuba	Good
11 Dec 1960	3016	Edens	Del Rio, Texas	Cuba	Good
3 Jan 1961	3018	Baker	Cubi Point	North Vietnam, Laos	Fair
4 Jan 1961	3019	Cherbonneaux	Cubi Point	" " "	Fair
4 Jan 1961	3020	Rand	Cubi Point	" " "	Good
9 Jan 1961	3023	Jones	Cubi Point	" " "	Good
10 Jan 1961	3024	Edens	Cubi Point	" " "	Poor
16 Jan 1961	3025	Baker	Cubi Point	" " "	Excellent
18 Jan 1961	3026	Cherbonneaux	Cubi Point	" " "	Good
19 Mar 1961	3028	Barnes	Del Rio, Texas	Cuba	Good
21 Mar 1961	3029	Knutson	Del Rio, Texas	Cuba	Good
6 April 1961	3030	Kratt	Del Rio, Texas	Cuba	Good
8 April 1961	3032	Rand	Del Rio, Texas	Cuba	Good
11 April 1961	3033	Jones	Del Rio, Texas	Cuba	Good
13 April 1961	3034	Edens	Del Rio, Texas	Cuba	Fair
15 April 1961	3035	Dunaway	Del Rio, Texas	Cuba	Good
15 April 1961	3036	Baker	Del Rio, Texas	Cuba	Good
16 April 1961	3037	Cherbonneaux	Del Rio, Texas	Cuba	Good
17 April 1961	3038	Barnes	Del Rio, Texas	Cuba	Good
17 April 1961	3039	Knutson	Del Rio, Texas	Cuba	Good
18 April 1961	3040	Kratt	Del Rio, Texas	Cuba	Good

TOP SECRET

Handle via BYEMAN
Control System

18 April 1961	3041	Rand	Del Rio, Texas	Cuba	Good
19 April 1961	3042	Jones	Del Rio, Texas	Cuba	Good
20 April 1961	3043	Edens	Del Rio, Texas	Cuba	Excellent
23 April 1961	3045	Dunaway	Del Rio, Texas	Cuba	Good
29 April 1961	3047	Baker	Del Rio, Texas	Cuba	Good
23 May 1961	3048	Cherbonneaux	Del Rio, Texas	Cuba	Good
15 June 1961	3049	Barnes	Del Rio, Texas	Cuba	Good
28 June 1961	3051	Knutson	Del Rio, Texas	Cuba	Good
29 June 1961	3054	Baker	Del Rio, Texas	Cuba	Good
15 Aug 1961	3055	Rand	Cubi Point	North Vietnam	Good
3 Sept 1961	3058	Cherbonneaux	Del Rio, Texas	Cuba	Good
26 Oct 1961	3060	Knutson	Del Rio, Texas	Cuba	Good
6 Dec 1961	3061	Barnes	Del Rio, Texas	Cuba	Good
19 Jan 1962	3062	Cherbonneaux	Del Rio, Texas	Cuba	Good
2 Feb 1962	3065	Rand	Del Rio, Texas	Cuba	Fair
21 Feb 1962	3066	Ericson	Tao Yuan, Taiwan	SEA, North Vietnam	Good
21 Feb 1962	3067	Baker	Del Rio, Texas	Cuba	Good
13 Mar 1962	3069	Ericson	Tao Yuan, Taiwan	SEA, North Vietnam	Poor
15 Mar 1962	3071	Edens	Del Rio, Texas	Cuba	Good
21 Mar 1962	3072	Ericson	Tao Yuan, Taiwan	SEA, North Vietnam	Fair
1 Apr 1962	3074	Barnes	Del Rio, Texas	Cuba	Good
7 Apr 1962	3076	Ericson	Tao Yuan, Taiwan	SEA, North Vietnam	Good

2

2 May 1962	3078	Rand	Del Rio, Texas	Cuba	Good
6 May 1962	6056	Knutson	Tao Yuan Taiwan	SEA North Vietnam	Good
22 May 1962	3079	Edens	Del Rio, Texas	Cuba	Excellent
6 June 1962	3080	Barnes	Del Rio, Texas	Cuba	Good
15 June 1962	3081	Cherbonneaux	Del Rio, Texas	Cuba	Good
18 June 1962	3082	Knutson	Del Rio, Texas	Cuba	Good
22 June 1962	6058	Baker	Tao Yuan, Taiwan	SEA, North Vietnam	Fair
29 June 1962	3083	Cherbonneaux	Del Rio, Texas	Cuba	Good
8 July 1962	3084	Knutson	Del Rio, Texas	Cuba	Fair
12 July 1962	3085	Cherbonneaux	Del Rio, Texas	Cuba	Good
21 July 1962	6060	Barnes	Tao Yuan, Taiwan	SEA, North Vietnam	Poor
5 Aug 1962	3086	Baker	Del Rio, Texas	Cuba	Good
29 Aug 1962	3088	Ericson	Del Rio, Texas	Cuba	Good
5 Sept 1962	3089	Edens	Del Rio, Texas	Cuba	Good
17 Sept 1962	3091	Baker	Del Rio, Texas	Cuba	Fair
26 Sept 1962	3093	Rand	Del Rio, Texas	Cuba	Good
29 Sept 1962	3095	Edens	Del Rio, Texas	Cuba	Excellent
5 Oct 1962	3098	Barnes	Del Rio, Texas	Cuba	Fair
7 Oct 1962	3100	Knutson	Del Rio, Texas	Cuba	Fair
5 Dec 1962	3201	Rand	Takhli, Thailand	Tibet	Good
10 Dec 1962	3203	Baker	Takhli, Thailand	Tibet	Good
27 Dec 1962	3206	Knutson	Takhli, Thailand	SEA, North Vietnam	Good
31 Dec 1962	3208	Rand	Takhli, Thailand	Tibet	Fair

3

TOP SECRET

3 Jan 1963	3210	Baker	Takhli, Thailand	Tibet	Fair
19 Jan 1963	3213	Cherbonneaux	Takhli, Thailand	Tibet	Good
22 Jan 1963	3215	Edens	Takhli, Thailand	Tibet	Good
1 Mar 1963	3218	Cherbonneaux	Takhli, Thailand	SEA, N. Vietnam	Fair
2 Mar 1963	3219	Cherbonneaux	Takhli, Thailand	SEA, NVN, Laos	Good
30 Apr 1963	3221	Knutson	Takhli, Thailand	SEA, NVN, Laos, China	Good
3 May 1963	3222	Rand	Takhli, Thailand	SEA, NVN, Laos, China	Good
13 May 1963	3224	Knutson	Takhli, Thailand	SEA, NVN, Laos, China	Fair
14 May 1963	3225	Rand	Takhli, Thailand	SEA, NVN, Laos	Fair
15 May 1963	3226	Baker	Takhli, Thailand	SEA, NVN, Laos	Fair
10 Aug 1963	6066	Knutson	Takhli, Thailand	SEA, NVN	Good
29 Sept 1963	3227	Barnes	Takhli, Thailand	Tibet	Good
10 Oct 1963	3230	Barnes	Takhli, Thailand	Tibet	Fair
11 Oct 1963	3231	Barnes	Takhli, Thailand	SEA, NVN	Good
26 Oct 1963	3235	Baker	Takhli, Thailand	SEA, NVN, Laos	Fair
29 Oct 1963	3236	Rand	Takhli, Thailand	Tibet	Good
10 Nov 1963	3238	Rand	Takhli, Thailand	China, NEFA	Good
14 Nov 1963	3239	Edens	Takhli, Thailand	SEA, Burma Border	Poor
15 Nov 1963	3241	Bedford	Takhli, Thailand	SEA, Burma, Laos	Fair
17 Nov 1963	3243	Edens	Takhli, Thailand	SEA, NVN	Excellent
3 Dec 1963	3250	Barnes	Ramey AFB, P.R.	Venezuela	Good
6 Dec 1963	3252	Ericson	Ramey AFB, P.R.	Venezuela	Good
13 Dec 1963	3253	Edens	Ramey AFB, P.R.	Venezuela, Guiana	Good
14 Dec 1963	3254	Barnes	Ramey AFB, P.R.	Venezuela, Guiana	Good
18 Dec 1963	3256	Ericson	Ramey AFB, P.R.	Venezuela	Good
19 Dec 1963	3257	Edens	Ramey AFB, P.R.	Venezuela	Good
29 Dec 1963	6070	Rand	Takhli, Thailand	Cambodia, SVN	Excellent
30 Dec 1963	6071	Bedford	Takhli, Thailand	SEA, NVN, Laos	Excellent

4

TOP SECRET

TOP SECRET

7 Jan 1964	0014E	Rand	Tao Yuan, Taiwan	SEA, SVN, NVN, Laos, Cambodia	Good
23 Feb 1964	0034E	Baker	Tao Yuan, Taiwan	SEA, SVN	Good
28 Feb 1964	0064E	Knutson	Tao Yuan, Taiwan	SEA, NVN	Poor
1 Mar 1964	S074E	Baker	Tao Yuan, Taiwan	SEA, NVN, Laos	Good
6 Mar 1964	S104E	Baker	Tao Yuan, Taiwan	SEA, NVN, Laos	Good
10 Mar 1964	S014A	Ericson	Takhli, Thailand	SEA, NVN, Laos	Poor
12 Mar 1964	S024A	Knutson	Takhli, Thailand	SEA, NVN, Laos	Fair
14 Mar 1964	S034A	Ericson	Takhli, Thailand	SEA, NVN, Laos	Poor
15 Mar 1964	S044A	Knutson	Takhli, Thailand	SEA, NVN, Laos	Good
16 Mar 1964	S064A	Knutson	Takhli, Thailand	SEA, NVN, Laos	Poor
17 Mar 1964	S074A	Edens	Takhli, Thailand	SEA, NVN, Laos	Poor
20 Mar 1964	S084A	Knutson	Takhli, Thailand	SEA, NVN, Laos	Excellent
24 Mar 1964	S114A	Ericson	Takhli, Thailand	SFA, NVN, Laos	Poor
31 Mar 1964	T124A	Edens	Takhli, Thailand	China, NEFA	Excellent
4 Apr 1964	S144A	Knutson	Takhli, Thailand	SEA, NVN, Laos	Fair
6 Apr 1964	S154A	Ericson	Takhli, Thailand	SEA, NVN, Laos	Fair
7 Apr 1964	S164A	Edens	Takhli, Thailand	SEA, NVN, Laos	Poor
12 Apr 1964	S184A	Knutson	Takhli, Thailand	SEA, Cambodia	Good
15 Apr 1964	S194A	Ericson	Takhli, Thailand	SEA, NVN, Laos	Good
24 Apr 1964	S214A	Rand	Cubi Point	SEA, NVN, Laos	Poor
19 May 1964	W224A	Barnes	RANGER	French Atomic Test	Excellent
22 May 1964	W234A	Edens	RANGER	French Atomic Test	Excellent
24 May 1964	T284A	Ericson	Charbatia, India	Tibet, Sino/Indian Border	Good
16 Dec 1964	T314A	Knutson	Charbatia, India	Tibet, Sino/Indian Border	Excellent
17 Dec 1964	T324A	Baker	Charbatia, India	Tibet, Sino/Indian Border	Excellent
20 Dec 1964	T344A	Schmarr	Charbatia, India	Tibet, Sino/Indian Border	Excellent

5

TOP SECRET

TOP SECRET

29 Oct 1965	S015A	Schmarr	Takhli, Thailand	Cambodia	Good
7 Nov 1965	S025A	Barnes	Takhli, Thailand	Cambodia	Excellent
27 Mar 1968	S018E	Hall	Takhli, Thailand	Cambodia Border	Excellent
3 Apr 1968	S028E	Hall	Takhli, Thailand	Cambodia Border	Excellent

6

TOP SECRET

Handle via B'EMAN
Control System

Personal Letter from President John F. Kennedy to Lt. Col. William Gregory, January 5, 1963

Dear Colonel Gregory:

It has recently been my pleasure to visit a number of the military units in the Southeast which took part in a very direct way in support of our Government's position in the Cuban crisis in October of this year. I thus had the welcome opportunity to personally congratulate their officers and men on the very real contribution they had made at a critical time in this Nation's history, and to express to them their Government's gratitude for a job well done.

Circumstances did not permit me to acknowledge openly your Detachment's significant and extended contribution to what was accomplished in the days and months prior to the climax of the Cuban situation. In spite of this, I want you, your fellow officers and men, your skilled civilian pilots, staff employees and supporting technical representatives, to know of my real and abiding appreciation for the fine job you have done so quietly for so long, not only in Cuba but in other areas of the world where vital intelligence must continue to be obtained in order to guarantee the cause of freedom. The dangers are no less real, the hardships no less difficult, and your achievement no less important to your country than those experienced by the men whom we can honor publicly.

Please accept assurance of my gratitude for your efforts, and extend to your entire command my sincerest thanks for their sustained superior performance.

With esteem and warm personal regards,

John Kennedy

Awards and Citations

Over the course of his 34-year Air Force career, Col. Gregory received numerous citations and awards, as shown below.

Legion of Merit with OLC*	Awarded by the US Armed Forces for exceptionally meritorious conduct in the performance of outstanding services and achievements.
Air Medal with eight OLC	Awarded for single acts of heroism or meritorious achievement while participating in aerial flight. In the Mediterranean Theater of World War II, the Air Medal was awarded in recognition of five combat missions, with OLCs awarded for each subsequent five missions.
Intelligence Medal of Merit Central Intelligence Agency	Awarded for performance of especially meritorious service or for an act or achievement conspicuously above normal duties which has contributed significantly to the mission of the Agency.
Air Force Commendation Medal	Awarded for sustained acts of heroism or meritorious service in direct contact with an enemy.
Presidential Unit Citation	Awarded to units for extraordinary heroism in action against an armed enemy. The unit must display such gallantry, determination, and esprit de corps in accomplishing its mission under extremely difficult and hazardous conditions to distinguish itself from other units in the same campaign.
Air Force Outstanding Unit Award with 2 OLC	Awarded for exceptionally meritorious service, specific acts of outstanding achievement, for excelling in combat operations against an armed enemy of the United States, or for distinction in military operations involving conflict with, or exposure to, a hostile action by any opposing foreign force.
American Campaign Medal	Awarded for service within the American theater during World War II.
European African Middle Eastern Campaign Medal with 4 Bronze Service Stars	Awarded for military service performed in the European or Mediterranean Theater during World War II. Service Stars are awarded for specific military campaigns. For Col. Gregory, those include the campaigns at Sicily and Naples-Foggia.

World War II Victory Medal	Awarded for military service during World War II.
National Defense Service Medal, with 2 Bronze Service Stars	Awarded for active duty service during national emergencies, such as the Korean War and the Vietnam Conflict.
Vietnam Service Medal with Bronze Star	Awarded for service during the Vietnam War.
Air Force Longevity Service Award with 4 OLC	An award equivalent to service stripes for other branches of service, to denote years of military service.
Air Force Reserve Meritorious Service Ribbon	Awarded in recognition of four years of honorable reserve service.
Small Arms Expert Marksmanship Ribbon	Awarded for expertise with either a rifle or handgun.
Republic of Vietnam Campaign Medal	Awarded to members of US military for support of operations in Vietnam.
* An Oak Leaf Cluster denotes subsequent decorations of the same medal. The small metal devices are attached to the award's ribbon. A bronze OLC represents each additional award; a silver OLC is worn in lieu of five bronze OLCs.	

Pilot ratings

Over the course of his career in the Air Force, Greg would fly 43 different aircraft, accumulating over 10,000 hours, and receive a series of ratings: Pilot, Senior Pilot, and Command Pilot.

Aviation Cadet badge, US Army Air Corps, September 27, 1941.

Pilot's badge, US Army Air Forces, April 29, 1942.

Senior pilot's badge, US Air Force, August 26, 1952.

Command pilot's badge: US Air Force, May 1, 1957.

Awards

First Legion of Merit

Awarded: January 27, 1960

Citation: Lt. Col. Gregory distinguished himself by his performance from May to August, 1958 while project officer for the RB-57D Test Group of the 4025th SRS" and as "commander of Operating Location Force 7 from January through April 1958.

Recommending officer: Col. A. J. Bratton, Commander, 4080 Strategic Reconnaissance Wing

Second Legion of Merit

Awarded: July 29, 1965

Citation: Colonel William J. Gregory distinguished himself by exceptionally meritorious conduct in the performance of outstanding service to the United States as Commander, Weather Reconnaissance Squadron (Prov IV), from 1 September 1960 to 14 June 1965. In this important assignment, the leadership, exemplary foresight, and ceaseless efforts consistently demonstrated by Colonel Gregory were instrumental factors in the resolution of many complex problems of major importance to the Air Force. The singularly distinctive accomplishments of Colonel Gregory reflect great credit upon himself and the United States Air Force.

Awarding Officer: Gen. J. P. McConnell, US Air Force Chief of Staff

Third Legion of Merit

Awarded: September 3, 1971

Citation: Colonel William J. Gregory distinguished himself by exceptionally rigorous conduct in the performance of outstanding services to the United States while assigned to the Directorate of Reconnaissance and Electronic Warfare, Deputy Chief of Staff for Research and Development, Headquarters United States Air Force from 8 August 1966 to 28 July 1971. In this important assignment, the leadership, exemplary managerial skill and ceaseless efforts consistently demonstrated by Colonel Gregory resulted in highly significant contributions to the operational effectiveness, programmed modernization, and long range development of reconnaissance and electronic warfare forces of the Air Force. The superior initiative, outstanding leadership, and personal endeavor displayed by Colonel Gregory reflect great credit upon himself and the United States Air Force.

Awarding Officer: Gen. John D. Ryan, USAir Force Chief of Staff

Fourth Legion of Merit

Awarded: August 31, 1975

Citation: Not available

Awarding Officer: General Frank J. Simokaitis, Commandant, Air Force Institute of Technology

Intelligence Medal of Merit

Citation: WILLIAM J. GREGORY, Lieutenant Colonel, United States Air Force is hereby awarded the INTELLIGENCE MEDAL OF MERIT for his meritorious contributions to the national intelligence effort. As leader of a small group engaged in operations of great importance and sensitivity, Colonel Gregory demonstrated professional abilities and leadership qualities of the highest order. His dedicated performance meets the highest standards of service to our Nation and reflects great credit on him, the United States Air Force, and the Central Intelligence Agency.
US Central Intelligence Agency

Air Force Commendation Medal

Awarded: September 19, 1960

Citation: Lieutenant Colonel William J. Gregory, 35829A, USAF, distinguished himself by meritorious service while assigned to the 4025th Strategic Reconnaissance Squadron, Light, Strategic Air Command, from 1 June 1956 to 19 April 1960. During that period he served, in turn, as Project Officer of the RB-57D Program, Deputy Squadron Commander and Squadron Commander. Through his personal endeavors, this squadron progressed from early testing stages to combat ready status in a minimum time. He also served as Detachment Commander for two overseas deployments of the RB-57D-2 aircraft and because of his personal direction, guidance, and overall supervision, the detachment missions were successfully accomplished and provided information of international significance. The outstanding devotion to duty and initiative displayed by Lieutenant Colonel Gregory reflect great credit upon himself and the United States Air Force.

Awarding Officer: Col. A. J. Bratton, Commander, 4080th Strategic Reconnaissance Wing

Air Force Outstanding Unit Citation

Awarded: February 4, 1963

Citation: The Weather Reconnaissance Sq, Provisional No. 4 is awarded the AF Outstanding Unit Award for exceptionally meritorious achievement or service in support of military operations from 1 Aug 62 to 3 Nov 62. BY ORDER OF THE SECRETARY OF THE AIR FORCE.

Awarding Officer: Curtis E. LeMay, Air Force Chief of Staff

Aircraft flown by Colonel Gregory

Piper Cub J3 1940 Murfreesboro, TN
Taylorcraft Coupe 1940 Waterloo, IA
Fairchild PT-19 1941 Uvalde, TX
North American BT-9 1941 Randolph Field, TX
North American AT-6 1942 Moore Field, TX
Lockheed P-38 1942–45 California, England, North Africa
(Models A, C, D, F, G, J, L)
Douglas B-23 1942 Hamilton Field, CA
Curtiss AT-9 1942 Hamilton Field, CA
North American BT-14 1942 Hamilton Field, CA
Piper L2A 1942 Hamilton Field, CA
Republic P-47 1943 Goxhill, England
Vultee BT-13 1943 San Diego, CA
Lockheed F-5 1944 Dallas to New York
Cessna UC-78 1944 Ontario, CA
Douglas A-25 1944 Ontario, CA
Curtiss SB-2C 1944 Ontario, CA
Beechcraft RA-24 1944 Ontario, CA
Beechcraft RA-25 1944 Ontario, CA
Beechcraft RA-29 1944 Ontario, CA
North American AT-23 1944 Ontario, CA
Douglas C-47 1944 Ontario, CA
Bell P-59 1945 Ontario, CA
North American P-51 1945 Ontario, CA (first jet fighter)
Beechcraft C-45 1946 March Field, CA
North American B-25 1946 March Field, CA
Beechcraft T-11 1947 Barksdale Field, LA
Martin B-26 1948 Barksdale Field, LA

Boeing B-50 1949 Barksdale Field, LA
Boeing B-29 1951 Barksdale Field, LA
Boeing KB-29 1951 Barksdale Field, LA
Convair T-29 1953 Ellington Field, TX
Boeing B-47 1954 Orlando, FL
Martin B-57C 1956 Albany, GA
Martin RB-57D 1956 Albany, GA
Martin RB-57D-2 1957 Del Rio, TX
Lockheed T-33 1959 Del Rio, TX
Fairchild U-3A 1960 Edwards AFB, CA
Lockheed U-2 1961 Edwards AFB, CA
Lockheed C-130 1961 Edwards AFB, CA
Boeing KC-135 1962 Edwards AFB, CA
Boeing KC-97 1963 Edwards AFB, CA
Cessna L-28 1963 Edwards AFB, CA
Grumman T-2A Navy 1964 Pensacola, FL

The year indicates the first time Gregory flew the aircraft.

Endnotes

Chapter 1

1   *Macon County Times*, Lafayette, TN, August 13, 1953, p. 1.
2   Trousdale County website: http://www.trousdalecountytn.gov/node/4.
3   "Cal's Column," *Macon County Times*, Lafayette, TN, June 11, 1959, p. 6.
4   Tennessee 4 Me, Confronting the Modern Era: Farming, see www.tn4me.org.
5   William Calvin Dickinson and Michael E. Birdwell (Eds), *People of the Upper Cumberland: Achievements and Contradictions,* University of Tennessee Press, 2017.
6   Patented in 1868 and initially sold as "Pitcher's Castoria," this cathartic was composed of senna, sodium bicarbonate, essence of wintergreen, taraxacum, sugar and water. It was promoted in one of the most significant campaigns in early mass advertising, and Castoria ads were seen across the United States.
7   Op. Cit. Tennessee 4 Me, Farming, see http://www.tn4me.org/article.cfm/a_id/152/minor_id/59/major_id/20/era_id/6; and Center for Historic Preservation, James E. Walker Library, Middle Tennessee State University, www.dsi.mtsu.edu/trials/work).
8   Op. Cit. Trousdale County, and *Tennessee 4 Me*; and Census, Tennessee, p. 1010 and ff.
9   "Look Back: Legacy of Payne's Store lives on today," John Oliver, Trousdale Historical Society, HartsvilleVidette.com; 1940 Census, Tennessee, table 5, p. 1024.
10 "The Tobacco Situation," September 27, 1939, TS-12, US Department of Agriculture, Bureau of Agricultural Economics, Washington, DC; and *SHARECROP Companion Guide*, Claudia Stack, 2017.
11 Op. Cit. *People of the Upper Cumberland*; and Tennessee 4 Me.
12 *Stepping Stone*, Trousdale High School Yearbook, Vol. XII, 1938.
13 That $270 Greg would earn during his nine months at Middle Tennessee would be equivalent in today's currency to just under $5,000. A fair amount of money, but still far short of what an academic year cost.
14 *Side Lines,* Middle Tennessee State Teachers College student newspaper, October 5, 1938, Vol. 12, No. 2.

Chapter 2

1   *Side Lines*, Middle Tennessee State Teachers College student newspaper, September 21, 1938, Vol. 12, No. 1.
2   Ibid, Sept. 27, 1939, Vol. 13, No. 1.
3   Ibid, Nov. 8, 1939, Vol. 13, No. 5.
4   Ibid, Nov. 9, 1938, Vol. 12, No. 4.
5   Ibid, Nov. 22, 1939, Vol. 13, No. 6.

6   Ibid, Dec. 13, 1939, Vol. 13, No. 7.

7   Ibid, Feb. 23, 1939, Vol. 13, No. 10.

8   Ibid, May 3, 1939, Vol. 13, No. 15.

9   Ibid, Dec. 12, 1940, vol. 14 No. 5.

10   Interview, Col. William Gregory, February 3, 2012, by James Crabtree, Texas Veterans Land Board Voices of Veterans Oral History Program.

11   Henry C. Herge, *Navy V-12 Program, Vol. 12*, Turner Publishing Company, 1996

12   "Putt Putt Air Force", the Story of the Civilian Pilot Training Program and the War Training Service, 1939–1944, Department of Transportation, Federal Aviation Administration, Aviation Education Staff, GA-20-84. The interested reader is also referred to the following: "Training to Fly: Military Flight Training, 1907–1945", Rebecca Cameron; the Virginia Aeronautical Historical Society at http://vahsonline.publishpath.com/; and "The Civil Aeronautics Administration Civilian Pilot Training Program (the C.A.A. Course)," Lawrence J. Hodgins Jr., November 29, 1940; and "The Civilian Pilot Training Program, Requirements for Participation Outlined by Authority," in Air Commerce Bulletin, Civil Aeronautics Authority, September 15, 1939, Vol. 11, No. 3.

    The CPT program eventually included 1,132 educational institutions, and 1,460 flight schools. By the time the CPT program was ended in 1944, it had provided flight training to 435,165 students, including several hundred female pilots. By mid-1942, CPT had trained over 125,000 pilots, including William Gregory and Breezy Foster. For a complete list of schools, see "They Flew Proud," by Jane Gardner Birch.

    For an example of the curriculum at the universities, see:

    https://ia800603.us.archive.org/4/items/southernillinoi194142sout/southernillinoi-194142sout.pdf

13   *The CAA Helps America Prepare for World War II*, Theresa L. Kraus, Historian, Federal Aviation Administration.

14   As will be seen, Neely would complete CPT and become an Air Force pilot, but his airsickness persisted for quite a while. His future Operations Officer, Richard Decker, related: "In late December (while in England) we received some P-38s and began flying camera gunnery passes against another plane. On one flight Lt. Neely was setting off to my side and not making passes. I called on the radio, but got not answer. Then I saw this white stuff coming from the window of his plane. As he began making passes at my plane, nothing more happened. [Later] I questioned him on the ground, and was told how he always became ill flying. He had lasted this long, and knew how to overcome the problem, so nothing was said to the others. You could certainly admire him for his determination." Interview with William Gregory, July 30, 2019, and *Autobiography of Richard Decker*, undated.

15   Dominick A. Pisano. *To Fill the Skies with Pilots.*

16   J-3 Piper Cub specifications from National Air and Space Museum, and Department of Transportation, Federal Aviation Administration, Aircraft Specification A-691, see: TheCubClub.Org.

17   *Daily News-Journal*, Murfreesboro, TN, April 2, 1941.

18   Edward L. Thorndike, "The Selection of Military Aviators: Mental and Moral Qualities," US Air Service, June 1919. The original study, entitled "Report of the Investigations of Physiological and Psychological Tests of Aptitude for Flying," dated July 5, 1918, is found at AFHRA Call no. 141.24-15, Vol. 2; IRIS No. 114256.

19   Greg was initially admitted to the Aviation Flight Program by the US Army Air Corp (AAC). In June 1941, the AAC was redesignated the US Army Air Forces (USAAF, or AAF). At swearing-in, Greg and his friends entered the USAAF.

Chapter 3

1   Op. Cit. Voices of Veterans.
2   W. F. Craven and J. L. Cate, *The Army Air Forces in World War II, Vol. VI, Men and Planes*, Chapter 17: Individual Training of Flying Personnel.
3   "The War Experiences of Arthur R. Driedger Jr., South West Pacific and Western Pacific, Jan. 10, 1943 to Jan. 4, 1946." Courtesy Carolyn Mastin.
4   William Mitchell, *From the Pilot Factory*, 1942.
5   Swanborough, F.G. and Peter M. Bowers. *United States Military Aircraft since 1909*. London: Putnam, 1963; and http://rwebs.net/ghostsqd/pt-19.htm.
6   Samuel Hynes, Flights of Passage: Recollections of a World War II Aviator, New York: Penguin, 2003.
7   Primary Flying School, Students' Manual, Army Air Forces Training Command, 1943.
8   Op. Cit. Craven.
9   Op. Cit. Craven.
10 Op. Cit. Craven.
11 AAF Training During World War II, Article 196138, National Museum of the US Air Force, Wright-Patterson Air Force Base, Dayton, OH. A single, or fixed-pitch propeller is one in which the blade pitch, or blade angle, is built into the propeller, giving optimal performance at specified rpm and airspeed. They are used on airplanes of low power, speed, range or altitude. The adjustable pitch propeller allows the blade angle to be adjusted to provide the best performance for particular flight conditions, or for particular flight instruction.
12 William J. Gregory, Pilot Flight Record and Log Book.
13 Robert L. Richardson, *The Jagged Edge of Duty*, Stackpole Books, 2017
14 Op. Cit. Hynes.
15 Aviation Archaeology Investigation and Research, 7644 S. 15th Ave. Phoenix, AZ 85041.
16 Warbird Alley, http://warbirdalley.com/bt9.htm, Belvidere, IL.
17 Op. Cit. Gregory, Pilot Flight Record.
18 Capt. Bob Norris, *The Dust Bowl to World War II: One Young Man's Journey of Survival*, Xlibris, 2014.
19 Bridgeman, Leonard. "The North American Texan," Jane's Fighting Aircraft of World War II. London: Studio, 1946.
20 Op. Cit. Norris.
21 Op. Cit. Aviation Archaeology.
22 In addition to the interviews of William Gregory noted earlier, the reader is referred to certain of his military records for this information. See: Gregory, William J., Recommendation for Promotion of Captain William J. Gregory, 12 December 1944.
23 Greg and Harold Ed parted company at Hamilton Field. Lt. Brown was eventually posted to the 364th Fighter Group, operating P-38s out of Honington Airfield in Suffolk, England. The group flew the full range of P-38 missions: bomber escort, dive-bombing, and strafing. Given Greg's comments above, it is ironic that 1st Lt. Harold Ed Brown was killed on February 24, 1944 while on a solo flight—a local high-altitude test flight to 30,000 ft.—and not as a result of close formation flying.
24 For a graphic illustrating the flight and squadron formation specified by the Air Force Standardization Board, see Appendix 1.
25 Specifications for the P-38G model are taken from the works of Joe Baugher. www.joebougher.com/usaf_fighters/p38_11.html.
26 Op. Cit. Aviation Archaeology.
27 Op. Cit. AFHRA Study 61.

28 Garry L. Fry, *The Eagles of Duxford: The 78th Fighter Group in World War II*, St. Paul: Phalanx, 1992 (MN, USA).

29 Transcript of an Interview with Colonel Robert E. Vickers, Center for Pacific War Studies, The National Museum of the Pacific War (Admiral Nimitz Museum), January 19, 2006.

30 RAF-112-squadron.org/78thfghonor_roll_mto.html.

31 Hoyt Davis would successfully complete his combat tour and return to his home in Trousdale County, TN.

32 William Gregory form R 605-12 dated December 18, 1944.

33 Loving, Woodbine Red Leader: A P-51 Mustang Ace in the Mediterranean Theater, 2003.

34 Wayne G. Johnson, *Whitey: From Farm Kid to Flying Tiger to Attorney: A Memoir*, Minneapolis, MN: Langdon Street Press, 2011.

Chapter 4

1 John W. Lambert, *The 14th Fighter Group in World War II*, Atglen, PA: Schiffer Publishing, 2008.

2 History of the 14th Fighter Group (TE), AAF, January 15, 1941–May 1943, AFHRA Documents 00077884 and 00077885; Combat Squadrons of the Air Force in World War II, Maurer and Maurer, edits, USAF Historical Division, 1969.

3 The document under which all AAF operations were conducted at that time was Field Manual 31–35, a document that was the culmination of years of internal debate—some would say strife—between the Army's ground commanders and those of the Army's Air Force. The primary point under argument had been vital: who should command these air assets? FM 31–35 resolved the debate by confirming that the Army Air Forces were subordinate to the ground force needs, and local battle conditions, that air support commanders function under the army commanders, that the army ground commanders could specifically allocate air assets in support of ground units, and that target priorities would be set by army units on the ground.

Against all widely accepted principles of aerial combat, air assets operating under FM 31–35 assumed a primarily *defensive* posture, and within these sharp tactical limitations, the losses to the fighter groups were immediate and substantial. Acting in defense of ground troops, the fighter groups that were part of Operation *Torch* flew very few interdiction missions against German airfields, with the result that air assets of the Axis forces were not degraded. With air superiority in German hands, the Luftwaffe would daily stage devastating attacks on Allied ground forces, inflicting severe losses on air forces in the process. The AAF policy embodied in FM 31–35 resulted in less protection for its ground forces, not more, and cost the AAF considerably in lost planes and pilots.

By the spring of 1943, FM 31–35 had been replaced by a new field manual, FM 100–20, based largely on the successful British model that had proven to be effective in the Eastern Desert. The AAF began operating under a wholly different set of strategies and tactics. New directives assigned air superiority as the first priority for air assets; second priority was air interdiction, and third was the close support of ground troops.

The organization of the American Air Forces in North Africa had also changed. B-17 heavy bombers, B-25 and B-26 medium bombers, and the P-38 units that would escort them were organized within the North African Strategic Air Force (NASAF), as part of the North African Air Force (NAAF).

Welcome as this change in Air Force policy was, it came too late to change the fate of the original 14th Fighter Group, which operated bravely but with high losses under the faulty policies of FM 31–35.

Interested readers are referred to the following sources: Field Manual (FM) 31–35, Basic Field Manual, Aviation in Support of Ground Forces, US War Department, April 9, 1942; War Department Field Manual FM 100- 20, Command and Employment of Air Power, Washington, 1944; and for a complete description of the AAF reorganization, see: http://en.wikipedia.org/wiki/Northwest_African_Strategic_Air_Force.

4 Robert W. Shottelkorb, *From Model T to P-38 Lightning: Celebrating the Life of William Frank Shottelkorb*, Missoula, MT: Pictorial Histories Publishing, 2003.

5 Mission History, 49th Fighter Squadron, Sgt. Ralph Holt, AFHRA IRIS 56631.

6 Interview, Harold Harper, August 14, 2014.

7 Mission Report, 37th Fighter Squadron, May 6, 1943, Capt. John McCarthy, S-2.

8 Biography of George Underwood, S/Sgt, 381st Bomb Sqdn, 310th Bomb Grp, 57th Bomb Wing, 12th AF, USAAF, James F. Justin Museum; and Steve Blake and John Stanaway, *Adorimini, A History of the 82nd Fighter Group in World War II*, Walsworth Publishing Co, 1992.

9 Op. Cit. Richardson.

10 Maurer (ed), *Air Force Combat Units of World War II*, Office of Air Force History, Washington, DC, 1983. Note that this document has an incorrect date for the arrival of the 14th FG to Telergma, a fact verified from other sources. Also, Op.Cit. Holt as the source of the combat mission information, in addition to AFHRA IRIS 56631, SQ-FI-49-SU.

11 Summary of Target Intelligence, AFHRA IRIS 232881 and 232885; and XII Air Force, A-2 Section, First Priority List.

12 Strategic Analysis, A-2 Section, NAAF, May 13, 1943, AFHRA IRIS 242239, and mission reports of the 14th FG.

13 JG 53 Pik As Claims in WWII, and www.lexikon-derwehrmacht.de/Gliederungen/Jagdgeschwader/JG53-R.htm.

14 Ibid, 14th FG Reports; and War Diary of the 49th Fighter Squadron, AFHRA IRIS 56630, SQ-FI-49-SU-OP; and National Archives Identifier: 2894478, National Archives, College Park, MD.

15 The North African Strategic Air Force included the 1st, 14th, 82nd, and 325th Fighter Groups, each with three squadrons. In total, the fighter groups were equipped with 144 fighter aircraft.

16 Due to a navigational error, the formation missed Millis and attacked instead the docs at Carloforte. The operational test was successful, however, since a large vessel was sighted there and sunk with two direct hits.

17 Commitment of German Air Forces on Sardinia and Corsica, Headquarters, European Command, Office of the Chief Historian, General Hubertus Hirshold, Document D-038.

18 Mission Reports, 14th FB, National Archives Document No. 2898242 and ff, and AFHRA and Mission Reports, 1st FG, AFHRA IRIS 77184, GP-1-SU-RE-D (FTR).

19 www.lexikon-der-wehrmacht.de/Gliederungen/Jagdgeschwader/ JG27-R.htm; en.wikipedia.org/wiki/Jagdgeschwader_27; and www.forgot- tenairfields.com/italy/sicily/trapani/trapani-mi-lo-s593.html.

20 cieldegloire.com/jg_027c.php.

21 Sortie Credits, Lt. William Neely. O-659836, 14th Fighter Group, February 16, 1943 to June 21, 1943. Also Op. Cit. to 14th Fighter Group: Mission Reports, 2894478.

22 War Diary of the 49th Fighter Squadron, AFHRA 56630, SQ-FI-49- SU-OP.

23 Interview, Harold Harper, August 14, 2014.

24 Foreign Airport Description, El Bathan, 3.6 miles SE of Tebourba, A-3 Section, III ASAC (SP). NARA Document 00244738; and El Bathan, Tunisia, NARA Document Folder 638.9351, Reference 00244738, June–September 1943.

25 Basic Airdrome Report, El Bathan, June 13, 1943, Capt. John C. Gillespie, NARA Document Folder 638.9351, Reference 00244738, June–September 1943.

26 Telergma Airport history at http://en.wikipedia.org/wiki/Telerg-ma_Airport.

27 Maurer, Air Force Combat Units of World War II.

28 Op. Cit. Blake and Stanaway.

29 Lloyd A. Guenther, *Under the Wings of a P-38 in North Africa*, unpublished memoir, copyright Lloyd Guenther and Kristine Guenther Sterbenz, May 2005.

30 John Steinbeck, *Once There Was a War*, 1943.

31 Interested readers are referred to: Roy R. Grinker and John P. Spiegel, *Men Under Stress*, McGraw-Hill Book Co, New York; and Marlowe, David H., *Psychological and Psychosocial Consequences of Combat and Deployment with Special Emphasis on the Gulf War*. Santa Monica, CA: RAND Corporation, 2001.

32 The details of missions flown on July 10, 1943, are taken from the mission reports of the units involved. This includes the 14th Fighter Group, the individual squadron reports for all three squadrons of the 14th, the 1st Fighter Group, the individual squadron reports for all three squadrons of the 1st, and the mission reports for all bomb groups involved: 2nd, 97th, 99th, and 301st BGs flying B-17s; 310th and 321st BGs flying B-25s; 17th, 319th, and 320th BGs flying B-26s. All reports were secured from either the Air Force Historical Research Office at Maxwell AFB, or from the National Archives. The 1st FG flew eight missions on D-Day, with each P-38 carrying a 500-pound bomb attacking targets of opportunity in the central part of south-eastern Sicily. Sources: 57826, 57828, 57327 Unit History 94th FS, 57182 Unit History 71st FS, 77183 History 1st FG and 56054 WSOR 27th FS.

33 Missing Air Crew Report, No. 100, Lt. Wallace Bland, July 13, 1943.

34 Missing Air Crew Report, No. 74, 2nd Lt. Allan Knepper, July 13, 1943.

35 War Diary, 49th Fighter Squadron.

36 Adolf Galland, *The First and the Last: The rise and fall of the Luftwaffe: 1939–1945*, New York: Henry Holt & Co., 1954

37 Sortie Credits, Capt. William J. Gregory, O-659810, 14th Fighter Group, February 16, 1943 to August 21, 1943.

38 Individual Deceased Personnel File, Lt. William Hester, O-427335.

39 49th Fighter Squadron unit histories, and Op. Cit. Lambert.

Chapter 5

1 Officer Military Record, William J. Gregory, Form AF11, dated April 3, 1974.

2 Maurer and Maurer (Editors), *Combat Squadrons of the Air Force, World War II*, USAF Historical Division, Air University, 1969; and Maurer and Maurer (Editors), *Air Force Combat Units of World War II*, Office of Air Force History, 1983).

3 Aviation Archaeology Investigation and Research, 7644 S. 15th Ave. Phoenix, AZ 85041.

4 Ibid.

5 *The Times of Shreveport*, March 9, 1937; September 1, 1938.

6 *The Times of Shreveport*, November 29, 1939.

7 *The Times of Shreveport*, May 19, 1941.

8 On a mission flown on December 28, 1942 Frank Mullinax downed two German aircraft before being shot down himself. Crash landing, he was captured immediately and held in Italian prison camps for nine months. While being transported through Carrito, Italy, Mullinax and two other Americans escaped and successfully evaded German troops in and around Carrito

for nine months before the region was liberated by Allied forces. When he returned to the 49th Fighter Squadron, he received a promotion to Captain and was transported back to the States, arriving in New York City on July 4, 1944. A video of an interview with Frank describing his military experiences are part of The Library of Congress Veterans History Project. Also see *The Hangman's News*, Newsletter of the 49th Fighter Squadron Association, Vol. 3, Issue 4 and Vol. 4, Issue 1, Paul Scoskie, squadron historian.

9   Frank Mullinax's grandson would be named after Greg: William Gregory Mullinax. And Greg's good friend Fred Bitter would name his first son after Greg as well: William Gregory Bitter.

10   Op. Cit. Aviation Archaeology, and National Archives, WWII Army and Army Air Force Casualties, Tennessee.

11   Trousdale County Historical Society, John Oliver, Historian.

12   Recommendation for Promotion of Captain William J. Gregory, Col. John O. Zahn, Commander, Ontario Army Air Field, December 12, 1944.

13   "Around the World in 90 Years, This is Your Life Greg Gregory," undated, provided by Cookie Ruiz.

14   Kenneth P. Werrell, *Who Fears? The 301st in War and Peace,* 1942–1979, Dallas, TX: Taylor Publishing Company.

15   It was not Greg's first association with the 301st Bomb Group. Just four years earlier, Greg's fighter group, the 14th, and the 301st Bomb Group, were both part of the North African Strategic Air Force. During the summer of 1943, Greg and his squadron had provided escort for B-17s of the 301st on many missions, principally in the days preceding and following the Allied invasion of Sicily. The 301st was heavily decorated during the war, earning two Distinguished Unit Citations, and was in continuous operation in the Mediterranean and European Theaters from the start of America's active combat until the fall of Germany. The group returned to the States in July 1945, was deactivated in October, reactivated a year later, and then assigned to the Strategic Air Command in November 1947. Upon reactivation, it had morphed from a Group to a Wing, had been reequipped with B-29 bombers, and had received an entirely new personnel contingent, most of whom were war veterans, but few of whom had any experience with B-29s. *Air Force Fifty*, the Air Force Association, Paducah, KY.: Turner Publishing Co, 1998; and the 353rd Bombardment Squadron (Medium) History, 301st Bombardment Wing, Barksdale AFB, LA, 1950.

16   Ibid. 353rd Bombardment Squadron.

17   Ibid, 353rd Bombardment Squadron.

18   Ruud van Dijk, *Encyclopedia of the Cold War, Volume 1,* Taylor and Francis, 2008.

19   Op. Cit. Aviation Archaeology and 353rd Bombardment Squadron.

20   Laurence K. Loftin, Jr., *Quest for Performance: the Evolution of Modern Aircraft,* NASA SP-468, NASA Scientific and Technical Information Branch, Washington, DC. 1985.

21   Ibid; and Vernon B. Byrd, *Passing Gas: The History of Inflight Refueling,* Byrd Publishing, 1994, pp 123–136; and blog post of JP Santiago "Tails Through Time." www.tailsthroughtime.com.

22   Richard K. Smith, *Seventy-Five Years of Inflight Refueling, Highlights, 1923–1998,* Air Force History and Museums Program, 1998.

23   Ibid.

24   Letter, Maj. Gen. Frank A. Armstrong, Jr, Comm 2nd AF, to Gen Curtis E. LeMay, CINCSAC, July 18, 1956.

25   Joe Baugher's encyclopedia of American military aircraft, Naperville, IL: Joe Baugher; and https://web.archive.org/web/20060618052842/ and http:/home.att.net/~jbaugher2/b29_22.html.

26   Unit History, 352nd Bombardment Squadron (Medium).

27   Ibid.

28   A modified aerial refueling method known as the probe and drogue system was soon developed to allow single seat aircraft to be refueled in the air. Several KB-29Ms were modified to use the new system, in which the refueling hose had a cone-shaped receptacle, and the receiving aircraft a mating probe on its nose or wing. By the time this new system was in place, Greg had already moved from the tankers to bombers.

29   Many websites contain pertinent information. See: http://www.navy.mil/navydata/ships/carriers/cv-list.asp; https://en.wikipedia.org/wiki/List_of_aircraft_carriers_of_the_United_States_Navy; https://en.wikipedia.org/wiki/USS_Forrestal_(CV-59); and https://en.wikipedia.org/wiki/Boe-ing_KB-29_Superfortress)

30   Op. Cit. Werrell.

31   Op. Cit. 353rd Bombardment Squadron.

32   History Stories: The Great Smog of 1952 at https://www.history.com/news/the-killer-fog-that-blanketed-london-60-years-ago.

33   And this same Air Force general would pin other decorations and awards on Greg's chest over the coming decade.

34   Op. Cit. 353rd Bombardment Squadron.

Chapter 6

1   Historical Snapshot, B-47 Stratojet, Boeing Aircraft Company.

2   Op. Cit. Quest for Performance.

3   John Lowery, "Mission Impossible", *Daedalus Flyer*, spring 2018.

4   Walter J. Boyne, "The B-47's Deadly Dominance", *Air Force Magazine*, February 2013.

5   The aircraft often operated from forward bases in the UK, Morocco, Spain, Alaska, Greenland, and Guam, and it remained the Air Force's primary nuclear deterrent aircraft until 1959 at which time the new B-52 aircraft began to be delivered to bomb wings. The B-47 continued in service as a bomber until 1965 and as a reconnaissance aircraft until 1969.

6   But the aircraft was not without its detractors: "There are those who did not like the B-47. Although it was often admired, respected, cursed, or feared, it was almost never loved." One former pilot claimed the Stratojet was difficult to land, unforgiving, subject to control reversal at high speeds, and had bad roll-due-to-yaw characteristics." Op. Cit. 353rd Bombardment Squadron.

7   Op. Cit. Smith.

8   Greg said goodbye to the 301st, which forged ahead with its transition to the B-47. The wing would later move from Barksdale to Lockbourne AFB in Ohio, and would add an electronic countermeasure capability in 1958. Its mission would change from a strike force to ECM—a critical support function for the remaining strike forces. The wing would conduct many clandestine intelligence missions, including ferret missions around the periphery of Soviet territory, and sometimes within it. Still later, the 301st would morph into SAC's first all jet-tanker wing—another support role with another aircraft, the KC-135. See: Strategic Air Command, www.strategic-air-command.com/wings/0301bw.htm; and https://en.wikipedia.org/wiki/301st_Air_Refueling_Wing; and the 353 BS History.

9   History of the 19th Bombardment Wing, Medium, from June 11 to July 31, 1954, Air Force Historical Research Agency (AFHRA) IRIS 448560.

10   History of the 19th Bombardment Wing, Medium, AFHRA IRIS 448560.

11   History of the 19th Bombardment Wing, Medium, AFHRA IRIS No. 448572 and 448560.

12 History of the 19th Bombardment Wing, Medium, AFHRA IRIS No. 448565.
13 History of the 19th Bombardment Wing, Medium, AFHRA IRIS No. 448564.
14 History of the 19th Bombardment Wing, Medium, AFHRA IRIS No. 448566.
15 History of the 19th Bombardment Wing, Medium, AFHRA IRIS No. 448569.
16 History of the 19th Bombardment Wing, Medium, AFHRA IRIS No. 448569.
17 History of the 19th Bombardment Wing, Medium, AFHRA IRIS No. 448571.
18 Op. Cit. AFHRA IRIS No. 448572.
19 History of the 19th Bombardment Wing, Medium, AFHRA IRIS No. 448573.
20 History of the 19th Bombardment Wing, Medium, AFHRA IRIS No. 448575.
21 History of the 19th Bombardment Wing, Medium, AFHRA IRIS No. 448577.
22 Interview, William Gregory, August 6, 2019.
23 History of the 19th Bombardment Wing, Medium, AFHRA IRIS No. 448579.
24 History of the 19th Bombardment Wing, Medium, AFHRA IRIS No. 448581.
25 Op. Cit. AFHRA 448579 and 448581.
26 Over the course of his career, Don Todt had logged more than 5,000 flying hours. During World War II, he had completed thirty-one combat missions, and during the Korean conflict, served as the chief navigator for Generals Douglas MacArthur and Matthew Ridgeway. He would serve as Chief Operations Officer for the 4080th Reconnaissance Wing, as Squadron Commander for the 381st Strategic Missile Wing, and as Chief of Systems Directorate at SAC headquarters in Omaha. He completed two tours of duty in Vietnam as Deputy Commander for Intelligence with the 450th Tactical Reconnaissance Wing, and served as Squadron Commander of the 15th RTC at March AFB in Riverside. He was the recipient of the Legion of Merit, the Distinguished Flying Cross, and the Bronze Star among other awards. He retired in 1971, and lived at Salt Lake until his death in 2002.

Chapter 7

1 Donald Hillman with R. Cargill Hall, "A Daylight Overflight of Soviet Siberia," in Symposium Proceedings, Early Cold War Overflights, 1950–1956, R. Cargill Hall and Clayton D. Laurie, editors, National Reconnaissance Office, 2003.
2 Op. Cit. Symposium, see: Robert M. McAllister, "Were Military Overflights Necessary?"
3 Intelligence Advisory Committee IAC-D-55/4, No. 7, (Prepared by the Central Intelligence Agency and Concurred in by the Intelligence Advisory Committee), 28 July 1953, Sub: The Foreign Intelligence Program.
4 Winston Churchill, radio broadcast, London, October 1, 1939.
5 Winston Churchill, in a letter to President Harry Truman, May 1945.
6 Michael Peterson, "Maybe You Had To Be There, The SIGINT on Thirteen Soviet Shootdowns of US Reconnaissance Aircraft," Cryptographic Quarterly, 1993.
7 Ibid.
8 Robert Perry, A History of Satellite Reconnaissance, Volume 1—Corona, National Reconnaissance Office, October 1973.
9 Larry Tart and Robert Keefe, The Price of Vigilance: Attacks on American Surveillance Flights, New York: Ballantine Books, 2013.
10 Op. Cit. Peterson.
11 Memorandum for Lt. Pusta, Headquarters, USAF/AFOIP-FL, for AFOIL-RC, January 10, 1950, Sub: Organization of Strategic and Tactical Reconnaissance.

12 Andrew J. Goodpaster, "Cold War Overflights: A View from the White House," in Symposium Proceedings, Early Cold War Overflights, 1950–1956, R. Cargill Hall and Clayton D. Laurie, editors, National Reconnaissance Office, 2003.

13 Project RAND, "Special Memorandum: Vulnerability of U.S. Strategic Air Power to a Surprise Enemy Attack in 1956," April 15, 1953, Rand Corporation. Interested readers are also referred to: "Denied Territory: Eisenhower's Policy of Peacetime Aerial Overflight," R. Cargill Hall, *Air Power History*, Winter 2009; and R. Cargill Hall, *Clandestine Victory: Eisenhower and Overhead Reconnaissance in the Cold War*, in *Forging the Shield: Eisenhower and National Security for the 21st Century*, Dennis Showalter, (Ed.), Chicago: Imprints Publications, 2005.

14 "Report of the Special Evaluation Subcommittee of the National Security Council," May 18, 1953, NSC 140/1, contained in *Foreign Relations of the United States*, 1952–1954, National Security Affairs, Volume II, Part 1, page 328. The report estimated that a Soviet attack in 1955 could result in the loss of 30 percent of the US atomic bomber fleet, the death of over six million Americans, and the paralysis of two-thirds of American industry.

15 Foster Lee Smith, "Overflight Operations: Another View," in Symposium Proceedings, Early Cold War Overflights, 1950–1956, R. Cargill Hall and Clayton D. Laurie, editors, National Reconnaissance Office, 2003. In the same proceedings, see: "Early Cold War Overflight Programs: An Introduction," by R. Cargill Hall.

16 R. Cargill Hall, "Clandestine Victory: Eisenhower and Overhead Reconnaissance in the Cold War," in *Forging the Shield: Eisenhower and National Security for the 21st Century*, Dennis Showalter, ed., Chicago: Imprints Publications, 2005.

17 Robert S. Hopkins III, *Spyplanes and Overflights, US Strategic Aerial Reconnaissance,* Vol. 1: 1945–1960, Hikoki Publications.

18 National Intelligence Estimate, Number 11-7-55, Soviet Gross Capabilities for Attacks on the US and Key Overseas Installations and Forces Through 1 July 1958, June 23, 1955, CIA document CIA-RDP79R01012A005200020004-0.

19 National Intelligence Estimate, Number 11–56, Soviet Gross Capabilities for Attacks on the US and Key Overseas Installations and Forces Through mid-1959, March 6, 1956, CIA document C00267689.

20 The four types of Soviet bombers were: Tupolev Tu-4 (Soviet B-29 clone); Tupolev Tu-16 (twin-engined jet bomber; Myasishchev M-4 (four-engined jet bomber); and Tupolev Tu-95 (four-engined turboprop). The number of bombers likely to participate in a surprise attack, their types, and their likely success were determined by many inter-related factors, including the specific launch base, bomb load, operating conditions and the aircraft performance. Of perhaps greatest significance was whether the strike aircraft would be refueled, permitting a return to base, unrefueled, in which case the mission would likely be a one-way suicide mission, a prospect that the CIA believed to be well within the Soviet psyche at that time.

21 George A. Brown, *Project Home Run Operations*, National Reconnaissance Office, document C051 06948.

22 Op. Cit. Cargill Hall.

23 David Lednicer, "Aircraft Downed During the Cold War and Thereafter." See www.sw.propwash.org/shootdown_list.

24 See: "Maybe You Had to Be There." This citation refers to a 1947 Army memorandum, subject: "Current Army Ferreting Operations," August 11, 1947.

25 Primary source for the above is Op. Cit. Peterson.

26 Op. Cit. Tart and Keefe.

27 "15 March 1953 Incident (Kamchatka Peninsula): Note from the American Embassy at Moscow to the Soviet Foreign Ministry," March 18, 1953. Contained in *American Foreign Policy 1950–1955*, Department of State Publication 6446, GPO 1957.

28 Op. Cit. Tart and Keefe.

29 In late August 1953, the English Electric Canberra would set twelve flight records, including a 14 hour, 21 min London–New York–London round trip in which the aircraft averaged just over 481 mph. Fred Hamlin and Eleanor Thayer Miller, (Editors), *The Aircraft Year Book*, 1956, Aircraft Industries Association of America, Lincoln Press, Washington DC.

30 Robert C. Mikesh, *Martin B-57 Canberra: the Complete Record*, Atglen, PA: Schiffer Publishing Ltd, 1995. Also see Peter W. Merlin, *Unlimited Horizons, Design and Development of the U-2*, NASA Aeronautics Book Series, 2015.

31 Fact Sheet, Martin RB-57D, National Museum of the US Air Force.

32 www.tailsthroughtime.com/2010/08/u-2s-antecedent-martin-rb-57d-canberra.html.

33 History of 4080th Strategic Reconnaissance Wing (L), US Air Force, May 1956, Air Force Historical Research Agency (AFHRA), IRIS No. 460380.

34 History of 4080th Strategic Reconnaissance Wing (L), AFHRA IRIS No. 460383 (August 1956).

35 Op. Cit. IRIS 460380; also see: Dedicated to Peace, 4080th Strategic Reconnaissance Wing, 1956–1966.

36 Dennis R. Jenkins, *Dressing for Altitude: US Aviation Pressure Suits – Wiley Post to Space Shuttle*, National Aeronautics and Space Administration, 2012.

37 From the podcast "Piloting the U-2," found at http://omegataupodcast.net/109-flying-the-u-2-dragon-lady/#t=3:36.745

38 Ibid.

39 Greg recalls: *Col. Maloney went with the initial deployment to Japan, but he was not in charge of it. They did one mission over the Soviet Union from Japan. It was not a very successful mission, and the Air Force got a lot of bad publicity from the mission. The deployment would last nine months, but the D-0s never flew another reconnaissance mission. The cameras were not nearly as good as the U-2s would be, and the "take" from the D-0 cameras was never really adequate.*

40 Op. Cit. Cargill Hall.

41 Electronic Warfare Branch, Historical Report Covering the Period 1 Jul 1954 to 31 Dec 1954, AFHRA IRIS No. 00470390.

42 Greg recalls: Frank Wyman was buried at Arlington, and I accompanied Jane there for the funeral. We remain good friends to this day. Years later, Gail called me from her home in Arizona, and made a trip to visit me. She wanted to talk about her father. I was happy that she did that, and I became close friends with Gail, even to this day. Gretchen would also later relate: "Gail has spent many hours with my dad trying to understand what happened and why. To this day she and I are in touch…part of my Air Force family." Greg would also recall: I had another experience like that involving the son of the landing signal officer. He wanted to know more about his father. He took a trip from LA to Austin, and I talked with him a long time about his father. It is typical of children who lost their father at an early age—it's a natural thing for them to want to do.

43 4080th Strategic Reconnaissance Wing, Laughlin Heritage Foundation, *The Ram*, Vol IV No. 7 and Vol IV No. 8.

Chapter 8

1 Operations Order 33–59, "Border Town," HQ 4080th SRW, December 19, 1958, Exhibit 5.

2 Op. Cit. Tart and Keefe.

3 Op. Cit. Cargill Hall.

4 History of 4080th Strategic Reconnaissance Wing (L), US Air Force, Air Force Historical Research Agency (AFHRA), K-WG- 4080-HI, IRIS 460409 (Jan 1959).

5   Ibid, History of 4080th Strategic Reconnaissance Wing (L), AFHRA IRIS No. 460411 (March 1959).

6   Ibid, History of 4080th Strategic Reconnaissance Wing (L), AFHRA IRIS No. 460412 (April, May 1959).

7   Ibid, History of 4080th Strategic Reconnaissance Wing (L), AFHRA IRIS 460409 (Jan 1959).

8   Ibid. History of the 4080th Strategic Reconnaissance Wing (L), AFHRA IRIS No. 460409.

9   "Capt. Martineau was the pilot of the D-2 that had the oxygen problem and was forced to descend. In fact, he landed at the wrong base. It was a miracle that he survived and was able to land. But he got it on the ground OK, and we had to get it a few days later. It was a really close call." Tony Martinez correspondence, October 12, 2018.

10 Ibid, History of 4080th Strategic Reconnaissance Wing (L), AFHRA IRIS 460412 (April, May 1959) and IRIS 460409 (Jan 1959).

11 Ibid, History of the 4080th Strategic Reconnaissance Wing (L), AFHRA IRIS 460409 (Jan 1959).

12 Ibid, History of 4080th Strategic Reconnaissance Wing (L), AFHRA IRIS 460410 (Feb 1959).

13 Ibid, History of 4080th Strategic Reconnaissance Wing (L), AFHRA IRIS 460412 (April, May 1959).

14 Ibid, History of 4080th Strategic Reconnaissance Wing (L), AFHRA IRIS 460410 (Feb 1959).

15 Commander, 2nd AF, Barksdale AFB to Commander 4080th SRW, RB-57 Conference, 17 Feb 1959, AFHRA K-WG-4080-HI, IRIS 0460412, April 1, 1959–May 31, 1959.

16 Ibid, History of 4080th Strategic Reconnaissance Wing (L), AFHRA IRIS 460410 (Feb 1959).

17 In practical terms, the RB-57-D-2 ELINT systems could identify and locate radar sites and record the electronic signature of the Soviet radar on magnetic tapes. Back at base the specific site signal could be compared with the location of the aircraft using the pilot's navigation radar, permitting an accurate location of the radar site by ground personnel.

The Fan Song, Spoon Rest and Tall King radar systems were the main defensive radars deployed in the Soviet Air Defense system.

The oldest of these systems, the Spoon Rest A radars, were ground-controlled early warning radars that had been first deployed in 1956 and superseded by the D variant by 1970.

The Fan Song radar series—Soviet designation SNR-75—was a trailer-mounted fire control and tracking radar used with the Soviet SA-2 Guideline surface-to-air missiles. The Fan Song could track a single target at a time, and could guide up to three missiles at once to the target. Identifying and locating the Fan Song radars was critically important to the Strategic Air Command because characterizing the frequency that they operated on would permit the Air Force to design a counter jammer to deny them the ability to steer the missile once it was launched.

The Tall King radar—Soviet designation P-14 2D—was an early-warning radar first reported in 1959. It was the first Soviet high-powered VHF radar, had a range of 250 miles, and was effective to an altitude of 200,000 ft. when operating on "high beam." It was produced in three variants, including one mobile system, all for the purpose of long-range detection and tracking of aerial targets. CIA report in 1965 estimated approx. 250 locations, deployed around the periphery and interior of the USSR.

See: Tall King Early Warning Radars, 25 March 1065, CIA-RDP78T05929A000800020039-9; and John Sheehan, Canberra SIG, by email of 11/7/18; and Tony Martinez correspondence of October 12, 2018.

18 History of the 4080th Strategic Reconnaissance Wing (L), AFHRA IRIS 460410 (Feb 1959).

19 History of 4080th Strategic Reconnaissance Wing (L), AFHRA IRIS 460412 (April, May 1959).

20 History of the 4080th Strategic Reconnaissance Wing (L), AFHRA IRIS 4605409 (Mar 1959).

21 History of 4080th Strategic Reconnaissance Wing (L), AFHRA IRIS 460412 (April, May 1959).

22 History of 4080th Strategic Reconnaissance Wing (L), AFHRA IRIS 460414 (July 1959).

23 Ibid.

24 Recommendation for the Award of the Legion of Merit, Col. A. J. Bratton, Commander, 4080th SRW, and Special Order GA-70, July 29, 1965, Gen. J.P. McConnell, USAF Chief of Staff.

Chapter 9

1 Op. Cit., Perry.

2 *The Corona Story*, The National Reconnaissance Office, apparent date December 1988.

3 Gregory Pedlow and Donald Welzenbach, *The Central Intelligence Agency and Overhead Reconnaissance: The U-2 and Oxcart Programs, 1954–1974*, History Staff, CIA/Washington, CIA document C00190094, 1992.

4 "Meeting the Threat of Surprise Attack: The Report to the President by the Technological Capabilities Panel of the Science Advisory Committee," February 14, 1955, Combined Chiefs of Staff 040 (11-2-43) BP 6A.

5 Op. Cit. Cargill Hall.

6 Op. Cit. Pedlow and Welzenbach; Merlin; and Chris Pocock, *50 Years of the U-2, The Complete Illustrated History of the "Dragon Lady,"* Shiffer Military History, Atglen, PA.

7 Op. Cit. Perry.

8 Op. Cit. Merlin.

9 Op. Cit. Pedlow and Welzenbach.

10 From CIA Memorandum, Director Allen Dulles, to President Eisenhower, dated 24 Nov. 1954: in recommending the U-2 to the President, Dulles said: "...There is not the prospect of gaining this vital Intelligence without the conduct of systematic and repeated air reconnaissance over the Soviet Union itself." In the same memorandum, with reference to the RB-57D aircraft, he also went on to advise: "[At 65,000 ft] the expectation that it would be detected is very low indeed, and the possibility that it would be intercepted and shot down is practically nil." As to the latter point, he was correct with regard to aircraft interception, but not SAM intercepts.

11 Organization and Delineation of Responsibilities—Project Oilstone, Joint CIA/USAF Memorandum, August 2, 1955, CIA Reading Room, document 743230.

12 Op. Cit. Merlin.

13 Op. Cit. Merlin.

14 Op. Cit. Merlin.

15 Peter W. Merlin, "Area 51 was rocked by atomic blasts." See: https://www.dreamlandresort.com/area51/nuke_effects.html

16 Op. Cit. Pedlow and Welzenbach.

17 *Corona Program History, Volume I, Program Overview*, CIA document RDP89B00980R000500070001-2.

18 Op. Cit. Perry.

19 "Sputnik," *Cold War*, Episode 8, CNN, 1998-11-15.

20 One year later, Eisenhower approved a second covert reconnaissance satellite program eventually known as GRAB, designed to collect electronic intelligence from Soviet air defense radars. The Naval Research Laboratory managed GRAB for the Director of Naval Intelligence and the National Security Agency (NSA). In this instance, GRAB used a solar radiation experiment for cover. GRAB 1, launched on June 22, 1960, operated in orbit for a number of months and became the country's first successful reconnaissance satellite. R. Cargill Hall, "Early Years

at the National Reconnaissance Office: Interagency Dynamics and Organizational Myths," from *Studies in Intelligence*, Vol. 46, No. 2, 2002).

21   Op. Cit. Perry.

22   "Radio Propaganda Report, Soviet Propaganda Treatment of the USSR's Strategic Rocket Capability," Foreign Broadcast Information Service, Research Series 26, April 23, 1959, CIA declassified document C 05704392.

23   "Recent Soviet Statements on ICBM capability," February 2, 1959, CIA document CIA-RDP61-00357R000300210006-7.

24   Op. Cit. Pedlow and Welzenbach.

25   Interview with Marty Knutson, Military Communications and Electronics Museum, Kingston, ON. Canada.

26   Francis Gary Powers, *Operation Overflight*, New York: Holt, Rinehart and Winston, 1970.

27   Op. Cit. Jenkins.

28   USAF Fact Sheet. Article 104560, September 23, 2015.

29   "U-2 modifications reduce decompression sickness," *US Air Force News*, November 18, 2013; and Jersey, Baril, McCarty and Millhouse, "Severe Neurological Decompression Sickness in a U-2 Pilot," *Aviation Space Environmental Medicine*, 2010, 81:64–8.

30   Edwin Land was co-founder of the Polaroid Corporation, and is credited with inventing inexpensive filters for polarizing light (Polaroid film), and in-camera instant photography. With his team, Land designed the optics for the U-2 aircraft, and was deeply involved in the Corona project. James R. Killian was the first science advisor at the White House. It would not be an overstatement that without these two men, the U-2 would not have been developed.

31   Op. Cit. Pedlow and Welzenbach.

32   The Open Skies proposal re-emerged thirty-four years later at the behest of President George H. W. Bush as a means of building confidence and security between NATO and Warsaw Pact countries, notably including the Russian Federation. The Open Skies Treaty was signed in 1992, entered into force in 2002, and establishes a program of unarmed aerial surveillance over the territory of treaty participants. Signators currently include the US, Russia, and most NATO and Warsaw Pact countries.

33   Andrew J. Goodpaster, "Cold War Overflights: A View from the White House," in Symposium Proceedings, Early Cold War Overflights, 1950–1956, R. Cargill Hall and Clayton D. Laurie, editors, National Reconnaissance Office, 2003.

34   Weather Reconnaissance Squadron, Provisional (1st) Letter Order #2, May 1, 1956, provided by Roadrunner Historian, Frank Murray).

35   Timeline of Events for the U-2, www.blackbirds.net, 1997.

36   Alexander Orlov, "The U-2 Program: A Russian Officer Remembers," *Studies in Intelligence*, Winter 1998-1999. Unclassified Edition, Central Intelligence Agency, 1998.

37   Op. Cit. Pedlow and Welzenbach.

38   "The Story of the First U-2 Spy Missions Over the Soviet Union," *The Aviationist*, February 27, 2014; and Op. Cit. Pedlow and Welzenbach.

39   Op. Cit. Pedlow and Welzenbach.

40   Op. Cit. Pedlow and Welzenbach.

41   Op. Cit. Pedlow and Welzenbach.

Chapter 10

1   Gregory Pedlow and Donald Welzenbach, *The Central Intelligence Agency and Overhead Reconnaissance: The U-2 and Oxcart Programs, 1954–1974*, History Staff, CIA/Washington, CIA document C00190094, 1992.

2   Jeffrey Richelson (ed.), *The Secret History of the U-2—and Area 51*, National Security Archive Electronic Briefing Book No. 434.

3   Powers was in the second class of CIA U-2 pilots, which started in May 1956 and graduated in August. He had been ordered to Incirlik with Detachment B, and made his first overflight of the USSR from Adana in November 1956.

4   "The Final Overflights of the Soviet Union, 1959–1960," NSA Archive No. C00190094.

5   Op. Cit. Pedlow and Welzenbach.

6   Op. Cit. Goodpaster.

7   Memorandum for Gen. Omar Bradley, Chairman, Joint Chiefs of Staff, from Robert A. Lovett, Secretary of Defense, August 12, 1952, Sub: Reconnaissance Requirements.

8   Op. Cit. Pedlow and Welzenbach.

9   Op. Cit. Cargill Hall.

10 Gretchen Davis, interview, January 2018.

11 "Reflections from an AF Brat," Cookie Gregory Ruiz, undated and unpublished memoir, received October 9, 2018.

12 With the increasing frequency of operational missions for Detachment G's U-2s, the development and testing programs at the North Base became increasingly a Lockheed responsibility during the period of Greg's command.

13 "On the Ground with the U-2, A Security Officer's view," based on an interview with Joe Murphy, former U-2 Security Officer, CIA document C05851448.

14 Project Idealist, CIA document CIA-RDP80T01137A000500020001-2.

15 Op. Cit. Cargill Hall.

16 "Aviation Navigation—Basic Navigation." *Virtual Skies*. National Aeronautics and Space Administration. "Pilotage: A method of navigation in which the pilot, flying at low altitudes, uses visual references and compares symbols on aeronautical charts with surface features on the ground in order to navigate."

17 Interview, Col. William Gregory, February 3, 2012, by James Crabtree, Texas Veterans Land Board Voices of Veterans Oral History Program.

18 The 4025th Strategic Reconnaissance Squadron had been deactivated on June 15, 1960 and the RB-57D aircraft were retired from service.

19 "History of the Office of Special Activities (OSA) from Inception to 1969," DDS&T Historical Paper, OSA_1, Helen Kleyla and Robert O'Hern.

20 Op. Cit. Pedlow and Welzenbach.

21 Greg followed each Detachment G mission with a checklist of his creation. Starting with #1—Receive Alert, and ending with #57—Prepare WX summary. This handwritten checklist, included in an inconspicuous little black book, is seen in Appendix 3. The little black book included his own codename—Bill Gray—and Kelly Johnson's private phone number,

22 Central Intelligence Agency Library, document CIA-RPD63-00313A000600090003-4.

23 Op. Cit Pedlow and Welzenbach.

24 Op. Cit. Pedlow and Welzenbach.

25 Op. Cit. Pedlow and Welzenbach; and Op. Cit. Kleyla.

26 Kevin C. Furrner (Editor), *Corona: America's First Satellite Program*, CIA History Staff, Center for the Study of Intelligence, 1995.

27 Op. Cit. Kleyla.

28 The Office of Special Activities was established on July 30, 1962, and Col. Jack Ledford was named Assistant Director on September 4, 1962. A former World War II B-29 bomber pilot, Ledford was promoted to the rank of Brigadier General in 1967, and retired in 1970 after holding a number of key Air Force positions. He was a command pilot, and the recipient of

numerous commendations, including the Distinguished Service Medal 9w/OLC), Legion of Merit, Air Medal, and the Purple Heart. Op. Cit. Kleyla. and Congressional Record, 90th Congress, First Session, Vol. 113, Part 3, page 3817.

29 Preliminary Plan for Activation of U-2 Detachment, CIA Library document CIA-RDP33-02415A000300080056-8; and Table of Org for Weather Recon Sq Provisional, CIA Library document CIA-RDP33-02415A000300080043-2.

30 Greg is describing what would later be termed the "tropopause"—an altitude where the air ceases to cool with height and becomes almost completely dry. It marks the upper end of the troposphere, and its altitude varies with latitude: roughly 58,000 feet at the equator, 29,500 feet in the polar regions.

31 In addition to these two crashes, three In Flight Refueling (IFR) versions of the U-2 were lost during operational missions. By 1967, only one IFR-configured U-2 was left in inventory. Op. Cit. History of OSA.

32 Op. Cit. Kleyla.

33 Op. Cit. Murphy

Chapter 11

1 In the fall of 1962, the nuclear imbalance can be summarized as follows:

The United States had an inventory of 1,595 bombers supported by 1,108 airborne refuelers, plus 204 ICBMs and 221 shorter range ballistic missiles based within range of the USSR.

The Soviet Union could field an estimated 160 bombers, 57 of which were equipped with the 300-mile-range Kh-20 cruise missile. Thirty-seven Soviet submarines carried a total of 104 missiles with ranges of between 80 and 750 miles. Also in inventory were six R-7 and 32 R-16 ICMBs. The Soviets also possessed an unknown number of SS-4 MRBM and SS-5 IRBMs. Victor Flintham, Cuban Missile Crisis, in Squarespace.com.

2 Graham Allison and Philip Zelikow, *Essence of Decision: Explaining the Cuban Missile Crisis*. 1999, New York: Addison Wesley Longman. pp. 94–95.

3 John T. Correll, "Airpower and the Cuban Missile Crisis." *Air Force Magazine*, August 2005.

4 Laurence Change and Peter Kornbluh (Editors), *The Cuban Missile Crisis*, 1962, New York: the New Press, 1992, 1998.

5 James H. Hansen, *Soviet Deception in the Cuban Missile Crisis*, CIA Center for the Study of Intelligence, Vol. 46 No. 1.

6 See Appendix 4 for a complete list of Detachment G U-2 missions during this period.

7 Op. Cit. Hansen.

8 For much of the information related to the Cuban Missile Crisis, Op. Cit. Pedlow and Welzenbach, and Op. Cit. Hansen.

9 U-2 Operations After May 1960, NSA Archives document C00190094, George Washington University.

10 The other USAF pilots at McCoy AFB during the Cuban Missile Crisis were Major Emerling, Major Brown, Major Qualls, Captain Herman, Captain Kern, Major McIlmoyle, Major Primrose, and Captain Schmarr. Correspondence from Tony Martinez, October 12, 2018.

11 Op. Cit. Hansen.

12 Rudy Anderson flew his first assigned mission, which was similarly successful. On his second mission, flown Oct. 27, his U-2 was shot down and he was killed—the only U-2 loss during that operation, but a loss that underscored the U-2's vulnerability to ground attack missiles.

13 Between October 23 and November 15, a total of 250 low-level sorties were flown, mostly by the RF-8s under Operation *Blue Moon*. Victor Flintham, *Cuban Missile Crisis*, Squarespace. Also see Peter Mersky, "RF-8 Crusader Units Over Cuba and Vietnam," Osprey Publishers, *Combat Aircraft, Vol. 12*, 2014.

14 Special Order G-13, Curtis E. LeMay, Chief of Staff, February 4, 1963.

15 Citation is undated and unsigned.

16 See Appendix 5 for the personal letter from President John F. Kennedy.

17 Op. Cit. Hansen.

Chapter 12

1 Hobson, Chris. *Vietnam Air Losses*, USAF, USN, USMC, Fixed- Wing Aircraft Losses in Southeast Asia 1961–1973. North Branch, Minnesota USA: Specialty Press, 2001. ISBN 1-85780-115-6.

2 Summary of U-2 Operational Missions Flown Since 1 May 1960, Chief, Operations Division, Office of Special Activities, 21 September 1962, CIA Library document CIA-RDP33-02415A000100220009-6; and History of the Office of Special Activities (OSA) from Inception to 1969, DDS&T Historical Paper, OSA 1, p. 1510 and ff, Helen Kleyla and Robert O'Hern.

3 Op. Cit. Kleyla.

4 Op. Cit. Pedlow and Welzenbach.

5 Op. Cit. Kleyla.

6 Op. Cit. Kleyla.

7 Memorandum for Deputy Director (Plans), Subject: Modified U-2 for Navy Aircraft Carrier Operation, May 16, 1960, Author redacted but believed to be Kelly Johnson, Lockheed. CIA Library document CIA-RDP74B00752R000100350001-7.

8 Ibid CIA-RDP75B00446R000100210015-3.

9 *The Aviationist*, June 28, 2015, Dario Leone; and CIA document C05701449, Memorandum for the Record, Project Whale Tale, August 7, 1963, author redacted.

10 Operating Instructions Manual for Carrier Operations, CIA documents contained in CIA-RDP7400836R0003000180001-8), and General Policy for Carrier Operations, Weather Reconnaissance Squadron Provisional (IV), Hiawatha Mohawk, Operations Officer, CIA Library CIA-RDP74B00776R000100130007-9.

11 Ibid.

12 Ibid, CIA-RDP75B00446R000100210015-3.

13 As a CIA U-2 pilot with Detachment B, James Cherbonneaux had once overflown the Soviet Semipalatinsk proving grounds during Operation *Soft Touch* only 4 hours before a half-megaton device was detonated. In fact, the U-2 unknowingly photographed the aircraft that was to drop the nuclear device. After joining Detachment G, Cherbonneaux flew 13 overflight missions, including eight over Cuba. James Barnes had also overflown Cuba many times in the days leading up to the Cuban Missile Crisis, and piloted a diversionary U-2 mission for *Grand Slam* on day Powers was shot down. "The CIA and Overhead Reconnaissance: The U-2 and OXCART Programs 1954–1974." NSA Archive document C01190094.

14 Commander Huber would remain with the detachment for 18 months, and Greg came to know him well. He was a Navy pilot himself, and spent a lot of his time training young naval aviators in landing on aircraft carriers. *Going through the carrier qualification program, I got to see how good he was.* Huber was later killed when his aircraft blew up in flight, leaving a four-year-old son. Years later, Huber's son would visit Greg in Austin, wanting to know more

about his father. Greg was pleased to meet with him—*there was a real need for these kids to know more about their father.*

15 Op. Cit. Kleyla.
16 Ibid CIA-RDP75B00446R000100210015-3.
17 France would conduct 41 atmospheric tests over Moruroa and Fangataufa between 1966 and 1974, 135 more between 1975 and 1991, and eight more between 1995 and 1996. See: http://navymuseum.co.nz/1945-1975-french-nuclear-testing-at-mururoa/. In a report related to the Aldebaran test, Greenpeace claimed that the test spread contamination across the Pacific as far as Peru and New Zealand.
18 Op. Cit. History of the Office of Special Activities.
19 Ibid.
20 Sources indicate the date was May 22. See Pedlow and Welzenbach.
21 Op. Cit. Pedlow and Welzenbach.
22 Op. Cit. Kleyla.
23 CIA Featured Story Archive, Eugene "Buster" Edens, April 24, 2015.

Chapter 13

1 Jan Goldman, ed. *The Central Intelligence Agency: An Encyclopedia of Covert Ops, Intelligence Gathering, and Spies*, Santa Barbara: ABC-CLIO, 2017
2 "SR71 Blackbird." PBS documentary, Aired: November 15, 2006. The SR-71's low radar cross-section, high altitude, and very high speed gave a very short time for an enemy surface-to-air missile site to acquire and track the aircraft on radar. By the time tracking was achieved, the SR-71 would be out of range of the SAM. During its operational life, no SR-71 was ever shot down.
3 History of the Oxcart Program, July 1, 1968, SP-1362, Lockheed Aircraft Corporation, Burbank, CA.
4 Peter W. Merlin, *Design and Development of the Blackbird: Challenges and Lessons Learned*, 47th American Institute of Aeronautics and Astronautics, Aerospace Sciences Meeting, January 2009, Orlando, Florida.
5 David Robarge, *Archangel: CIA's Supersonic A-12 Reconnaissance Aircraft*, CIA Center for the Study of Intelligence, 2012.
6 Thomas P. McIninch, *The Oxcart Story*, CIA Library, Studies Archive Indexes, Vol 15.
7 T. D. Barnes, *The Archangels, Book Two, the CIA, Area 51 Chronicles, The Complete Illustrated History of the CIA at Area 51*, 2018.
8 Op. Cit. McIninch.
9 Op. Cit. McIninch.
10 Op. Cit. Robarge.
11 Project Oxcart and Operation Black Shield, Briefing Notes, October 20, 1965.
12 "OXCART vs Blackbird: Do You Know the Difference?", CIA Featured Story, November 12, 2015.
13 Op. Cit. McIninch.
14 Op. Cit. History of the Office of Special Activities.
15 Robert S. Hopkins III, *Spyplanes and Overflights, US Strategic Aerial Reconnaissance, Vol. 1:1945–1960*, Hikoki Publications.
16 Op. Cit. Pocock.
17 History, 19th Bombardment Wing, AFHRA IRIS No. 448581, April 1956.
18 Census of Population: 1960, Vol. I, Characteristics of the Population, Part A, Eighteenth Decennial Census of the United States.

19   Census of Population and Housing, US Census Bureau, 1960.

20   Op. Cit. Pocock.

21   Department of the Air Force, Washington, Special Order GA-70, July 29, 1964, J. P. McConnell, General, USAF Chief of Staff.

22   Within a year Col. Ledford, by then Director of Special Activities, would also be reassigned, returning to the Air Force in August 1966.

23   During the year-long Operation *Silver Javelin*, the A-12 achieved a maximum speed of Mach 3.29, an altitude of 90,000 feet, a sustained flight time above Mach 3.2 of one hour and fourteen minutes, and a maximum endurance flight of over six hours. The aircraft was declared operationally ready in November 1965, three years and seven months after its first flight. For a number of reasons having more to do with international diplomacy that the aircraft's operational effectiveness, and despite repeated requests by the CIA, deployment of the A-12 was delay until May 1967. The deployment, operating from Kadena, Okinawa under the command of Col. Hugh Slater, flew its first operational mission on May 3, 1967—an event that would be the culmination of ten years worth of effort and expense.

As early as November 1965, the costly A-12 program fell under the scrutiny of the Bureau of Budget, even as it was coming to operational readiness. Following consideration and debate by the CIA Director, the Secretary of Defense, and the Science Advisor to the President, President Lyndon Johnson ordered the termination of the Oxcart program by January 1, 1968, with the provision that the A-12 unit then on deployment to Kadena would maintain capability through 1967. Before returning to Groom Lake, the A-12 detachment would complete 26 reconnaissance missions over North Vietnam, and three over North Korea.

Col. Slater, and his second in command, Col. Maynard N. Amundson, would each be awarded the Legion of Merit. Slater would also receive the CIA Medal of Merit. The 1129th SAS would receive the Air Force Outstanding Unit Award.

Chapter 14

1   Fitzhugh Lee, US Navy Commandant, National War College, to William Raborn, Director, CIA, November 22, 1965, CIA Library, document IA-RDP80B01676R000100090003-1.

2   Guide in the Selection of Personnel to be Nominated as Students to Attend the Course of Instruction Conducted at the National War College, CIA Library, document CIA-RDP80B01676R000100090003-1, undated. "Q"-level security clearance dates to the immediate postwar years, and the formation of the Atomic Energy Commission in 1947. This level of clearance was for those individuals who required access to restricted data and security exclusion areas, with particular reference to atomic or nuclear activities.

3   National War College Yearbook, Academic Year 1965–1966, Washington, DC.

4   National War College website: www.nwc.ndu.edu.

5   By the time of Greg's admission, its mission was: "To conduct a course of study of those agencies of government and those military, economic, scientific, political, psychological and social factors of power potential, which are essential parts of national security in order to enhance the preparation of selected personnel of the armed forces and State Department for the exercise of joint and combined high-level policy, command and staff functions and for the planning of national strategy." Op. Cit. Yearbook.

6   The author's leading paragraph reflects the uncertainty within the JCS regarding the situation in Vietnam and the academic freedom that was part of the NWC: "After reviewing the documents that your staff provided, I have enclosed my thoughts on the current situation in South Vietnam. At this time, we have already deployed Marine main force elements and have

completed a limited bombing operation in North Vietnam. The deployment of these units concerns me because I don't think we have a clear understanding of the situation in Vietnam. We have crossed the Rubicon with little more than the Johnson administration's guidance to 'kill more VC' and maintain the current status quo."

The discussion that followed that presentation would have been fascinating.

7   "Agrarian Reforms and Their Implications for Future Stability of the Mexican Government," William J. Gregory, Colonel, US Air Force, Individual Research Paper, National War college, Washington, DC, January 19, 1966.

8   Citation to Accompany the Award of the Legion of Merit, Second Oak Leaf Cluster, Department of the Air Force, John D. Ryan, Air Force Chief of Staff, Special Order GB-612, September 3, 1971.

9   Virginia's first husband was killed in a car crash three months before her son William was born. It would be the third of an eventual four marriages for Virginia; her second marriage to an abusive alcoholic ended in a divorce, and later a remarriage that lasted until his death in 1967; she was married to Jeff Dwyer in 1969 until his death in 1974, whereupon she married her final husband, Richard Kelley, in 1982 and remained married until her death in 1994.

10 The source for this information is an exceptionally well documented article in Wikipedia. See: http://en.wikipedia.org/wiki/Recipients_of_the_Legion_of_Merit.

Chapter 15

1   "Around the World in 90 Years, This is your life Greg Gregory," Cookie Ruiz, unpublished document. Undated. Presumably prepared on the occasion of William Gregory's 90th birthday, August 5, 2010.

2   Cookie Ruiz, personal correspondence, October 9, 2018.

3   For the MTSU posting of Greg's address, see: https://mtsunews.com/gregory-military-lecture-spring2015/. For the associated video, see: https://www.youtube.com/watch?v=2AWZ 9qqEvzg. For the MTSU Alumni News profile, see: https://mtsunews.com/a-flying-start/.

4   www.olli.utexas.edu/lamp.

5   Gretchen Davis, email October 3, 2018.

Appendix 2

1   Steve Blank, The Secret History of Silicon Valley, Part 14: Weapons System 117L and Corona, January 18, 2010.

2   Op. Cit. Perry.

3   National Intelligence Estimate, NIE 11-8/1-61, September 21, 1961.

4   Op. Cit Perry.

5   Everet Clark, "Satellite Spying Cited by Johnson," New York Times, March 17, 1957.

6   Op. Cit Perry.

Appendix 4

1   Source for this data is History of the Office of Special Activities, From Inception to 1969, Directorate of Science and Technology, Helen Kleyla and Robert O'Hern.

Index